History of
Medieaval Hindu India

History of Medieaval Hindu India

Early History of Rajputs (750 to 1000 A.D.)

By

C.V. VAIDYA

Vol. II

GYAN

Published by

Gyan Publishing House
5, Ansari Road
Daryaganj, New Delhi-110002
Phone: 011-47034999, 9811692060
E-mail: books@gyanbooks.com

Distribution Network
gyanbooks.com
India, USA, Canada, UK, Australia, France

ISBN : 978-81-212-0006-6 (Set)
978-81-212-1940-2 (HB)
First Published, 1924

2nd Impression 2022

Printed at: Gyan Press, Delhi.

History of Medieaval Hindu India:
Early History of Rajputs (750 to 1000 A.D.) (Vol. II)
Author: C.V. VAIDYA

CONTENTS.

BOOK III.

THE ORIGIN OF THE RAJPUTS.

Chapter.	Subject.	Page.
1.	The Rajputs	1
2.	Theory of Foreign Descent	7
3.	The Exploded Myth of Agnikulas	12
	Note—The Value of the Prithvirāja Rāsā	18
	,, The 36 Rajput Clans or Royal Families	22
4.	Are Agnikulas Gujars ?	27
	Note—The Skanda Purāṇa list of countries	39
	,, The meaning of the word Rajput	43
5.	The Gotras of the Rajputs	49
	Note—Gotra and Pravara	56
6.	Aryan Settlements in Rājputāna	64

BOOK IV.

THE SECOND SET OF HINDU KINGDOMS.

1.	The Guhilots of Mewad and Bappā Rāwal	70
2.	The Successors of Bappā	77
	Note—Are the Guhilots foreigners ?	83
3.	The Chāhamānas of Sambar	90
4.	The Imperial Pratihāras of Kanauj	98
5.	The Chāvadas of Anhilwad Pātan	114
6.	The Paramāras of Dhar	117
7.	The Chandellas of Bundelkhand	124
	Note—Smith's wrong view about the origin of the Chandellas	130
8.	The Kalachūris of Chedi	134
9.	The Pālas of Bengal	138
10.	The Rāshṭrakūṭas of the Deccan	144
11.	The Other Kingdoms of India	157
12.	Contemporary Arab writers	162

BOOK V.

GENERAL SURVEY.

Chapter.	Subject.	Page
1.	Language	167
	Note—Extracts from Dr. Grierson's Linguistic Survey of India	173
2.	Caste and Social Condition	175
	Note—The Smṛiti Law of Anuloma Marriage	193
3.	Religious Condition	196
4.	Kumārila and Śaṅkara	206
	Note—Date of Śaṅkara	218
5.	Political Condition	220
6.	Civil and Military Administration	229
7.	The 9th and 10th centuries A.D. the happiest period of Indian history	247

APPENDIX.

I.	The Solar and Lunar Races of Kshatriyas in the Vedas ..	259
II.	Some Inscriptions in the original	301
III.	Extracts from important Smṛitis showing the freer social intercourse of the period	308
IV.	Genesis of the dictum कलावाद्यन्तयोः स्थितिः	312
V.	The Mahārāshtra kingly families were Maratha Kshatriyas ..	313
VI.	Rai Bahadur Gaurishankar Ojha on Bappā Rāwal ..	332
VII.	Recent Research and new light on the history of the period.	389
VIII.	List of contemporary kings from 750 to 1000 A.D.	
IX.	Map (religious and political) of India ,,	
	Index	i—xxi

PREFACE

In this second volume of our history is presented to the reader the history of the second sub-period of mediæval Hindu history of India. As stated in the beginning of the preface to our first volume, the mediæval Hindu period of Indian History extends, according to our view, from 600 A.D. to 1200 A. D. roughly, i. e. from the accession of Harsha, the last Buddhist Emperor of India to the death of Prithvīrāja, the last Hindu Emperor of India. This period of about 600 years curiously enough falls into three sub-periods of about 200 years each, in which appear on the stage of Indian history different sets of Hindu kingdoms. In the first volume we presented to the reader the history of the first set of Hindu kingdoms led by the Varmās of Kanauj and the Chālukyas of Badāmī. Indeed, throughout the Hindu period, Kanauj in the north appears to have been the acknowledged capital of India and there was always a competing kingdom in Mahārāshtra struggling to divide imperial honour with it in the south. These first imperial Hindu kingdoms at Kanauj and at Badāmī disappear about 800 A. D. with other kingdoms, and the second set of Hindu kingdoms come in, led by the Pratihāras in the north and the Rāshtrakūtas in the south. These again disappear about the end of the second sub-period, i. e. about

1000 A. D. and the history of this second set of Hindu kingdoms is presented to the reader in this volume. A third set of Hindu kingdoms appear hereafter led by the Gaharwārs of Kanauj and the later Chālukyas of Kalyan in the north and the south respectively; and their history will be given in our third volume.

The most remarkable thing about the second set of Hindu kingdoms is that they are ruled by kings who call themselves Rajputs. In fact, the Rajput clans which exist today in India trace their descent to kings who established their rule about this time. And hence this period is conspicuously characterised by the rise of Rajput families. We have consequently given a second name to this volume, namely, the Pristine History of the Rajputs; and this volume chiefly contains the initial account of several Rajput families. Even Tod, the historian of the Rajputs could not give this history in sufficient and well authenticated detail owing to the absence of the epigraphic material which has since been so amply collected. This history, therefore, will be particularly interesting to Rajputs and to all those who admire the noble qualities of that heroic race.

Who were these Rajputs is a question which has puzzled almost all European scholars and many Indian antiquarians. For most of the historians and researchers who have laboured to collect and interpret the epigraphic evidence relating to this period have been misled in this respect by the theory first put forward by Tod that the Rajputs are the descendants of the Getœ and other foreign races, which invaded India from the first to the sixth century A. D. Kielhorn, Fleet, Smith, Buhler and Johnson and Bhandarkar D. R. and other Indian scholars who have laboured in this field and whose labours must be thankfully acknowledged here as on their elucidation of the epigraphic records of this period, this history is chiefly based, have been misled by this theory of the foreign descent of the Rajputs, and have represented them as descended from foreign peoples like Śakas and Hūṇas, or in some cases aboriginal peoples like Gonds and Bhars of Central India.

But the riddle of the appearance of the Rajputs on the stage of Indian history about the middle of the eighth century A. D. has to be solved differently. The history of India is nothing if not religious. The march of events and the change of social or political conditions in India are dominated by religious upheavals, and thus the appearance of Rajputs at this stage of Indian history is to be explained by the nature of the religious events which took place in India at this time. Not only was the supplanting of Buddhism by the philosophy of Kumārila instrumental in reforming and re-enforcing Hinduism about 700 A. D. but the conquest of Sind by the Arabs, moving over the then known world under the influence of a new virile religion sent a shock through India and roused the forces of opposition to foreign faith and domination among the orthodox population. The Rajputs came forward under this impulse from among the ranks of the orthodox Khshatriyas of what is modern Rājputana and Central India, where Hinduism was particularly strong (See Map attached to the first volume). And their successful efforts led to the establishment of new kingdoms under new kingly families. Thus about 750 A. D. the Guhilots of Mewad under Bappā Rāwal, the Chāhamānas of Sāmbhar under Sāmanta and the Pratihāras of Māndor under Nāgabhata, as the reader will see in this volume, obtained renown by their opposition to the Mlenchhas surging eastwards from Sind towards Rājputana for conquest as well as conversion. We find from inscriptions that these leaders of opposition were all orthodox Hindus worshipping Śiva, and we are led to conclude that the Rajputs were descendants of orthodox Vedic Aryans who fought for their independence and their ancient religion against the ferocious onslaughts of Mahamedan Arabs.

In Book III, in the beginning of this volume on the origin of Rajputs, we have, therefore, first answered the arguments which are usually advanced to support the theory of a foreign origin. And then we have given in chapters V and VI those arguments which strike one as going to prove affirmatively that the Rajputs are the descendants of Vedic Aryans. The reader's attention is particularly drawn to the chapter on the exploded myth of the Agnikulas or Fire-born septs, which had been the principal support of the theory of foreign extraction of the Rajputs, and which has now been proved to be baseless from the ancient records of the very families which believe themselves to be fire-born.

In the next Book IV we have given the history of the several Rajput kingdoms which were founded about this time and notably of the Guhilots of Mewad and the Imperial Pratihāras of Kanauj. In particular, it was necessary to examine the theory put forward by Dr. D. R. Bhandarkar about the Guhilots of Mewad that they were Nagar Brahmins and hence Mers or foreigners !!! This theory suggested by the general idea about the foreign origin of the Rajputs, no doubt, finds apparent support (at least with regard to Bappā Rāwal, the founder) in the ancient records of the family. But this view cannot be sustained, as we have shown at length, on a careful examination of these records. And Rai Bahadur Gaurishankar Ojha has also no doubt that the Guhilots are Solar race Kshatriyas, as shown in a special note on the subject in the Appendix. It may further be mentioned that the date of Bappā Rāwal as traditionally believed in in the Mewad family, namely Samvat 191, was difficult of explanation, even from the days of Tod, and the solution which we have offered of this difficulty will, it is hoped, generally recommend itself to our readers. Finally, the statements of Arab writers about the various kingdoms of this period have been collected together and explained in a special chapter. Their evidence is very valuable for this period, as the evidence of Hiuen Tsang was with regard to the previous period.

As in the first volume, we have in the last book (V) taken a general survey of the condition of India during this period, and dealt with several important topics such as language, caste, religion, political ideas and administration civil and military. It is necessary to draw the special attention of the reader to the chapter on Kumārila and Śankara, two master-minds which gave to Aryanism its present form after overthrowing Buddhism in India. Hinduism, as it exists today, was then formed and this religious upheaval led not only to the remodelling of religion, but also of the social and even political condition of the country. In fact, as stated before, the rise of the Rajputs was due to this religious upheaval and the idea firmly gained ground that only Kshatriyas or Rajputs could rule. These Rajput rulers were naturally of a highly religious turn of mind (witness Bappā Rāwal and others) and were men of high moral character. They were, what is strange to our sight, even abstainers from wine. Arab travellers have recorded that kings in India abstained from drink; and any one indulging in it was considered unfit to rule. This religious revival was instrumental in raising the moral fibre not only of kings, but of the people also and there being only one religion in the land, namely Hinduism, this period was according to our view, the happiest period in Indian history. In the last chapter, we have tried to show at length how this period was the happiest in many ways. In fact, in our Marathi edition of this history, we have styled it the history of the rise, the prosperity and the fall of Hindu kingdoms; and truly enough, this period is the period of the highest prosperity of Hindu kingdoms, from which, in the next period they declined and eventually fell. Why they did so, is a very interesting and difficult question, which we shall have to deal with in our third volume.

We look upon the Rajputs as undoubted descendants of Vedic Aryans of the solar and lunar race, and there was no third race or Vaṁśa, according to our view (namely the Agnivaṁśa). In the Appendix, we have, therefore, re-published our paper read before the Bombay Branch of the R.A.S. on the Solar and Lunar Kshatriya races in the Vedas, which will show how this idea of two races goes back even to the Vedas. Next, some important inscriptions are given in the original Sanskrit for the benefit of Sanskrit-knowing readers. A question raised by Mr. Rajawade, the well-known historical researcher of Mahārāshtra, about the ruling families of the Deccan in this period, is next examined, as he has doubted their being treated as Marāthās. Rai Bahadur Gourishankar Ojha's views on Bappā Rāwal have been discussed in a special note, and some facts discovered in recent research and not embodied in this history have been noticed in a special appendix. A map of India, giving the political divisions in this period and showing in different colours the prevailing religions has been appended, and will be found as useful and interesting as the map appended to the first volume.

This volume is printed in Monotype and effort has been made, as far as possible, to secure correct printing for which thanks are due to Mr. C. R. Naidu, the Monotype-operator of the Jagaddhitecchu press,

Indian printing, however, has yet to make good progress and an errata is yet a necessary evil which has to be tolerated by the reader. An index, prepared by Mr. N. N. Kulkarni B. A., of the Bhandarkar Institute for which my thanks are due to him as also to Mr. M. R. Moghe B.A., LL.B., for the preparation of the index of the 1st Volume, has been added which will facilitate easy reference. The attention of the reader is particularly drawn to the statement, given at the end, of contemporaneous kings prepared for the period 750 to 1000 A.D. which will show at a glance what kings ruled in the several kingdoms of India at any particular time, and thus will assist the reader in understanding the history of India as a whole during this period (800-1000 A.D.). Lastly I have to thank Dr. N. G. Sardesai L.M. & S., Manager, Oriental Book Supplying Agency Poona for carrying the book through the press.

POONA,
February 15, 1924.

C. V. VAIDYA.

BOOK III.

THE ORIGIN OF THE RAJPUTS

CHAPTER I.

THE RAJPUTS.

With the beginning of the ninth century A. D., the face of Indian history completely changes. Aryan India and Aryo-Buddhistic India have ended and Hindu India, as it practically is at present, is presented to us. Buddhism has entirely disappeared from the land, except in a few isolated places like Magadha. While, in the map appended to the first volume of this history, the reader finds about three-fourths of India painted rose, being Aryo-Buddhistic, in the map appended to this volume, nearly the whole of India is painted soiled red, being Hindu. But if Buddhism has disappeared from the land, Vedic Aryanism too exists no more. The sentiment of aversion to animal sacrifice had been too deeply implanted in the Indian heart to allow the Pūrva Mīmānsā doctrine which supplanted Buddhism to remain long supreme. In fact Buddhism and Pūrva Mīmânsā, so to say, killed each other. While respect for the Vedas revived and gained strength, respect for Vedic sacrifices was gone. The doctrine of the efficacy of the Vedic sacrifices inculcated by the Pūrva Mīmānsā no doubt gained credence for a time after the death of Harsha about 650 A. D.; but by 750 A. D., the aversion to animal sacrifice had again asserted itself so strongly that Vedic animal sacrifices died again and died finally. Modern India with its Hinduism does not countenance these sacrifices and the Pūrva Mīmānsā doctrine is dead so far, along with Buddhism which it killed. The founders of the first set of Hindu kingdoms generally signalised their assumption of royal greatness by the performance of the Aśvamedha; the second set of Hindu kingly families which now began to establish themselves were indifferent to these sacrifices. The new kings were devout worshippers of the Puranic gods now enthroned supreme viz., the five deities of modern Hinduism, Śiva, Vishṇu, Sūrya, Devī, and Gaṇesha and chiefly of the first. The Śiva cult too of modern India is different from the same cult as it flourished in the previous period of Indian history. Its nature assumed a less revolting form and the offensive practices and the absurd doctrines which belonged to the Tāntric worship of Śiva of the days of Pushyabhūti, the founder of the Thanesar dynasty, were no more in vogue or obtained popular favour. Thus, religiously considered, modern Hindu India practically commences from about the beginning of the ninth century of the Christian era.

One most prominent feature of this Hinduism, a feature which subsists to-day in all its strength, is the strengthened belief in the sacredness of the cow and the bull. The cow has been sacred indeed from Vedic times; but Vedic ritual included the sacrifice of cows and bulls. The now strongly entrenched sentiment of Ahimsā, made the slaughter of cows and bulls even for Vedic sacrifices one of the five most heinous sins and even the maiming of cows came to be looked upon as sinful. Both Śiva and Vishṇu worships which were now enthroned supreme contributed to this strong belief in the sacredness of the bovine animal. The bull was sacred to Śiva and the cow to Vishṇu in his highest incarnation as Śri Kṛishṇa. That great root cause of the terrible conflicts between Hindus and Mahomedans acquired its supreme influence at this time, an influence which subsists to-day in all its strength. In all Hindu States the killing or maiming of cows and bulls is even to-day a heinous crime under the Penal Code.

Socially also, modern Hindu India can be traced back to the beginning of the ninth century A. D. Caste was till then not so exclusive as it is at this day, nor had castes sub-divided themselves into minor ramifications. The final overthrow of Buddhism and the inclusion of people who had previously professed that faith in the Hindu society probably led to the formation of sub-castes in the next sub-period within the main castes and though the modern sub-castes can not be traced back to the ninth century or rather the second sub-period of Mediæval Hindu India, the origin of it and its probable cause may be traced to that sub-period, viz., the difference of local tendencies due to the conversion of Buddhists into Hindus worshipping Puranic deities. The food of the people again generally became vegetarian and the accentuation of this fact contributed its share to the formation of more sub-castes within castes in the next period.

What is more remarkable still is that the language of the people too changed markedly from this time. The modern vernaculars of India arose about this time for reasons which we shall try to elucidate in a separate chapter. It is sufficient here to state that the history of the modern vernaculars of India can be traced back continuously to this period and not beyond it; and hence it may be said, speaking historically, thaī the modern languages of India began to be formed about thist time. While in previous centuries the ancient Prākṛits Saurasenī, Māgadhī, Mahārāshtrī and Paiśāchī or their Apabhraṇśas appear to have still been spoken, from the ninth century onward we find Hindi, Bengali, Marathi, Gujarati and Panjabi appearing as new developed spoken languages of north, east, south and west India.

But the greatest phenomenon of this period was the rising into political prominence of new kingly families—families which subsist as kingly families down to this day. It may in fact be said that modern *political* Hindu India as it is to-day also commences from this period. This phenomenon is marked by Indian historians and Sir V. Smith among them properly observes that the Rajputs about this time enter upon the stage of Indian history. The former kingly families are gone. The Guptas and the Vardhanas who were probably Vaiśyas were the leading kingly families of India during the Aryo-Buddhistic period and there were foreign kingly families also such as the Yavanas, the Śakas and the Hūṇas. These gradually disappeared in the first sub-period of Mediæval Hindu India. There were some Kshatriya families then also who are described as Kshatriyas even by Hiuen-Tsang, but these did not call themselves Rajputs and the Maitrakas of Valabhī or the Varmas of Kanauj in the north and the Chālukyas of Badāmi and the Pallavas of Kāñchī in the south are styled Kshatriyas but not Rajputs. These too disappeared about this time and new Kshatriya families arose all over India at this time which delighted to call themselves Rajputs, not a new name, however. And the wonder is that these Rajput kingly families subsist, though with diminished importance, as kingly families to this day. Indeed there are no other kingly families at this date in the whole world which can trace their pedigree back in a continuous line to the 9th century A. D. For this reason alone if not for anything else, the Rajputs of India deserve a prominence peculiarly their own.

But the Rajputs deserve much greater renown than this. In fact their greatness as a chilvalrous and valiant people has not adequately been realised by us. They shed a glory on the history of this time which deserves as great a record in the history of the world as the glory of the most heroic peoples in that history. The Śisodias of Mewad and the Chāhamānas of Sāmbar deserve the foremost mention in world's history for chivalry and heroism, for the orthodoxy of their faith and for the persistence of their struggle against a foreign faith and dominion. In fact, the flood of Arab conquest which westward inundated the north of Africa and pouring even over the straits of Gibralter rushed into Spain and crossed the Pyrenees into France was only dashed to pieces against the rock of the valour of the Franks on the banks of the Loire. The flood of the same Arab conquest led by the same fanaticism of a new religion, which rushed eastward and engulfed Mesopotamia, Iran, and Baluchistan and crossing the Indus submerged Sind in India received its shattering at the hands of the heroic Gehlots. Had it not been for Bappā Rāwal who justly deserves the veneration in which his name is held by the Rajputs and who can fitly be styled the Charles Martel of India, the whole of India would have fallen before the Arabs and to use the eloquent words of Gibbon, professors of the Arabian faith might to-day have preached to a circumcised population in the city of Benares. But this fate was averted by the heroism of Bappā Rāwal and his Rajputs and it is refreshing to observe that his descendants throughout their long and glorious history down to this day have always upheld the banner of independence and of Hinduism against the Mahomedan conquerors. The last upholder of Svadharma and Svarājya in Indian history was a descendant of this hero viz., Sivaji who fought with the Mahomedans in the Deccan and re-established the independence and the religion of the Marathas.

There is, however, one great difference between the Aryans of the west and the Aryans of the east. The Spaniards remained in a deadly grip of fight for a thousand years nearly with the Moors on the banks of the Tagus in Spain when suddenly the Moors lost in strength and were immediately overthrown by the Spaniards and driven out of Europe. In India the Arabs followed by the Turks remained similarly grappled in conflict for about five hundred years, near about the Indus, with the Rajputs, the Indo-Aryans. In this tug-of-war, however, the Rajputs eventually gave way and were overthrown by the Turks and the Afghans about the end of the third period of our history. Though the Rajputs preserved their independence and their honour, their religion and their valour in the sands and hills of Rajputana, India as a whole lay prostrate at the feet of the Mahomedan conquerers. The Mahomedans were not only not beaten back out of India as in Spain but they eventually engulfed the whole of this country. Why unlike their Aryan brethren of the West, the Rajputs of India failed is a question which the historian of Mediæval Hindu India has to answer and we shall try to do so in the volumes which are now before us.

Who are these Rajputs who arose at this time and for five hundred years at the least beat back the Mahomedan onslaughts and whence did they come? We have already said that they were Indo-Aryans, the most chivalrous representatives of the Vedic Aryans of India. They defended their ancient faith with heroism and may well be called the defenders of the Hindu faith.

Were they new proselytes to Hinduism from the ranks of foreigners, the remnants of Huns and Śakas, of Yue-chi and Geetœ as many European and native antiquarian researchers think? We propose to discuss this subject at great length in this book as in spite of the verdict of anthropometry that the facial characteristics of the Rajputs show them to be true Aryans, noted historians like Sir V. Smith still adhere to the theory that the Rajputs are the descendants of foreign peoples who invaded India about the sixth century A. D.

CHAPTER II.

THEORY OF FOREIGN DESCENT.

The Rajputs who now came to the front and who by their heroism diffuse such glory on this period of Mediæval Indian History can not but have been descendants of Vedic Aryans. None but Vedic Aryans could have fought so valiantly in defence of their ancestral faith. It is true that converts sometimes exhibit more virulence and more violence in the defence of their adopted religion but this is more by way of exception than the rule. It is, therefore, natural to infer that these Rajputs were the descendants of Vedic Aryans. Their own traditions also declare that they belonged to the well-known Solar and Lunar races of Kshatriyas, or as we have elsewhere interpreted the terms, that they were the descendants of the two hordes of Aryan invaders who in pre-historic times entered India by way of the Panjab and the Gangetic valley. Thirdly, anthropometric measurements taken at the time of the census of 1901 fully substantiate the claim of the Rajputs to Aryan descent. Their straight noses, their long heads and their tall statures unmistakably show them to be Aryans, as these characteristics of Aryan races have been marked all over the world. And many European observers like Nesfield and Ibbetson have no doubt whatever about the truth of this claim of the Rajputs to be treated as Aryans, as descendants of those ancient Kshatriyas who settled in India in Vedic times.

But inspite of ethnology, of tradition and of probabilities, other European historians and scholars and many Indian antiquarians believe and maintain that the Rajputs who now began to figure on the stage of Indian history were the descendants of foreign barbarian races. Tod the famous historian of the Rajputs no doubt started this theory but in his days historical research and the science of anthropometry were in their infancy.

were perhaps non-existent. But that historians like Sir Vincent Smith, after the discovery of so much historical material and the present progress of anthropometry, should still seek to forward the same theory is to be wondered at, nay, deplored. Setting aside the conclusions of ethnology "as of no use to the historian" Sir V. Smith observes (E. H. I. 3rd Edn. P. 322) on the origin of the Rajputs," In thi splace I want to draw attention to the fact, long suspected and *now established by good evidence* that the foreign immigrants into Rajputana and the upper Gangetic valley were not utterly destroyed in the course of their wars with the native princes. Many of course perished but many survived and were mixed in the general population of which no inconsiderable part is formed by their descendants. These foreigners like their fore-runners the Śakas and the Yue-chi universally yielded to the wonderful assimilative power of Hinduism and rapidly became Hinduised. Clans or families which succeeded in winning chieftainships were admitted readily into the frame of Hindu polity as Kshatriyas or Rajputs and there is no doubt that the Parjhārs and many other famous Rajput clans of the north were developed out of the barbarain hordes which poured into India during the fifth and sixth centuries. The rank and file of the strangers became Gujars and the castes ranking lower than Rajputs in their precedence. Further to the south, various indigenous or aboriginal tribes and clans underwent the same process of Hinduised social promotion in virtue of which Gonds, Bhars, Kharwas and so forth emerged as Chandels, Rathors, Gaharwars and other well-known Rajput clans duly equipped with pedigree reaching back to the sun and the moon." The extract is long but necessary to show how European scholars and historians interpret the appearance of Rajputs in the history of India about this time and how they treat the most famous Rajput clans of the present day, the Guhilots and the Rathors, the Chandels and the Pratīhārs, as in reality either barbarians (Huns etc.) or aborigines (Gouds etc.) in origin, in spite of their vaunted claim to Aryan descent.

Whether these Rajput clans which play so brilliant a part in Indian history both in mediæval and modern times are Aryan by descent or Scythian or Dravidian does not really matter in the least. That they are a virile and a chivalrous people cannot be denied and their importance does not diminish by the supposed *descent* in their ancestry. But we are really concerned here with history, with the question whether this view of the origin of the Rajputs is historically correct. This view is supported if not originated by some Indian researchers like Dr. D. R. Bhandarkar and naturally enough is also accepted by the last erudite editor of Tod's Annals of Rajastan. Mr. William Crooke who has just edited this famous history with notes based on up-to-date research thus observes in his introduction: " Recent research has thrown much light on the origin of Rajputs. A wide gulf lies between the Vedic Kshatriyas and the Rajputs of mediæval times which it is now impossible to bridge. It is now certain that the origin of many clans dates from the Śaka or Kushān invasions or more certainly from that of the White Huns who destroyed the Gupta empire about 480 A. D. The Gurjar tribe connected with the latter people adopted Hinduism and their leaders formed the main stock from which the higher Rajput families sprang. When these new claimants to princely honour accepted the faith and the institutions of Brahmanism the attempt would naturally be made to connect them with the heroes of the Mahābhārata and the Rāmāyaṇa. Hence arose the body of legend recorded in these annals by which a fabulous origin from the sun and the moon was ascribed to these Rajput families " (P. XXXI). Mr. Crooke further on remarks " The group denoted by the name Kshatriya or Rajput depended on status rather than on descent and it was therefore possible for foreigners to be introduced into these tribes without any violation of the prejudices of caste, which was then only partially developed. But it was necessary to disguise this admission of foreigners under a convenient fiction. Hence arose the legend how by a solemn act of purification or initiation under the superintendence of the ancient Vedic Rishis, the *fire-born* septs were created to help the Brahmins in repressing Buddhism and other heresies. This privilege was confined to four septs known as Agnikula or fire-born—viz., the Paramār, Parihār, Chālukya and Chanhān." This long extract would also show how the latest English researchers do not believe in the generally accepted

2

view of the Rajputs that they are the representatives of Vedic Kshatriyas and it also shows how the now generally accepted legend about Agnikula Rajput families is twisted into a support for the theory of foreign descent started by western scholars and antiquarians.

We have tried in our first volume to refute many of these arguments. We have shown in that volume how Mr. D. R. Bhandarkar's theory that the Gujars are foreigners (Khizars) who came along with the Huns in the beginning of the fifth century is baseless, inasmuch as it is admitted by even Smith that there is no historical evidence either of native tradition or foreign record to suggest, much less to prove that the Gujars *came* into India from outside about this time and further because we find that the history of the Khizars proves that they never left their own country. We also showed that the characters of the two people are diametrically opposed. While the Khizars are stationary in habits and traders by profession, the Gujars are of roving habits and cattle-grazers by profession. It was also shown that the Gujars of India are distinctly Aryan by features, that their noses are more prominent than the noses of even Parisans, that in short the whole theory based on the premiss that Gujars are foreigners is mistaken for the Gujars are not foreigners and Scythians but are distinctly Aryans. We will, therefore, not repeat in this volume what we have urged already in refutation of this theory. We have also shown that foreigners like the Huns and the Śakas could not have left many descendants behind, that ruling races generally disappear when their rule is gone. We will, however, address ourselves in this volume to the second part of Mr. Bhandarkar's theory accepted by Sir Vincent Smith and Mr. William Crooke that it is established *on good evidence* that the Rajputs are the descendants of Gujars. In fact we may say that while we have refuted the second premiss of Dr. D. R. Bhandarkar's argument in our first volume, we will in this volume try to refute his first premiss. For Dr. Bhandarkar's argument may in syllogistic form be stated thus: "1st The Rajputs are the descendants of Gujars; 2nd the Gujars are foreigners. Therefore, 3rd the Rajputs are the descendants of foreigners." We have already shown that the

Gujars are not foreigners but are true Aryans, and hence even if the Rajputs are descendants of Gujars they cannot be classed as Non-Aryans. But we go further and will prove in this volume that the Rajputs are not descended from Gujars but from Kshatriyas who may well be believed to be the representatives of the Vedic Kshatriyas. Dr. Bhandarkar's theory has been elucidated principally in his papers on the Gujars (J. Bom. R. A. S. 1903) and on Foreign Elements in the Indian Population (Ind. Ant. XXI). Many of his arguments advanced in these papers have been accepted by historians like Smith and Crooke from whom we have quoted above at length. These arguments have always derived a strong support from the tradition relating to the Agnikulas current among the Rajputs themselves. It is here that we see the immense value of research. For research has already established that this tradition or myth of Agnikulas is indeed a myth, a creation and a modern creation of a poet's brain; and we see here how false traditions once set up by poets and accepted in popular belief not only delude the people themselves but even historians like Smith and Crooke and researchers like Bhandarkar and Johnson. Indeed one can demonstrate the value and usefulness of historical research by the example of this very baseless myth of fire-born races which has so strongly supported the theory of the foreign descent of the Rajputs.

CHAPTER III.

THE EXPLODED MYTH OF AGNIKULAS.

Gibbon, in explaining the doctrine of Transubstantiation, remarks truly that in popular belief what is originally rhetoric becomes subsequently logic. Most popular traditions arise in this way in poetical fancies which are eventually accepted as undeniable truths. No sane man believes that human races could have sprung from the sun or the moon. Such beliefs are certainly absurd, but the tradition of solar and lunar origins of Indo-Aryan races is of very ancient date and even goes back to the Ṛigveda. This tradition, therefore, absurd as it is, has a historical importance and we have already elsewhere noted the inference derivable from this tradition viz., that the Indo-Aryans must have come into India in two different hordes, an inference first suggested by Sir R. Grierson on linguistic grounds. The traditions similarly of the origins of different Rajput clans have some historical importance if they are of long standing and unvarying character. The tradition about the origin of Agnikulas might thus have been of use historically and might have supported the theory of foreign peoples being incorporated into Hindu society, if it had not been proved beyond the shadow of a doubt that it originated in a poet's brain, nay it may be shown further that it is based on a misconception of that poet and is finally of quite recent date. Research has amply shown this but unfortunately western scholars have not sufficiently recognised the fact and drawn the necessary inference from it.

As is generally known, this story of four warrior clans having been created out of fire by Vaśishṭha was first told by Chand the bard of Pṛithvirāj in his epic the Pṛithvīrāj Rāsā on the exploits of this last chivalrous Rajput king. The story shortly is that when this world was oppressed by Rākshasas or Mlechchas, Vaśishṭha created from his sacrificial fire four warriors in succession viz., first the Paramāra, then the Chālukya, then the Parihāra and when these could not destroy the Rākshasas, the terrible Chāhomāna from whom the poet's hero Pṛithvīrāja was decended. This story along with the Rāsā became by and by extremely popular and was eventually accepted by all Rajputs and what is strange by the descendants of these four clans themselves. Naturally the great historian of the Rajputs Col. Tod accepted it and incorporated it in his history. These four clans, it is now currently believed, cannot trace their pedigree to the sun or the moon as the other Kshatriyas do, but are fire-born thus giving colour to the theory that these clans are really foreigners who have been transformed into Kshatriyas by the Brahmins by a fiction of purification by fire.

Now it will be a revelation to many to know that this story is not only a poet's fancy but further arises from a misconception of even that fancy. For as a matter of fact it seems that even Chand himself did not wish to represent that these Kshatriyas were *newly created* Kshatriyas. For epigraphic evidence unequivocally proves that these four or at least three of these, in the ninth century A. D., represented themselves as and were believed to be descended from the solar and lunar Vaṁśas. Thus the Pratihāra clan which established its empire at Kanauj which Dr. Bhandarkar and others strive to show to be Gujar in origin and therefore foreign is distinctly said in a stone inscription of the 10th century to belong to the solar line. This Gwalior Bhoja inscription is very important in this connection and states that the imperial Pratihāras of Kanuaj were descended from Lakshmaṇa brother of Rāma, the hero of the solar race, Lakshmaṇa being Rama's Pratihāra or door-keeper. As already stated we attach no value to such traditions except in so far as they represent the beliefs current at particular times. This tradition proves that the Pratihāra clan was in the ninth century treated as solar in race. How can Chand then in the 12th century represent these Pratihāras as Agnikulas? Similarly the Chāhamānas are also said in records previous to Chand's Pṛithvīrāj Rāsā distinctly to belong to the same solar line. The Harsha stone inscription (Ep. Ind. II. p. 119) gives the line of the

Chāhamānas from one Gūvaka and to our mind clearly conveys that this clan is solar in descent. (तन्मुक्त्यर्थमुपागता रघुकुले भूचक्रवर्ती स्वयम्.) Mr. Harbilasa Sarda of Ajmere has, in his paper in R. A. S. 1903 on Pṛithvīrāj Vijaya—a poem by a contemporary poet in the Darbar of Pṛithvīrāj himself, shown that the poem describes Pṛithvīrāj as born of the solar line. Hammīra Mahākāvya again declares that the Chāhamānas were descended from the sun, as also a stone inscription in the Ajmere Museum. It is, therefore, certain that from the ninth century down even to the thirteenth and the fourteenth, the Chāhamānas were considered to belong to the solar line of Kshatriyas. The third clan Solankhi or Chālukya of Anahillapāṭaṇ is, in epigraphic records described as belonging to the lunar line. It must be remembered that the Chālukyas of Badāmi were different from these. Here it is sufficient to state that these Chālukyas belong to the Bhāradvāja gotra and are so described even in the Pṛithvīrāj Rāsā. Now this gotra of these Chālukyas is given in an inscription of the Haihayas of Chedi. The Bilhari stone inscription (Ep. Ind. I. p. 253-9) states that Keyūravarsha Haihaya married Nohalādevī, daughter of Avanivarman Chālukya of the Bhāradvāja gotra. This inscription which has been assigned to the beginning of the 11th century A. D. gives a different version about the origin of these Chālukyas from that of the southern Chālukyas given by Bilhaṇa as also by Eastern Chālukya kings and states that the first ancestor of these Chālukyas was created out of the water in his handful by Droṇa Bhāradvāja for *killing Drupada*, and hence belonged to his gotra. As Bhāradvāja belonged to the lunar line, the Chālukyas of Bhāradvāja gotra also belonged to the same line. Now since in this inscription, the Chālukyas were believed to belong to the lunar line and were also believed to be created by Droṇa, how can Chand in the 12th century represent these same Chālukyas as created by Vaśishṭha from his fire ?

These three clans, it is now admitted by researchers (see introduction by Mr. Crooke himself to Tod's Rajastan page XXXI) do not belong to the Agnikula creation origin, but the necessary inference from this is not drawn by them. If the Chāhamānas and the Prātihāras, the two most important clans who were supposed to be Gujars transformed into Kshatriyas by purification, are proved to be no longer Agnikulas but on the contrary were believed to be solar in descent in the 9th and 10th centuries, does not the whole theory of foreign descent fall to the ground ? But this is not all. Even the fourth, the Paramāras are not Agnikulas as represented by Chand. In fact stone inscription records of these Paramāras from the 12th century though giving the origin of the Paramāras from the fire of Vaśishṭha, do not give the story of the Rāsā, but an entirely different story. Vaśisṭha is said therein to have created the first Paramāra to *chastise Visvāmitra* who was taking away the divine cow belonging to the former. The Udepur Praśasti for instance (Ep. Ind I.) gives this story and states that the gotra of the Paramāras is consequently Vaśishṭha. This gotra is still claimed by the Paramāras all over India and is also given by Chand.

How can then the story given by Chand in the Rāsā be taken to be a correct representation of the traditions prevailing in his time and in earlier centuries about the lineage of Pratihāras and Chāhamānas, of Chālukyas and Paramāras, and recorded even in contemporaneous poems ? The only explanation is that either the Pṛithvīrāja Rāsā is a forgery, a later work produced in Mahomedan times when inscriptions had been forgotten, or that the story as given by Chand in his poem is misinterpreted. The authenticity of the Rāsā as a poem written by a contemporary poet is questioned by Shyamaldas Pandya. Our views on the subject will be given in a note as it is not necessary to discuss this subject here at length. For one can see and say that the Rāsā merely gives here a poetical *imaginary* story which has subsequently been taken to be a real story. These four races, we know, came to the front by their fights with the Mlechhas and hence have been brought together in this story. But it seems that the story even as given by Chand is misinterpreted and it appears that Chand did not intend here to set forth a third lineage for Kshatriyas viz., the fire in addition to the two well-known Puranic lineages the solar and the lunar. This is clear from the fact that Chand mentions only three lineages (1) the solar (2) the lunar and (3) the Yādava for the famous thirty-six royal families enumerated by him. He does not give the Agnikula lineage at all but assigns the four supposed Agnikula clans the Parihāra, the Paramāra, the Chāhamāna and the Chālukya under the old two or three lineages. The enumeration of the 36 Rajput families in the Rāsā begins thus रंवि ससि जाधव वंस । ककुत्स्थ परमार सदावर । चाहुआन चालुक, । छंदक सिलार आभियर ॥ Here it is clear that he puts the three Paramāra, Chāhamāna and Chālukya under the three old recognised Vaṁśas, the solar, the lunar and the Yādava. We think Chand's story has entirely been misconstrued. In describing the four warriors, Paramāra, Pratihāra, Chālukya, and Chāhamāna as coming out of fire at the call of Vaśishṭha, he did not intend to convey that these warriors were heroes *newly created* by Vaśishṭha. He simply wanted to convey that four warriors out of the already existing clans came out of the fire at Vaśishṭha's bid to fight the Rākshasas.

This story of Chand being so misinterpreted gained popular credence from the 16th century A. D. along with his now generally accepted Epic so much so that these four clans forgot that their ancestors in their historical records on stone represented themselves nowhere as Agnikulas but as solar and lunar race Kshatriyas. And their bards too forgot the fact so completely that a new Chand viz., Surajmal Bhata of Bundikota wrote another Hindi epic poem in glorification of his patron's family the Chāhamāna clan in which he completed the mischief caused by this misinterpretation of Chand, by assigning five Vaṁśas for the Kshatriyas. In this Vaṁśa-Bhāskara by Sūrajamal of Boondi we find the story of the Yajnakunda of Vaśishṭha given with greater detail, nay with the exact date when the first Chāhamāna warrior was created from the fire (the date comes to about 6632 B. C. being 3531 years before Kali began) and the following verse gives the five Kshatriya Vaṁsas which now for the first time were enumerated as भुजभव, मनुभव, अर्कभव, सासिभव, छत्रन वंश । है चउतिम, शुर्चवंस हुव पंचम प्रथितप्रशंस. The Hādās of Boondi-Kotā accepted the new Vaṁśa assigned to them by their poet and thus the myth of Agni-Vaṁśa which at the earliest commenced in about 1200 A. D. became a logical fact in about 1700 A. D. when the four clans themselves accepted a new Vaṁśa for themselves. Col. Tod could not but believe in this tradition and he set his final seal upon it by his well-known history of the Rajputs.

Such is in short the story of this Agnikula myth, a story begun in a poet's brain and being misconstrued by another poet finally commanding acceptance even from the deluded Rajputs themselves. The value of historical research cannot be illustrated more vividly than in the exploding of this myth from stone and copper records of these clans themselves. And we now clearly see that no such story was really put forth by Chand and that these four clans* represented themselves as and were believed to be solar or lunar by race in the 9th to the 13th century A. D. The theory of the foreign descent of these Rajput clans loses, therefore, its strongest support viz., the myth of purification by fire ; though it may still be contended by the propounders of this theory that these clans might as well have affiliated themselves to the solar or lunar race, as they are known to be Gujars from various records. We have, therefore, to examine the question whether there is any argument to prove that these clans of Rajputs are Gujars by descent.

---

* Even the Paramāras seem to be treated as solar race Kshatriyas, for the Paramāras among the Marāthas who have the same Vasishṭha gotra are treated as Solar-race Kshatriyas in their Vaṁśāvalis

NOTE

THE VALUE OF THE PRITHVĪRĀJA RĀSĀ.

The Pṛithvīrāja Rāsā purports to be a poem composed by Chand Bardai, a friend and contemporary of Pṛithvīrāja who fought the last battle of the Hindus with Mahomedans for independence on the usual battlefield of India viz., the plain of Panipat in 1191 A. D. Kavirāja Śyāmaldās questioned the authenticity and the antiquity of this poem in a learned article published in J. R. A. S. Bengal Vol. V (1887), pointing out many inaccuracies of date and even of the histories of the several Rajput royal families of Rājastān and notably the fact that Samarasi king of Mewad, mentioned by the Rāsā as contemporary and brother-in-law of Pṛithvīrāja lived many years after him and could not have fought along with him at Panipat. The recent editors of this poem (published by Nāgarī Prachāriṇī Granthamālā at Benares 1911) viz., Mohanlal Pāndya and Śyām Sunderdas, however, maintain that the poem is authentic and as old as Chand, the reputed contemporary of Pṛithvīrāja and have tried to answer the arguments adduced by Kavirāja Śyāmaldās. Sir Vincent Smith has long ago recorded his opinion that the poem has little historical value (1881 and also Note E. I. H.). It is necessary to give our view on the subject here, inasmuch as a history of the Rajputs cannot proceed without the help of this great epic in the Hindi language and especially that of Pṛithvīrāj must seek help from it.

In our opinion the epic Pṛithvirāja Rāsā resembles the Mahābhārata in most essential points and especially in this question of its antiquity and authenticity. On this point truth lies half way between the two opposite views. While the nucleus of the peom is authentic and ancient, the poem has been amplified at least by two additions. As we have shown in our book-the Mahābhārata Mīmānsā in Hindi-the present Mahābhārata is the second amplified form of the original poem of Vyāsa (first amplified by Vaiśampāyana) given us by Sauti. Similarly it seems that Pṛithvīrāja Rāsā must have originally been written by Chand, then amplified by his son and again amplified by an unknown writer about the 17th century A. D. In many essentials too the two poems completely resemble each other. For example, the poet Chand is himself an actor in the plot of the poem in the same way as Vyāsa the poet of the great war is an actor in the great war itself. Again Chand could not have been invested with miraculous powers (expressed in the epithet Bardai) like Vyāsa by himself. It was either his son who invested him with these superhuman powers or the last editor. And the poem is related by Chand to his wife just as Vaiśampāyana, Vyāsa's first disciple, recites his Bhārata to his patron king Janamejaya. These facts make it imperative that Chand's original work must have been amplified by others at least twice.

That we must concede an original nucleus by Chand cannot possibly be denied. This poem if fabricated by some unknown poet in the 17th century A. D. in the name of Chand, could not have attained that authority in Rajputana which the Rāsā unquestionably enjoys. In fact for the Rajputs the Rāsā enjoys an authority next only to the Mahābhārata. The Mahābhārata centres round a terrible fight, so lovable to a Kshatriya and the Rāsā too centres round the terrible fight which the Kshatriya warriors of modern India waged under Pṛithvīrāja with the Mahomedans for independence. As Indian Kshatriyas love to trace their ancestry to some hero in the Bhārata fight like the Greeks who loved to trace their origin to the heroes of the Iliad, so the present Kshatriya families love to believe that some one of their ancestors was present in the fight of Pṛithvīrāja with Ghori. A spurious work cannot gain such popularity without the help of a nucleus of a generally popular well-known work of a popular reputed poet. If there had not been any poem of Chand Bardai in existence, an unknown poet could not have suddenly sprung a work upon the people under the name of Chand. Chand Bhāt like Vyāsa must have been a well-known poet among the Rajputs and subsequent poets must have only taken advantage of his name and work and tried to make additions not out of their imagination solely but on the basis of popular legends which always gather round national heroes and national bards and national events. In this respect also to our mind the Rāsā exactly resembles the Mahābhārata and as an original nucleus of the Mahābhārata composed by Vyāsa is conceded by all, so we must concede a similar nucleus by Chand for the Rāsā.

These subsequent additions to the Rāsā, it is, however, difficult to separate as in the Mahābhārata, though certain considerations can be adduced which will tolerably assure us that particular portions are additions. We have tried to indicate these considerations with regard to the Mahābhārata in our book 'The Mahābhārata : a criticism'; but we cannot make a similar attempt for the Rāsā which being in old Hindi is not as completely open to us for inspection.

It is, however, certain that the poem in being amplified has made a conscious attempt to imitate the Mahābhārata and we would point out a few glaring examples of this conscious similarity. In the first place the poem aspires to the same length as the Mahābhārata viz., 100,000 Ślokas which ponderous length appears to have become in India a traditional one. To write a शतसाहस्री संहिता* is the ambition of great poets and the Rāsā has partially succeeded in attaining this enormous length. Then again

* Mohanlal interprets सत सहस्र as seven thousand.

various outside legends have been incorporated into the poem, of great length, which of course is unavoidable if the poem is to reach its avowed portentous dimension. The great credit again of this poem as of the Mahābhārata is its numerous detailed and yet interesting descriptions of fights and battles. It is really difficult to describe ancient battles and much more difficult to invest them with different details which will invest each fight with an interest of its own. There is again a conscious attempt to describe different scenes and incidents and especially the different seasons, (the poetic artifice employed by the Rāsā in giving a description of all the seasons together is indeed unique), to give an insight into different philosophies and into all kinds of knowledge, and to discuss the intricacies of government and administration and wordly life or Sansāra which, while it imitates the Mahābhārata, has a peculiarity and a beauty of its own establishing the claim of the poem to be called a great epic.

But what seems most interesting and similar is the conscious effort of the poet to introduce riddles after the fashion of the Kūta Ślokas of the Mahābhārata and many of these riddles are based like those in the latter on number. The most glaring example of this is the Ananda Vikrama era in which all the dates in the poem are given. We do not believe with Kavirāja Śyāmaldās that the dates given in the Rāsā are *Wrong*. The ingenious explanation of these dates given by Mohanlal Paṅdya appears plausible since we find that all the Samvat dates given in the Rāsā are mistaken by the same number 91 and this shows, as Mohanlal contends, that the poet has used a special era called Ananda Vikrama era which was either really in use or which the poet purposely invented. It is necessary to quote here the two verses which give the poet's first date and which in our view are riddle verses. They are as follows :— एकादससे पंचदह विक्रम साक अनंद । तिहि रिपुजयपुरहरनको भय प्रिथिराज नरिंद ॥ एकादससे पंचदह विक्रम जिम ध्रमसुत्त । तृतिय साक पृथिराजको लिख्यो विप्र गुन गुप्त ॥ २ ॥ Now Ananda here is not Ānanda as Mohanlal Pāndya rightly contends; it does not suit versification nor can Ananda (taking benefit of the poetic license to shorten the first syllable of Ānanda) be poetically introduced here. But strangely enough the explanation given by Mohanlal does not also fit in as Ananda would simply mean less by ***nine*** not ***ninety-one*** as he tries to make out. Of course his view must be accepted that a new era has been constructed here which gives dates in the usual Vikrama era less by 91; but how to arrive at that figure from the word Ananda is a riddle. Then the next verse is equally a riddle. Mr. Mohanlal Pandya tries to make some sense out of it (Vol. I p. 145) by introducing Brahmagupta; but firstly, विप्र गुन गुप्त cannot lead to Brahmagupta; secondly, so far as is known, Brahmagupta never held that Yudhishṭhira preceded Vikrama by 1115 years. The Indian astronomers all hold that Yudhishṭhira Śaka at the beginning of the Vikrama Śaka was 3044. It is the Purāṇas notably the Bhāgavata, which hold that Yudhishṭhira preceded the corona tion of Nanda by 1015 years. (यावत्परीक्षितो जन्म यावन्नन्दाभिषेचनम् । एतद्वर्षसहस्रं तु ज्ञेयं पञ्चदशोत्तरम्). It is probably this verse from the Bhāgavata which Chand has in his mind when he introduces Nanda in the first verse and Dharmasuta or Yudhishṭhira in the second. But it is still difficult to explain how Chand places 1115 years between Vikrama and Dharmasuta and in what manner he forms his third Śaka of Pṛithvīrāja. It seems that लिख्यो विप्र गुन गुप्त means that the Brahmin poet has written this in a riddle after making calculations and that there is no reference here to Brahmagupta the astronomer.

The view that Pṛithvīrāja Rāsā must have a nucleus by Chand himself and that it is not wholly a fabrication of the 17th century is strongly supported by the list of the 36 Royal Kshatriya families which is given by the Rāsā and which cannot be so late as the 17th century. The verse सोरोसे सतोत्तरे विक्रमसाक बदीत । दिल्लीधर चितोडपे लेवेंगा बलजित ॥ indeed records a prophecy that the Delhi Mahomedan emperor will take Chitod again in Samvat 1677 and may make this verse of the Rāsā an interpolation of the 17th century A. D. (Even in this the Rāsā resembles the Mahābhārata wherein as shown by us in Mahābhārata Mīmānsā there is a prophetic reference to Udayana). But that does not make the whole poem spurious and of so late a date. We will discuss the list of 36 Royal families in the next note and show that it cannot be of a date later than that of Pṛithvīrāja. The question whether Samarasi was a contemporary of Pṛithvīrāja or not we do not mean to discuss here as we shall have to discuss it in our third volume. Unfortunately we have not come across the explanation which Mohanlal Pandya has offered on this point and which he has reserved in his note on this subject (Vol. I page 145) in the Rāsā.

---

* If it were possible to make a guess, Nanda may stand for 91 which perhaps was the period of the reign of the nine Nandas and not 100 as stated in Purāṇas.

NOTE

THE 36 ROYAL CLANS OR RAJPUT FAMILIES.

It seems certain that from ancient times the Rajputs consider themselves as consisting of 36 Kulas or clans which are allowed to give and take daughters from one another. This confining themselves to a close group must have taken place about the end of the second or the beginning of the third sub-period of the Mediæval Hindu age, as we know that caste in the three Aryan higher grades was fluid during the first sub-period. For though the list of 36 clans cannot be traced earlier than the poem of Chand yet the number 36 is mentioned before him by Kalhaṇa who wrote his Rājataranginī in 1148 A. D. (VII 1617 wherein it is said that the Rajputs in their pride would not concede a higher position to even the sun). And the enumeration by Chand seems to be as old as the days of Pṛithvīrāja and cannot be treated a later interpolation as we shall presently show. Tod has given five lists of which one dates earlier than the Rāsā but he does not say how old this first list is; it was obtained from a Jati in the old city of Nadol in Marwad but since it gives some names such as Jhālā which are of later date, it appears that the list in the Rāsā is really the oldest we have. The third list is from Kumārapāla-charita a contemporary work of Chand but it does not give 36 names. In short it seems that the Rāsā first enumerated the 36 and the enumeration together with the number has become traditional inasmuch as the Rāsā became to the Rajputs what Homer's Iliad was to the Greeks.

Strangely, however, there is a great discrepancy in the interpretation of these verses of the Rāsā and we think that even the latest editors of the Rāsā have misunderstood their meaning. We will first give the verses here for the curious reader and then give our rendering of them.

रवि ससि जाधव बंस । ककुत्स्थ परमार सदावर ॥
चाहुवान चालुक । छंदक सिलार अभयिर ॥
दोय मत्त (दोयमत) मकवान । गरुअ गोहिल गोहिलपुत ॥
चापोत्कट परिहार । राव राठोर रोसजुत ॥
देवरा टांक सैधव अनिग [अनंग] । यौतिक प्रतिहार दधिषट्ट ॥
कारट्टपाल कोटपाल हुल । हरितट गोर कला [मा] ष भट ॥
धन्य [धान्य] पालक निकुंभवर । राजपाल कविनीस ॥
कालच्छुरकै आदि दे । बरने बंस छतीस ॥

The few variations given above in brackets are taken from the copy of the Rāsā we personally saw and inspected at the Udepur Museum Library. Now people generally and Tod and even Mohanlal Pandya in the interpretation he has given in the recent edition of the Rāsā enumerate 1. Ravi 2. Śaśi and 3. Jādhava among the 36. But this inclusion would make the number more than 36 as we proceed to show. Let us take the list from the bottom so that we shall at once be able to see that 1. Ravi 2. Śaśi and 3. Jādhava cannot be included. These names are :—

1. Kālachchhuraka.
2. Kavinīsa (omitted by Mohanlal but not by Tod.)
3. Rājapāla.
4. Nikumbhavara.
5. Dhānya-pālaka (omitted by Tod but not by Mohanlal).
6. Mata (omitted by Tod.)
7. Kamāsha (Kalāsha).
8. Gaura.
9. Haritaṭa (omitted by Tod).
10. Hula. (Mohanlal wrongly interprets it as Hūṇa).
11. Koṭapāla.
12. Kārattapāla.
13. Dadhishaṭ (Tod gives Didiot).
14. Pratihāra.
15. Yautika (Tod gives Pātaka).
16. Aniga (Tod gives Anaṅga).
17. Saindhava.
18. Tāka.
19. Deorā.
20. Rosajuta (omitted both by Tod and Mohanlal).
21. Rāthoda.
22. Parihāra.
23. Chāpotkaṭa.
24. Guhilota (Gohilaputra). [Tod mentions Gohil only.]
25. Gohila.
26. Garua (omitted both by Tod and Mohanlal).
27. Makavāna.
28. Doyamata.
29. Abhīyara.
30. Silāra.
31. Chhandaka.
32. Chālukka.
33. Chāhuvāna.
34. Sadāvara.
35. Paramāra.
36. Kakutstha.

Now we need not detain the reader on the inaccuracies of Tod as he has made out a list of 30 only by omitting many and even after including wrongly 1. Ravi 2. Śaśi and 3. Jādhava. Let us, however, see how Mohanlal is mistaken in including these. He has first omitted (2) Kavinīsa which even Tod admits (20) Rosajuta and (26) Garua. It is not possible to suggest that Rosajuta is an adjunct of Rāthod which has already one viz., Rao (and which itself may be treated separately). And Garua cannot be an adjective of Gohila for though Guhilots were certainly famous Gohilas were not. It is thus that Mohanlal has been wrongly induced to add 1. Ravi 2. Śaśi and 3. Jādhava.

But the most convincing proof why these three cannot be included in the 36 is that these were never the names of any clans in the sense the other names are. For the chief importance of these clan names is that they are practically for Rajputs what gotras are for Brahmins in respect of marriage. No Kula or clan out of the 36 can marry in the same clan. A Chālukka cannot marry a Chālukka and a Chohan cannot marry a Chohan. Ravi, Śaśi and Jādhava, especially the first two are not clan names in this sense. They are the names of races in which the 36 clans may be grouped. The Sūryavaṁśa, the Chandravaṁśa and the Yaduvaṁśa are the famous Vaṁśas of the Purāṇas and they do not indicate clans for purposes of marriage. There is no objectoin for a Sūryavaṁśī to marry a Sūryavaṁśi. As a matter of fact the Guhilots of Udepur and the Kachhavāhas of Jaipur are both Sūryavaṁśis but they do intermarry. The Purāṇas also do not show that Sūryavaṁśa or Chandravaṁśa was prohibitive of marriage within itself. Rāma and Sītā were both Suryavaṁśī and so were Arjuna and Draupadī both Chandravaṁśī. In Purānic times the Kshatriyas were observers of gotras only and Rāma being of Vaśishṭha gotra and Sītā of Gautama gotra could marry. In modern times the Kshatriyas have adopted the clan system to determine who cannot marry whom, and as we have already shown, it practically fulfils the gotra law of the Smṛitis. The argument why Ravi, Śaśi and Jādhava cannot be treated as clans like the other names will, therefore, be clear and we are certain that Chand merely indicates here the three great vaṁśas or races in which all the following 36 were to be grouped. The word vaṁśa used here only is of importance and has a meaning different from the same word used at the end (बरने बंस छतीस).

The question may here be asked why the Yadu-vaṁśa has been separately counted when it comes under the Chandravaṁśa. But it seems that the Jādhavas were always separately counted from the other Chandravaṁśis. Even in the Rigveda, the Yadū-Turvaśas are separately mentioned, the Turvaśas eventually disappearing. The Yādavas are again separately treated in the Purāṇas they having no right to be kings owing to the alleged curse of Yayāti. They were probably still pastoral in habits and hence their separate mention. It is, therefore, not strange that the Yaduvaṁśis are separately mentioned from the Chandravaṁśis. Their clans viz., Bhāti, Jadejā and others can intermarry as has already been shown and hence it is evident that Jādhava is not a clan like any of the 36.

It will be clear, therefore, that 1. Ravi 2. Śaśi and 3. Jādhava have not to be counted in the enumeration of the 36 families and the only way of making up the number is as shown above viz. , by treating Garua, Rosajuta and Kavinīsa as separate clans. The same thing is clear from the fact that Sūrajmal author of Vaṁśabhāskara treats Ravi and Śaśi as races and not families when he numbers them as five instead of three, viz., the old four, Bhujabhava, Manubhava, Arkabhava, Śaśibhava and the fifth Śuchibhava (fire-born). Bhujabhava means those created by Brahmā himself from his arms and Manubhava those born of Manu, while the Arka or Sun and Śaśi the moon are treated as the remaining two. We have already quoted this verse of Sūrajamal and we hold that there can be no possible doubt that Chand treated 1. Ravi 2. Śaśi and 3 Jādhava as races and not clans or families of which he has given the number as 36.

Now this list of the 36 cannot be dated in the 17th century A. D. when the Rāsā is supposed to have been fabricated but seems to be as old as Chand Bhāta of Pṛithvīrāja's court. We have the mention of many clans here which had no existence in the 17th century and Tod himself is in a difficulty as to their identity. And many clans or families which were well-known in the 17th century find no mention in the list. Thus Rosajuta, Anaṅga, Yautika, Dadhishat, Kārattapāla, Kotapāla, Haritaṭa, Kamāsha, Maṭa, Dhānyapāla, Rājapāla and Kavinīsa are difficult to be traced; while Bhāṭī, Jhālā, Bais and other modern tribes are conspicuous by their absence. Thirdly, some names are rather obscure though their identity is not doubtful. Kakustha is equated to Kachhavāha and Sadāvara to Tuar by Mohanlal Pandya properly, though it is very doubtful whether these names were ever in use. On these grounds it seems almost certain that this list given in the Rāsā is very old in fact as old as the 12th century A. D.

We may here discuss the propriety of the identification of each tribe as given by Mohanlal in his edition of the Rāsā (Vol. I p. 54). Chhanda is treated as Randel but this is probably a misprint for Chandel. The Rāsā sometimes uses the word Chand as a short form for Chandel.* Doyamata as Dāhima is again doubtful; Aniga as Anaṅga is also obscure. Parihāra and Pratihāra are both given in the list and must be distinct. Now which of the two is the Padhihar of Mandor? That question is unsolved. Kāraṭṭapāla is certainly not Kāthi who are not admitted to be one of the 36 Rajput families. Koṭapāla is left unexplained and Maṭa cannot be jāt who are not admitted to be Rajputs. Lastly, Dhānyapāla and Rājapāla are not identified. We may add that Garua who are omitted by Mohanlal may be said to be Gujara which in Prākṛit would be Guar which by transposition becomes Garua. The Bīra Gujars are a well-known family of Rajputs. Gujara and Ābhīra or Ahīra are noted names of

* e.g. राज चंद नहीं जाय ।

Śūdras and Vaiśyas indeed but they have been taken as the names of certain kingly families which ruled over these people and which were, however, Kshatriya families.

Before concluding, we may notice the argument advanced by many that after all Hūṇa was admitted to be one of the 36 royal clans and thus the inclusion of foreign races as true Kshatriyas stands proved by admission; and state that Hūṇa is not one of the 36 according to the enumeration of the Rāsā. The name given there is Hula with short u and l and not Hūṇa. By no rules of transformation Prākṛit or other can Hūṇa become Hula. It may be argued that the inscriptions do mention the marriage of Kshatriya kings with Hūṇa princesses and that there is also mentioned a Hūṇa kingdom in India in the inscriptions of the time. Both these facts may be admitted but they do not prove that the Hūṇa kings were treated as Kshatriya kings. Kings then married and marry still wives from Vaiśya and Sūdra and even Mlechchha families but that does not prove that any of the latter were treated as Kshatriyas. For example some Rajput princes have taken even now Hūṇa princesses i. e. princesses from English or French or Spanish families. But none of these people are, therefore, Kshatriyas nor are the ladies themselves treated as Kshatriyas nor their progeny. And in Mahomedan times Rajput princesses were given in marriage to Mogul and other Mahomedan emperors and kings. But such relations do not establish the proposition that these Moguls or Mahomedans were treated or looked upon as Kshatriyas. It is, therefore, not possible to argue from these marriage relations that the Hūṇas were treated as Kshatriyas.

Who were the Hula mentioned among the 36? We are not bound to answer the question for there are many unidentifiable names among the 36 clans enumerated by Chand. In the Hindi census report of Marwar, however, there appears a branch by name Hula of Śisodia Rajputs. This fact shows that there was and is still the name Hula current in Marewar (see report for 1891 and 1895 Vol. III in Hindi, page 6). The name is taken as the name of a branch of Guhilots; but probably they may be a distinct clan and family by themselves. Any how the name appearing in the list of 36 by Chand is Hula and not Hūṇa and this has been verified by us even in the copy of the Rāsā in the Udepur Library. That they were distinct from Hūṇa is further proved by the fact that among the clans which assist Bappā Rāwal in his fight with Mahomedans are mentioned both Hūṇas and Hulas (see Tod's Rajastan by Crooke Vol. I. p. 290). Although these catalogues of Rajput clans gathering frequently to assist the Guhilots of Mewad are of later date, they at least prove that Hula was a clan of Rajputs which was differentiated from Hūṇa,

CHAPTER IV

ARE THE AGNIKULAS GUJARS ?

Dr. D. R. Bhandarkar in his paper in Indian Antiquary, Vol. XL (1911) tries to prove that the so-called four Agnikula clans viz., Pratihāra, Paramāra, Chālukya and Chāhamāna are Gujars (see his paper on Foreign Elements in Hindu population). It is not difficult to show that this view is incorrect and in this chapter we propose to answer the arguments adduced by him in this paper.

The ancient Vedic history of caste and marriage has been much misunderstood by Dr. Bhandarkar and the inferences he draws in the beginning of his paper must be accepted with caution. There is no doubt that in Vedic times there was for a time a great commingling of the Aryan race with the Dravidian race which originally inhabited this country. Among the Aryans themselves, caste was then rather a class distinction, the three castes Brāhmins, Kshatriyas and Vaiśyas freely intermarrying. But there was in this no mixture of races as the three castes were Aryan by race. When after settling in India these classes began to take Śūdra wives, then only the fusion of races began and for a time this fusion was unchecked. The Nahusha episode in the Mahābhārata (Vana Parva Chap. 180) affords distinct proof that such mixture of blood went on for a time.* But opinion soon gathered strength against the marriage of higher caste men with Śūdra women, as the result of such marriages was found to be extremely unsatisfactory. Especially Pratiloma marriage with Śūdras was found to be disastrous and this view is embodied in the following observation of Manu जातो नार्यामनार्यायामार्यादार्यो भवेद्गुणैः । जातस्त्वनार्यादार्यायामनार्य इति निश्चयः ॥

---

* जातिरत्र महासर्प मनुष्यत्वे महामते । संकरत्वात्सवर्णानां दुष्परीक्ष्येति मे-मतिः । सर्वे सर्वास्वपत्यानि जनयान्ति सदा नराः । तस्माच्छीलं प्रधानेष्टं विदुर्ये तत्त्वदार्शिनः ।

"A person born of a non-Aryan woman from an Aryan man might be Aryan by qualities, but a person born of a non-Aryan man from an Aryan woman is most certainly non-Aryan by qualities." In consequence Pratiloma marriage with Śūdras was soon stopped and by imitation Pratiloma marriage among higher castes also. Anuloma marriages with Śūdra women continued to take place infrequently no doubt but, as Yājñavalkya distinctly said that he was of the opinion that a Śūdra wife should not be taken, a prohibition began to be observed even in this direction.

Such then was the state of caste and the law of marriage in the time of Megasthenes who lived in India about 300 B. C. He distinctly states that "No one is allowed to marry out of his own caste or to exchange his profession for another. An exception is made in favour of the philosopher who for his virtue is allowed this privilege." (McCrindle's Ancient India Megasthenes pp. 85-86). This shows that caste was already a water-tight compartment in the days of Megasthenes i. e. about 300 B. C. How could then the Śakas and Yavanas have been admitted into Indian castes? Even if they became Buddhists or Hindus, they remained a distinct caste as is proved by the very fact that they are, even after becoming Buddhists or Hindus, called Śakas or Yavanas in the inscriptions quoted by Dr. Bhandarkar himself. Maga Brahmins too remained Magas and, therefore, a distinct sub-caste. We do not know whether the Magas came after Megasthenes even as the Śakas and Yavanas unquestionably did. The fact that they were and are called Maga Brāhmins shows that they remained separate and did not merge their blood with that of the other Brāhmins.

We have the historical evidence of Megasthenes relating to the state of caste in 300 B. C. We have similarly a distinct foreign piece of evidence with regard to the state of castes about 600 A. D. in the writings of Hiuen Tsang and we have already quoted his statement in our first volume. He says "the members of the caste marry within the caste" (Vol. I p. 60). Now here the exception noted by Megasthenes is not mentioned and caste appears now as an entirely confined body. Inscriptions, however, show that the Brāhmins sometimes did marry Ksha triya women especially when daughters of kings (see Vol. I p. 61) and Kshatriya kings married daughters of Vaiśya kings. The difference, however, in the result of such marriages may be noted. In most ancient times the progeny of such marriages was treated as of the caste of the father as in the case of Vyāsa and others. In later times an intermediate position was assigned to the progeny and this led to the formation of intermediate mixed castes*. But later still, in the days of Harsha and subsequent centuries it appears from inscriptions that the progeny was treated as belonging to the caste of the mother.† This is at least certain in the case of Brāhmins. For example we are told in an inscription of the Pratihāras that a Brāhmin married a Brāhmin wife and a Kshatriya wife and the progeny of the Brahmin wife became Padhihar Brahmins while the progeny of the Kshatriya wife became Padhihar Kshatriyas. From roughly the 11th century onward, as we shall show in our third volume, marriage outside the caste was treated as illegal by a Kalivarja text. This history of the development of caste (see Note) if borne in mind will dispel many of the doubts created by stories in the Purāṇas quoted by Dr. Bhandarkar.

With these preliminary remarks we now proceed to discuss the cogency of the particular arguments adduced by Dr. Bhandarkar to prove that the four supposed Agnikula tribes were Gujars who were allied to the Huns and therefore foreigners. It is necessary at the outset to say that because a tribe is mentioned along with another and foreign tribe in any connection, therefore it does not follow that the first tribe is also a foreign tribe. Because Bāṇa says in Harsha-charita that Pratāpavardhana the Thanesar king conquered the Huns and also the Gujars, therefore it would be absurd to argue that the Gujars were a foreign

* Smṛitis generally embody this state of the marriage law. There was indeed a previous intermediate step, however, which is contained in the Manu Smṛiti. This was to the effect that if the wife was of the next caste only the progeny was to be treated as of the caste of the father. But this intermediate step soon disappeared and other Smritis do not contain this provision but declare the progeny to be of an intermediate mixed caste.

† Later Smṛitis such as Vyāsa contain this provision which means a further tightening of caste.

tribe allied to the Huns and came to India along with them. On this evidently fallacious argument Dr. Bhandarkar tries to prove that the Haihayas also were foreigners, simply because they are mentioned in the Purāṇas along with foreigners. "As the Haihayas are classed (?) with Śakas, the Yavanas, the Pāradas, the Kāmbojas there can be little doubt that they were regarded as Mlechhas at about the 4th century A. D. when the Harivaṁśa was composed" (p. 19). This is certainly illogical, for we must have a distinct statement to hold that the Haihayas were themselves regarded as Mlechchhas. Though they might have taken the aid of Mlechchhas in their wars, they themselves cannot thereby become Mlechchhas. But the case of the Haihayas is still stronger. For the Harivaṁśa itself and all the Purāṇas agree in stating that the Haihayas and their ancient king Sahasrārjuna were Aryans belonging to the Lunar Vaṁśa. Not only this, throughout Indian history and down to the present time the Haihayas are treated as some of the best Kshatriyas. As shown in our first Volume (p. 345) their anthropometrical characteristics are also distinctly Aryan*. While again the Haihayas are distinctly Aryans and are treated as Aryans and the best Kshatriyas, the Huns were distinctly mentioned as foreigners and were treated as foreigners by the orthodox Hindus. A Kshatriya recorded as marrying a Hūṇa princess in ancient days no more makes a Hun an Indian and a Kshatriya than a Native prince in these days marrying a Spanish lady makes the Spanish, Indians or Kshatriyas. The Huns were never treated as one of the 36 Royal families as we have already shown in our note and Dr. Bhandarkar like many others is mistaken in looking upon them as Kshatriyas. With these unavoidable further preliminary observations which are, however, necessary, we proceed to examine one by one the case of the four Agnikulas whom Dr. Bhandarkar believes to have been Gujars,

* Dr. Bhandarkar mentions here the unnecessary fact that the Kāyastha Prabhus claim descent from Sahasrārjuna. Perhaps this is intended to hint that these Prabhus too are foreign by race. But it is clearly proved that the Kāyastha Prabhus are Aryans by their features as also by their tradition. Perhaps Dr. Bhandarkar does not wish to leave out any higher caste from his theory of foreign descent.

even though this also would not make them foreigners. For Gujars as stated many a time before are not foreigners but are anthropometrically Aryans with the best Aryan noses and are historically the Vaiśyas of the Vedas and the Smṛitis.

The first and foremost supposed Agnikula tribe is the Pratihāra to which the Imperial Pratihāras of Kanauj belonged. Now Dr. Bhandarkar admits that they never call themselves Gujars in their inscriptions, that their names are Aryan names like Vatsarāja, Nāgabhata and so on, that they represent themselves in their inscriptions as Sūrya-Vaṁśis, that even Rājaśekhara a noted poet in their time calls them Raghukulatilakas. These facts should have induced Dr. Bhandarkar to examine carefully the arguments which appear to show them as Gujars. Instead of that, he twists these facts themselves into arguments to hold " how wonderfully soon foreign tribes were assimilated with the Hindus and were even treated as Kshatriyas and solar race Kshatriyas " ! ! ! As a matter of fact ancient Hindus and Hindus of the 8th century A. D. too were as strongly against the amalgamation of varṇas as they are now; and Dr. Bhandarkar should rather have laid stress on these facts in order to see that the other facts which appear to show them as Gujars must be explained in another way (see p. 23 Ind. Ant. XL. 1911).

But what are these opposing facts and how are they to be explained ? The first argument adduced is that a minor Pratihāra dynasty ruling in the south-east of modern Jaipur territory calls itself Gurjara Pratihāra in an inscription found at Rājor. Now since the Pratihāras of Kanauj never call themselves Gujars, these Pratihāras call themselves so, simply to distinguish themselves from other Pratihāras, and the method of such distinction is the natural one viz., that based on the mention of the country of residence. As there are Nāgar and Kanojia Brāhmins i.e. of Nāgar and Kanauj, these Pratihāras call themselves Gujar Pratihāras because they inhabited the Gujar country. Dr. Bhandarkar has himself shown here that this part of the country was and is inhabited mainly by Gujars. Nay, this part was alone called Gurjaratrā or Gujarat in those days and Dr. Bhandarkar is right when he says that Gurjaratrā in the 8th and 9th centuries was not modern Gujarat but southern Rajputana extending up to the south-east part of the present Jaipur State. It is, therefore, not at all strange that these Pratihāras in order to distinguish themselves call themselves Gurjara Pratihāra from the country they ruled or resided in and not because they were themselves Gujars by caste. In any case the Imperial Pratihāras cannot be looked upon as Gujars on the basis of this inscriptional statement*.

But Dr. Bhandarkar has adduced the further argument that these Pratihāras of Kanauj were called Gujars by the Rāshtrakūṭas in their inscriptions and also by the Arabs in their accounts of travel. These two facts cannot be contested and the Rāsṭrakūṭas and the Arabs often were allies in their fights with the Pratihāras of Kanauj. When the Rāshṭrakūṭa grants refer to their battles with Gurjaras they mean the Kanauj kings, for these alone were powerful enough to fight with them and these indeed were the overlords of a very large part of Northern India; and so also the Arabs speak of the kingdom of Kanauj when they speak of the kingdom of Juzr. But does this fact prove that the kings of Kanauj were Gujars by caste? Because Indians call the Mahomedans Yavanas does it prove that the Mahomedans are Greeks by race or descent? In the thirteenth century and later the Rajputs called all Mahomedans Turakadā from their first fight with the Turks viz., Mahmud of Ghazni; does that show that every Mahomedan that came to India whether he be Afghan or Persian was a Turk by race or caste? The argument is in short ineffectual and cannot weigh against the facts which distinctly show that the Pratihāras were Śūrya-Vaṁśi Rajputs or Kshatriyas by caste. As the Arabs of Sind were on the east bounded by the Gurjaratrā country which was then the name of South Rajputana and as the country was ruled by the Pratihāras it was but natural that the Arabs called the country and the king by the name of Juzr and indeed the Rāsṭrakūtas too called them Gurjaras for the same reason.

Still more flimsy is the argument based on the legend of the Pratihāra origin given in certain inscriptions (p. 24 ditto) viz.

* The phrase Gurjara Pratihāra need not be interpreted to mean Prātihāras who were Gurjaras but should be interpreted as Pratihāras of the Gurjara country.

a certain Brahmin had a Brahmin wife and a Kshatriya wife and the progeny of the Brahmin wife became Padhihar Brahmins while the progeny of the Kshatriya wife became Padhihar Rajputs. "The marriage of a Brahmin with a Kshatriya woman with the result as noted in this inscription is curious and can only be accounted for as being of foreign importation." Such marriage with such result, as shown in the beginning of this chapter is *not* curious but is normal; but even if it were, that it should be treated as an argument for the foreign extraction of the Pratihāras is certainly very curious. In this manner indeed, any inference can be drawn from this legned, the inference e. g. that these people were cannibals and so on. Thus so far as Pratihāras are concerned we find that all the three opposing arguments which Dr. D. R. Bhandarkar adduces are ineffectual and cannot weigh against the facts which show that the Imperial Pratihāras were Rajputs. Having thus far refuted Dr. D. R. Bhandarkar's strong case we will proceed to examine the case of the second supposed Agnikula clan, the Chālukya or Solankhi.

Dr. D. R. Bhandarkar admits that there is *no epigraphic* evidence in their case but he argues that "since Gujarat of to-day bears this name since the Chālukyas occupied or conquered the country, if the Chālukyas had not been of Gujar extraction, it is inconceivable how this province came to be called Gurjaraṭrā when it was till their advent known as Lāta" (p. 24). Now there is no doubt that Gujaratrā in the 8th and 9th or even 10th centuries was the name of southern Rajputana as inscriptions of that period show. Lāṭa was not, however, the name of the whole of modern Gujarat. It was the name of southern Gujarat *i. e.* Surat and adjacent parts. Central Gujarat was Ānarta while northern Gujarat was sometimes called Sārasvata, Mandala though all the three were sometimes called Lāṭa. Now it seems that these three parts have latterly acquired the name Gujarat because of the Gujarati language and not because of the establishment of the Chālukya rule. The modern languages of India, as we have already observed, arose about the 9th century and the language of these parts generally assumed the modern Gujarati form. How old the Gujarati language is and how old the word

Gujarati is, it is difficult to determine. For while the word Mahārāshtrī as the name of a language is as old as Vararuchi of the 1st century B.C. the word Mahārāshtra as the name of a country is much later, certainly later than Varāha Mihira of the fifth century A. D. It is, therefore, not difficult to suppose that Mahārāshtra assumed this name for the country from the common language namely modern Mahārāshtrī. Similarly it would be proper to believe that the name Gujarat for the province was adopted owing to the prevalence of the Gujarati language.

But that question does not really concern us; whatever may be the reason of the name Gujarat appertaining to the province, it would be absurd to argue that because the province began to be called Gujarat about their time, therefore the Chālukyas were Gujars by caste. The names of countries arise in different ways and stick for extremely different reasons. England, for example, began to be called England after the Norman conquest and yet the Normans were not Angles. The Angles themselves were an insignificant people compared with the Saxons and yet the name of the country has remained Angle-land ignoring the Saxons altogether. France began to be called France when the Franks were no longer masters and had been entirely merged in the general Gaelic population and had lost their German character and affinities. So also in India the English called the eastern districts of the Madras Presidency by the name of Carnātik when they were not ruled by Carnātik kings and when even the language was not Carnātik; but they simply continued the name given to the country by the Marathas who looked upon the whole of southern India as Karnātaka. It is, therefore, extremely illogical to argue that the Chālukyas were Gujars because from about their time the province began to be called Gujarat.

Going on to the third supposed Agnikula clan the Paramāras, we find that Dr. D. R Bhandarkar is at a loss to find any argument which could make these also Gujars and is driven to observe that though we do not know to what race they belonged *it is morally certain* that they were of foreign extraction. It is for the first time we read of moral certainty in a case like this where there are no considerations of morality in discussing the race of a people.

The reader will leave Dr. D. R. Bhandarkar to his moral views and will hold with us that there is no proof or argument to show that the Paramāras were Gujars or even foreigners.

Lastly, we come to the consideration of the case of Chāhamānas or Chauhans to prove whose Gujar extraction Dr. D. R. Bhandarkar is at the worst pains and begins from some old Sassanian coins found in the north-west of India and ends with the Himālayan Siwalik hills. The whole argument savours so completely of the Pickwickian method of research that it is a wonder that a man of Dr. D. R. Bhandarkar's capacities should have fallen a prey to it. We are certain if he had not been obsessed by his theory of the foreign or Gujar descent of the Rajputs, he would himself have seen the absurdity of his own argument. Let us see how his argument is transparently based on pure imagination.

Certain coins have been found in Northern India on which is read the legend Sri Vāsudeva Vahman in Nāgarī characters and in Pehlvi "Takkān, Jabulistān and Sapardalakshān." First Dr. D. R. Bhandarkar to suit his purpose reads Vahman as Chāhman "because the characters of the letters v and ch in old days were so close to each other that one might be easily mistaken for the other." "And Chāhman, it need scarcely be said, stands for Chāhamāna (ma lenghtened into mā) so that Vāsudeva of these coins is a Chāhamāna and since Vāsudeva iṣ mentioned in Pṛithvīrāja Vijaya as the founder of the Chāhamāna family of Śākambarī, *that founder must be the same* as the Chāhmaṇ of these Sassanian coins. "Rājaśekhara's Prabandha-kośa also gives one Vāsudeva as the founder of the Chāhamāna family for whom he gives the date 608 V. E." This date is a serious difficulty in establishing the identity of these two Vāsudevas. But Dr. D. R. Bhandarkar is not at a loss. He naively observes that the kośa gives a date which is *rather early* and the proper date to be assigned appears to be 627 A. D. concluded from the type of coins which are an exact copy of the coins of Parveiz Khuśru. So Dr. D. R. Bhandarkar cannot only change letters but also dates to suit his theory, but what is still more strange is that he can change the race also at his sweet will. Cunningham held that Vāsudeva of the coins was a Hūṇa and Prof. Rapson thinks that he was a Sussanian (from the legend of the coins as also from their type). But Dr. D. R. Bhandarkar thinks that he was a *Khazar* why he alone knows. It is sufficient to place this whole argument before the reader in detail to enable him to come to the conclusion that Dr. D. R. Bhandarkar has failed signally in showing that the Chāhamānas were Gujars.

But the greatest mistake which Dr. D. R. Bhandarkar has committed in this connection is that of placing the town of Ahichchhatra and the country Sapādalaksha in the Siwalik hilly region of the Himālayas. He has in fact in doing so distorted the natural course of Indian history and represented Brahmins and Kshatriyas, as moving south from this place. But how can we believe that Rajputs spread from the Siwalik hilly regions into India even if they were Gujars? If Gujars were foreigners who had come along with the Huns as conquerors, they would settle in the inviting plains of the Panjab and not go to the difficult Himālayas to settle. As a matter of fact history and tradition tell us that Brāhmins and Rajputs went into these sub-montane inhospitable regions in historical times from the Panjab, in consequence of the inroads of foreign invaders down to the Turks, in the same way as many took shelter in the sands and hills of Rajastan. It is, therefore, absurd to point to the Siwalik hills as the original *habitat* of either the Rajputs or the Gujars. The identification of Sapādalaksha with Siwalik hilly region is absurd and we need not go to Babar for an explanation of that word. Babar gives perhaps the current explanation when the original and correct explanation was forgotten. We give in a note an extract from the Skanda Purāṇa giving the list of countries in India about the 9th century A. D. and the traditional number of villages assigned to each. Sapādalaksha is a name which is given in this list to four or five countries and the first of them is Śākambhara or the land of the Chauhāns. It is also given to Karnātaka and to Mewad and also to Varendu which is not identifiable, but which probably means the Delhi region*. When the coins noticed by

* Or it might mean the region about Multan for Al–Masandi relates that around Multan these were one hundred and twenty thousand towns and villages (Elliot I p. 23).

Dr. D. R. Bhandarkar mention Takkān, Zabulistān and Sapardalakshān they probably mean the Panjab with Ghazni on the west and the Delhi province in the south-east which three probably comprised the territory ruled by Vāsudev Vahman, a Sassanian king. In any case Sapādalaksha does not indicate 1¼ lakhs of hills but 1¼ lakhs of villages and this number is traditionally assigned to Śākambhara, Mewad, Delhi and Karnātaka as the evidence of the Skanda Purāṇa conclusively proves.

Ahichchhatra again is wrongly placed in the Himālayan region. It is undoubtedly the famous capital of North Pāñchāla as mentioned in the Mahābhārata and Cunningham has properly identified it from Hiuen Tsang's description with Rampur. The words " being flanked by mountain crags" need not suggest the Himālayas at all and this Ahichchhatra was properly enough the place to which Brahmins and Kshatriyas in the south looked as their original habitat. The Pāñchāla country is famous in Vedic literature as the residence of learned Brahmins. It was also the country of the valiant Pāñchāla Kshatriyas and Dr. D. R. Bhandarkar need not wonder that the founder of the Chāhamāna family is said to have come from Ahichchhatra. The Chāhamānas did not take the word Sapādalaksha to the new country for it was not a name like Holland which could be taken to other places but it was a word denoting a number of villages which comprised their territory. Again Karnātaka or Dhārwār was called Sapādalaksha because it contained that number of villages. The name was not taken and could not be taken from the north to Dhārwār. The strange conclusion which Dr. Bhandarkar derives from this word used for Karnātaka viz., that the habitat of the Chālukyas like that of the Chāhamānas was also the mountain region called Sapādalaksha and hence they too were foreigners is, therefore, absurd and the whole theory which he has built on the wrong identification of Ahichchhatra and Sapādalaksha is to say the least mistaken. We, therefore, think that Dr. D. R. Bhandarkar's attempt to prove that the four supposed Agnikula clans were Gujars has signally failed and his theory must be abandoned. It must be mentioned that Mr. Har Bilas Sarda of Ajmer has already pointed out that Sapādalaksha meant the Sambar country though he thinks Ahichchhatra should be identified with Nagore in Marwad. Whether the Chāhamānas came from Rampur or were originally of Nagore, it is certain that there is not a scrap of evidence to show that they were Gujars and we shall not further dilate upon this untenable theory of the foreign extraction of the Rajputs started by Dr. D. R. Bhandarkar and accepted by Jackson and Smith. We will instead in the next chapter indicate the positive arguments which in our opinion go to prove that they are the representatives of the ancient Vedic Aryans of India.

NOTE.

THE SKANDA PURĀNA LIST OF COUNTRIES IN INDIA WITH THE NUMBER OF VILLAGES IN EACH COUNTRY.

The Mahābhārata list of countries or rather peoples in India is important for Indian history preceding the Christian era. Varāha Mihira's list is similarly important for the fifth century A.D., while Hiuen Tsang's travels supply us with accurate and detailed information about the peoples of India in the beginning of the 7th century A. D. There is a list of countries in India (not peoples) in the Skanda Purāṇa, Kumāra Khaṇḍa, Chapter 39 which is equally important for Indian history and gives us pretty accurate information about the 9th century A. D. This Purāṇa can clearly be assigned to the 9th or 10th century from this very list; as therein the old names of countries or rather peoples find no place and new names occur denoting countries or rather provinces which generally well fit in with the 9th century and which mostly subsist to this day, though there are many names which are unidentifiable. Below are specially marked those names which can be identified and also their extent and importance. The numbers assigned to each country are mentioned as numbers of villages and there is no vagueness about them though in many cases the numbers are palpably unbelievable. But some numbers are corroborated from inscriptions of the time and we must recognise the fact that countries or provinces had at this time been assigned a fixed number of villages by tradition.

The list begins from the north and correctly reflects the political condition of India in the 9th century A. D. We first have Nepāl with one lakh of villages and immediately next naturally comes Kānyakubja with 36 lakhs. This shows that the Kanauj empire was at its height, an extensive empire covering Oudh, the Gangetic valley, part of the Panjab and Gwalior territory and the valley of the Jumna. Now this number of villages of Kanauj is also mentioned in the Prabandha Chintāmaṇi. What Gājaṇaka is, which next follows with 72 lakhs cannot be surmised. Probably in the usual fashion of the Purāṇas facts and fictions are jumbled together in order to make up the total of 96 crores and 72 lakhs of villages, an exaggeration befitting the Purāṇas, for the whole of India. Then comes the Gauda country or Bengal with 18 lakhs which means a territory half of the Kanauj empire which is not impossible. Next we have Kāmarūpa and Oddiyāna or Orissa with the same extent as Kāmarūpa or Assam *i. e.* 9 lakhs or half of Bengal or Gauda. The same extent is assigned to Dāhala or Bundelkhand which is described as Vedasamjna meaning probably that it consisted of four parts. Next we have Jālandhara and Lohapura or Lahore each with the same number of 9 lakhs. Next we recognise Raṭarajya or the kingdom of the Rāshtrakūtas with 7 lakhs of villages and we are reminded of the 7½ lakhs Rattapāḍi mentioned in inscriptions of this and the preceding period. We, hereafter, come across names which we do not recognise but we come next to countries to which the number assigned is 1¼ or Sapādalaksha. We have already explained how Dr. Bhandarkar has committed a mistake in interpreting the name and how he identified it with the hilly range at the foot of the Himālayas called Śiwalik hills. This list in the Skanda Purāṇa clearly establishes the fact that about 7 countries were then known as Ṣupādalaksha countries viz., Varendu, Atilāngala, Sayambhara, Medapāta, (these two unquestionably are Sambhar and Mewad), Tomara, Karnāta and Pungala, followed closely by Mālava which is assigned the exact figure 1 lakh 15 thousand and 180. One of these may be the Siwalik region though we are not certain about it but at any rate the word Śiwalik need not be derived from 1¼ lakhs of hills in that region.

The next important countries which we recognize are Gurjarātrā 70000, Sind 20000, Kachhamandala 16020, Saurāshtra 55000, Lāta 21000, Konkana 36000 and Laghu Konkana 16000. Here the form used is Gurjarātra and it is distinct from Lāta. Moreover, Gurjarātra appears to be yet southern Marwad and hence it seems probable that the Skanda Purāṇa is not later than the 11th century A. D.

The extent of Kashmir given in this list is 68000 which is corroborated by Kashmir records as already observed in our Vol. I. Then follow many countries which are traditional though imaginary and must come in a list of Indian countries, such as Ekapāda and others. But we can identify Kāmboja, Kabul, Kośala (C.P.), Vidarbha, (Berar) with 5 lakhs or 2\3 of Mahārāshtra, Vardhamāna (Wadhwan), Magadha 68,000 and lastly Mulasthānapura 25000. In all there are said to be 72 countries (the actual number of countries named comes, however, to 75), into which India was divided with 96 crores and 72 lakhs of villages. 36000 velākulas are also mentioned which we interpret as meaning so many *Kos* of coast line and one is reminded here of the fact that even in the days of Alexander, the length of the coast line of India was accurately reported to him by Indian informants.

Before concluding, we may give here the mountains and rivers of India as enumerated in this Skanda Purāṇa in imitation of the Mahābhārata which apparently it has an ambition to equal. These are given in this same chapter 39 of the Kumāra Khanda. The chief mountain ranges, or Kulaparvatas as they are called here also, are the same seven viz.

Mahendra, Malaya, Sahya, Śuktimān, Riksha, Vindhya and Pāriyātra. The first four are the well-known Eastern Ghats, Malaya, Western Ghats, and Girnar. Riksha is the Aravali range while Vindhya is the well-known range that stretches across India. But Pāriyātra is difficult to identify. It is described as the range to the south of which lies the Kaumāra Khanda; and from it rises the Veda—Smṛiti and other rivers. This description does not assist us much though we suspect that Pāriyātra now is some portion of the Western Vindhya range. The Narmadā and Sarasā properly rise from Vindhya but how can Śatadru and Chandrabhāgā rise from the Riksha range? Rishikulyā and Kumāri rise from the Śuktimān mountain of Kathiwar. The Tāpī, the Payoshṇī, the Nirvindhyā, the Kāverī, the Kṛishṇā, the Veṇī, the Bhīmarathī rise from the Sahya which must be interpreted as including the Sātpura. And strangely the Godāvarī is conspicuous by its absence. The Kṛitamālā and the Tāmraparṇī rise from the Malaya Mountains while the Triśanu and the Rishyakulyā rise from the Mahendra. Probably the writer or recaster of the Purāṇa had not much acquaintance with northern or southern India and was a native of Gujarat or Malwa as he has described the Stambha (Khambayat), Prabhāsa, Avanti and Nāgara Tīrthas with a fulness which bespeaks his partiality for and his familiarity with them. With these remarks we give the Skanda Purāṇa list of countries below:

1. Nīvṛit 4 crores.
2. Bālāka 2½ crores.
3. Sāhaṇapura 1¼ crore.
4. Andhala 4 lakh.
5. Nepāla 1 lakh.
6. Kānyakubja 36 lakh.
7. Gājaṇaka 72 lakh.
8. Gauda 18 lakh.
9. Kāmarūpa 9 lakh.
10. Dāhala 9 lakh.
11. Kāntipura 9 lakh.
12. Lohapura 9 lakh.
13. Pāmbīpura 7 lakh.
14. Raṭarāja 7 lakh.
15. Hariyāla 5 lakh.
16. Drada 3½ lakh.
17. Māchīpura 9 lakh.
18. Oddiyāna 9 lakh.
19. Jālandhara 9 lakh.
20. Bambhaṇavāhaka 3½ lakh.
21. Nilapura 21 thousand.
22. Amala 1lakh.
23. Varendu Sapādalaksha
24. Atilāngala 11 thousand.
25. Mālava 1,18,180.
26. Sayambhara Sapādalaksha.
27. Mevāḍa Sapādalaksha.
28. Vāguri 88 thousand.
29. Gujarātra 77 thousand.
30. Pānduvishaya 70, thousand.
31. Jahāhuti 42 thousand.
32. Kāshmīra 68 thousand.
33. Konkaṇa 36 thousand.
34. Laghu Konkaṇa 1,600.
35. Sindhu 22 thousand.
36. Kachchha 36 thousand.
37. Saurāshṭra 55 thousand.
38. Lāṭadesha 21 thousand.
39. Atisindhu 10 thousand.
40. Aśvamukha 10 thousand.
41. Ekapāda 10 thousand.
42. Sūryamukha 10 thousand.
43. Ekabāhu 10 thousand.
44. Sañjāyu 10 thousand.
45. Śivadesha 10 thousand.
46. Kālahayañjaya 10 thousand.
47. Liṅgodbhava 10 thousand.
48. Bhadra 10 thousand.

49. Devabhadra 10 thousand.
50. Chaṭa 36 thousand.
51. Virāta 36 thousand.
52. Yamakoṭi 36 thousand.
53. Romaka 18 crores.
54. Tomara Sapādalaksha.
55. Karnāta Sapādalaksha.
56. Pingala Sapādalaksha.
57. Strīrājya 5 lakh.
58. Pulastya 10 lakh.
59. Kāmboja 10 lakh.
60. Kosala 10 lakh.
61. Bālhika 4 thousand.
62. Laṇkā 36 thousand.
63. Kuru 64 thousand
64. Kirāta 1½ lakh.
65. Vidarbha 5 lakh.
66. Vardhamāna 14 thousand.
67. Sinhala 10 thousand.
68. Pāṇḍu 36 thousand.
69. Bhayāṇaka 1½ lakh.
70. Magaḍha 66 thousand.
71. Mūlasthāna 25 thousand.
72. Yāsana 40 thousand.
73. Pakshabāhu 4,000.
74. Pāṅgu 60,000.
75. Varendeka 30,000.

NOTE

THE MEANING OF THE WORD RAJPUT

The Rajputs pride themselves on being Kshatriyas of noble descent belonging to the Vedic Aryan race. Unfortunately native writers impelled by bigotry and even by ignorance, owing to the fact that many Kshatriyas during the Aryo-Buddhistic period gave-up Aryan religion and Aryan practices and turned Buddhists, have expressed an opinion that the Rajputs are not pure Kshatriyas and go so far as to invoke a questionable statement in the Purāṇas to the effect that in the Kali age there would remain no Kshatriyas nor Vaiśyas (for the Vaiśyas also, even in greater number, had turned Buddhists) but only two Varṇas Brahmins and Śūdras. What is the value to be attached to these statements in the religious books of the Hindus and what is the true meaning of the term Rajput is a question which must be answered at the same time that we refute the adverse opinion of western scholars.

There is not the least doubt that these statements of the Purāṇas are valueless and historically considered they are interpolations in the Purāṇic texts promoted not indeed by malice but by bigotry and through enmity to the Buddhists. It will not be difficult to prove that earlier texts exist which show that the word Rajput is not a new word coined in about the 9th century A. D. but an old, a very old word and that it was usually used in a very honourable sense. Words sometimes do take up double meanings, one a good and the other a bad one, but it is well to remember that the bad sense is usually a later growth. Many examples may be given but the very word Brahmin will suffice. It originally indicated the highest Varṇa or caste to whom the duty of preserving the Brahma or Veda was entrusted. But later on, we find that the duty of supplying water and even of cooking fell to the lot of this caste and hence the word Brahmin now-a-days often means a cook or a waterman (A Hindi saying has it that a Brahmin meant *Babarchi, Bhisti, Bhikhari*). In this way the term Rajput is sometimes applied to the illegitimate progeny of Kshatriyas or kings born of mothers of lower castes. But that this is not its original or general meaning will appear from the following disquisition.

At Alwar it was stated to us by some Pandits that the word Rajput meant a mixed-caste man as stated in a verse of the Parāśara Smṛiti "वैश्यादंबष्ठकन्यायां राजपुत्रः प्रजायते." Now it may be stated at once that there is no such line in the Parāśara Smṛiti as it is ordinarily known. If any copy of the Smṛiti has this line it is plainly an interpolation. There is also this contradiction of this supposed statement of Parāśara that the author of Śūdra-Kamalākara looks upon Ugra as one who is popularly known as Rajput. An Ugra is the son of a Kshatriya from a Śūdra woman and the author of Śūdra-Kamalākara adds the explanation अयं च रजपूत इति भाषाप्रसिद्धः "An Ugra is called Rajput in the spoken language." Now this view is also wrong but it undeniably shows that the text of Parāśara quoted above is spurious*.

Rajput is a word which is indeed used sometimes in common parlance to denote the illegitimate sons of Rajput chiefs. But that it is not its ordinary meaning can be proved by the fact that the word is used so far back as the Mahābhārata in a good sense. In that ancient epic it indicates a Kshatriya generally (एते रुक्मरथा नाम राजपुत्रा महारथाः। रथेष्वस्त्रेषु निपुणा नागेषुच विशांपते ॥ २० ॥ द्रो० अ० ११२), but often times not an ordinary Kshatriya but one who is descended from a crowned king. It is sometimes urged that the Amarakośa does not give Rājaputra as a synonym of Kshatriya. This is true but the Amarakośa cannot claim to be an exhaustive dictionary and even if a word is not given in a Kośa or dictionary, it is no proof to hold that it has no existence or has not a particular meaning. (Words in dead languages are to be known from use by classical authors and the word Rājaputra has been used in the sense of a Kshatriya in hundreds of places in the Mahābhārata.) One instance of such use in the Mahābhārata will suffice. Other ślokas might be quoted using the word Rajput in the same or higher sense even in the Mahābhārata; but it is unnecessary to quote many instances. The following verse from Śāntiparva Adhyāya 64 shows that Rājaputra is often used in the simple sense of a Kshatriya: भैक्ष्यचर्यां ततः प्राहुस्तस्य (शूद्रस्य) सद्धर्मचारिणः । तथा वैश्यस्य राजेन्द्र राजपुत्रस्य चैव हि ॥. Rājaputra is very often used in a higher sense also, nay even the word Rājaputrī is often used in the Virāta Parva in addressing Draupadī, where the sense 'daughter of a king' does not appear to be intended, but merely a high-born Kshatriya lady. It may further be noted that Bhavabhūti of the 7th century A.D. uses the word Rājaputrī in addressing Kausalyā where the same sense is intended, viz., not the daughter of a king; but merely a high-born Kshatriya lady. Bāṇa in the Harshacharita similarly uses the word Rājaputra to denote a Kshatriya soldier.

It may be objected that the word Rājaputra occurs in Pāṇini where a sense somewhat different from Rājanya is intended to be conveyed by it. The Sūtra is very important and clearly shows that the word

---

* The Parāśara Smṛiti is intended for the Kali age and if it had intended to preach that there were no Kshatriyas in the Kali age, it could not have contained many provisions specially prescribed for the Kshatriyas.

Rājaputra has been in use since even the days of Pāṇini. It is used there not in its etymological or literal sense but it plainly has an acquired individual meaning. The sūtra is as follows: गोत्रोक्षोष्ट्रोरभ्रराजराजन्य राजपुत्रवत्स मनुष्याजाद्वुञ् (4-2-41). This precedes another Sūtra तस्य समूहः (4-2-39) and means that where the sense of collection is intended the affix वुञ् or क is to be added to these words. Thus Rājaka would mean a collection of Rājas; Rājanyaka would mean a collection of Rājanyas or Kshatriyas and Rājaputraka would mean a collection of Rajputs. Now it is not necessary here that Rājanya and Rājaputra should have different senses, for Pāṇini is more concerned with words than with meanings. However, this point apart, it is clear that Rājaputra is not used here in its literal sense i. e. son of a king for a collection of sons of a king would be meaningless. It may be used in the sense of princes generally as one may speak of a collection of many princes i. e. sons of different kings. In short in our view this sūtra does not show that the word Rājaputra has only a literal sense or has any bad sense in it. On the contrary as stated above it shows that Rājaputra may mean something more than a Rājanya or ordinary Kshatriya i. e. a high-born Kshatriya, one who not only belongs to the varṇa or caste of a king but is born in a kingly family. It seems that the word is often used in this sense in the Mahābhārata though it is also often a synonym of Rājanya which means an ordinary Kshatriya.

It is at least certain from Pāṇini and from the Mahābhārata that the word is an old word in use from thousands of years and not a word which came into use in the 9th century A. D. (as some believe) and does not mean an illegitimate son or a mixed-caste man. Even in Bāṇa's Harshacharita the word is used in the sense of a high-born Kshatriya. Bāṇa's use of the word is good proof of the fact that the word is not a new word. How and why it came into prominence in about the ninth century or the the tenth or even eleventh may be explained as follows. After the expulsion of Buddhism from India, caste began to stiffen gradually till it became rigid in the third sub-period of our history as we shall show in our third volume. We may anticipate a little and state that every caste began to limit its field, especially for purposes of marriage, to families which were known to be pure and unmixed. That there were kingly families in India in the 7th century which belonged to the Kshatriya varṇa is undisputed from the statements of Hiuen Tsang quoted in our first volume. But Kshatriyas had turned Buddhists by scores and lost touch with the Aryan practices pertaining to Kshatriyas. Such families were now rigorously excluded. And further distance made it difficult to determine the exact nature of the caste purity of families and it became the tendency not only among Kshatriyas but among Brahmins and Vaiśyas also to form sub-castes based on provinces, so that the question of the purity of families residing in distant provinces might not arise

Hence it is that about the beginning of the 11th century Rajputs confined themselves to the tract where the Kshatriya kingly families were chiefly gathered. And the status of Kshatriya was naturally confined to those who could prove descent from undoubted Kshatriya kings within the memory of the generation and had not to depend on bardic legends, broken as they were by many centuries of Buddhist and foreign rule. The word Rājaputra became, therefore, of special importance and the thirty-six royal families of Kshatriyas were enumerated, marriage within which group was considered proper. We need not wonder that those families were chiefly confined to what is now called Rajaputana and the adjoining portions of Central India where, as the religious map appended to our first volume shows, Hinduism was very strong even in the days of Hiuen Tsang and Buddhism had not much hold upon the people, Kshatriyas and Rajputs outside these limits were looked upon as not undoubted Kshatriyas. And it is thus that the gulf between the central tract Rajputs and the Kshatriyas of Bengal and the Deccan arose. It must be noted that Rajputs who have now given their name Rājputānā to this central tract can all trace their descent step by step to some known king ruling in the 7th and 8th centuries A. D. It may seem strange but it is nevertheless true that such descendants of one man in the 9th century or even the 12th may be reckoned at this day by thousands. The Rajput has thus preserved the purity of his race unquestionably from the 8th century onward down to this day in a manner not to be found in any other caste, not even Brahmins in India, or any people in the whole world.

Inspite of the extreme purity of race which the Rajputs have preserved through nearly a thousand years of their history, it is indeed almost a mystery, how the myth could arise that in the Kali age there were only two varṇas viz., the Brahmins and the Śūdras, a myth which has so banefully influenced writers of commentaries on the sacred texts of Smṛitis. This mystery will, however, disappear if one looks at the religious map appended to Vol. I. These writers of commentaries and treatises on law belong to the south and Buddhism prevailed far more extensively in these parts and even in the north than in the middle land. The Kshatriyas in these parts had also contracted marriage relations with Non-Aryan local tribes more extensively than those in the middle land. The Kshatriyas of the south, the Marathas, consequently lost communion with the Kshatriyas of Rājputāna when caste became rigid, as also the Kshatriyas of the east and the north. The Kshatriyas of Bengal and Oudh had contracted marriage relations with the Khasas and other Mongolian races of the north. The orthodox Kshatriyas, therefore, of the middle country excluded these Kshatriyas of the east and the south from their fold; and to this day they still adhere to their unwillingness to form marriage relations with Kshatriya families of the south and the east.

The Brahmins had not turned Buddhists in any great numbers and had not lost touch with the Vedas and the Vedic sanskāras or practices. The other two varṇas on the other hand had become Buddhists in thousands and had lost all touch with the Vedic religion. When, Buddhism being overthrown, these came back to Hinduism, most of them had forgotten their gotras and had no knowledge of the gāyatri and they were naturally looked upon as Śūdras. They still adhered to certain practices of their own and kept their distinctness as Kshatriyas and Vaiśyas. The bigoted Brahmins could not assign to the descendants of Pulakeśin and others who had performed the most orthodox Vedic sacrifices, the status of Kshatriyas in the newly constituted Hindu society and gradually the opinion gained strength that in the Kali age there remained only two varṇas the Brahmins and the Śūdras, and found expression in the Purāṇic text कलावाद्यन्तयोः स्थितिः. When this happened is not quite clear but that it is an interpolation of a date later than the 10th century A. D. and that it arose in the south or the east cannot be gainsaid.[1] The existence of Kshatriyas in the south was never disputed in the 1st century A. D. as may be seen from the expression खतिय दपमान दमनस्स in one of the Nasik cave inscriptions of Gotamīputra (Ind. Ant. p. 37) which means "who crushed the pride of Kshatriyas." It is wrongly stated here that "these Kshatriyas are the native Indian princes of Rājputāna, Gujarat and Central India." These parts were never invaded by Gotamīputra. What the epithet means is that Gotamīputra Śātakarṇi who was a Śūdra and who came from Dhanakataka had humbled the pride of the Kshatriyas, of course, of the Deccan itself. There were Kshatriyas in the Deccan itself at that time viz., the Rāshtrakūṭas and others and one need not go to Rājaputāna of the modern day to find Kshatriyas in the 1st century A. D. Then again we know that there were Kshatriyas in the Deccan and the South in the 7th century A. D. Not only Hiuen Tsang describes the Pallavas of Kāṇchi and the Chālukyas of Badāmi as Kshatriyas, but the stone and copper records of these families distinctly state that they had performed Aśvamedha and other Vedic sacrifices and that they claimed to be Kshatriyas e. g. in the epithet श्रीक्षत्रचूडामणिः inscribed on the walls of a temple at Madurā. It seems, therefore, certain that the theory that there were no Kshatriyas in the Kali age had not arisen till the seventh century A. D.

This theory again is contradicted to our mind by the Parāśara Smṛiti itself which is specially intended for the Kali age. In this Smṛiti various texts give special provisions for Kshatriyas and Vaiśyas. If indeed in the Kali age there were no Kshatriyas and Vaiśyas where was the necessity of making the special provisions intended for these varṇas? The Smṛiti does not contemplate, therefore, the non-existence of these varṇas and as this Smṛiti may be assigned to the 7th or 8th century one may infer that this view had not arisen yet. The Parāśara Smṛiti to our mind belongs to the south as the sanctity of the Setu Tirtha is specially extolled in it. But whether it arose in the south or the north, it certainly does not look upon Kshatriyas as non-existent in the Kali age.

The Śūdra Kamalākara was composed at Benares and by a Deccani Brahmin. It, therefore, reflects the sentiment of the south and the east. Kshatriyas of the central part where the word Rajput came into special vogue looked down upon Kshatriyas of the south and east, not in the 9th and 10th centuries but later, as we shall show that marriage relations between these continued to take place in these centuries. It seems, therefore, that this view arose in later centuries and it arose in the east and the south. Legal writers took it up and worked it to its natural consequences. Even the Rajputs who then prided and still pride themselves upon being good Kshatriyas were consequently looked upon by these writers as Ugras and the theory further grew that Kshatriyas had no gotras of their own but took the gotras of their Purohitas. It is not necessary here to pursue the subject further; but we may conclude by saying that the dictum that the Rajputs are Ugras is not only not correct but is further based upon a view of later growth that there were no Kshatriyas in the Kali age. The text कलावाद्यन्तयोः स्थितिः is historically speaking an interpolation. At best it must be explained by interpreting it to mean not that there would be no Kshatriyas in the Kali age throughout, but from some time in later centuries when the Kali age would be at its extreme point. We have for the present to ignore this text and to hold that Kshatriyas do exist still and that the Rajputs are the purest portions of them, the word Rajput meaning a high-born Kshatriya.

CHAPTER V

THE GOTRAS OF THE RAJPUTS

Having examined the evidence which is supposed to prove that the Pratihāra and other Rajput tribes were Gujars originally, and found it insufficient to establish the conclusion that these tribes are foreigners, we will proceed to sketch the evidence which goes to show that the Rajputs are the descendants of Vedic Aryans. And the first item of evidence which presents itself to us is the fact that the Rajputs have the same gotras and Pravaras as those laid down in the Vedic Sūtras and have carefully preserved their memory to this day. The gotra and Pravara system as laid down in the several Sūtras of the Vedas preserves among Indo-Aryans the memory of descent in a manner not to be witnessed anywhere else in the world. The Indian Aryans who profess the Vedic faith have to recite at every religious ceremony, their gotra and Pravara before beginning the ceremony and in this way the memory of the Vedic ancestors from whom the reciter is descended is kept alive from day to day and generation to generation. The Brahmins of India have thus kept up the memory of their descent for at least 3000 years *i. e.* from the time when the Vedic Sūtras were mostly composed and possibly for 5000 years, before which time the Vedas were probably composed. The Kshatriyas or Rajputs too have kept up the memory of their gotras religiously and tenaciously. In fact epigraphic evidence extending over two thousand years shows that the Kshatriyas and the Rajputs were careful and proud to record their gotras in their inscriptions. And the gotras of the principal Rajput families of the present day are the same as those mentioned in their ancient records on stone and copper and we may, therefore, well believe that the Rajputs are the descendants of the Vedic Kshatriyas. Thus the gotras of the supposed Agnikula clans are from their gotrochchāra recorded by Col. Tod, (the word gotrāchāra is probably wrongly used here by Tod; it should have been gotrochchāra which means the recital of one's gotra) are as follows: the Chāhamānas are of the Vatsa gotra with five pravaras; the Chālukyas are of the Bhāradvāja gotra with three pravaras and the Paramāras are of the Vaśishṭha gotra with three pravaras. (The Pratihāra's gotra has not yet been ascertained from inquiry or from record.) Now the same gotras are mentioned in ancient inscriptions of these tribes as we have already shown. The gotra of the Paramāras is thus mentioned in the Udepur Praśasti and in many other records, notably for instance in the following line-वसिष्ठ-गोत्रोद्भव एष लोके ख्यातस्तदादौ परमारवंशः ॥ in the Pātanārāyaṇa inscription (Ind. Ant. XLV); and the Paramāras all over India whether in the Deccan or in Rajputana still possess the same gotra. The gotra of the Chālukyas again is mentioned in the Haihaya record already noticed while the gotra of the Chāhamānas is mentioned in the Bijolia inscription (J. Ben. R. A. S. Vol. LV. p. 41) in the line विप्र श्रीवत्सगोत्रेऽभूदहिच्छत्रपुरे पुरा ।. The gotra of the Rāthodas is Gautama while that of the Guhilots is Baijavāpāyana as mentioned in their records. The gotras thus mentioned in ancient records are still the gotras professed by these Rajput clans and it may, therefore, well be inferred that both the possession of gotras and their continual recital and remembrance to this day go to support if not to establish their descent from Vedic ancestors.

This evidence, however, of long standing tradition is sought to be impeached on the ground that when these Rajput clans were transformed from barbarians into orthodox Kshatriyas about the sixth or seventh century A.D. they took these gotras from their Brahmin Purohitas; and the rule as given in the Sūtras that the Kshatriyas are to use their Purohitas' gotras (पुरोहित-प्रवरो राज्ञाम्) is quoted in support of this view. Now this is another example of how wrong ideas arise by misconception among ourselves and how such misconceptions of some of our own Pandits lead astray western scholars and antiquarians. The author of the famous commentary Mitākshara on Yājñavalkya Smṛiti has indeed wrongly laid down the maxim that the Kshatriyas have no gotras of their own and that they are to use the gotras of their Purohitas. This comment of Vijñāneśvara on the text of the Smṛiti making marriage of Dvijas or Aryans outside the gotra alone as valid has now-a-days become generally accepted and European scholars naturally resort to it when they explain the mention of gotras in inscriptions by Kshatriya kings. But the mention of gotras by kings in inscriptions cannot have been of any importance if these gotras of the kings were adventitious and were to be borrowed from their Purohitas and were liable to be changed with the change of Purohitas. The Chālukyas of Badāmi for instance and the Pallavas of Kāñchī would not have cared to record in every grant they made मानव्यसगोत्राणां चालुक्यानाम् and भारद्वाजसगोत्राणां पल्लवानाम्, if these gotras were not their own. The rule of the Sūtras (पुरोहित-प्रवरो राज्ञाम्) has evidently been misinterpreted by Vijñāneśvara and we have not the smallest doubt that the Kshatriyas of ancient days had and the Rajputs of modern time have gotras of their own. When, therefore, in ancient records we find mention of gotras we must hold that the Kshatriyas must have mentioned the gotras from pride in mentioning their gotra showing their descent from Aryan ancestors. Nay in ancient times the gotra was the only method of distinguishing families and Brahmins and Kshatriyas mentioned their gotras both from pride and from necessity to distinguish their families as we mention the surnames now-a-days which are in fact derived from gotras themselves. Thus in an inscription on a Torana at Barhut we have गार्गी पुत्तस !बिसदेवसपुतेन गोपुत्तस अगराजस पुत्तेन वछी पुतेन धनभूतिना कारितं तोरणं which Cunningham has translated as follows "Gateway erected by king Dhanabhūti born of the queen of the Vatsa family, son of Agarāja son of queen of Gota (Kautsa) family and grandson of king Bisadeva son of queen of Garga family." Here the different gotras of the queen-mother, grand mother and great grand-mother are honourably mentioned with the object of showing that the queens in the several generations were also of Aryan gotras. But Cunningham here observes "Queens among Rajputs are still known by their family names. These names are gotra names . The explanation of this fact is that *in accordance with the precept of the Smṛitis*, the Rajas were considered to be of the gotras of their Purohitas." Here is the same dictum wrongly interpreted by Vijñāneśvara responsible for the misapprehension of so noted a scholar and antiquarian as Cunningham (see Cunningham's Barhut pp. 127-130). For if the gotra is not of the Raja's family but of his Purohita, where is the incentive to mention it especially with regard to the family of the queens? Evidently the rule was not then understood as it is now and as we proceed to show in the detailed note on this subject the dictum of the Śrauta Sūtras really meant that when kings had to perform sacrifices they were to select the Adhvaryu and other priests of the same Pravara as his Purohita; for the king himself could not continually sit as the Yajamāna or the sacrificer and had always to give power to his Purohita as his substitute and hence the sacrificial priests should be of the same Pravara (and not gotra) as the Purohita; in view of the fact that sacrificial procedure differed in different Pravaras. We have not the smallest doubt as shown in our note that the provisions of the several Śrauta Sūtras themselves show that the Kshatriyas have gotras of their own and that Vijñāneśvara's dictum in his Mitākshara is wrong.

But if any doubt remains, it will be dissipated by the epigraphic evidence itself already noted. Vijñāneśvara lived in the 12th or 13th century in the Deccan Karnatic at Kalyan where there were few or no Rajput families. The evidence of inscriptions of the 10th and 11th centuries of Rajputs in Northern India show no trace of the maxim that Kshatriyas have no gotras of their own and have to take the gotras of their Purohitas or preceptors. These inscriptions show that the gotras of the different Rajput clans were indicative of their *descent* from those ancestors. Thus when Vaśishṭha created the first Paramāra and gave him his gotra he did not do so because he was his Purohita but because he was his creator. Similarly in the Kalachūri Haihaya inscription noticed before, the Chālukya warrior born from the handful of water in Droṇa's hands has Droṇa's gotra viz., the Bhāradvāja not because Droṇa was his preceptor or Purohita but progenerator. The line distinctly is क्षितिधर--परि-

पाटीसूत्रिते तत्र गोत्रे । अभवदवनिपमौ विश्वविख्यातकर्मा. Then again the Chāhamānas were of the Vatsa gotra and the legend given in one of their inscriptions is that they were born *from* a Brahmin of the Vatsa gotra (विप्रः श्रीवत्सगोत्रेऽभूदहिच्छत्रपुरे पुरा । सामन्तानन्त सामन्त पूर्णतल्ला-नृपस्ततः). In another inscription the first Chāhamāna is said to have been born from the eyes of the Vatsa Ṛishi himself. These instances will suffice to prove that in the 9th and 10th centuries no such idea was entertained as is done by Vijñāneśvara. These stories of the birth of warriors from the fire of Vaśishṭha or the handful of Bhāradvāja are plainly myths but they clearly are based on the fact that the Paramāras and the Chālukyas in the 10th and 11th centuries were reputed to be of Vaśishṭha and Bhāradvāja gotra by descent and not by discipleship. Thus gotra even for Kshatriyas meant descent from the gotra ancestor and hence the poetic bards invented some stories showing the descent of these clans from these ancestors. Thus interpreted these inscriptions clearly prove that in centuries preceding the Mitākshara, Rajputs and Kshatriyas were certainly believed to have gotras of their own, gotras which indicated descent. It seems probable that at the time of the Mitākshara, Kshatriyas in the south had begun to forget their gotras; and that Brahmin orthodoxy was not willing to accept as Kshatriyas those who during Buddhistic times had entirely lost touch with Aryan ceremonies and were being now received back into Hinduism. Having forgotten their own gotras in Buddhistic times they were held to belong to the gotras of their Purohitas. Vijñāneśvara interpreted the sūtra पुरोहित-प्रवरो राज्ञाम् in a convenient manner and propounded the theory that Kshatriyas had no gotras of their own but had according to Vedic precept to take the gotras of their Purohitas or preceptors.

Whatever the explanation of this wrong statement of the Mitākshara, there is no doubt about its being wrong and of the fact that Kshatriyas and Rajputs from centuries preceding the Mitākshara had gotras of their own, gotras which indicated descent. In fact even now the Rajputs of Rajputana and elsewhere have gotras which are different from the gotras of their *Purohitas* as we ascertained from inquiries specially made on the subject, the result of which is embodied in the note attached hereto. The question may here be asked, how it is that Kshatriyas and Brahmins and even Vaiśyas have the same gotras. How is it that Kshatriyas of the solar and lunar lines could have Brahmin Ṛishis for their ancestors? We will discuss this question also in detail in our note, but it is necessary to indicate here the answer to this question. It will be a revelation to many persons that in ancient times down to the period at which we have arrived, caste in India was not hard-bound as it is to-day, especially in the three higher castes which formed the Aryan element in the population. Not only Brahmins and Kshatriyas married from one another's caste but even changed their caste easily. Thus many Vedic and Puranic legends show how Kshatriyas became Brahmins and Brahmins became Kshatriyas. The Ṛishis of Pravaras and even of gotras it will be a revelation to many are both Kshatriyas and Brahmins indiscriminately, that is to say, in the Pravara Ṛishis of many Brahmins there are Kshatriya kings as ancestors and in the Pravara Ṛishis of Kshatriyas there are Brahmin Ṛishis also. It is indeed a really unsectarian affair viz., the Pravara system as it has been laid down from the Vedic age; though some attempt is made in the Śrauta Sūtras to differentiate between Brahmins and Kshatriyas it is only the beginning of the cleavage between the two; but in actual practice through all the intervening centuries down to this day the gotras and Pravaras are the same for Brahmins and Rajputs and even for Vaiśyas, the three classes of the Aryan race. Consequently we may be sure that the Rajput claim to Aryan descent, to descent from the Kshatriyas of the Vedic times is not at all ill-founded but is founded on long tradition extending back to thousands of years before the Christian era. When and why these Vedic Aryans migrated into Rajputana we shall try to discover in the next chapter from legend as well as from history.

Note—Gotras of Modern Rajput families with the gotras of their Purohitas.

No.	State.	Rajput family.	Gotra.	Gotra of the Purohita.
1	Udepur, Dungarpur etc.	Guhilota	.. Baijavāpa	.. Samnāyana.
2	Jodhpur, Rutlam etc.	Rāṭhoḍ	.. Gautama	.. Bhāradvāja.
3	Jaipur and Alwar ..	.. Kachhavāha	.. Mānava	.. Vatsa.
4	Bundi-Kota ..	.. Chauhān	.. Vatsa ..	.. ....
5	Bijolia in Udepur	.. Paramāra	.. Vaśishṭha	.. ....
6	Dhar (Maratha)	.. Paramāra	.. Vaśishṭha	.. Karisha.
7	Bhavanagar ..	.. Guhila	.. Gautama..	.. Kāshyapa.
8	Dholera, Taluka Dhunduka.	Chudasama	.. Atri ..	.. ....
9	Kachchha, Navanagar Gondal Morvi Rajkot, etc.	Jādeja	.. Atri ..	.. ....
10	Dhrangdhra, Limdi, Vakaner, Patan.	Jhālā ..	.. Mārkandeya	.. ....
11	Lunavada in Rewa-Kantha & Pethapura.	Chālukya (Solankhi).	.. Bhāradvāja	.. ....
12	Rewa Bundelkhand ..	Vāghela (Solankhi).	.. Bhāradvāja	.. Vaśistha (new Chandrātri).
13	Kashmir ..	.. Jammuval	.. Bhāradvāja	.. Vaśishṭha.
14	Gidhaur, Bengal	.. Chandella	.. Chandrātreya	.. Kāśyapa.
15	Delhi represented by Pātaṇ (Jaipur)	Tuar ..	.. Vaiyaghrapadya	Bhāradvāja.
16	Kanauj ..	.. Gaharwar	.. ....	....

NOTE

GOTRA AND PRAVARA

We have already stated our view that Kshatriyas have gotras of their own and that Vijñāneśvara's dictum in the Mitākshara that they, having no gotras of their own, have to borrow those of their Purohitas, is wrong. But the question is often asked how can Brahmins and Kshatriyas have the same gotras, if gotras are to indicate descent and not discipleship? For it is believed that the Kshatriyas are not descended from Brahmin Rishis but are born in the solar or lunar Vaṁśas. This doubt often puzzled bards and poetic writers of inscriptions who, therefore, invented fanciful stories about the origin of Kshatriya families. We think that a minute examination of the subject of gotra and Pravara will solve this difficulty and we accordingly proceed to examine the subject from the beginning.

According to the latest view the gotra—Rishi is a son or rather a descendant of one of the seven Rishis (सप्तर्षि) with the addition of the eighth Agastya who is outside the well-known Saptarshis (see the dictum) of Baudhāyana: सप्तानां सप्तर्षीणामगस्त्य ष्टमानां यदपत्यं तद्गोत्रमित्याचक्षते. This means that the original Indo-Aryan families were considered to be eight viz., 1. Viśvāmitra, 2. Jamadagni, 3. Bharadvāja, 4. Gautama, 5. Atri, 6. Vaśishṭha, 7. Kāśyapa and 8. Agastya.

But an important śloka in the Mahābhārata takes us still further back and states that there originally were four gotras only मूलगोत्राणि चत्वारि समुत्पन्नानि भारत । अङ्गिराः कश्यपश्चैव वसिष्ठो भृगुरेव च ॥ (शां. अ. २९६). These ancient four gotras 1 Angiras 2 Kaśyapa 3 Vaśishṭha and 4 Bhṛigu are supported by the Pravarādhāyas also in the several Sūtras which always begin with the Bhṛigu Pravara. (It is hence that the Bhagavad-gīta has the line महर्षीणां भृगुरहम्. He is indeed the first of the great or Pravara Rishis). Now this shows that when the first or solar race Indo-Aryan invaders came to India there were four family stocks viz., 1 Bhṛigu, 2 Angiras, 3 Vaśishṭha and 4 Kaśyapa. These were the patriarchs so to say being the mind-born sons of the creator. And they were progenitors of all the three Aryan classes (which were not castes yet) Brahmins, Kshatriyas and Vaiśyas. They in fact were not Brahmin Rishis but Aryan Rishis.

Now Bhṛigu's name does not appear in the Saptarshi but that of his descendant Jamadagni does; so also Angiras is substituted by his two grandsons Bharadvāja and Gautama. Therefore, in order to constitute the later 8 stocks we have to add Atri, Viśvāmitra and Agastya. It is clear that the Atri stock represents the second horde of Aryan invaders viz., the lunar race Aryans, as the moon is looked upon as a son of Atri and the lunar race Aryans have generally the Atri gotra. Agastya is entirely a new addition but it also took place in Vedic times, for Agastya is a Vedic Rishi while Viśvāmitra an Indo-Aryan Kshatriya became a Brahmin and a Pravara Rishi by his austerities, also in Vedic days when caste was still of the nature of class and families could give up their hereditary avocation and take up another, especially the priestly intellectual one. Viśvāmitra's, therefore, was a Solar race Kshatriya stock which became priests by his intelligence and his high religious merit. Thus the old history of gotra as preserved in the Mahābhārata shows that the ancient Rishis can well be the progenitors of Brahmins and Kshatriyas.

The same conclusion is further supported by a study of the Pravaras, What is Pravara is not known generally even to the most learned Pandits for this question is rarely studied by them. A study of the Pravarādhyāyas of the several Sūtras discloses the fact that Pravara Rishis are those ancestors in one's family who have composed hymns in the Rigveda and who have praised Agni by those hymns or sūktas. The sacrificer in reciting Pravara is supposed to pray to Agni and tell him that he is the descendant of those Rishis who have praised him by their hymns in the Rigveda. In fact the sacrificer calls upon the Agni by the name of his Rishi. The Āpastamba Sūtra आर्षेयं वृणीते is thus commented on " आर्षेयमृष्यपत्यसंबन्धं प्रार्थयते संकीर्तयति । अथवा ऋषेरपत्यमग्निं यजमानस्य ऋषि सन्तानत्वात् तं वृणीते प्रार्थयते होमादिभिः ॥" It is clear from this that the sacrificer is connected with the Pravara Rishis by descent and not by discipleship. The word Rishi is explained by another Sūtra (मंत्रकृतो वृणीते) as meaning the composers of mantras or hymns. Now the gotra Rishi may not be a Mantrakrit or composer of hymns. He is any famous descendant of the Pravara Rishi who gave his name or a fresh start to the particular branch sprung from him. This proves the truth of the dictum that gotras are innumerable, while the number of Pravaras is fixed, for the composers of Vedic hymns must be fixed in number. Now the Sūtras further declare एकं वृणीते द्वौ वृणीते त्रीन् वृणीते न चतुरो वृणीते न पंचातिवृणीते " One may recite one, two, three, but not four, nor more than five, Rishis." That is to say even if there are more than five composers of hymns in one's ancestry, one cannot mention more than five. This explains how there are usually three and sometimes five Pravara Rishis but never four nor more than five. The gotra Rishi is either one of these Rishis or their descendants.

Thus for expample, the Bhāradvāja gotra has three Pravaras Āngirasa, Bārhaspatya and Bhāradvāja, Bharadvāja the gotra Rishi being one of the three Pravara Rishis. But the Vatsa gotra has five Pravaras Bhārgava, Chyāvana, Āpnavāna, Aurva and Jāmadagnya, Vatsa not being one of these but some noted descendant of Jamadagni who gave his name to a special branch. One more provision of the Sūtras must be noticed before we proceed. The Sūtras declare that the Adhvaryu priest should recite the Pravara Rishis in the order of ascent while the Hotā is to recite them in the order of descent. This further shows that Pravara and gotra mean descent and not discipleship. Thus Angiras, Bṛihaspati, and Bharadvāja is the descending line as also Bhṛigu, Chyavana, Apnavāna, Urva and Jamadagni.*

Now it may be asked how a Kshatriya born in the lunar or solar line *i. e.*, from the moon or the sun can have these Pravara Rishis or composers of Vedic hymns in their ancestry. But if we scan the list of the Pravara Rishis, we find therein many names of kings of the solar and lunar line. In fact it would be a revelation to many that the composers of Rigveda hymns were drawn from all classes, Brahmins, Kshatriyas and Vaiśyas. Thus, for instance, Māndhātā, Ambarīsha, Yuvanāśva, Trasadasyu, Purukutsa etc. who are Pravara Rishis are names of noted solar line kings. while Śunahotra, Ajamīdha etc., are lunar race kings. It seems that the Bhṛigu gaṇa and the Āngirasa gaṇa Pravaras mostly contain names of Kshatriya kings, a fact which we proceed presently to show. But we may first notice the fact that an examination of the several Pravaras given in the Pravarādhyāyas also shows that many Kshatriyas became Brahmins even in Vedic times. We will enumerate these cases. First we have the case of Garga who was originally a Kshatriya being a son of Bhumanyu, son of Vitatha, son of Bharata, son of Dushyanta a well-known lunar line king. This Garga and his descendants became Brahmins as is stated in the Vāyu Purāṇa also, दायादाश्चापि गर्गस्य ।शिनिबद्धाद्बभूव ह । स्मृताश्चैते ततो गार्ग्याः क्षत्रोपेता द्विजातयाः ॥ १६१, अ. १९०. Now the Pravarādhyās show that the Gārgyas are mentioned among the Āngirasa gaṇas. Thus Āśvalāyana says गर्गाणामाङ्गिरस बार्हस्पत्य भारद्वाज गार्ग्य शैन्योति ॥ आङ्गिरस शैन्य गार्ग्येति वा । Here we have to explain how the Gargas could go into the Āngirasa stock, being themselves lunar race Kshatriyas. The only explanation possible is that they were, when they became Brahmins, adopted into the Āngirasa stock through Śini. The alternative idea of Āchāryaship cannot be entertained as started by Mr. Pargitar who has touched this subject in his study of the Purāṇas and of the solar and lunar dynasties and who observes (J. R. A. S. 1919 Pānchāla dynasty) "Kshatriyas who became Brahmins were incorporated into Brahmin families, either in the Āchārya gotra or by adoption and were not allowed to start a new line like Viśvāmitra." For the idea of Āchārya gotra is inconsistent with the basic idea of Pravara viz., that the Yajamāna or sacrificer has to pray to Agni

* भार्गवच्यावनाप्नवानौर्वजामदग्न्येति होता जमदग्निवदूर्ववदप्नवानवच्च्यवन-वद्भृगुवदित्यध्वर्युः ॥

and identify him with his ancestral Vedic Rishi. The only way Garga could do this was by way of adoption into the Āngirasa family for he could then pray to Agni " Kindly look upon me as my ancestor Angiras who has praised thee in such and such a hymn." The second thing we glean from this episode is that these Brahmins are called by the Vāyu Purāṇa क्षत्रोपेता द्विजातयः or Brahmins endowed with Kshatriya power. From this we can gather the importance of the term Brahma-Kshatra-Kulīna often applied to Kshatriyas, an importace of which we will take notice further on.

Similar is the case of the Kāṇvas. Kaṇva was born in the Lunar line and was an ancestor of Dushyanta. His Pravara is Āngirasa, Ājamīdha, Kāṇva. Similar again is the case of Vishṇuvardhana whose Pravara is Āngirasa, Pāurukutsa, Trāsadasyava. The Vāyu distinctly states that Vishṇuvardhna was a descendant of Trasadasyu who was a son of Purukutsa, a Solar king and he became a Brahmin attaching himself to the Āngirasa stock. Another example is that of Mudgala who was a son of Bharmyaśva of the lunar line. His descendants became Brahmins and attached themselves to the Āngirasa Paksha, मुद्गलस्यापि मौद्गल्याः क्षत्रोपेता द्विजातयः। एतेऽह्यङ्गिरसः पक्षे संश्रिताः कण्वमुद्गलाः ॥ वायु. Hence their Pravaras are Āngirasa, Bhārmyaśva, Maudgalya. Now here an alternative Pravara is given by Āśvālayana तृक्षमुद्दैकेऽङ्गिरसः स्थाने तार्क्ष्य भार्म्यश्व मौद्गल्येति. Here Ṭriksha who is substiutted for Āngirasa is a Kshatriya king and an ancestor of Bharmyaśva, Triksha, Bharmyaś and Mudgala being all Kshatriyas of the Pānchāla lunar line. This, therefore, is a Pravara wherein no supposed Brahmin comes in but all are Kshatriyas. The same is the case with the Haritas. Their Pravara is Āngirasa, Āmbarīsha, Yauvanāśva. Herein also an alternative is allowed and Āngirasa is to be substituted by Māndhātṛi. The Pravara would then be Māndhātṛi, Āmbarīsha, Yauvanāśva. Now these three are the names of three famous Solar line kings and in this Pravara no Brahmin enters. The Vāyu gives the line as follows :— तस्यामुत्पादयामास मान्धाता त्रीन्सुतान् प्रभुः। पुरुकुत्समम्बरीषं मुचुकुन्दं च विश्रुतम् ॥ अम्बरीषस्य दायादः युवनाश्वः परः स्मृतः। हरितो युवनाश्वस्य हरिता :शूरयः स्मृताः। एते ह्यङ्गिरसः पुत्राः क्षत्रोपेता द्विजातयः ॥ These lines show that the Brahmins with the Hārīta gotra have a Pravar ın which all are Kshatriya kings. These changes, it must be remembered, took place in Vedic times. The descendants of Harita became Brahmins though he was born in the solar line with Yauvanāśva, as father, Ambarisha as grandfather and Māndhātṛi as great grandfather who are all Pravara Rishis *i. e.*, composers of Vedic hymns. If Brahmins have Kshatriya kings as Pravara Rishis, where is the wonder that Kshatriyas have Brahmins as Pravara Rishis ? If in Vedic times Kshatriyas could become Brahmins (which is the Pratiloma or revers process) ; surely Brahmins could become Kshatriyas (which is Anulom process). Indeed this change of a higher caste into a lower could take place down to mediæval times, for we know Brahmin families like those of Chacha and Lalliya of Sind and Kabul became Kshatriyas and the Kshatriya Bhatis became Vaiśyas in later times still.

To return to our subject, we have said that such instances of Kshatriyas being Pravara Rishis occur in the Āngirasa and Bhṛigu stocks. We will now give instances from the latter stock The Āśvalāyana Sūtra contains the following Pravaras which consist plainly of Kshatriyas (1) श्येतानां भार्गववैन्यपार्थेति. Here Pṛithu and Vena are clearly Kshatriya kings and the Śyetagotris attach themselves to the Bhṛigu Paksha, (2) मित्रयुवां वाध्र्यश्वेति त्रिप्रवरं वा भार्गवदैवोदासवाध्र्यश्वेति Here also Divodāsa and Vadhryaśva as well as Mitrayu are Kshatriya kings and the Pravara is attached to Bhṛigu Paksha: (3) शुनकानां गृत्समदेति त्रिप्रवरं वा भार्गव-शौनहोत्र-गार्त्समदेति. Now Gṛitsamada is a king and a Kshatriya; he is the noted author of the hymns in the second Maṇḍala of the Rigvada. His story is given in the Mahābhārata (Anu. Ch. 30). Gṛitsamada was the son of king Vītahavya and became a Brahmin by the simple word of Bhṛigu. Gṛitsamada was adopted by Śunahotra. Gṛitsamada's son was Suhotra whose son was Varchas in whose line was born Śunaka who gave his name to a gotra. Therefore the Śunaka-gotris have the simple Pravara Gṛitasmada or the triple Pravara Bhārgava, Śaunhotra, Gārtsamada. These instances show that Kshatriya Pravaras occur also in the Bhṛigu stock. There are some stray instances of Kshatriya names in the Pravara gaṇas of Viśvāmitra and Atri but not of Vasishtha and Agastya so far as we can see.

The above details will show that in Vedic times even, certain Kshatriyas became Brahmins and in doing so affiliated themselves to certain Pravaras or rather stocks of Brahmins. The instances recorded of Brahmins becoming Kshatriyas are rare and we remember only one instance viz., that of Bharadvāja who gave himself as son to Bharata who had left no issue. But it is natural to expect that such cases of Brahmins becoming Kshatriyas must have happened; and as stated above they did happen down to mediæval times. Kshatriyas then must have had gotras and Pravaras firstly as Aryans and descendants of the original four Aryan stocks. Then again they must have had gotra and Pravara as descendants of Kshatriya Mantrakrit or composers of Vedic hymns. Lastly even by adoption for purposes of sacrificial ritual they must have taken to certain Pakshas or gotras and Pravaras, there being differences of ritual among the different Pravaras in minor matters.

Whatever the proper explanation, one fact is unquestioned and appears from the several Śrauta Sūtras themselves, viz., that the Kshatriyas from ancient times had gotras and Pravaras and these were the same as those of the Brahmins. For the Pravarādhyāyas do not declare that the Pravaras given are those of Brahmins. Take for instance the Āpastamba Sūtra. It gives first the rules for Pravara and their recital. Then comes the sūtra पुरोहितस्य प्रवरेण राजा प्रवृणीते इति विज्ञायते. Here the word used is Rājā or king and the commentator adds अत्र च वचनात् ब्राह्मणोपि राज्यं प्राप्तः पुरोहितस्य प्रवरेण प्रवृणीते which means that even when a Brahmin becomes a king he is to use the Pravara of his Purohita. A king has many emergent duties to perform and whenever he sacrifices, he does not, nay cannot, personally attend to the sacrifice. He has always to appoint his agent viz., the Purohita and hence when the king sacrifices and appoints the Hotā, Adhvaryu and other priests, he must use the Purohita's Pravara and select priests of the same Pravara in order that there may be no hitch in the proper performance of the sacrifice.

This sūtra was misunderstood in later times but it plainly appears here that it applies to a king and not to all Kshatriyas. The Sūtra proceeds to give the Pravaras beginning with Bhṛigu without distinction for Brahmins and Kshatriyas. The special provisions for Kshatriyas come at the end which are very important; अथ क्षत्रियाणां यद्वाह सार्षे प्रवृणीरन् एक एवैषां प्रवरः । मानवैडपौरूरवसेति होता ॥ The word सार्षे is not properly understood and it appears as सार्ष्ठें in Āśvalāyaua There is plainly here an attempt to bring in the Purānic genealogy. But it also appears that these old Sūtras which date probably from the 5th to the 1st century B. C. contemplate the Purāṇas not as they exist now, but as they existed in those days. For this Pravara offers a puzzle which we placed before many Vaidikas but which has not yet been solved. Ida or Ila is Manu's son but Pururavas is not Ida's son but the son of Ila changed into the woman Ilā according to modern Purāṇas. And secondly, this Pravara cannot be used by the solar race Kshatriyas among whose ancestors Purūravas does not come. Thirdly, Manu may be a Mantrakṛit but we know no Rigveda Mantra composed by Ida. He cannot be a Pravara Rishi.

Whatever this may be, it is clear that this sūtra only offers an alternative Pravara for the Kshatriyas based probably on the Purāṇas, which they might use if they liked. The following sūtras make the matter clear with regard to the ordinary Pravaras. अथ येषां मंत्रकृतो न स्युः सपुरोहितप्रवरास्ते प्रवृणीरन्. The Kshatriyas even in pre-Christ times had begun to forget their gotra and Pravara owing to Buddhistic influences or under the stress of foreign invasions and perhaps through the natural indifference which a profession of arms creates towards troublesome religious ritual. And for these this sūtra provides that those who have no Mantrakrit Rishis, should use the Pravara of their Purohitas. But the next Sūtra adds अथ येषां स्युरपुरोहितप्रवरास्ते —Those who have

Mantrakṛit ancestors cannot use Purohita's Pravara ; but must use their own Pravara as the commentator adds आत्मीयानेव प्रवरान् प्रवृणीरान्नित्यर्थः । However a fourth sūtra adds that even they from convenience (न्यायेन) can use Purohita's Pravara, not gotra it must be remembered. These sūtras convincingly show that the Kshatriyas had their own gotras and Pravaras from the most ancient times and epigraphic records dating from before the Christian era show that Kshatriyas actually mentioned their own gotras in inscriptions. Not only the Śrauta Sūtras but the Smṛitis also contemplate that Khsatriyas have gotra and Pravara of their own. How could otherwise the Smṛiti rule असमानार्षगोत्रजाम् . be applied to Kshatriyas ? The rule "one must not marry a girl of one's own gotra and Rishi (Pravara)" applies to Kshatriyas and Brahmins and hence Kshatriyas must have had their own gotra and Pravara. The method suggested by Vijñāneśvara in the Mitākshara is useless, for if marriage is to be settled on the Pravara of the Purohita, this Pravara may change from time to time or may be even changed specially when a difficulty arises and thus two families which can not intermarry may effect such marriages by change of Purohitas. The modern Kshatriyas and even Vaiśyas observe this law in effect by adopting the system of clans or nukhs.

Lastly, we may notice an important Sūtra from Kātyayana Laugākshi ; अथ हैके मानवेत्येकमार्षेयं सार्ववर्णिकं प्रवृणीते । कस्य हेतोरिति । मानव्या हि प्रजा इति । तदेतन्नोपपद्यते । न देवैर्न मनुष्यैरार्षेयं प्रवृणीते ॥ तदेतदन्यत्र ब्राह्मणक्षत्रियाभ्यामितरासां प्रजानामुक्तं भवति । "Some say that only one Pravara should be used for all Varṇas or castes viz., Mānavya, for all are born from Manu. But this is not proper. For you are to recite your Pravara neither by gods nor by men (a sūtra of Āpastamba), but by Vedic Rishis or composers of hymns, (Manu being a man cannot be a Pravara). This is spoken of other people except Brahmins and Kshatriyas." This Sūtra distinctly places Brahmins and Kshatriyas on the same level. It shows that Kshatriyas had still generally kept up the memory of their gotra and Pravara like the Brahmins and were bound by the same rules. It may be added that even according to the Purāṇas gods, Rishis and men are distinct categories. Such Kshatriyas who had kept up the memory of their Pravara Rishis were probably called in later times Brahma-Kshatra. *i.e.*, Kshatriyas who were endowed with Brahma *i.e.*, who had kept up their connection with the Vedic Rishis. The epithet ब्रह्मक्षत्रकुलीन thus is applied to the Paramāras in one inscription. It means in our view that this family is one of those Kshatriyas who have Mantrakṛits for their ancestors. The Paramāras are of the Vasishtha gotra and are supposed to be even born of Vasishtha and hence they are ब्रह्मोपेतक्षत्रेण कुलीनाः. The explanation is often given that Brahma-Kshatra may be explained आदौ ब्राह्मणः पश्चत्क्षत्रियः and there is no objection even to accept this meaning, since the Kshatriya families having gotra and Pravara were certainly looked upon as born from Brahmins, whether directly or by adoption. And this adoption may have taken place even in Vedic times. Thus a careful study of the Sūtras relating to gotra and Pravara leads us to the conclusion that Kshatriyas have gotra and Pravara of their own which are the same as those of Brahmins and that the Pravara Rishis contain many names of noted Kshatriya kings, there being a time, as indeed the Māhābhārata distinctly asserts, when the Varṇa difference was not rigid, when in fact there was only one Varṇa, the Aryans of India.

CHAPTER VI

ARYAN SETTLEMENTS IN RAJPUTANA

The Rajputs or rather their ancestors the Vedic Kshatriyas settled in Rajputana in not very ancient days and we have mention of such settlements in the two ancient epics of India. It must be remembered that this part of the country is very inhospitable and could not have ordinarily invited settlements. The sands of the western and the hills of the eastern part of Rajputana were not fit places for the settlements of Aryans who were, as stated in Vol. I, generally tillers by occupation and were consequently fond of what is called a Jāṅgaladeśa that is a dry fertile plain country. It is, therefore, no wonder that this part of the country remained inhabited, from pre-historic times for long, by Ābhīras, Bhils and other aboriginal tribes of the Dravidian race only. The Aryan settlers of the lunar race or second horde of Aryan invaders who spread from Mathurā toward the south avoided this country and passing through it settled in the level and fertile lands of Ānarta and Saurāshtra. We know from the Mahābhārata that Śri Kṛishṇa himself, when troubled in the Madhya Deśa "or middle country the favourite land of the lunar race Aryans" by Jarāsandha, went to Saurāshtra and founded Dvārakā. He was led to this country probably by the consideration that the king of Ānarta (or North Gujarat) was the father-in-law of Balarāma. Dvārakā and Ānarta were thus the first settlements of the Aryans in modern Kathiawar and Gujarat. When these Aryans had to visit the "middle country" they had to traverse no doubt what is modern Rajputana but they did it with great trouble and reluctance. Balarāma for instance in the Mahābhārata is shown to have gone along the track of the Sarasvatī which river, it is said, disappeared in the sands of Rajastan for fear of the Śūdra Ābhīras. Arjuna similarly was troubled by the same people when he escorted to the old country the widows and families of the new Aryan settlers in Saurāshtra after Śrī Kṛishṇa's death. The people here are called Dasyus and Mlechchhas which Dr. Bhandarkar wrongly interpretes as banditti and foreigners. (Bhandarkar, 'Foreign elements in Indian population Ind. Ant. XL.) Dasyu is the appellation given in the Vedas to the aboriginal people of India while Mlechchha is not necessarily a foreigner. For the Dravidas of the south are also called Mlechchhas in the Mahābhārata (Mlechchhas were those who pronounced Sanskṛit inaccurately and they were as well the aboriginal Dravidians as foreigners of the Turanian or Scythic race.). The Ābhīras were not therefore foreigners but aboriginal people of the Dravidian race and they inhabited this sandy part of the country in the time of the Mahābhārata, that is, about 250 B. C.

There are two more references to the Maru desert in the Mahābhārata which must be noticed here as giving us an idea as to how Maru was made habitable. When Śrī Kṛishṇa was returning to Dwārkā—his home—after the Great War, he was accosted on the skirts of the Maru desert by Uttanka who appears to have been the first Brahmin to establish his Āśrama there. He complained to Śrī Kṛishṇa that he often felt thirsty and got little water to drink. The latter asked him to remember him whenever he felt thirsty and thereafter sent clouds whenever Uttanka remembered him, clouds which gave plentiful of water and quenched Uttanka's thirst. Since his days certain clouds appear in Maru in hot days which are called Uttanka clouds (Mahābhārata Asvr. P. Ch.) The second legend refers to the hot winds that blow from the desert and Uttanka was troubled by these hot winds also, These were supposed to be the breathings of Dhundhu a demon, who lay concealed beneath the sands of the desert or dried sea. Uttanka sought and obtained the help of the solar race king Kuvalāśva of Ayodhyā. The latter dug out the sand and discovered the demon. Many Kshatriyas died in the hot fire emitted by the demon but eventually the fire was quenched by water brought by the king and the demon was destroyed. Kuvalāśva was thence-forth called Dhundhumāra (Vana P. Chap. 204). This story is again told in the Mahābhārata and is told in the Rāmāyaṇa also. It thus appears to be a favourite legend and shows that the first settlement in Maru was led by the Solar Kshatriyas.

The Rāmāyaṇa too of the first century B. C. speaks of this part as still inhabited by the dread Ābhīras. In the Yuddha Kāṇḍa Sarga 22, Rāma takes out an arrow to throw at the recalcitrant southern ocean who, appearing bodily, asks Rāma to forgive him and requests him to let his arrow fly against a northern part of himself called Drumakulya where many people headed by the Ābhīras who are described as "Dasyus of terrible appearance and deed" drink his water and whose proximity he can no longer bear. The arrow was accordingly sent and the country became devoid of water except in a well which was pierced by the arrow and which became famous as Vraṇa Kūpa*. What Drumakulya country was and where this Vraṇa Kūpa is, cannot be ascertained but certain it is that Indian poets have taken the most natural view of this part of India in its geological aspects viz., that Rajputana was probably once a sea which is now dried up and that there is very little water to be got except in some well-known wells. This part, however, was blessed by Rāma in return for its undeserved punishment and it became† very fertile and healthy. Apparently, therefore, about the beginning of the Christian era this part was first entered and settled by Aryans, after subjugating the fierce and uncouth aborigined people. The road became thus clear for settlement and it was found that Maru (desert) was fertile and healthy and capable of maintaining large stocks of cattle and raising different kinds of grain. In short, we may gather that the Aryan settlers first came to Maru, probably by the beginning of the Christian era.

The hilly tracks of eastern Rajputana must have been invaded by the Aryans earlier than the Maru desert. For the Mahā-

---

* उग्रदर्शनकर्माणो बहवस्तत्र दस्यवः । आभीरप्रमुखाः पापाः पिबन्ति सलिलं मम । तैर्न तत्स्पर्शनं पापं सहेयं पापकर्मभिः ॥ ३०; ३१ ॥ स बभूव तदा कूपो व्रण इत्येव विश्रुतः । सततं चोत्थितं तोयं समुद्रस्येव दृश्यते ॥ ३५ ॥

† वरं तस्मै ददौ विद्वान् मरुेऽमरविक्रमः । पशव्यश्चाल्परोगश्च फलमूलरसैर्युतः बहुस्नेहो बहुक्षीरः सुगन्धिर्विविधौषधिः । रामस्य वरदानाच्च शिवः पंथा बभूव ह ॥३९ ॥

bhārata speaks of the Pushkara Tīrtha situated near Ajmer as the holiest in India. In fact even now it is looked upon as one of the three holiest viz., 1 Pushkara, 2 Kurushetra and 3 the Ganges. But though early discovered, the Pushkara lakes were described as situate in Pushkarāraṇya or the Pushkara forest. Hence like Dandakāraṇya, Pushkrārṇya must have remained unsettled for a long time. Only Brahmin settlements must have first been founded as in Dandakāraṇya and Kshatriyas must have followed only after a long interval as in Mahārāshtra.

The route of communication between the valley of the Jumna and Gujarat in ancient days must have been the same as at present viz., along the Rajputana Railway. And the next spot which must have attracted attention after the Pushkara lake of Ajmer was naturally the high mountain peak of Abū. This high mountain in an otherwise level country must have suggested to the ancient Indo-Aryans the idea that this mount was a son of the Himalaya mountain. This poetic idea based on a natural aspect gave rise to the story of the Arbuda mount related by Chand. In fact the main part of this story is as old as the Mahābhārata itself where in Vana Parva Chap. 82, we have a reference to the Arbuda Tīrtha and therein Arbuda is described as a son of the Himālaya and it is further stated that there was here formerly a deep hole in the earth, to fill which the mountain had been brought from the north. The name of Vaśishṭha is again long connected with this mount as the Mahābhārata mentions the Āśrama of Vaśishṭha on this mount as a holy place.

The story of the digging of the hole by Uttanka is given in the same epic in two places. In the first, he is said to have dug up this deep hole in the earth to pursue the Takshaka Nāga to the nether world. In this hole Vaśishṭha's cow fell and he it was who conceived the idea of bringing a son of the Himālaya to fill up the deep fissure. Himālaya at first refused to give any help as the place was unholy but Vaśishṭha promised to make the country pure and eventually one of the sons of Himlāaya went and filled up the hole. Vaśishṭha thereupon lived there himself and built a temple to Śiva who, therefore, was given the name of Achaleśvara or lord of mountain. Even at present as throughout Rajput history the Achaleśvara temple is a holy place on this mountain. This story related here is thus probably very old and was subsequently amplified with details by the Skanda Purāṇa in its Arbuda Khaṇḍa Chapter 3. (The name of the mountain in the Purāṇa is Nandivardhana while Arbuda is the name of the great serpent seated on whose back the Nandivardhana mount came from Himālaya to this country). The Skanda Purāṇa story, however, makes no mention of any sacrifice by Vaśishṭha which plainly is Chand's addition to the ancient legend. From this account of the rise and growth of the Arbuda legend we may conclude that the Abu mountain was a holy place as early as about 250 B. C. and was first inhabited by some Aryans of the Vaśishṭha family. It is no wonder that the Paramāras who came to prominence in this part of the first country later on, take Vaśishṭha as their gotra.

These settlements of the Vedic Kshatriyas in the inhospitable sandy and hilly regions of Rajastan before and about the beginning of the Christian era, it is not difficult to imagine, must have been impelled by the pressure of foreign invaders on their ancient homes in the Panjab and the Gangetic valley. In fact throughout Indian history Rajputana appears to have afforded a sheltering ground to the Indo-Aryans, whenever they were thrust out of their richer lands, blessed with plentiful water, by barbarian hordes like the Śakas, the Kushans, the Huns and lastly the Mahomedan Turk's and Afghans. The last of the Rajput families which thus took shelter in the sands of Rajastan, we know from authentic history, were the Rāṭhods of Kanauj, who after the defeat and death of Jayachand came from the Gangetic valley to the sands of Marwar. In fact Rajputana has got this name—the land of Rajputs—from Mahomedan times only. History furnishes proof, though not certain, of many such immigrations in times previous to the advent of the Rāṭhods. The first historical mention is that of the Mālavas, the Malloi of Greek historians. From coins discovered at Nagar in Rajputana, Cunningham inferred that the Mālavas were there in their migration from the Panjab to Malwa about the first century B. C. as the coins bear the simple legend Jaya Mālavanam" (Cunningham's Arch. Survey Report

Vol. XIV). The next mention we have is that of the Madhyamikas who had a kingdom somewhere near Jaipur and who were invested by Śakayavanas. The Gaur Rajputs appear from tradition to have come from Gauda Deśa *i. e.* the region about Thanesar (not Bengal as people wrongly think) and settled in Ajmer where they were subsequently supplanted by Chāhamānas. The Gurjaras of Bhinmal were in our opinion not foreigners as Smith and Bhandarkar believe but were, on the contrary, Vedic Aryans pressed by foreigners from their homes in the Panjab taking shelter as usual in the sands of Marwar and preserving their independence. We have no record left of other Kshatriya tribes founding settlements in Rajputana in the 3rd and 5th centuries onsted by Kushans and Huns. But it may be surmised that the Kshatriyas or Rajputs who now came to prominence in the 8th century by their heroic conflicts with the Arabs were descendants of Vedic Aryans who had come to Rajastan being driven out of better homes in the Panjab and the Gangetic valley by foreign invaders. The religious map of India which we have appended to our first volume shows that this part of India was not predominently Buddhist nor Hindu Buddhist, but predominently Hindu. Here in the deserts and hills of Rajputana, the Vedic Kshatriyas had preserved their independence as well as their Vedic religion and when here also they were attacked by new foreigners who, to the cruelties of invaders, added the ferocious intolerance of a new idol-breaking faith, the Vedic Kshatriyas or Rajputs rose to the height of their efforts in defence of their religion and their independence. It is hence we see the phenomenon that in Rajputana, new Kshatriya clans came into prominence about this time and not only beat back the Arabs but by their new vigour founded the second set of Hindu Kingdoms which ruled India in the second portion of the mediæval Hindu period. Of these Rajputs the Guhilots, the Chāhamānas, the Pratihāras and the Paramāras were the most prominent and we proceed to sketch the history of these and other clans and the kingdoms they founded in our next book, beginning of course with the Guhilots to whom by the unanimous consent of modern Rajputs the palm of chivalry and pure Kshatriya blood has been properly conceded.

BOOK IV

THE SECOND SET OF HINDU KINGDOMS.

THE GUHILOTS OF MEWAD.

The foremost and the most renowned among the new royal families which came to the front about the beginning of the ninth century A. D. in consequence of their valorous resistance to the Mahomedan onslaughts on inner India, were undoubtedly the Guhilots of Mewad. We shall begin our history of the second set of Hindu Kingdoms by relating the story of this most chivalrous clan. Tod observes rightly that the Rajput tribes yield unanimous suffrage to the prince of Mewad, the legitimate heir to the throne of Rāma, as the first of the thirty-six royal tribes ; and has further properly noted the fact that the State of Mewad is the only one (with the exception of Jaisalmere) which has outlived eight centuries of foreign domination and in the very lands where it was founded in the second half of the 8th century A. D.—a circumstance which certainly adds to the dignity of the Rāṇā of Mewad. But the dignity of the Mewad royal family is not only due to the stability of their rule and dominion but to the long continued and determined resistance which they offered to the Mahomedans in spite of great reverses now and then, a conflict—almost always successful—which has become the most glorious episode in Indian history hallowed by the names of a succession of great heroes such as the legendari Bappā, Khumana, Samarasi, Bhīma, Hamīra Sāṅgā, Pratāpa and others. In fact the heroism of this family and its sustained tenacious effort for the preservation of its independence* and its religion are as stable as their fortune and their dominion.

Of this most illustrious family Bappā Rāwal was the reputed founder and it is no wonder that many strange legends have gathered round the birth, the youth, the exploits and even the end of this great hero, as around the lives of most heroes in ancient and even modern history of the world. Tod has recounted them in his monumental history but we shall content ourselves here with giving the most simple account leaving out all miraculous events and testing each fact in the crucible of probability, aided by inscriptions which too require to be submitted to the same test; for it can never be accepted that because certain facts are recorded on stone or copper they are therefore reliable or true. We find that facts especially those belonging to former times recorded in inscriptions are often based on untrue and unreliable legends and hence the need of applying this same test even to inscriptions. Col. Tod made most searching inquiries about oral and written traditions of this family, collected genealogies and inscriptions and had the advantage of personal acquaintance with the historical localities of Mewad and he has done well in recording traditions which he also looked upon as doubtful. For the shrewd observation of Hume which Tod has quoted must here be borne in mind viz., "poets though they disfigure the most certain history by their fictions and use strange liberties with truth when they are the sole historians have commonly some foundation for their wildest exaggeration." We will use the legends given by Tod in connection with the founder of the Mewad family under the same test in giving the following account, differing in many respects from that of Tod. With due deference to this great historian of the Rajputs, we must say that he was much influenced by the wrong theory of the foreign descent of Rajputs started by him and further observe that historical research was only in its infancy in his days, many im-

* It may be noted that none of the Mewad Chiefs submitted to the Mogul empire entirely or ever attended the Delhi Darbar of the Mogals. Even under the British rule which the family have accepted, the Mewad prince did not attend the last Delhi Darbar alleging their long tradition which the British government was good enough to respect.

portant and incontrovertible facts being now known or finally established. With these prefatory remarks and duly honouring and recognising the work done by the great historain, we proceed to sketch our story of Bappā Rāwal and his successors during the Mediæval period of Indian history. It may be stated here that Mewad history is certain and unquestionable only from Hamīra onwards, the history of the family from the foundation to the end of the twelfth century A. D. being still shrouded in doubt on many points and our account is only an attempt to rationalize story and is therefore liable to be modified as future research may discover new facts or new arguments.

Bappā Rāwal the reputed founder of the Mewad family was the Charles Martel of India against the rock of whose valour, as we have already said, the eastern tide of Arab conquest was dashed to pieces in India. He was further a contemporary of Charles Martel and strangely enough his life also resembles the life of that hero of the Franks who signally defeated the Arabs in the west and turned the tide of Mahomedan conquest in Western Europe in 732 A. D. Like Charles Martel who was a prince himself being Duke of Austria under the king of France. Bappā Rāwal was a minor prince under the Mori king of Chitore. He ruled in Nagada (Nagahrada) a small town a few miles to the north of Udaipur among Bhils whom he enlisted in his force just as Shivaji in later history enlisted the Mawlas in his fight against Bijapur. He was a small prince or Rāwal a term which does not mean, as Dr. Bhandarkar suggests, an ascetic of a particular sect. The word applied to such ascetics is simply by borrowed meaning for we know that even the word Mahārāja which really signifies a great king is applied to Brahmins and ascetics in a borrowed sense. Rāwal means a small Rao or prince and Bappā Rāwal ruled in Nagada among the hills and ravines inhabited by Bhils of the Aravalli range. He belonged to the Guhila family of Rajputs which was an offshoot from the royal family of Valabhi first established at Idar and subsequently taking refuge from Mahomedan inroads among the hills at Ahara, as usual among the Rajputs throughout their history. To this family belonged Bappā Rāwal a Rajput prince among

Bhils with whom he freely associated and whom he disciplined and engaged in service for his own preferment.

Like Shivaji, Bappā Rāwal was an intensely religious man and he equally hated the new invaders of India who were cow-killers. From their base in Sind which they had conquered in 712 A. D., the Arabs had begun to overrun India south and east. They had attacked the kingdom of the Moris of Chitore who were, as stated in Volume I, the relatives of Sāhasi king of Sind and who had even laid claim to that kingdom when usurped by Chacha. To traverse deserts was not a difficult task for Arabs and they had begun to harass Chitore with great force. We actually find it recorded in the inscription of the Navasāri Chālukya grant of 739-740 A. D. (Bombay Gazetteer Vol. I part I, p. 465) that the Arabs had attacked the Maurya (necessarily of Chitore) along with Chavoṭaka, Kachchha and other states. Bappā Rāwal was a great devotee of Śiva whose image of Ekalinga was near Nāgadā and a disciple of the noted Śaiva sage who lived there named Hārīta. We need not believe the story given in the Achalagada and other inscriptions that Hārīta foretold Bappā's greatness and gave him the golden anklet indicative of sovereignty in return for his devoted services to himself. But we may surmise that Hārīta saw the greatness inherent in his disciple and advised him to go to Chitore, enter the king's service and fight with the infidels, the breakers of idols and killers of cows. Bappā accordingly took service with his clansmen and his Bhils with the Mori king (perhaps he was already a Sāmanta of that king) and soon rose to importance and was chosen as the leader of the forces deputed to repel the recurring Arab invasions. Like Charles Martel, the Mayor of the Palace at Paris, Bappā Rāwal was probably the commander-in-chief of the Mori forces opposed to the Arabs and like Charles Martel Bappā seems to have achieved a signal victory over them. Naturally his renown was now greater than ever. We do not believe the legend that the Sardars of Chitore hereafter revolted and deposing the Mori king of Chitore placed the crown on Bappā's head. Bappā was too religiously minded to depose his king; although such an event is not unlikely. Like Charles Martel's son Pepin who, setting aside Childeric, the puppet king of the Merovingian line on the throne of Paris, himself became king of the Franks, Bappā might have, from the renown and power which he had acquired by his signal defeat of the Arabs, set aside the decrepit Mori king; but we prefer to believe that the then Mori king of Chitore died childless like Sāhasi in Sind or like Shahu at Satara in Maratha history, and Bappā became the king of Chitore like Chacha in Sind or the Peshwa Nanasaheb in Poona. Whatever the nature of the revolution, it is certain that the Mori line ceased and Bappā the conqueror of the Mahomedans founded an illustrious line of kings at Chitore, a line which subsists to this day after twelve centuries. This was also like what happened in France where Charles Martel became the progenitor, through his grand-son Charles the Great, of a renowned and long continued line of kings.

Unlike Charles Martel, however, Bappā Rāwal lived long and marrying many wives had a numerous progeny. He is the progenitor of the Guhilot Rajputs who have several branches and whose number at this day cannot be less than one hundred thousand. Bappā was in fact so long lived that he eventually retired in favour of his son and became a Śaivite recluse and died at a very ripe old age. We do not believe, as the legend recorded by Tod relates, that he in old age retired and went to Persia, again married there and founded a second royal family. It is far more in consonance with his highly religious nature that he retired and became a devotee as stated in the Ekalinga inscription.*

It remains to fix the dates of Bappā's birth, his accession to the throne of Chitore and his abdication. The traditional date of his abdication is given as V. Samvat 820 or 763 A. D. This date does not seem to be incompatible with the date which is found in the inscription of Maun Mori at Chitore given by Tod in his history (Appendix Vol. II Tod's Rajastan by Crooke) viz.,

* The above account is detailed from the following two ślokas :— हारीतराशिवचनाद्वरमिन्दुमौलेरासाद्य स द्विजवरो नृपतिर्बभूव । पर्यग्रहीन्नृपसुताः शतशः स्वशक्त्याऽजैषीच्च राजकमिलां सकलां बुभोज ॥ दत्वा महीं मध्वगुणाय सूनवे नवेन्दुमौलिं हृदि भावयन्नृपः । जगाम बाप्पः परमेश्वरं महो महोदयं योगयुजामसंशयम् ॥

770 V. S. or 713 A. D. Maun Mori is supposed to be the last king of the Mori line. The accession of Bappā to the throne of Chitore may be placed between 713 and 763 or somewhere about 730 A. D. It is given by Tod on the basis of Mewad tradition as 728 A.D. (see Tod by Crooke Vol. I p. 285). The Arabs conquered Sind in 712 A. D. and must have made incursions into kingdoms of inner India thereafter. The incursion on Maurya kingdom as stated above must have taken place sometime before 738 the date of the Navasāri inscription and we may safely place Bappā's accession in 740 A. D. and even earlier in 730 A. D. His rule, therefore, may be taken to have lasted 33 years not a long period however. It is difficult to say what his age was when he sat on the throne of Chitore. If he was comparatively young, we may take him about 30 years old and his birth may be assigned to 700 A. D. Now there is a strong traditional belief among the Guhilots of Mewad that Bappā was born in St. 191 a date which Tod says neither the bards nor the reigning prince of Udepur were willing to give up (see Tod by Crooke Vol. I p. 268). How to explain this figure was a riddle before Tod and he solved it by going to the Valabhī era and the sack of Valabhī by the barbarians. Now for both these Tod assigned dates which have been proved wrong from inscriptions. For the latter he assigns A. D. 524 but as a matter of fact we know that the last Śilāditya of Valabhī has left a grant dated 766 A. D. The explanation given by Tod, therefore, fails and we are driven to say that the Guhilot bards stick to a false and fanciful date for the birth of Bappā or we must offer some other explanation. We think we can explain this figure by looking upon it as given in the era of the founding of the Valabhī kingdom by Bhaṭārka, the date of which is 509 A. D. as given in our genealogy of the Valabhī kings (see Vol. I page 250). If we add 191 to this we get 700 A. D. It is not at all strange that the Idar branch of the Valabhī dynasty should have kept up the memory of the kingdom founded by Bhaṭārka as the branch was founded by a son of Guhasena whose date is 565 A. D. The Indian dynasty bards kept up, even keep up now, by calculation of their own, such eras or Samvats by adding the number of years for each reign and thus the memory of St. 191 for Bappā's birth from the foundation of Valabhī rule is not strange.

Whether Bappā is, as sometimes represented, a nickname only and whether he is to be identified with Khumāna or some other Guhilot king ruling later on, we shall discuss fully in a note. Here it will suffice to state that though the word Bappā sometimes means a Bāvā or recluse, it originally means father (Marāthi Bāpa) and is found actually applied to the founder of a kingly family as shown by the epithet बप्पपादानुध्यात applied to kings of Nepāl in their many inscriptions. But we do not believe that Bappā was an epithet so bestowed by later kings on the founder of the Guhilot family; we think it was his own proper name, for we do find Bappā as a proper name even in these times and in earlier times also. Thus Bappabhaṭṭi is the name of a Jain Āchārya of the time and Bappārya of a Brahmin donee in an inscription of the time; and among Kshatriyas the name Śrivallabha Bappa is mentioned as that of the Dūtaka in the Bagumra grant of A. D. 655 (Ind. Ant. XVIII p. 269).

CHAPTER II.

THE SUCCESSORS OF BAPPĀ.

The Guhilot line of Rajput kings of Chitore in Mewad founded by Bappā is certainly the most unique line in the history of the world. Founded by Bappā in 730 A. D. in Mewad it still subsists after the lapse of nearly twelve hundred years and in the same lands and the fortress of Chitore is still in its possession though the capital is not now Chitore but Udepur. But what is more wonderful is that the kings of this line, however diverse their fortune, were, each and all, chivalrous and virtuous, lovers of independence and supporters of their ancestral faith. Indeed we may say that the sublime character of the hero-god Rāma as a man and a king whom they look upon as their progenitor still exercises its influence over the kings of this line and equally reigns the influence of the life of the actual founder Bappā who was a highly religious and independence-loving, valorous king. The praise bestowed* upon him by the Chitoregad and Achaleśvara inscriptions is not untrue and the Guhilot line of kings equally deserves the praise bestowed upon it†.

---

* Bappā was given a golden valaya for his foot, indicative of sovereignty, by the sage Hārīta for his great devotion to the Ekalinga Śiva idol (संप्राप्ताद्भुतमेकलिंगचरणांभोजप्रसादात्फलं यस्मै दिव्यसुवर्णपादकटकं हारीतराशिर्ददौ । बप्पाख्यः स पुरा पुराणपुरुषप्रारंभनिर्वाहनात्तुल्योत्साहगुणो बभूव जगति श्रीमेदपाटाधिपः ॥ (B. I. P. 75) See also हारीतात्किल बप्पकोऽङ्घ्रिवलयव्याजेन लेभे महः क्षात्रं धातृनिभाद्वितीर्य मुनये ब्राह्मं स्वसेवाच्छलात् ॥ (B. I. 85). This does not necessarily show that Bappā was a Brahmin and Hārīta was a Kshatriya. The poet simply means that Bappā's service of the sage was a Brahmin mahas (greatness) and it was repaid by the Kshatriya mahas viz: the golden anklet of a king.

† See यद्वंशो गुहिलस्य राजभगवन्नारायणः कीर्त्यते तत्सत्यं, कथमन्यथा नृपतयस्तं संश्रयन्तेतराम् । मुक्तेः कल्पितवेतसः करतलव्यासक्तदण्डोज्ज्वलाः प्राणत्राणधियः श्रियः समुदयैर्न्यस्तापहस्ताः सदा ॥ and एतेऽद्यापि महीभुजः क्षितितले तद्वंशसंभूतयः शोभन्ते सुतरामुपात्तवपुषः क्षात्रा हि धर्मा इव ॥ B. I. Page 85.

The several inscriptions yet known relating to this line, however, are very difficult to reconcile one with another, regarding the names of the successors of Bappā step by step and the matter is further complicated by the finding of a fresh copy of the Ātapurā inscription which was before Tod also. In this new copy certain names appear which are not in Tod's copy and the number of kings down to Samarasinha the reputed contemporary of Prithvīrāja with whom our history will *end* about the beginning of the 13th century A. D. is about 30 which gives approximately $(\frac{1200-740}{30}=\frac{460}{30})$ 15 years per reign, not an improbable figure. If we, however, take the number of kings as given by the new copy of the Ātapurā inscription we have from Bappā (or Guhila) to Śaktikumāra whose inscription of V. S. 1034 or A. D. 977 has been found, 20 kings excluding Bappā and this gives $(\frac{977-763}{20}-\frac{214}{20})$ 11 years which is rather improbable. But looking to the fact that during the period with which our second volume is concerned, the Mewad kings were constantly fighting with the Mahomedans who harassed them from their base in Sind, we need not wonder at this shortness of the average reign. For example, we find four kings mentioned from 1008 to 1034 V. E. or a period of 26 years only viz., Allaṭa, Naravāhana, Śālivāhana and Śaktikumāra. Or it may be possible that this Ātapurā inscription brings together contemporaneous kings of different branches of the Guhila tree, as was done by Tod himself, for we are already told that this family had many branches (vide the Chitoregad inscription*). We are, therefore, not yet certain about the successors of Bappā during the second subperiod of Mediæval Hindu Indian history, (The two kings Śīla and Aparājita whose inscriptions of the 7th century A. D. have been found must be considered to be Bappā's ancestors and if these names recur in the Ātapurā new copy they are descendants having the same names). But we will give here the most important of these kings, mainly following the Chitoregad and Achaleśvara inscriptions for details.

---

* शाखोपशाखाकुलितः सुपर्वा गुणोान्वितः पत्रविभूषितांगः । कृतास्पदो मूर्द्धनि भूधराणां जयत्युदारो गुहिलस्य वंशः ॥ (B. I. P. 85.)

The son of Bappā who came to the throne of Mewad was Guhila and he had many tough fights with enemies, of course, the Arabs from Sind. In fact throughout our period the Guhilot kings of Chitore fought hard-fought battles with foreigners, so much so that the whole country was strewn with flesh and the meda (fat) of the evil warriors slain and thus acquired the name Medapāta (undoubtedly a poetic fancy suggested by the name Medapāṭa, Prakṛita Mewad, but yet proving the terrible battles which the heroic Rajputs and the equally heroic Arabs fought on this soil.)* Guhila gave his name, it is said in both these inscriptions, to the family which consequently became known as Guhilot, Skt. Guhilaputra, (the termination ota from *putra* Skt., is now generally used in Rajputana to denote descendants of any famous king).

The successor of Guhila was Bhoja and his successor was Śīla. Both these fought with the Arabs but Śīla's successor Kālabhoja is described as having fought harder battles still. The son of Kālabhoja is said to be Bhartṛipaṭṭa and his son was Sinha. These as usual were great warriors and fought battles with enemies. The son and successor of Sinha was Mahāyaka and his son was Khommāṇa of whose exploits these inscriptions sing great praises. Now Tod refers to a poem called Khommāṇa Rāsā in which after the fashion of the Rāsās an attempt is made to bring together the various Rajput clans which assembled to assist in the defence of Chitore against the hereditary foe—the Mahomedans from Sind. The Ātapurā inscription mentions two Khommāṇas before this Khommāṇa, the first of them being the son of Kālabhoja and the second being son and successor of Sinha. In whose time did this great invasion take place? Tod has given a short account of the invasions of the inner country by Mahomedans from Sind during the time of the several Khalifas who succeeded Walid. It seems probable according to Tod that this invasion took place in the first quarter of the ninth century. If we take Bappā as resigning in 763 A. D. and this invasion as taking place about 825 A. D., we have a distance of about 62 years which ordinarily

* मेदःक्लेदभरेण दुर्जनजनस्याप्लावितः संगरे । मेदपाटाभिधाम् ॥

would cover three reigns but in this line of short reigns we might assign five kings between Bappā and Khommāṇa. As some kings are not mentioned in these inscriptions between Bappā and Mahāyaka who are mentioned in the Ātapurā inscription (Ind. Ant. XXXIX p. 191) it seems probable that Khommāṇa who fought valiantly with the aid of other Rajputs with the Arabs was the son and successor of Kālabhoja.

The poem Khommāṇa Rāsā has not been available to us and it is very difficult to say how far it is historically valuable. The bringing together of various Rajput clans is a favourite artifice with poets introduced to display knowledge of Rajput clans just as Homer brings all the then known Greek tribes together in some places in his Iliad. But it may be accepted that many Rajput clans did actually come to the help of Chitore in this their first great struggle with Mahomedans just as Rajputs came together to oppose Mahmud of Ghazni and they came to the assistance of Prithvirāja in his fight with Shahbudin. It is, however, unnecessary to discuss here which Rajput tribes came to the assistance of Khommāṇa and we will leave the details to Tod's work (Vol. II) as these details are probably not historical but imaginary.

The son and successor of Khommāṇa (the third) who was also a great warrior is in these two inscriptions said to be Allaṭa. The mother of this king was Mahālakshmī born of a Rāshtrakūta family*. We have a separate inscription of Naravāhana, son and successor of Allaṭa, in which also Allaṭa is said to be a son of Mahālakshmī but this inscription does not give the name of his father who may be either Khommāṇa or Bhartripaṭṭa, son and successor of Khommāṇa, as stated in the Ātapurā inscription. The son and successor of Allaṭa was Naravāhana whose successor was Śaktikumāra (but the Ātapurā inscription puts one Śālivāhana between Naravāhana and Śaktikumāra). The Ātapurā inscription belongs to the time of Śaktikumāra and is

* The Nilgunda inscription of Amoghavarsha I. dated 866 A.D. states that Amoghavarsha conquered the Gurjaras, of course, of Kanouj and those who dwell in the hill fort of Chitrakūta. This shows that Chitorewas a substantial kingdom and had come into conflict with the Rāstrakūtas of the Deccan.

dated Vikrama Samvat 1034 equivalent to 977 A.D. Śaktikumāra's successor was Śuchivarman. We have an inscription of Śuchivarman himself which is dated V. E. 1038. The Chitore inscription closes with the mention of king Naravāhana and the line is carried on upto Samarasinha of V. S. 1338, in the Achaleśvara inscription. We will speak of this latter portion of the line in our third volume and we close here our account of the Guhilot kings of Chitore with Śuchivarman who probably reigned about 1000 A. D. Who the king of Chitore was when Mahmud of Ghazni invaded the Chitore territory we shall discuss in Book VI. We append a list of the Guhilot kings from Bappā to Śatikumāra and give for comparison the list given in the Mewad Gazetteer by Erskine with a few remarks of our own explaining our view.

GENEALOGY OF GUHILOT KINGS.

Ātapura Ins. St. 1034	Achalgadh Ins. St, 1342	Bānapur Ins, St, 1496	Mewad Gaz.
Guhāditya or Bappā retired in V.S. 820.		Bappā	.. A.D. 763
1 Guhila ..	Guhila ..	Guhila	
2 Bhoja ..	Bhoja ..	Bhoja.	
3 Mahendra ..	— ..	—	
4 Nāga ..	— ..	—	
*5 Śila ..	Śila ..	Śila	
*6 Aparājita ..	— ..	—	
7 Mahendra II ..	— ..	—	
†8 Kālabhoja ..	Kālabhoja ..	Kālabhoja	
†9 Khommāna ..	— ..	—	.. 836
10 Mattata ..	— ..	—	
11 Bhatripatta ..	— ..	—	
12 Sinha ..	Sinha ..	Sinha	
13 Khommāna II ..	— ..	—	
14 Mahāyaka ..	Mahāyaka ..	Mahāyaka	
15 Khommāna III ..	Khommāna ..	Khommāna	.. 936
16 Bhatripatta II .. married Mahālakshmi of the Rāstrakūtas.	— ..	—	
17 Allata ..	Allata ..	Allata	
Ins. V. E. 1008—16	..		.. 951

18 Naravāhana	Naravāhana	Naravāhana	
V. E. 1028			971
19 Śālivāhana	—	—	
20 Śakti-Kumāra	Śakti-Kumāra	Śakti-Kumāra	
V. 1034			977
21 Śuchivarman—V. S. 1038			1,000

* Inscriptions dated V. E. 703 and 718 have been found of kings of these names but they are not these kings according to our view.

† It is sought to identify either of these two kings with Bappā by Dr. Bhandarkar and others, because if Guhadatta is identified with Bappā we have 20 kings from 820 V. E. to 1034 which gives 10 years for each reign. Dr. D. R. Bhandarkar looks upon the 9th Khommāna as the Bappā of the Guhilot tradition which will give 214 (1034-820) years for 11 kings or an average of 20 per king. But it seems to us that for securing the usual average of 20 years per king it is not advisable to upset the whole tradition. If Khommāna is taken to be Bappā the whole line of successors is upset; you do not get Guhila, Bhoja, Śīla and Kālabhoja as descendants of Bappā which they were believed to be at the time of the Achalagadh ins. You can not set at naught the tradition current in the thirteenth and even in the eleventh century (see Naravāhana Ins.,), for merely securing the usual average. It may be that this line of kings had a specially short average or it may be that the Ātapurā ins. repeats some kings wrongly or brings together kings of different branches who were contemporaries? for instance Śālivahana is unnecessary very probably being king not in Chitore but in Ātapurā itself where a younger branch may have continued ruling. If the Achalagadh inscription is alone relied upon, we get 11 kings only after Bappā to Śaktikumāra *i. e.* from 820 to 1034 V. E. In any case it is practically impossible to equate Bappā with Khommāna as the successon would be entirely different and we have no hesitation in identifying him with Guhadatta of the Ātapurā inscription.

NOTE

ARE GUHILOTS FOREIGNERS ?

Dr. D. R Bhandarkar in his paper on Guhilots (Bengal R. A. S. New Series Vol. V, 1909 pp. 176-187) has attempted to show that the Mewad Guhilot family of Rajputs was founded by one Guhadatta who was a Nāgar Brahmin from Vadnagar and who consequently was a foreigner and a Mer, the Nāgars and the Maitrakas of Valabhī being in fact foreigners who came to India along with the Huns in the sixth century A. D. like the Gurjaras. He has thus killed two birds (nay three) with one throw and degraded the Guhilots of Mewad who are considered to be the best Kshatriyas by the whole of India, from their high Aryan ancestry, along with the kings of Valabhī from whom they claim their descent and the Nāgar Brahmins one of the chief Brahmin sub-castes, into Mers ! ! ! We propose to examine this theory of Dr. Bhandarkar in this note and to see how far it is sound and believable.

We may at once say that the second part of this theory is absurd and based on the usual fallacies and prejudices. In beginning this part of his theory, Dr. D. R. Bhandarkar himself admits that he is not quite on *terra firma*. He argues that the names of certain Nāgar Brahmin donees in the Alīna inscription end in Mitra. On this he cannot resist the temptation to hold that Mitra was the name by which Nāgar Brahmins were distinguished from other sub-caste Brahmins. Now the Valabhī kings in their inscriptions are called Maitrakas. " We thus see that the Nāgar Brahmins and the Valabhī kings belonged to the same ethnic stock *viz.*, " Maitra " (P. 184.) ! As Mitra and Mihira are names of the same sun, " there seems reason to identify the Maitrakas with Mihiras the well-known tribe of Mehers or Mers." And further this rise of the Maitraka (Valabhī) power took place about 500 A. D., the period when the Huns came to and conquered India. " This *seems* to show that the Maitrakas were like Gujars a tribe allied with Hūṇas and entered India with them ") !! And finally " Now we see that Nāgar Brahmins were Maitrakas and the Maitrakas were like Gujars a foreign race. When a stranger tribe settled in India the priests of the foreign tribe became Brahmins and the warriors became Kshatriyas." Thus the Nāgar Brahmins who were Mitras and consequently Mers are foreigners and the Guhilots who are descended from Nāgar Brahmins are also Mers and foreigners by race. Even if they were descended from the Maitraka kings of Valabhī, they belonged, according to Dr. D. R. Bhandarkar, to the same ethnic stock *viz.*, Mers and are allied to Gujars and Huns *i. e.*, are foreigners and Mers by race ! ! !

It is plain that the argument as stated above is so flimsy and illogical that it is needless to enter into any refutation of it. The reader will hold with us that even if the Guhilots were proved to be descended from a Nāgar Brahmin they cannot be treated as non-Aryan for nobody will agree with Dr. D. R. Bhandarkar in holding that Mitra is another name of Mihara and, therefore, of Mer the well-known outcast people of Kathiawar. It is, however, the first part of his theory that requires a searching examination as it goes directly against the ancient traditions of the Mewad Rajput family, viz. that it is descended from the Maitraka Valabhī kingly family founded by Bhatārka who traces his descent through Kanakasena to Rāma, the solar-race hero of Indian mythology.

It must be admitted at the outset that this part of Dr. Bhandarkar's theory is based on many inscriptions. But, as we have said already, because a statement is recorded on stone or copper that does not make it invulnerable. Statements in inscriptions must be submitted to the same tests as any other statements *e. g.* of witnesses. Now we have first to point out that there is no contemporary evidence to show that Bappā Rāwal was a Nāgar Brahmin. He lived, as we have seen, from 700 A.D. to 763 A.D. There is no record of this period which throws any light upon the question who Bappā was and how he rose to power. It is well-known that stories gather round the life of great heroes and founders of ancient families. We have to test these stories and traditions and reject such as are obviously absurd or as are likely to have naturally subsequently arisen. Now we have, on this ground, rejected the tradition current in Mewad that Bappā or one of his ancestors was born of a pregnant queen in a jungle where she had taken refuge after the destruction of her husband's clan and kingdom. This story is told in India of many founders of royal families; it is told of Vanarāja; it is told of the founder of the Chālukya family of the Deccan and recorded even in an inscription of the Eastern Chālukyas (see Ep. Ind. VI, p. 367). Moreover, from unquestioned evidence the last king of Valabhī was alive and on the throne of Valabhī in 766 A. D. *i. e.* three years even after Bappā Rāwal had finished his career. We have, therefore, to see first whether such traditions are likely to arise and whether they are supported by contemporaneous evidence or not.

Now the inscriptions found which first state distinctly that Bappā Rāwal was a Brahmin are the Chitoregad and Achaleśvara inscriptions both written by the same man. These inscriptions are dated V. E. 1331 and 1342 equivalent to A. D. 1274 and 1285 *i. e.*, more than 500 years after Bappā lived. The first states "May the city with name beginning with Ānanda prosper from which a Vipra named Bappā etc." Here there is no doubt whatever that Bappā is said to be a Vipra or Brahmin from Ānandapura. All later inscriptions or records are mere echoes of this statement and naturally embody this tradition. The Ekalinga Māhātmya and the Ekalinga inscription thus follow and embody this belief. The origin of all these is, as stated expressly in यदुक्तं पुरातनैः कविभिः of the

Ekalinga Māhātmya, the verse in the beginning of the Ātapurā inscription a copy of which was even before Tod the historian of the Ra puts and which has been edited again from a fresh and probably original copy obtained by Dr. Bhandarkar. That verse is as follows. आनन्दपुरविनिर्गत विप्रकुलानन्दनो महीदेवः । जयति श्री गुहदत्तः प्रभवः श्री गुहिलवंशस्य ॥. It is this verse which we have to examine closely and see what it really means though even this Ātapurā inscription is 300 years later than Bappā.

Now it seems that the later writers misconstrued this verse and gave rise to a wrong tradition much in the same way as the misinterpretation of Prithvīrāja Rāsā verses gave rise to the spurious tradition of Agnikulas now exploded from inscriptions themselves. For there is firstly nothing to show that Ānandapura in this verse is the Ānandapura or Vadnagar of the Nāgar Brahmins, as it is admitted by Dr. Bhandarkar himself that Ānandapura is the name of many towns including Ātapurā itself where this Rajput family first lived and ruled. And there is further nothing whatever to prove that the supposed Brahmin founder was a *Nāgar* Brahmin. The writer of the two long poetical praśastis of Achaleśvara and Chitore of V. E. 1342 and 1331 was a Nāgar Brahmin himself as he distinctly states at the end of his Achaleśvara record that the Praśasti at Chitrakūta was composed by a Brahmin belonging to the Nāgar caste (Nāgarajñātibhājā). Had the supposed founder of the Mewad royal family been a Nāgar Brahmin, the Nāgar Brahmin writer of the Praśastis would probably not have missed the opportunity to state that the founder too was a Nāgar Brahmin. The Ekalinga Māhātmya has no historical value and may be left out of consideration entirely, especially as it is of a very recent date.

But the chief point in connection with the verse in the beginning of the Ātapurā inscription is whether the word Mahīdeva is to be interpreted as Brahmin or king, for the word is used in both meanings. It is possible that it means here a king as pointed out by Mohanlal Pandia in his answer to Dr. D. R. Bhandarkar; for विप्रकुलानंदनो विप्रः seems to be incongruous and it further appears that this verse equates the name Guhadatta with Bappā. Dr. D. R. Bhandarkar does not do this and thinks that Bappā is the nickname of some later king either Mahendrajit or Kālabhoja* (See also Mewad Gazetteer where Erskine adopts this view of Dr. Bhandarkar). Dr. Bhandarkar further says that Guhila is the same as Guhadatta which is not correct. In most inscriptions Guhila is the name of Bappā's son who succeeded him. Here it is necessary to point out that Guhadatta and Bappā must be the same. Dr. Bhandarkar observes " It is true that some records speak of Bappā or Bappaka as the progenitor of the family but they are comparatively

* This seems doubly absurd if we are to suppose according to the Achaleśvara inscription that Bappā was a Brahmin. Was Kālabhoja a Nāgar Brahmin ?

much later inscriptions." This is not correct. Both the Achaleśvara and Chitoregad inscriptions represent Bappā as the founder of the Mewad family. The Ātapurā inscription is dated V. E. 1034 or A. D. 979 and mentions no doubt Guhadatta but there is an earlier inscription of Naravāhana which is dated V. E. 1028 or A.. D. 971 in which Bappā distinctly appears to be the founder. Though the inscription is broken and illegible here and there, his name appears in the beginning and the word Guhilagotranarendrachandra would point to him as the founder and no other name is given before his (See Bhavn. Ins. page 59); and since Bappaka *king* is to be indentified with Guhadatta we have to interpret Mahīdeva as meaning a king and not a Brahmin.

The name Bappā as the founder's name given in the Naravāhana inscription is, therefore, as old as A.D.971, it is in fact the oldest inscription we have and we may be tolerably certain that he was not then looked upon as a Brahmin. But this word Mahīdeva appears to have been misinterpreted into meaning a Brahmin in later times and later inscriptions such as those of Chitoregad and Achaleśvara of A.D. 1274 carried on the misconception later still. How did this misconception based upon a misinterpretation of the word Mahīdeva arise we may try to surmise from the contemporary records of other kingly families.

The stories about the origin of founders of families usually arise from misconceptions and have always, it must be noted here, to be disregarded. When Chālukya inscriptions say that the founder of the family was born from the chuluka or handful of Bhāradvāja Droṇa, there is nothing more in the story than a poetic interpretation of the name Chālukya. Similarly, when Pratihāra is said to be a name given to the family from Lakshmaṇa who was always the door-keeper or Pratihāra of Rāma, we may treat this also to be a fictitious origin assigned to it which may safely be disregarded. Even Vedic Rishis delighted in exploiting names in this fanciful way and assigned fanciful origins to founders of family. Dr. Bhandarkar makes capital out of the story in the Vedas that Vasistha was born of the Apsaras Urvaśī whom, again, later Purāṇas represented as a gaṇikā or prostitute; but we may at once set aside such stories as poetical fancies carrying no historical importance. Vaśistha and Agastya are said in the Vedas to be the sons of the twin-god Mitrā-Varuṇa who put in a kumbha or pot, his seed emitted at the sight of Uravaśī and hence Agastya is called Kumbhayoni. Bṛigu is similarly said in the Vedas to be the son of Varuṇa. Now all such legends are simply poetical and have to be omitted out of consideration. Such legends obtained even among the Greeks and other Aryan branches also, assigning strange origins to heroes and the founders of families. Similar disregard has to be paid to unbelievable stories which gain currency about the origin and even the exploits of founders of families who lived in historical times. It is, however, possible to find the cause of such misconceptions and false ideas and we may suggest the following reason why Bappā was looked upon as a Brahmin. As we have elsewhere shown at length, the Rajput families kept up the memory of their gotras religiously and the Udepur family gotra was Baijavāpa. It was a puzzle *in mediæval times* to explain how Kshatriyas could have the same gotras as Brahmins and the puzzle continues down to this day. Though we have tried to solve the question in our note on Gotras some doubt may still be entertained by many on the subject. The latest theory of the 13th century A. D. noted by Vijñāneśvara was that these gotras were borrowed by Kshatriyas from their purohitas which as we have shown is untrue and incorrect. It appears that in the earlier centuries these gotras were explained on the theory that the Rishi of the gotra was the progenitor of the family. The Paramāra inscriptions thus say that their gotra was Vasishṭha because Vasishṭha created the first Paramāra warrior from his fire. The Chedi inscription which we have already noticed similarly professes to believe that the first warrior of the Chālukya family was sprung from the chuluka not of Brahmā but of Bhāradvāja and hence it was that the Chālukyas professed to be of the Bhāradvāja gotra. The case of the Chāhamāna is distinctly in point. While certain inscriptions give an independent origin, the Bijolia inscription says that there was a Brahmin in Ahichchhatra of the Vatsa gotra from whom was born the Chāhamāna king Sāmanta Now the Chāhamānas from ancient times have professed this gotra an. this legend tries to explain the gotra by supposing that the progenitod of the Chāhamānas was a Brahmin of the Vatsa gotra. But if the Chāharmānas were represented as Solar Kshatriyas in other inscriptions how ca- they be born of a Brahmin of the Vatsa gotra living in Ahichchhatra n This idea changed into another idea and another origin of the Vats? gotra of the Chāhamānas is given in the Sunda hill inscription of Chāchagadeva of Samvat 1319 and therefore of the same period as the Chitoregaiand Achaleśvara inscriptions. It says that the first Chāhamāna hero w d born from the eyes of Vatsa Rishi himself when he threw out tears of jo^a^s Now all these attempts are fanciful attempts to explain the gotras of Ray. put families which were being made from about the tenth century an] later. And it is no wonder if like the ancestor king Sāmanta of the Chāhad māna Rajputs who was said to be born of a Vatsa gotra Brahmin of Ahichchatra, the chief ancient town of the Chāhamānas, so Bappā Rāwal wabelieved in the thirteenth century A. D. to be born of a Brahmin of ths Baijavpā gotra of Anandpura, the chief town of the Guhilots. The worde Mahīdeva must have originally meant king but it was interpreted in later times under wrong gotra theories to mean a Brahmin. As said above we have generally to discard all such theories about the founders of families whether of Rajputs or Brahmins and take as little as possible from legends which are inconsistent with probabilities.

But we go a step still further. Even if we grant that Bappā or Guhadatta was a Brahmin and a Nāgar Brahmin from Ānandapura alias Vadnagar, how does that make the whole Guhilot family of Rajputs foreigners—irrespective of the fact we have already noticed that Nāgar Brahmins could not be treated as foreigners. We have already shown in Vol. I and in this volume also that at that period of Hindu history, Brahmins often married Kshatriya wives especially kings' daughters and the progeny of such unions was treated as Kshatriya and probably of the sept to which the mother belonged. The theory of putrikāputra has always been accepted in Hindu Law and moreover the Guhilot family, king by king, as mentioned in later inscriptions has always married into Kshatriya families. How can then the fact of one Brahmin coming in affect the race of the whole family ? We believe that Bappā's being a Brahmin is a misconception of later inscriptions but we argue that even if he were a Brahmin, his marrying a Kshatriya princess is not at all inconsistent with the customs of the period. His wife must have belonged to the Guhila family of Idar or of Nāgadā and their son being a putrikāputra or daughter's son taken into the grandfather's family was a Guhila himself. He might have been named Guhila even for this reason just as the son of Durlabha-vardhana king of Kashmir who married the sole daughter of the preceding Kashmir king of the Gonandīya dynasty was called Pratāpāditya (See Vol. I, p.206). The inscription at Achaleśvara distinctly says that Bappā's son was Guhila and the whole family afterwards was called Guhilot after him. It seems then that even if we accept the idea that Bappā was a Brahmin, there is nothing strange if he married the daughter of a Guhila Kshatriya king of Nāgadā and became famous as many Brhmins did in his time *e. g.* Chacha of Sind or Lalliya of Kabul whose history we have already given in Vol. I and the descendants of these kings were Rajputs for all practical purposes for we know they gave daughters to and married daughters from Rajput families. But here in the Guhilot family all subsequent kings were treated as Kshatriyas and married Kshatriya ladies and we have a detailed list of them all. How can, even if Bappā were conceded to be a Brahmin, the whole line be treated as foreign by race ?

In closing this subject then we will give our view of the matter in plain and simple terms. We do not believe that Bappā was a Brahmin; he belonged to the Guhila Vamśa as stated in the Naravāhana inscription of St. 1028 or 971 A.D. which is even earlier than that of Ātapurā which contains the disputed verse. The lines of the Naravāhana inscription are important. They declare that Bappā was a *king* (क्षितिपतिः) who was moon to the Guhila Vamśa*. This shows that there was a line of Guhila princes at Nāgadā which was most probably a branch of the Idar family founded by a Gūhāditya belonging to the Valabhī line of kings and hence called Guhila. To this line belonged Aparājita and Śīla whose inscriptions belonging to the seventh century A.D. have been found. They were kings before Bappaka who was like the moon to the stars of that family. Bappā was a great devotee of Śiva and a disciple of Hārīta a great saint and worshipper of Ekalinga and was himself a highly religious man. By his valour

* यस्मिन्नभूद्गुहिलगोत्रनरेन्द्रचंद्रः श्रीबप्पकः क्षितिपतिः क्षितिपीठरत्नम् ॥

and fortune Bappā became eventually king of Chitore and having married many wives like all great Indian kings was the father of a numerous progency in so much so that numerous clans numbering together several thousand descendants at this day claim descent from him. In his old age he retired to a forest and became a Śaiva Sanyāsi* (he did not go to Persia to marry Mahomedan women). In order to distinguish his descendants from the previous Guhilas, the latter were called, in the usual Rajput manner, Guhilaputras or Guhilots. It is extremely probable that Bappā was his own name as we find in an inscription a king with this name of a very early date (Ep. Ind. Vol. IX:—Bappabhattāraka pāda Bhattarasa). In short our view is that the word Mahīdeva in the Ātapurā inscription means a king and not a Brahmin.

But even if it does mean a Brahmin we add that there is nothing to show in any inscription that he was a *Nāgar* Brahmin. Ānandapura is the name of many towns besides Vadnagar. Nay it seems certain from the below quoted ślokas that the Chitoregad inscription looks upon Nāgāda as Ānandapura.† And is it to be granted that a Brahmin coming from Vadnagar must necessarily be a Nāgar Brahmin ? And lastly, even if it be granted that he was a Nāgar Brahmin there is no truth whatever in the theory that Nāgar Brahmins are Mers and foreigners. It is not necessary to write a note on this subject refuting the flimsy arguments of Dr. Bhandarkar and show that Nāgars are not Mers.

---

* The Ekalinga inscription has the following verse about Bappā on retirement :—दत्वा महीमच्छगुणाय सूनवे भवेन्दुमौलिं हृदि भावयन्नृपः । जगाम बप्पः परमैश्वरं महो महोदयं योगयुजामसंशयम् ॥

† अस्मिन्नागहूदाव्हयं पुरमिलाखण्डावनीभूषणम् ।, जीयादानन्दपूर्वं तदिह पुरमिलाखण्डसौन्दर्यशोभि ।

CHAPTER III.

THE CHĀHAMĀNAS OF SAMBHAR.

The next Rajput clan that came to the forefront about the same time as the Guhilots were the Chāhamānas or Chauhāns of Sambhar. They are rightly described by Tod as " the most valiant of the Rajput races " not excluding even the Guhilots of Mewad and the Rathors of Marwad ; for Tod adds that though these two " would be ready to contest the point, impartial decision with a knowledge of their respective merits must assign to the Chauhāns the van in the long career of arms ". This position they have well maintained through the long period of twelve hundred years. Though the Chauhāns no longer possess their original seat of power like the Guhilots, they have the three important kingdoms of Bundi, Kotā and Sirohi still, in Rajputāna and the chiefs of these have always been known as the most valorous princes through both the Hindu and the Mahomedan periods of Indian History. Nay more, under Pṛithvīrāja Chauhān and his grand-father Vīsaladeva also, they once enjoyed the imperial power in India and though Pṛithvīrāja was the *last* Hindu emperor of India, this unfortunate country being permanently enslaved after him, he has, unlike many last emperors of ancient and modern times shed such glory over the Rajput name by his chivalry and heroism that the Rajputs still love to believe that some one of their ancestors was with Pṛithvīrāja in his last memorable struggle with Shabuddin Ghori on the plain of Panipat. Indeed the Chauhāns for these reasons would have been entitled to be considered the first among the 36 royal clans, had it not been for the fact that in later history they accepted a position of subordination to the Mahomedan emperors of Dehli and some Chauhān sub-clans even embraced the Mahomedan faith to save their lands and their chiefships. It is for this reason that the Chauhāns stand second to the Guhilots whom they resembled, as we shall presently see, in many most important virtues.

The history of the Chauhāns, however, differs from that of the Guhilots in the fact that we have very little information about the founder of the greatness of this most valiant Rajput clan. We have already discarded the Agnikula myth originated by Chand Bardai, the bard of Prithvīrāja. The first hero named Chāhamāna (or sometimes Anahila in later records) may be regarded as fabulous as also the date assigned to him by Surajmal Bhat, author of Vaṁśa-Bhāskara and bard of the Bundi kings. Again the 136 kings mentioned by him as Chāhamāna's successors down to Prithvīrāja we are also compelled to treat as unhistorical. Even the kings mentioned in the Prithvīrāja Rāsā, 36 in number, as successors of Chāhamāna upto Vīśaladeva are unhistorical (for they are not borne out by inscriptions found relating to this family). It seems indeed strange that Chand Bardai a contemporary of Prithvīrāja of 1167 A. D. should not have been able to give a correct or even reliable genealogy of the family before Vīśaladeva who belonged to the tenth century A. D. For the period, therefore, of which we are treating in this volume (800 to 1000 A.D.), we have very meagre information indeed and we have to rely for meagre details chiefly on the Harsha stone inscription (Ep. Ind. Vol. II p. 119) in which two dates are given V.E.1013 and 1030 or 955 and 972 A.D., this being the oldest inscription available for this line of kings. This inscription is supported to a great extent by the Bijolia inscription which is about 200 years later being dated St. 1226 or 1169 A.D. (A. S. J. Bengal LV. p. 41). Copies of both these inscriptions are given in the appendix for the curious reader. Many other inscriptions belonging to this line have been found but they do not give any information before the above mentioned date viz., 972 A.D. and some of them confine themselves to one king only. There are thus three inscriptions of the Chāhamānas of Nadul V. E. 1218 (Ep. Ind. IX. p. 68) and Sunda hill inscription of Chāchiga Deva St. 1319 (Ditto) published by Kielhorn and several inscriptions of the same line (Ep. Ind. XI p. 169) published by Dr. D. R. Bhandarkar and the inscription of Chāhad Deva of Ranathambhor (Ep. Ind. XII. p. 224).

According to the bards of the Chāhamānas, the original seat of power of the family was Māhishmatī on the Nerbudda and they enjoyed, it is believed, sovereignty of the whole of India many a time. We may treat this as unhistorical though we actually find the Chauhāns spread over almost the whole of India from the Panjab in the north to Mahārāshtra in the south. Their first historical seat of power was unquestionably Sambhar or the Śākambhari land which was a kingdom to the north of Mewad and which included Ajmer also. This country contained or was reputed to contain 1¼ lakhs of villages and hence was called Sapādalaksha country. (We have already quoted the list of Indian kingdoms with their reputed number of villages given in the Skanda Purāna Kumāri Khanda Chap. 39 (See note p. 40). Dr. Bhandarkar mistaking this Sapādalaksha country for the Siwalik hills country wrongly assigns that place as the original home of the Chāhamānas. The mistake has already been pointed out by Mr. Harbilas Sarda of Ajmer who also pointed out that Ahichchhatra which the Bijolia inscription mentions as the original city of the Chāhamānas was not situated in the Siwalik hills as was propounded by Dr. D. R. Bhandarkar but was Nagaur in Rajputana. On this point we are not quite sure and Ahichchhatra may have been the famous Ahichchhatra of the Pānchāla country mentioned in the Mahābhārata. But this question we have already alluded to in detail elsewhere and we may confine ourselves here to the remark that when the Chāhamānas are called Sapādalakshīya kings they are undoubtedly referred to as the kings of Sambhar or Sayambhar for we also find that they are usually called Sambharī Rais or kings of Sambhar in Prakrit poems and records.

Who was the first king that established his power in this Sambhar country it is difficult to state. The Harsha stone inscription begins its description of the Chāhamāna family with

Gūvaka and when it uses the word Adya or first we are tolerably certain that the word being taken with king and not with Gūvaka shows that the inscription looked upon him as the first great king of the Chāhamānas of Sambhar. The Bijolia inscription, however, begins with a verse which is not quite clear in its meaning, saying "There was a Brahmin (we take the reading *vipra* as suggested by Dr. Bhandarkar instead of *viprah* of the edition in A. S. R. LV) of Śrivatsa gotra formerly in Ahichchhatrapura. From him was (descended or born) king Sāmanta of many Sāmantas or Sardars. (पूर्णतल्ल (Purṇatalla) remains unintelligible) ; or we may translate the verse as " There was a Brahman of Śrīvatsa gotra in Ahichchhatra formerly, named Sāmanta. From him was born Purṇatalla (a proper name) who had many Sardars." Whatever the correct translation, it is clear that this verse gives the goby to the later myth started by Chand that the first founder of the Chāhamāṇas was *created* by Vaśishtha on Mount Abu from his sacrificial fire. That story as we have already shown emanates from a poet's imagination only. But even this story given in this verse of the Bijolia inscription viz., that a Brahmin of the Vatsa gotra was the founder of the family is imaginery and suggested by a desire to explain the Vatsa gotra of the Chāhamāna Rajputs. We may, however, believe that there was a powerful Chāhamāna chieftain by name Sāmantadeva supported by many Sardars who belonged to Ahichchhatrapura (either Rampur or Nagaur) and who came to the Sambhar country and founded a kingdom there, since the Pṛithvīrāja Rāsā also gives the first great king after Chāhamāna as Sāmantadeva.

It may be said that the Harsha hill inscription does not begin with Sāmantadeva but with Gūvaka I and therefore does not also give the successors of Sāmanta upto Gūvaka I mentioned in the Bijolia inscription viz., 1 Jayarāja, 2 Vigraha, 3 Śrīchandra, 4 Gopendra and 5 Durlabha ; but it is satisfactory to note that the two inscriptions give almost the same line from Gūvaka I onwards upto Durlabharāja in whose reign the first inscription was recorded in V. E. 1030. There is a difference in one name only viz., that of (5) Vākpatirāja who must be equated with Bappayarāja—Vindhya Nripati, the name of Vākpati coming again in the latter (No. 10) being treated as Vākpati II. The two lists are as follows :—

Harsha Stone Ins. V. E. 1030.		Bijolia Inscription.
1. Gūvaka I	(circa 868 A. D.)	1. Gūvaka I.
2. Chandra	(„ 883 „)	2. Chandra (Śaśi)
3. Gūvaka II	(„ 898 „)	3. Gūvaka II.
4. Chandana	(„ 913 „)	4. Chandana.
5. Vākpatirāja	(„ 928 „)	5. Bappayarāja Vindhyanripati.
6. Sinharāja	(„ 943 „)	6. Sinha.
7. Vigraharāja	(„ 958 „)	7. Vigraharāja.
8. Durlabharāja	(„ 973 „)	8. Durlabha.

It is, however, strange that the list given in Rajputana Gazetteer Vol. III. B. page 65 omits the name of Gūvaka I after (8) Durlabha I though this name is given distinctly in the Bijolia inscription which this list follows and also in the Harsha stone inscription. The list requires to be corrected by the addition of this king who certainly was a conspicuous king of the line and who may even be looked upon as the founder of its greatness.

We shall try to assign probable dates to and Sāmantadeva Gūvaka I. We cannot assign to this line 20 years per reign on an average. We know that Vigraharāja was alive in V. E. 1030 or A. D. 973. His grandfather was Vākpatirāja who had a younger son Lachhmana who founded the Nadul branch and for him we have a date V. E. 1039 or 982 A. D. in the inscription. His father Vākpati therefore cannot be put in 933 A.D. or 40 years earlier than Vigraha but we might put him 30 years earlier *i. e.*, in 943. We may take, therefore, 15 years as average for each reign in this line and we thus find that Gūvaka I must have reigned in 868 A.D. (973—105). And Sāmanta may be placed 195 years before 973 A.D. or in 778 A.D. The Rajputana Gazetteer assigns 750 A.D. as the date for Sāmanta which is not improbable, though it is not apparent on which definite data this date has been assigned to him. By probable calculation we can only arrive at rough dates only but the two dates given above are probable and also well fit in with the course of Indian history at this period. Sāmantadeva must have attained to fame by his conflicts with Mahomedans at about the same time as or a little later than Bappā Rāwal and established his power in Sāmbhar in the middle of the 8th century. One of his descendants *viz.*, Gūvaka I became still more famous in the conglomeration of Indian kings and established his power firmly in that kingdom. The expression in the Harsha inscription " who obtained the fame of a warrior in the great kings' sabhā of Nāgāvaloka " has been interpreted to mean that Gūvaka I obtained fame as a Sāmanta or Sardar in the court of the Imperial Pratihāra king Nāgabhata. Kielhorn started this theory but subsequently changed his opinion (Ep. Ind. IX. p. 62) and yet again changed his view and reaffirmed his first opinion as appears from Stein Konow's paper on the Hansot inscription (Ep. Ind. XII. p. 67). It is, however, not probable that Gūvaka I was a dependent king though Sāmantadeva might have been. The Nripasabhā does not necessarily mean the Darbar of an emperor but may be translated as " an assemblage of kings called by Nāgāvaloka, who himself might be taken to be an imperial king. It is further not quite certain if the Hansot inscription is related to the Chāhamānas, for even there the word Chāhamāna is not clear and is only read by surmise. Its date again is St. 813 or A. D. 756 which does not fit in with Gūvaka I and we prefer to say that Gūvaka was an independent king who established his fame among kings by his exploits against the Mahomedans. He also in this respect resembled Bappā the founder of the Mewad Rajput family of Guhilots.

Gūvaka I further resembles Bappā in being a devotee of Śiva. The Harsha stone record clearly shows that the Chāhamāna kings of Sambhar were devotees of the Śiva god named Harsha himself on the Harsha hill as the Guhilots were devotees of Ekalinga. It is even stated in the first verse of the Harsha inscription that Gūvaka I built the temple to Harsha Śiva on the hill and from the following verses it appears that many succeeding kings showered wealth upon the Harshadeva temple. It even appears that Harshadeva was the family god of this line and to his favour they believed that their greatness was due, just as the Guhilots believe that their greatness is due to the favour of Ekalinga whose ministers they merely profess to be. The line श्रीहर्षः कुलदेवोस्यास्तस्माद्दिव्यः कुलक्रमः " Śṛiharsha is the family god of this line of kings and from him is derived the splendid career of the family" indicates this clearly and shows that at that time the worshippers of Śiva generally came forward to defend the religion and the independence of the Aryans of India. The Śiva cult of Lakulīśa was then in the forefront as appears from this inscription also, for the priests of Harshadeva whose devotees the Chāhamāna kings were belonged to the Lakulīśa sect like the priests of Ekalinga also from Hārīta onwards. About this sect and their importance in the development of religious thought in India we shall speak later on; but of their influence on the political condition of the country by generating enthusiasm in orthodox Rajput families this inscription as well as the Guhilot Ekalinga inscription are sufficient proof.

Gūvaka's successor was Chandrarāja and his son was Gūvaka II. His son and successor Chandana is described as having defeated a king of Tomara race named Rudreṇa and thereby obtained fame. The Tomaras had, it appears, established by this time, their kingdom at Delhi and being their immediate northern neighbours the Chauhāns had constantly to fight with these Tomarras. Chandana's son was Mahārāja Vākpati who seems to be the greatest of this first portion of the Chauhān line. He is said in the Harsha inscription to have defeated a king Tantrapāla of what country it is not stated (Ananta pārśva cannot be identified). The Bijolia inscription calls him Vindhya Nṛipati; perhaps his power extended so far. The Rajputana Gazetteer Vol. III. B, identifies him with Manikrai of the Prithvīrāja Rāsā on what ground is not stated; but this king's younger son Lachhmana founded the Nadul line from which the kings of Sirohi derive their descent and his date may be taken to be 943 A. D. as shown above. Vākpatirāja's elder son Sinharāja ascended the gaddi at Sāmbhar and he gave much wealth to the Harshadeva temple and covered the tremple roof with golden plate. He is described as the equal of Harischandra (their ancient ancestor) in wealth, munificence and success in battle. He defeated the Tomara king with Lavaṇa, defeated other kings in all directions and imprisoned many. His son was Vigraharāja "the equal of his father in all respects." In his time two villages were granted to Harshadeva temple and being the king during whose reign the Harsha inscription was recorded, he is naturally extolled the most. His brother and successor Durlabha is equally praised and we close our account of the Chāhamānas in this volume with Durlabharāja who reigned probably about the end of our period *i.e.*, about 1000 A.D. Who the king was in Sāmbhar when Mahmud of Ghazni invaded India, we will discuss in Book VI in the next vloume.

From the Harsha stone inscription it appears that the Chāhamānas in the tenth century A.D. believed themselves to be of the solar race. The same fact appears from many other records which we have already noticed . Even so late as 1400 A.D. when the Hammīra Kāvya was composed the same belief prevailed. The story given in this poem about the origin of the Chāhamāna family and their next seat of power viz., Ajmer with its Pushkara lake is as follows : " Brahmā once formed a plan of performing a sacrifice and as he was moving in the sky to look for and settle upon a suitable spot, the lotus in his hand fell on the earth and the spot became known as lotus or Pushkara. Brahmā performed a sacrifice there and in order to protect the sacrifice the sun created a hero by name Chāhamāna." This legend explains at one throw why there is Brahmadeva's solitary temple in India at Pushkar, why the lake was called Pushkar and how the solar race Kshatriyas the Chauhāns came to rule over the land. But the story also proves that the different legends about the origins of the founders of families are all imaginary, each poet being at liberty to frame a story of his own. Any how it is certain that Chand's story of the fire origin of the Chāhamānas is imaginary ; in fact, as we have shown he himself treated it as such and did not mean that these Kshatriyas were new creations. The Chāhamānas, therefore, must be treated as solar race Kshatriyas or of the first race of Aryan invaders of India, though their descendants in modern times believe themselves to be fire-born.

CHAPTER IV.

THE IMPERIAL PRATIHĀRAS OF KANAUJ.

The third clan of Rajputs which came to the fore at about the same time and by about the same causes as the Chauhāns and the Guhilots was that of the Pratihāras and they soon became the most powerful clan in Northern India, having conquered the imperial city of Kanauj from Chakrāyudha the last Varmā emperor of Kanuaj (See Vol. I. p. 341). Tod, the historian of the Rajputs, describes the Pratihāras as the least important of all the Rajput clans, probably owing to the fact that they were insignificant during the Mahomedan times and have left no kingdom of their own at the present day. But inscriptions discovered since the days of Tod and well interpreted by scholars especially Smith and Bhandarkar have established beyond doubt the fact that the imperial power of Northern India was wielded by the Pratihāras in the 9th and 10th centuries A. D. in succession to the Varmās described in our first volume. The history of the Imperial Pratihāras of Kanauj has been well told by Sir Vincent Smith from the inscriptions found up to date in J. R. A. S. 1909 and we rely chiefly on his paper therein in the following account of the kings of Kanauj. Of course Smith's view that the Pratihāras were Gujars and therefore foreigners has already been refuted on both grounds; for firstly the Pratihāras were not Gujars and secondly even if they were, they could not be foreigners as Gujars were not foreigners. With this one exception the account given by Sir Vincent Smith may safely be followed and we add certain further observations which appear on a perusal of the original inscriptions referred to by him.

The history of the origin of the family and its early kings can be gathered from the Sāgaratāla inscription of Bhoja published in Arch. Survey Report for 1903-04, a copy of which is purposely given in the appendix for the curious reader. The first king of this family who according to this inscription acquired power was Nāgabhata to whom Smith assigns a reign from 728 to 740

A. D. We have already noted the fact that this inscription assigns the Pratihāra clan to the solar race, being descended from Lakshmaṇa the pratihāra or doorkeeper of Rāma the hero-god. " In this family bearing the emblem of Pratihāra was born Nāgabhata who appeared as if he were four-armed owing to his weapons flashing in the destruction of the army of the *Balana* Mlechchha king, the enemy of virtue." This shows that Nāgabhata first acquired renown by his defeat of the Arab invaders the breakers of Hindu idols, who having conquered Sinḍ tried to extend their conquests eastward. He thus established a kingdom in the same way as Bappā Rāwal of the Guhilots or Sāmantadeva of the Chauhāns. It is indeed to be regretted that this detailed inscription does not mention where Nāgabhata founded his kingdom. Framers of inscriptions usually forget to mention this fact; perhaps to them it was always so obvious as not to require any mention. But future historians are often in a puzzle over this question. Smith says that Nāgabhata was king of Bhinmal but it is not certain where Nāgabhata the first illustrious king of the Pratihāras founded his power. It may be that his capital town was Mandor which certainly was the Pratihāra capital in the days of Prithvīrāja and whose king Nāhararai as stated by Tod immortalized his name by his stubborn fight against Prithvīrāja. Mandor again has very ancient ruins of an extensive character and has also ancient inscriptions in Pāli (See Tod by Crooke Vol. I p. 210). Mandor was certainly the capital of Marwar before the Rathods came to it; and the Rathods first took shelter under the Pratihāras of Mandor whom they subsequently treacherously supplanted. The Rathods removed the capital to Jodhpur which they newly founded only at a distance of a few miles from Mandor. All these facts raise the presumption that Nāgabhata the first Pratihāra king must have reigned at Mandor. Bhinmāl and Mandor are, however, both in Marwar or the desert and probably must have been in the same kingdom viz., Gurjaratrā as Marwar was then called. The ancient name of Marwar was unquestionably Gurjaratrā as is evidenced by inscriptions, while modern Gujarat was then called Lāla (See Ep. Ind. Vol. IX p. 277). The family ruling in Bhinmāl before this period was undoubtedly the Chāpa family of Vyāgramukha (mentioned in Vol. I p. 357) and it is hence not probable that Nāgabhata ruled in Bhinmāl. It is in short not possible to determine exactly where Nāgabhata ruled; but his country was undoubtedly Gujaratrā or Marwar and it was exposed to the attacks of the Arabs as completely as or more completely than either Sāmbhar or Chitore. And it is no wonder that the Pratihāra chief Nāgabhata acquired by his determined resistance to foreign invasions and the signal defeat of an Arab army. This must have happened a few years after 712 A. D. the date of the Arab conquest of Sind.

The successor of Nāgabhata was his nephew Kakustha or Kakkuka to whose reign Smith assigns the date 740 to 755 A.D. His brother and successor was Devaśakti or Devarāja and his son was Vatsarāja the next illustrious king of the family. Devaśakti has been assigned a reign from 755 to 770 A. D. and Vatsarāja from 770 to 800 A.D. The great exploit of Vatsarāja was that he conquered the king of Kanauj and "wrested the imperial power from the famous family of Bhandi" (Khyātad Bhandikulat etc.) "unassailable as it was by the wall of rutting elephants," "by the single help of his own bow." The importance of each word in these lines has not been sufficiently realised and we proceed to draw the attention of the reader to it.

In the first place the idea of a Sāmrājya or empire and a Samrāṭ or an emperor of Northern India had long been established in India on a firm footing. It is first mentioned in the Mahābhārata itself wherein Śrīkṛishṇa says (Sabha P. chap. 14) that "the Kshatriyas for fear of the Brahmins had established a confederacy and had appointed an emperor and that Jarāsandha of Magadha was then the emperor of India." Whether the Pāndavas became emperors of India or not, after destroying Jarāsandha, this statement of the Mahābhārata shows that there were emperors in Magadha at least in about 300 B.C. (the date of the Mahābhārata) probably beginning with the Nandas. The idea of an empire was further consolidated by the power of Chandragupta and the greater power of Aśoka and Pātaliputra became the seat of the empire. Later on many imperial dynasties ruled there, the last being that of the Guptas and Samudragupta and Chandragupta were the two great emperors of this last line in Pātaliputra. The empire of the Guptas having been overthrown by the Huṇs, Pātaliputra lost its importance as the seat of empire and eventually, as shown in Vol. I, Kanauj became the next seat of the Imperial power in India under Harsha whose extensive and beneficial reign has already been described, supported as it was by an army of 60,000 elephants (Vol. I. p. 13). In the mediæval period of Indian History of which we are treating, it was, therefore, the ambition of powerful subordinate kings to seize Kanauj and establish power there as it was the ambition of Mahomedan heroes in Mahomedan times to seize Delhi and establish an imperial line there. It is hence that we see Vatsarāja of Mandor raising his hand against Kanauj. As stated many a time before, kingly families decline in about 200 years and hence about every 200 years also we have the political phenomenon of one imperial line supplanting another. The Varmā line of emperors of Kanauj was now in its decline and it is no wonder that the ambitious king Vatsarāja of Gurjaratrā vanquished the emperor of Kanauj and wrested the imperial power from him.

It does not appear from this inscription whom he vanquished but probably it was Indrarāja. Again the date of the conquest seems to be about 780 A.D. from an important piece of evidence which has been discovered in the colophon of a Jain work. The verse quoted by Smith in his paper is fit to be requoted here and is thus translatable. "In the Śaka year 703 when the king by name Indrāyudha was ruling the north and Śrīvallabha son of Kṛisṇa was ruling the south and king Avanti was ruling the east and Vatasarāja the west and the territoty of the Sauryas was protected by Jayavarāha."* This shows with undeniable certainty that Indrarāja or Indrāyudha was on the throne of Kanauj and Vatsarāja on the throne of Marwar in Śaka 705 or A.D. 783. (It seems the word Avanti Bhūpati has been wrongly translated as king of Avanti, for Avanti or Malwa cannot

* शाकेष्वब्दशतेषु सप्तसु दिशं पञ्चोत्तरेषूत्तराम् ।
पातीन्द्रायुध-नाम्नि कृष्णनृपजे श्री-वल्लभे दक्षिणाम् ॥
पूर्वां श्रीमदवन्ति-भूभृति-नृपे वत्सादिराजेऽपराम् ।
सौर्याणामधि-मण्डले जययुते वीरे वराहेऽवति ॥

be in the east. The proper translation should be king Avanti, Avanti being the name of a king). It follows that Indrāyudha though defeated in 780 A.D. by Vatsarāja was still on the throne of Kanauj. This is not at all strange; for we find from the histories of all countries and of Indian empires in particular that the last kings of a tottering dynasty are allowed to reign under control, nay new puppet emperors are raised for a time, in deference to popular sentiment, before the line is finally uprooted. This is what happened at Delhi under the Marathas and even under the English. Nay the parallel goes still further. When an imperial line is tottering there rises a rivalry between powerful contending kings as to who should become the protector or guardian of the emperor. Such rivalry arose in India in the 18th century between the English, the Marathas and the Afghans. The English were powerful in the east, the Marathas in the south and the Rohillas in the west. The same thing happened about a thousand years before. And Vatsarāja from the west eventually became the master of India. Gopāla (Avanti) king of Bengal opposed him from the east and the Marathas of the 8th century viz., the Rāshtrakūtas. from the south; for inscriptions of the Pālas and the Rāshtrakūtas show to us the contentions that took place about this time. Gopāla of Bengal was defeated by Vatsarāja and *two* royal umbrellas were taken by him, probably the royal emblems of Gauda and Vanga or western and eastern Bengal. But Vatsarāja was in his turn defeated by the Rāshtrakūta king Dhrūva who carried away these two trophies and who "confined Vatsarāja to his own country viz., the desert Gurjaratrā."

These meagre but important facts appear from a Rāshtrakūta record. We do not know the places where these decisive battles were fought nor the manner of fighting or the actual forces engaged. It seems, however, that Vatsarāja from the desert country had no elephant force. He had bowmen and probably cavalry also, the Marwar Rajputs being still known as good riders. Both Bengal and Deccan forces had the elephant arm which was also the chief arm of Kanauj inherited from the days of Harsha. Although Vatsarāja could defeat Kanauj and Bengal, he could not defeat the Rāshtrakūtas as probably the Marathas were well-known both for their elephant arm and their cavalry (See the description of them by Hiuen Tsang and by Bāṇa in Harshacharita).

Although Vatsarāja was deprived of the fruit of his victory over Kanauj, his son Nāgabhata named after the founder of the family obtained what his father had vainly sought. The four verses recorded in praise of this king in the Sāgaratāla inscription give important particulars. He first defeated many kings. Āndhra, Saindhava, Kalinga, Vidarbha and others. These probably were the feudatories of Kanauj and had to be first defeated. Or as usual with Indian ambitious kings, Nāgabhata II must have made a Digvijaya before he seized the central power. The defeat of these kings does not mean the annexation of their kingdoms, but simply their humbling. The Samrājya or empire in pre-Mahomedan times, as stated many times before, did not mean annexation but merely the establishment of suzerainty evidenced by payment of tribute. Having established his power by a sort of Digvijaya, Nāgabhata II defeated a Vaṅga king who had before him vanquished Indrarāja and placed a young king Chakrāyudha in his place. Nāgabhata conquered Chakrāyudha also on the pretext that he had leaned for support on another (the Vanga king) and had thus exhibited his *lowness* " (sphutanīcha-bhāvam). It raises a smile in us to note that conquerers in all times have put forward the same pretext. Shah Alum took shelter with the English and the Marathas for that reason deposed him and placed on the throne another scion of Babar's family. Nāgabhata, however, seems to have tolerated Chakrāyudha on the throne for some time more ; for the words here used " he shone with his body bent in modesty " show that Nāgabhata shone brighter by humbling himself (before the puppet emperor). It seems, however, certain that Chakrāyudha was eventually set aside and Nāgabhata ascended the imperial throne at Kanauj and made it his capital. The Buchakalā inscription (Ep. Ind. IX. p. 198) describes both Vatsarāja and Nāgabhata as Parama Bhattāraka Mahārājādhirāja Parameśvara *i.e.*, gives imperial titles to both and thus confirms the fact that Vatsarāja had really " wrested Sāmrājya" from Kanauj and that Nāgabhata II too was emperor ; but whe ther he ruled from Kanauj is not quite clear, for even this inscription does not mention the kingdom or place where Nāgabhata ruled. We are, therefore, not quite sure if in 815 A.D. the date of the Buchakalā inscription Nāgabhata was emperor in Kanauj. Smith, however, surmises that Nāgabhata made Kanauj his capital sometime about 810 A.D. while 816 A.D. is given as the date of the end of the Varmā line (Vol. I p. 134).

Having established himself as emperor, Nāgabhata II had naturally to make his power felt by the subordinate kingdoms and he is said in verse 3 to have forcibly taken possession of forts in the countries of Ānarta (North Gujarat), Mālava, Kirāta (Vindhya hills), Turushka(?), Vatsa (Allahabad), Matsya (Jaipur) and other countries also. This shows the extent of the empire of Kanauj which in the north extended to the Himalayas and in the south-west to Kathiawar. In the east it was bounded by Allahabad and in the west by Panjab. The word Turushka in this document of 850 A. D. is an enigma which we will discuss in a note as it is difficult to equate it with Arab as Smith does.

Smith assigns to Nāgabhatta II a rule from 800 to 825 A.D. He had defeated the king of Bengal (probably Dharmapāla) who had placed Chakrāyudha on the throne of Kanauj and had thus made his power firm. He is said to have, however, been defeated by the second rival struggling for balance of power; the Rāshtrakūtas, in an unpublished grant by Govind III, but this defeat was not such as to oust him from the imperial throne at Kanauj since we know for certain that eight successors of Nāgabhatta II ruled as emperors in Mahodaya alias Kanauj hereafter.

The first of these was Rāmachandra, Nāgabhata's son, who ruled from about 825 to 840 A. D. and he was followed by Mihira alias Bhoja who was indeed the most powerful emperor of the Pratihāra line. He had a long reign from 840 to 890 A.D. and had very extensive dominion. The Sāgaratāla inscription already mentioned was recorded in his time and naturally gives him the utmost praise. But it seems that his power was really acknowledged upto the Vindhyas from sea to sea, he having again conquered even his formidable foe the ruler of Bengal. He was, however, defeated by the Gujarat Rāshtrakūta king

Dhruva Nirupma whose Bagumrā grant dated 867 A.D. (Ind. Ant. XII p. 184) mentions the fact that Dhruva defeated Mihira even though his power had extended through all quarters (dhāma-vyāpta-digantara). Here also the army of Mihira is described as consisting of good cavalry (sadvaśyavāhānvita). From the Bilhauri and Benares inscriptions (Ep. Ind. I. p. 252 and II p. 300) it seems certain that Kokkalla-deva of the Chedi Haihayas was a contemporary independent king who claimed to have *supported* Bhoja in the north and Krishṇa in the south. The verse in the latter record is rather boastful (whose hand gave abhaya, freedom from fear to Bhoja, Vallabharāja, Śrīharsha, the king of Chitrakuta and king Śankaragana), but it may be granted that the Chedi king Kokkala was really an independent soverign *in alliance with* Mihira Bhoja and that in the south-east the Jumna was the boundary of the Kanauj empire and the kingdom of Chedi or Tripura.

The internal administration of Bhoja is extolled by Al Masudi, an Arab traveller, who in 851 A.D. wrote "The king of Juzr maintained a powerful army with the best cavalry in India and plenty of camels. He was extremely rich and no country in India was more safe from robbers" (Elliot I p.4). This confirms what we have already stated that while under the Varmās the elephant arm was strong at Kanauj, under Pratihāras cavalry was well maintained. As the Pratihāras came from Gujaratrā or Marwar they were naturally more fond of horses and even of camels. The Arabs call the Kanauj empire the kingdom of Juzr or Gurjaras firstly because, as stated already, that was the country to which the Pratihāras belonged and secondly because the country immediately in contact with Sind (where the Arabs ruled) was this Gurjaratrā country. The Rāstrakūtas who were friends of the Arabs, and enemies of the Pratihāras, also called the Pratihāras Gurjaras for the same reasons. But we have to remember the fact that the imperial Pratihāras of Kanauj never call themselves Gurjaras in their records.

Bhoja was succeeded by his son Mahendrapāla alias Nirbhayarāja. His guru or preceptor was the famous poet and dramatist Rājaśekhara who always speaks of himself in his works as guru of Mahendrapāla and also of his son Mahīpāla. The empire inherited from his father remained intact under him and epigraphic evidence amply proves that it included Saurāshtra, Oudh and the Karnal district of the Panjab. His reign is assigned between the years 890 and 908 A.D. The plates of Balavarman (Ep. Ind. IX. p. 1) dated Valabhī Samvat 574 or 893 A.D. come from Kathiawar and style Mahendrapāla as Mahārājādhirāja Parama Bhattāraka and Parameśvara and therefore the overlord of the Chālukya prince Balavarman who made the grant. The Dighwa-Dubauli grant issued from Mahodaya or Kanauj itself makes the grant of a village in Vālayikā Vishaya or pergana of the Śrāvasti Mandala and Bhukti *i.e.* district and division and shows that Oudh was under the direct rule of Kanauj. The Siyadoni inscription (found near Lalitpur) dated 903 A. D. also belongs to the reign of this emperor and shows how subordinate chiefs ruled in this empire and contains many other interesting details regarding administration which we will notice later on.

Mahendrapāla was succeeded by his elder son Bhoja II who, however, had a short reign from 908 to 910 A.D. and he was succeeded by his brother Mahīpāla who is mentioned in many records and who reigned probably from 910 to 940 A.D. (Smith J. R. A. S. 1909 p. 269). His other names are Kshitipāla and Herambapāla or Vinayakapāla. The power of the Kanauj Pratihāras seems to begin to decline from his time; for we are told in a Rāshtrakūta record that Indra III captured Kanauj between 915 and 917 (Ep. Ind. VII, 30, 43) and the same incident is probably referred to by the Kanarese poet Pampa when he states that Narasinha Chālukya father of his patron Arikesarin Karnāta defeated Kanauj and bathed his horses at the confluence of the Ganges and the Jumna. He must, no doubt, have been a feudatory of Indra III and present with his army when he conquered Kanauj. But, as usual, Kanauj still lived on under Mahīpāla with perhaps undiminished glory and Rājaśekhara's play Bāla Bhārata or Prachanda Pāndava was performed before Mahīpāla at Kanauj. The Haddāla plates dated Dec. 22, 914 A.D. show that Mahīpāla was still the overlord of Kathiawar when the Chāpa king Dharanīvarsha made the grant as Sāmantādhipati (Ind. Ant. XII 190) . He clearly states that his overlord was Mahīpāla as he was "ruling by the grace (prasāda) of Mahīpāladeva Parameśvara Rājādhirāja." We know for certain that Mularāja Chālukya (Solankhi) founded an independent kingdom in Anahilvad by supplanting a Chāpa dynasty in 961 A.D. It follows that Kathiawar must have been lost to Kanauj after 914 A. D. and before 961 A.D. Govinda III inflicted a defeat on the Gurjaras probably in the time of Mahīpāla and Smith thinks that he must have lost Kathiawar long before 961 A.D. and very soon after 916 A.D. the date of Indra's conquest of Kanauj. The two inscriptions of Asni and Benares (Ind. Ant. XVI. p. 173 and XV p. 138) dated 917 A.D. and 913 A.D. respectively belong to the same reign of Mahīpāla though the names are Mahishapāla and Vinayakapāla as the grants are issued from Mahodaya and these show that the eastern limit of the dominion of the empire of Kanauj was Benares in Allahabad or Pratishṭhāna district.

The Arab traveller Al Masudi visited India in 915 A.D. again and writing in 950 A.D. about his travels says that the king of Juzr possessed many horses and camels and considered himself as equal of any king on earth. A fragmentary inscription from Khajurāho states that Kshitipāla was enabled to regain his throne by the aid of a Chandel king (probably Harshadeva). This must have been after the capture of Kanauj by Indra III in 916 A.D.

Mahīpāla was succeeded by his son Devapāla who is assigned a reign from 940 to 955 A.D. A reference in the Khajurāho inscription dated 948 refers to him as suzerain and shows that the imageof Vaikuṇṭha or Vishṇu set up by Yaśovarman Chandel in a temple there was received by him from Devapāla who had obtained it from a Śāhi king of Kīra in exchange for a force of elephants, who again had obtained it from a king of Bhota (Tibet) who lastly had obtained it from Kailasa (Ep. Ind. I. 134). This shows that Devapāla was in a sense inferior in power to the Chandel king and was under obligation to him for reasons already stated.

Devapāla was followed on the throne by his half-brother Vijayapāla who must have reigned from 955 A.D. to about

990 A.D. He is mentioned as overlord by a subordinate chief Mathanadeva in the Rajaur inscription (Ep. Ind. III p. 266). We have already commented on the word Gurjara Pratihāra occurring in this inscriptuion as the clan to which Mathanadeva belonged. The empire of Kanauj declined still more in the time of Vijayapāla. Gujarat (modern) was now independent under Mūlarāja Solankhi. The Paramāra kingdom of Malwa was also fully independent as we shall show elsewhere, Munja its greatest king being contemporary of Vijiayapāla. The kingdom of Jajhoti under the Chandellas was also powerful and independent and had apparently taken possession of the Gwalior territory, the actual feudatory there being Vajradāman a Kachhawāha chief (A.D. 977, also mentioned in an inscription dated 1083 A.D. Ind. Ant. XV p. 35). Very little information is available about the reign of this king. Possibly he may have been present at the battle which was fought by Jaipāla of the Panjab against Sabaktegin in 990 A.D. The confederacy of kings called by Jaipāl included Kanauj. Vijayapāl was succeeded by Rājyapāla who is assigned a reign by Smith from 990 to 1020 A.D. As the fall of the empire of Kanauj took place during his reign owing to the conquest and occupation of Kanauj by Mahmud of Ghazni, we shall have to come to him again in our third volume.

The above summary shows that the Pratihāra line was founded by Nāgabhata I in Gurjaratrā or Marwar by defeating the Arabs in about 725 A.D. and that his grandson again named Nāgabhata II founded its greatness by conquering Kanauj and making it the capital about 815 A.D. Bhoja and Mahendrapāla were the greatest emperors of this line which ruled from about 800 to 1000 A.D. They had an extensive empire comprising almost the whole of Āryāvarta and ruled it justly and secured to the subjects peace and orderly administration. The records and grants of these kings use naturally the forms of writing and address laid down by the great emperor Harsha. Each emperor signs his deeds of grants and attaches a seal which recites the names of kings in succession in the same way as Harsha's grants do or Moguls' seal did in later times. For instance the Daulatpurā grant of Bhoja and the Dighwā-Dubauli grant of Mahendrapāla recite the genealogy as follows in the seal, giving the religion and the mother of each monarch.

1. Parama Vaishṇava Devarāja, queen Bhūyikādevī.
Son 2 Parama Māheśvara Vatsarāja, queen Sundarīdevī.
Son 3 Parama Bhagavatī-bhakta Nāgabhata, queen Iśatādevī.
Son 4 Paramāditya-bhakta Rāmabhadra, queen Appādevī.
Son 5 Paramabhagavat..Bhoja, queen Chandrabhattārikād.
Son 6 Do. Mahendrapāla, queen Dehanāgādevī.
Son 7 Parama Vaishṇava Bhoja.
Brother Paramādityabhakta Mahīpāla.

This seal certainly puts us in mind of Harsha's seal where the religion and mother of each king is given in detail. There is this change in this seal that while Harsha's seal makes mention of Saugata Rājyavardhana this seal makes no mention of a Saugata or Buddhist emperor. The people and the kings of Āryāvarta had given up Buddhism entirely; now the kings were devotees of different Hindu gods especially the five gods Śiva, Visṇu, Sūrya, Devī and Gaṇesha. The importance of this change we will notice further on but it is necessary to remark here that there is nothing strange in the change of deity for each king. Tolerance yet reigned in India. As in former times the father might be a Māhesha and the son a Saugata without troubling the serenity of the family, so in this epoch (between 800 and 1000 A.D.) kings could be devotees of different Hindu gods without imperilling the happiness of the family. The verse quoted by the writer in I. A. here " Antah Śāktā " etc. has no room here for application as it is intended to level redicule against the practices of *hypocrites*. The change of deity can not be ridiculed in the case of this kingly line for the kings were real and hearty devotees of their special gods but were at the same time no so bigoted as to hate the other gods of the Hindu panchāyat tana. This stage came on later as we shall have to record in our next volume.

The documents and grants issued by the Pratihāra kings resemble those of Harsha in another point *viz.*, that they are terse and do not indulge in praise of each emperor. Other aspects of these grants will be noticed later on. There is, however, one peculiarity of these grants *viz.*, that each king has a special Biruda or name taken by him and it is mentioned in a verse at the end. For example one grant has the line "Śrimad-Bhāka-prayuktasya śāsanasya sthirāyatch" followed by a similar line giving the name of the emissary who proclaimed the grant on the spot. It appears thus that Bhoja had taken the title of Prabhāsa, Mahendrapāla Bhāka and Mahīpāla Śrī Harsha (Ind. Ant. XV. p. 141). Mihira alias Bhoja appears to have taken another Biruda *viz.*, Ādi Varāha and many coins have been actually found with this name. It seems that this emperor struck numerous coins in this name and the Siyadoni inscription dated 1020 A.D. contains mention along with others of–Ādi Varāha drammas or rupees.

NOTES.

THE PRATIHĀRA LINE OF THE GHATIĀLĀ INSCRIPTION.

It is necessary to add a note on the line of the Pratihāra kings mentioned in the Ghatiālā inscription published by Dr. D. R. Bhandarkar in Ep. Ind. Vol. IX. 277 and to examine its relation with the Imperial Pratihāra line. Strangely enough, this relation does not seem to be discussed. The inscription was found in Ghatiālā which is a village 18 miles from Jodhpur and presumably near Mandor. It speaks of a column raised by a king named Kakkuka in St. 918. Now the genealogy given here is as follows. "A Brahmin named Harischandra married a Kshatriya wife named Bhadrā and had a son named Rajjila from whom was born Narabhata from whom came Nāgabhata and then in succession 1 Tata 2 Yaśovarman 3 Chandaka 4 Śiluka 5 Bhota 6 Bhillāditya 7 Kakka and 8 Kakkuka from queen Durlabhādevī". This gives approximately for Narabhata a date somewhere about 701 A.D. (918-160 St.—758St) which is not far behind the date we have assigned to the founder of the Imperial Pratihāra line, Nāgabhata (725-740 A.D.) The name Kakkuka also appears in that line. It is therefore possible to argue that this was a younger branch from Nāgabhata. This Kakkuka founder of the column appears to be a valorous as well as a learned prince. The countries where he established his fame are mentioned as Travaṇi, Valla, Māda (Jaisalmer is still called Māda as Dr. Bhandarkar says), Ārya, Gurjaratā, Lāta and Parvata. Ārya and Parvata are not quite identifiable but Gurjaratrā is Marwar and Lāta is Gujarat according to Dr. Bhandarkar himself. He therefore appears to be a subordinate branch prince of the Pratihāra line who distinguished himself in the several dominions of the empire and probably ruled at Mandor, the ancient seat of the Pratihāras. The subhāshita verses composed by Kakkuka given at the end of this inscription are really interesting.

It may be objected that this inscription does not mention the rule of any imperial soverign of Kanauj, as subordinates are expected to state. But perhaps Kakkuka belongs to the same family and therefore omits to mention it. The Buchakalā inscription (ditto Ep. Ind. p. 199) mentions the overlord, being recorded by बीड्गनक भुंसुवक husband of a daughter of Jajjaka son of Bappaka of the Pratihāra gotra. Or it may be that Kakkuka considered himself equal of the imperial Pratihāras being born of the same ancestor Nāgabhata.

II—THE DATE OF DAULATPUTRĀ AND OTHER INSCRIPTIONS·

This Daulatpurā inscription evidences a grant made by Bhojadeva of a village in Dendavānaka Vishaya in Gurjaratrā and the year is Samwat 100. This was first treated as Harsha era but eventually Dr. Bhandarkar suggested that the figure should be read as 900. Dr. Bhandarkar has indeed set right a very disputed chronology and as already stated, he has the honour duly of setting right the Pratihāra line chronology. How 100, however, could be read as 900 has not been explained. There is the further fact that the Pehewa inscription of the time of Bhoja is recorded in Harsha Samvat era, though the word Harsha is not mentioned. It seems Harsha's Samvat still confinued in the empire in use. Curiously enough after about 950 A.D., Vikrama Samvat became universally established in Northern India while in the south the Śaka era became equally universal. No king thought it fit to start a new era of his own or use any other era than Vikrama in the north and the Śaka in the south. The cause of this shall have to be discussed later on.

III—BBHANDIKULA.

The Sāgaratāla inscription of Bhoja says that Vatsarāja wrested empire from the family of Bhandi. Who was this Bhandi? The only other mention of Bhandi is found in Harsha-charita of Bāṇa wherein this is the name of the maternal uncle of Harsha. We know for certain that Indrāyudha was the king of Kanauj who was conquered by Vatsarāja. The only inference possible is that he belonged to the Bhandikula. Is the former Bhandi to be assigned to the same kula? There is no reason why this may not be done. The uncle of Harsha as we have said in Vol. I (p. 38) and his mother Yaśomati must have belonged to some subordinate kingly family. They might have been of this Bhandikula itself. They might have belonged to an unimportant branch of the Maukhari family which ruled in Kanauj before Harsha and when after the death of Harsha and his sister the throne of Grahavarman became vacant, a representative of this branch must have sat on the throne of Kanauj and founded the later Varmā kingly family there, described in Vol. I Chap. XIV. It is possible in this way to connect the two mentions of the name of Bhandi.

IV—TURUSHKA.

The mention of Turushka in the Sāgaratāl inscription dated about 850 A.D. is a mystery. The Turks were not probably known to the Indians as conquerers until the days of Sabaktegin *i.e.* about the end of the tenth century. They are equated by Smith with the Arabs, but the Arabs were called Tajikas and perhaps Berbers but could not have been called Turushkas in 850 A.D. It seems possible to explain that the Arabs as a conquering people lost vigour by about 800 A.D. From about 600 to 800 A.D. their powerful outgoing force was spent and the Caliphs at Baghdad after Harun Al Rashid became steeped in the pleasures of empire. The Turks began now to come forward and they were employed as mercenary soldiers by the Caliphs in place of ruling Arabs. It might thus be that the army of occupation in Sind from 800 A.D. onward consisted mostly of Turks. There might also have been minor chiefships of Turks at least in Sind in about 850 A. D. and these were conquered by Mihira Bhoja. So far as is known the word Turushka does not occur in the Mahābhārata but it does so in the Bhāgavata which undoubtedly is a Purāṇa which came into existence about the ninth century A.D. (See Vol. I. p. 353).

GENEALOGY OF THE PRATIHĀRA IMPERIAL LINE OF KANAUJ

I. Nāgabhata of Bhinmal or Mandor A.D. 725-740.

II. Nephew Kakkuka A.D. 740-755.

Nep. III. Deva-Śakti A. D. 755 to 770.

IV. Vatsarāja A.D. 770-800 (king of the west, conqueror of Kanauj in 780 A.D.)

V. Nāgabhata II emperor of Kanauj A.D. 800- 825.

VI. Rāmachandra A. D. 825-840.

VII. Mihira alias Bhoja (most powerful emperor) A.D. 840-890.

VIII. Mahendrapāla A.D. 890-908.

IX. Bhoja II A.D. 908-910.

X. Mahīpāla (Kshitipāla, Vināyakapāla etc. A.D. 910-940.

XI. Devapāla A.D. 940-953.

XII. Vijayapāla A.D. 955-990.

XIII. Rājyapāla A.D. 990-1018.

Kanauj being seized and plundered by Mahmud of Ghazni this line of emperors of Kanauj ends with Rājyapāla though some further descendants ruled for some time more.

CHAPTER V.

THE CHĀVADĀS OF ANHILWAD PĀTAN.

The history of these Chāvadās can only be given from several Prabandhas or Bakhars so to speak of Jain and other writers consulted by the author of the Bombay Gazetteer Vol. III (Gujarat). Most of these Prabandhas are not available to us as they were to that author except Prabhanda Chintamaṇi and Sukrita Sankīrtana and there are unfortunately no inscriptions to support or refute the story of these Prabandhas. The legends given in the Prabandhas, as in Marathi Bakhars of later history, are not always reliable and they always contain a mixture of fact and fiction which it is very difficult to separate. It is undoubted that the Chāvadās of Patan did establish a rule in the Sārasvata Mandala (north Gujarat) during the period we are dealing with in this volume; but though they are said to be independent, it seems that they were subordinate throughout their history to Kanauj. With these important remarks we give below a short account of these Chāvadās from the Bombay Gazetteer Vol. III supplemented by a few facts from Sukṛita Saṅkīrtana and Prabandha Chitamaṇi.

These Chāvadās, appear to be or may be treated as a branch of the Chāpotkatas or Chāpas of Bhinmal. There was a small chiefship of Chāpas at Panchāsar and the last chief, it is said, was killed by one Bhūyada. Who this Bhūyada was it is not known. The pregnant queen wandered in a forest and gave birth to a vigorous son who became famous as Vanarāja. This story of Vanarāja is thus the same story as that of Bappā Rāwal or of the founder of the Deccan Chālukya line or of other princes in later history. But while these latter may be treated as copies, we think the story of Vanarāja is the original. He grew a stout valiant man who first commenced his career as a freebooter and having like Śivāji in later times had an opportunity to waylay and seize a convoy of treasure * going to Kānyakubja to which the country was subject, was enabled to lay the foundations of a kingdom viz., the enlistment of an army and the founding of a capital. He founded the city of Aṇahillapura in what is modern North Gujarat. This city is said to have been founded in 746 A.D.† This period was the period of the decline of the first imperial line of Kanauj kings, when many similar kingdoms were founded by heroic Rajputs such as the kingdom of Chitore by Bappā and of Sāmbhar by Sāmantadeva and the kingdom of Mandor by Nāgabhata. Whether Vanarāja had to fight with the Arabs we do not know; but it is certain from the Navasāri grant noticed many a time before, that the Arabs in their attempts to invade the Deccan had defeated some Chāpa kingdom. Whether Vanarāja had to fight with Arabs or not, he succeeded in establishing a strong kingdom at Aṇahilwad which under the Solankhis two centuries later was destined to become one of the then powerful and independent kingdoms of India.

Vanarāja is believed to have had like Bappā, a long reign and a long life. He is assigned a rule from 765 to 805 A.D.; why his rule is taken to begin later than the founding of Anhilwad i. e, 746 A.D. does not appear. He was succeeded by his son Jogarāja, (Yogarāja is the name given in Sukṛita Sankīrtana) who is said to have ruled from 806 to 841 A.D. He must have been a subsordinate chief to Bhoja the emperor of Kanauj who ruled about this time. Yogarāja was succeeded by Ratnāditya and he by Vairisinha. Khemarāja was the next king who ruled from 856 A.D. and was succeeded by Mundarāja (S. S. and not Chāmunda) who was also called Bhūyada in 881 A.D. His successor was Ghaghada or Rāhapa who came to the throne in 908 A.D. The last king was one unnamed king (Bombay Gazetteer) who ruled from 937 to 961 when the kingdom was seized by

* Prabhanda Chintamaṇi states that a *Paacha Kula* came from Kanauj to collect tribute from the land of Gujarat and he was taking away, after six months' stay, twenty-four lakhs of silver drammas when Vanarāja killed him in a pass and seized the treasure.

† A paper based on an old ballad in Ind. Ant. IV. p. 147 gives the date of the founding of Anahilawad as St. 802 which comes to the same year 746 A.D. The same date is given by Meruttunga in the Prabandha Chintamaṇi.

his sister's son Mūlarāja Solankhi. The name of this king is given as Bhūbhata in Sukṛita Saṅkīrtana.‡

Except these names and these dates which are given by later Jain Prabandhakāras, we have very little information about these Chāvadās of Patan. The city does contain some relics of Chāvadā rule. They appear to have been Śaivas like almost all Rajputs who came to the fore at this time and later on they probably patronized Jain Pandits. As they remained feudatories of Kanauj, they do not appear to have had many wars with neighbouring kings. We will close this short notice of these Chāvadās with an account of a minor branch of the Chāpas of Vardhamāna (Wadhwan) which ruled at about the same time from an inscription of Dharaṇivarāha in Ind. Ant. XII p. 193.

This grant of Dharaṇivarāha is dated Śaka 839 or 917 A.D. It admits that he was a dependent chief ruling under the emperor Mahīpāla "ruling by the grace (prasāda) of Rājādhirāja Parameśvara Śri Mahīpāladeva". Now this Mahīpāla must be the Mahīpāla of Kanauj and not of a Chūdāsama family ruling in Kathiawar. This grant mentions four predecessors *viz.*, Vikramārka 2 Addaka 3 Pulakeśin 4 Dhruvabhata, before the grantee Dharṇivarāha and taking 20 years and not 26 per generation we may put Vikramārka in about 837 A.D. during the reign of Bhoja Mihira of Kanauj. The Chāpas are herein said to be born from the Chāpa or bow of Śiva. As Dr. Bühler remarks, this legend belongs to the order of etymological myths, an order which has often been the cause of much confusion. The grant is made to an Āchārya of the Āmardaka Santāna (Śiva sect) and it seems certain that in Gujarat at this time Śiva worship was much prevalent and these Śaiva ascetics lived in Maṭhas built for them as the Buddhists lived in Saṅghāramas in previous centuries.

---

‡ Prabandha Ch. gives the following names and dates.—

1. Yogarāja till St. 878	4. Chāmunda till St. 938
2. Ratnāditya till St. 881	5. Akadadeva till St. 965
3. Khemrāja till St. 922	6. Bhuyagadadeva till St. 991 = 943 A.D.

No. 5. built Ākadeśvari temple and Kantheśvari and No. 6, built Bhuyadeśvari in Patan and the rampart.

CHAPTER VI.

THE PARAMĀRAS OF DHĀR.

The fourth Rajput tribe which established a renowned kingdom in the second sub-period of our history was the Paramāras of Abu and subsequently of Dhār. Tod has described it as the most potent of Agnikulas and the most extensively spread, quoting the bardic saying "the world is the Paramāras'." "But they never equalled in wealth and power the Solankhis of Anahilwad and the Chauhāns of Ajmer." Like the greatness of the Pratihāras whom Tod wrongly considered to be least of the Agnikulas, that of the Paramāras has certainly been less understood by Tod because of the then absence of inscriptions and because they have left very few representatives at the present day. Their power under Bhoja was certainly very extensive and their renown for learning was equally great. The Paramāras are represented at the present day by minor chiefs only, such as the chief of Bijolia under Mewar reputed to be the descendant of the ancient kingly stock of Dhār, the Vihāl branch of Chandrāvati at the foot of Aravali, the Sodha prince of Dhat in the desert and the Sānkhlā chief of Pugal in Marwar. The Umra and Sumra were noted in Mahomedan times but have now become Mahomedans.

When did the Paramāras rise in power and how did they do so? It seems that Tod is wrong when he states that they held Chitore when the Guhilots seized and conquered it in 730 A.D. The Moris are indeed given as the first Śākhā of the Paramāras but they must be treated as different from the Mauryas at Pātaliputra or the Moris of Chitore mentioned in an inscription. The Mauryas are not given by Chand among the 36 royal tribes though they are given as one of them in other lists. We have already shown (Vol. I) that the kings of Sind who were distinctly described as Śudras by Hiuen Tsang were relatives of the king of Chitore who were certainly Mauryas and consequently Śudras. It is not therefore possible to assign to the Paramāras any rise before the ninth century A.D. Unfortunately unlike Pratihāras their earliest inscriptions do not speak of any king before Krishṇa nor do they state how he rose to power and when. The Udepur Praśasti dated about the twelfth century A.D. gives the names of some kings before Krishṇa which are, it seems, fictitious for bards and poets have a fancy to multiply the number of generations by repeating names. The learned note of Bühler in Ind. Ant. Vol. I p. 223 which compares all the Paramāra genealogies found in different inscriptions and then proceeds to give a detailed account of the Paramāras of Dhār and Ujjain cannot be entirely followed though it has been so followed by some modern historians; for it appears that these Paramāras cannot be assigned a rise so early as 800 A.D. a date which this note assigns to Kṛishṇarāja for the following reasons.

It is admitted that the land grants of Vākpatirāja alias Munja and Bhoja (Ind. Ant. VI. p. 488) mention the pedigree as Kṛishṇa, Varisinha, Sīyaka and Vākpati, carried on by the later inscriptions to Sindhurāja and Bhoja. The Udepur Praśasti alone mentions the first king as Upendra and puts Varisinha I, Sīyak I and Vākpati I before Vairisinha. This is as said above a reduplication of names which is suspicious and intended probably to carry back the genealogy to a longer anterior period. Then again the Nagpur Praśasti begins with Vairisinha only and omits all the four kings before him. Thirdly, it is not possible to believe that the Paramāras could have founded an independent kingdom in the days of Nāgabhata II emperor of Kanauj who ruled from about 800-825 A.D. and who is expressly stated to have reduced Mālava to subjection*. Lastly, if we omit these three or four kings *viz.*, Vairisinha I, Sīyaka I and Vākpati I, we shall be making a dynasty which is historically sound and which makes the epithet Kṛishṇapādānudhyāta as applied to Vairi-

* And it seems probable that before Nāgabhata Mālava was in possession of the Rāstrakūtas. The Baroda grant of Karkarāja dated 812 A.D. has the following "he stretched his arm like an iron bar to a door (Argala) for the protection of Mālava attacked by the Gurjara king proud of his conquering Gaud." As in later history Malwa alternately belonged to the emperors of the north and the south.

simha in Vākpati's grants not far-fetched. These grants, terse and official documents as they are, should in our opinion be followed strictly and not the Udepur Praśasti of much later date.

The first king, therefore, of this line appears to be according to our view Kṛishṇarāja who probably distinguished himself first as a subordinate chief and then as an independent king in about 910 A.D., when the Kanauj Pratihāra empire had began to decline and had received shock from the Rāshtrakūta king Govinda III, in the days of Mahīpāla who has been assigned a rule from 908 to 940 A.D. We know that the earliest grant found of Vākpati alias Munja is dated in A.D. 974. If we suppose that he began to rule in 970 his father Sīyaka may be assinged a reign from 950 to 970, his grandfather Vairisinnha from 930 to 950 and his great-grand-father Kṛishṇarāja from 910 A.D. to 930 A.D. These grants apply the titles P.B. Mahārājādhirāja and Parameśvara to all the three kings before Vākpati. Although these are imperial titles they may well be assumed by an independent sovereign and do at least show that Kṛishṇarāja was an independent king. The Paramāras appear first to have reigned in Avanti or Ujjain and then removed their capital to Dhārā which was not founded by them for it already existed and is mentioned in an inscription of the seventh century A.D. (No. 51, plate No. XXXII Corpus Inscriptionorem Vol. III). They made Dhārā their capital probably because they had constantly to fight with their adversaries and neighbours the Solankhis of Anahilavāda. The next imaginary kings Varisinha I, Sīyaka I and Vākpati I have to be omitted according to our view and Bühler himself says that "their descriptions in the Udepur Praśasti are conventional nor is a single historical fact recorded about them in any document." We come, therefore, to the real successor of Kṛishṇarāja Vairisinha who was also called by the people Vajrata. His son was Sīyaka otherwise called Śri Harsha (Sīyaka being an abreviation of Śri Harsha itself and not Sinharāja) and he is mentioned in Navasāhaśāṅka, also in Prabandha Chintāmaṇi. Two things are recorded of him. He conquered the Huṇas (Navasāhaśānka) these being a branch of Kshatriyas or they may be foreigners *viz.*, Arabs, the word Huṇa being extended to them and secondly he like Garuda (snake-eater, this being the emblem of the Paramāras as shown in their grants) seized the wealth of king Khottiga (Nagpur Praśasti). Now Bühler says that this Khottiga is the Rāshtrakūta king of Mānyakheta who made a grant on a solar eclipse day 22, October 971 and who certainly died before September 972 on which day the Kardā plates of his nephew Karkarāja are dated. This shows that Malwa was also at feud with the Rāstrakūtas of Malkhed as with Gujarat and that Sīyaka and Khottiga were contemporaries. The period which may be assigned to Sīyaka's reign is 950-973. For Dhanapāla poet says that he composed his work (Paiyyalachhi) "in 1029 V. E. when Mānyakheta had been plundered by the ruler of Malwa" and Bühler thinks that this must refer to the attack on and defeat of Khottiga by Sīyaka. (V.E. 1029 or 972 A.D. which is the date of the book must also be the date of the plunder of Mānyakheta). This does not also contradict Vākpati's first land grant of 974 A.D.

Sīyaka's son and successor was the famous Vākpati alias Munja. He takes other titles also in his grants viz., Amoghavarsha and Pṛithvīvallabha, perhaps from the Rāshtrakūtas whom he or his father had humbled. There is no doubt about the identity of Vākpati with Munja as the Nāgpur Praśasti mentions this name only. He was a great poet and a great vanquisher. He was also a liberal patron of poets and many noted names in Sanskrit literature belong to authors patronised by him such as Padmagupta, Dhanika, Halāyudha and Dhanapāla. He is as conqueror also well-known. He defeated the Rāshtrakūtas and along with them the Karanātas, Cholas and Keralas (as stated in Uḍepur Praśasti) and also the Haihayas of Chedi, Yuvarāja being their king. These latter were the allies and relatives of the Rāstrakūtas. But Meruttunga's story that he conquered Tailapa sixteen (recently corrected to six) times, each time releasing him and then was defeated and taken prisoner himself by Tailapa is probably a myth of the same type as the story of Pṛithvirāja conquering Shabuddin six times and each time releasing him and himself being finally defeated, taken prisoner and beheaded. Such stories are the natural suggestions of poets' brains and they gain credence within a couple of centuries nay even earlier. But the story of Munja is further embellished by poets who borrowing details from the story of Udayana and Vāsavadattā state that Munja was in his regal confinement attended by the sister of Tailapa (this is on the face of it absurd among Rajputs) who eventually fell in love with him and who was asked to enter into a conspiracy to run away with him. The plot being discovered by her to her brother, Munja was ill-treated and finally beheaded by Tailapa. This legend is too poetical to be true and not being supported by any statement in any contemporary or later epigraphic record may be discarded. One may, however, believe that Munja more than once defeated Tailapa who was leniently treated after each defeat but that he finally was himself defeated by the latter and killed in battle.

He was succeeded by his brother Sindhurāja who was himself after a few years' reign succeeded by his son Bhoja whose greatness had been already foreseen by his uncle Munja. Bhoja was by far the greatest monarch of the Paramāra kings of Malwa; but as his reign falls in the period from 1000 to 1200 A.D. and as he was a contemporary of Mahmud of Ghazni, we have to reserve his reign to our third volume. It is, however, necessary to state here that the story that Munja wished to kill him in his boyhood as it was foretold that the latter would eclipse him is also another unhistorical myth and has to be treated as the creation of a poet's imagination*. The question when Sindhu-

* With regard to this the accession of Bhoja and the death of Munja we may cull the following from Ep. Ind. I. p. 230. It is not true that Vākpati alias Munja appointed Bhoja as his successor, nor that he wanted to kill him. The following sentence from Navasāhasāṅka dispels these ideas. "Vākpati placed the earth in Sindhurāja's hands when he started for Ambika's town." This clearly shows that when Munja started on his last fatal expedition against the Rāstrakūtas he left behind Sindhurāja probably as Yuvarāja and when he died on the field of battle, the latter succeeded to the throne by natural succession. This is further supported by another sentence in Nava-Sāhasāṅka "When His Majesty Vākpati was about to ascend to heaven he put a seal on my lip. Sindhurāja the younger brother of that brother of poets now breaks it." This means that Vākpati had appointed Padmagupta as the court poet and Sindhurāja on accession again conferred that post upon him. N. J. Kirtane thinks that when Vākpati died, Bhoja the intended successor was a minor

rāja died and Bhoja succeeded may be discussed here. Munja is proved to have been alive in 994 A.D. as Amitagati says in the colophon to his work Subhāshita-Ratna-Sandoha that he composed his work in Vikrama Saṁvat 1050 (994 A.D.) during the reign of Munja which may, therefore, be taken to end in 997 A.D. R.B. Gaurīshankar Oza in his recent brochure on the subject assigns 1010 A.D. as the date of the death of Sindhurāja which he thinks took place in a fight with Chāmuḍarāja Solaṅkhi of Patan. This fact he culls from a description of the latter in the Badnagar Praśasti of Kumārapāla dated V. E. 1208 or 1157 A.D. in which the word Sindhurāja was wrongly translated by Bühler as king of Sind. " It is probable, nay almost certain"* Gaurishankar contends, " that this word means Sindhurāja king of Malwa" and we may accept the story of Sindhuraja being killed in a conflict with Chāmuṇḍarāja of Gujarat.† But the date of this fight does not appear in any document and we are not yet certain whether Sindhurāja died in 1010 A.D. The date of the accession of Bhoja is yet uncertain but cannot be much later than 1010 and cannot be 1021 A.D. as stated in Bhoja Prabandha of Subhāśita as we have a grant of his dated 1020

---

about eight years old and therefore must have been placed on the throne at eighteen *i. e.* about ten years after Munja's death in 995 or in about 1004. But as the story of his being named a successor is not credible we may say that Bhoja succeeded in the natural course when Siṅdhurāja was killed in battle in about 1010 A.D. with the king of Anhilwad.

* It may be stated here that the attempt of Indian kings to seize the capital of each other is not strange. An adversary is considered humbled when his capital is seized; see for instance the attempt by the Germans in European history to seize Paris or Rome. We need not, therefore, wonder if Paramāras seized Mānyakheta or Rāshtrakūtas seized and plundered Dhārā or Kanauj.

†This is supported by the following line in a Jain work of Jayasinhadeva Sūri Ind. Ant. XII. p. 197.

राजा चामुण्डराजो ऽथ,—
सिन्धुराजमिवोन्मत्तं सिन्धुराजं मृधेऽवधीत् ॥
तस्माद्वल्लभराजोभूत् यत्प्रतापाभितापितः ।
मुंजोवनीश्वरो धीरो यंत्रेपि न घृतिं दधौ ॥

The second verse creates some difficulty again.

A.D. made in memory of his conquest of Konkan (Ep. Ind. XI p. 81 also Ind. Ant. VI. p. 48). This conquest must have happened a few years at least after he came to the throne and not immediately. We must, however, admit that the dates assigned to each king in this line are yet approximate only.

Mr. Lele in his early history of Dhār in Marathi says that Munja excavated many tanks in Dhār which he first made his capital and one beautiful tank is still called Munjasāgara while there is another tank known after Sindhurāja alias Kuñja known as Kuñjasāgara. There is a Munja tank at Mandogadh also. Munja also built ghats and temples at Ujjain, at Maheś-vara on the Nerbudda and at Omkar and Dharmapuri.

GENEALOGY OF PARAMĀRA KINGS OF DHĀR—

Kṛishṇarāja.
Circ. 914-934 A.D.
|
Vairisinha alias Vajrata.
Cir. 934-954 A.D.
|
Sīyaka or Śri Harsha.
954-973 A.D.
|
Vākpati or Munja.
973—997 A.D.
|
Sindhurāja or Kuṇja.
997 to circ 1010 A.D.
|
Bhoja, famous in the Paramāra line.

CHAPTER VII.

THE CHANDELLAS OF JAJHOTI OR BUNDELKHAND.

Oral tradition recorded by Vincent Smith states that Bundelkhand or Jejākabhukti was occupied by the Ghaharwārs and after them by the Pratihāras before the Chandellas came to it (J. R. A. S. B. 1881 part I). But oral traditions, though there may be some grain of truth behind them, often confound dates. Whether the beautiful lakes abounding in Bundelkhand were constructed by the Gaharwārs before the Chandellas came to Bundelkhand as oral tradition relates is not certain. It is quite possible that people orally assign builders to constructions that preceded them by centuries, but further this oral tradition is contradicted by the historical evidence of Hiuen Tsang who records in about 640 A.D. that there was a Brahmin king in Jajhoti. We have already stated that this Brahmin must have been a governor under Harsha. The Maukhari or Varmā empire after Harsha must also have retained this near province under its direct control while it was strong and we may surmise that an independent or semi-independent power set itself up in Jajhoti only when the Varmā empire was tottering and when Indrāyudha was being replaced by Chakrāyudha on the imperial throne of Kanauj by a foreign power.

Epigraphic records also support this historical inference; for the Benares inscription of Dhanga the most famous king of the Chandella line (Ep. Ind. I. p. 123-125) sets out a pedigree which reaches back to about the same time viz., the beginning of the ninth century *i. e.*, when the first Kanauj empire fell. The first king of this family who founded the kingdom is said in this record to be Nannuka who may be assigned by calculation backwards and who has been assigned by Smith from tradition a reign from 831 to 850 A.D. The exact year 831 A.D. is based by Smith on the years 204 and 225 given by the Mahoba Kanungos to Smith as the dates of the supplanting of the Parihāras by the Chandellas. These are Harsha years and undoubtedly show that the Harsha empire was still hovering over them. These dates are equivalent to 810 and 813 A.D. and while the first date may be taken to represent the coming to prominence of the Chandellas in some battle, the second may be taken to represent the accession of Nannuka to the rulership of Jajhoti. Nannuka's successor was Vijaya from 870 to 890 A.D. In the above inscription two brothers are mentioned Jayaśakti and Vijayaśakti while in another inscription of Harsha of about the same time (Ibid) the name appears as Jejjaka. The name Jejjaka is derived sometimes from the names of these two kings but it is to be noted that the name of Jajoti (derived of course from Jejākabhukti) is mentioned by Hiuen Tsang two hundred years before. The word Bhukti or province certainly indicates that it was then a province directly ruled from the capital whether it be Kanauj or Ayodhyā (under the Guptas) and the name Jejaka must have come to this king of about 870 A.D. by repetition. Vijaya's successor was Rāhila (890-910) and he seems to be the first powerful king of this line. His capital was Mahoba and the large tank near Mahoba named after him Rāhilya Sāgar and the fine granite temple on its bank commemorate his name in the province. His exploits are mentioned even by Chand Bardai poet of Prithvirāja. His daughter Nandā Devi was married to Kokkalla, the contemporary famous king of the neighbouring Chedi kingdom. His son and successor was Harsha who married Kanchukā of a Chāhamāna family and his rule may be assigned to about 910-930 A.D. The race of his queen is given by Smith as the race of Gangā. What Gangā meant is not known but probably it is the name of a Chāhamāna family.

Harsha's son was Yaśovarman who raised the family to its highest eminence by conquering the famous hill fort of Kālan jara which was then in the possession of the Kalachūri kings. The fortress of Kālanjara is noted throughout Indian history. Kālanjara is also noted as a holy place from the days of Mahābhārata. The kings of Chedi called themselves by the epithet Kālanjarapuravaiādhiśvara "lords of the great city of Kālanjara"; but this title was wrested from them by the Chandella king Yaśovarman. This exploit of his is mentioned in this inscription as also the fact that he conquered Gauda, Khasa, Kosala, Kashmir, Mithilā, Mālava, Chedi, Kuru and Gurjara. This list is long and probably exaggerated. But Chedi was the Kalachūri king from whom Kālanjara was conquered and Gurjara must be treated as the Pratihāra emperor of Kanauj. Now it is recorded that Harsha the father of Yaśovarman had assisted Devapāla of Kanauj during his fight with the Rāshtrakūta Indra III of the Deccan. His son Yaśovarman must have defeated the already weakened king of Kanauj subsequently and obtained from him a renowned image of Vaikuṇṭha or Vishṇu. This Chandella king appears to be Vaishhṇava and the Khājurāho inscription records that a famous image of Vishṇu was obtained by Mahīpāla from Shahi king of Kīra who had obtained it from the king of Bhota or Tibet. This fact recorded in this inscription is very important and shows that Jajhoti was already independent. In fact as Smith has observed (E. H. I.) the later kings of Chandella line must be considered as independent, the earlier being subordinate to Kanauj during the days of the emperors Bhoja and Mahendrapāla. The inscription of Dhanga of Samvat 1053 (A.D. 999) describes Harsha as Paramabhattāraka and Parameśvara as also Yaśovarman and we may conclude that Harsha was the first independent king (Ind. Ant. XVII. p. 202). Secondly the Khājurāho inscription describes Devapāla as Hayapati the lord of horses. It has already been pointed out that the Kanauj kings coming as they did from Marwar were strong in cavalry and it may be noted that Hayapati, Gajapati, Narapati and Bhūpati began to assume special signification as titles of kings from this period.

Yaśovarman may be assigned a rule from 925-950 A.D. His successor was Dhanga, the greatest king of the Chandella line as usual being the third from Harsha. The Khajurāho inscription (Ep. Ind. I. p. 123-35) gives the limits of his kingdom (which is rather unusual in inscriptions). He ruled from the Jumna on the north to Bhāsvat on the Malwa river on the south and from Kālanjara fort on the east to Gopādri (Gwalior fort) on the west. The Malwa river mentioned must be taken to be Betwa (and not Dasān which is a river of Daśārṇa) and Bhāsvat has properly been identified with Bhaillasvamin or Bhilsa of modern days.

Dhanga has left many inscriptions and three have been known dated 954, (the Khajurāho inscription already noted) 998 and 1002 A.D. In the second inscription he is described as equal of Hammīra. This certainly refers to his fight with Sabaktegin along with other princes of India fought beyond the Indus somewhere near the Krammu in about 989 or 990 A.D. Ferishta also says that Jayapāla of Lahore was assisted by Kālanjara with men and money in his war against Sabaktegin. This inscription records that Dhanga was the equal of Hammīra while Mahomedan historians record that the Hindus were defeated in this battle. Probably it was a drawn battle but the details of this fight and the further history of the Chandella line which continued upto 1200 A.D. in glory we have to leave to our third volume.

Dhanga had a long reign and a long life also and he is believed to have ended his life by drowning himself at the confluence of the Ganges and the Jumna which is religiously considered to be a meritorious act of self-destruction. Rājendralāl however thinks that he died a natural death, the expression used in inscription No. 3 dated 1002 being merely figurative.* Dhanga

* So far as we think the expression is not figurative. The verse is as follows (Ep. Ind. I. p. 146).

रक्षित्वा क्षितिमम्बुराशिरशनामेतामनन्यायतिं ।
जीवित्वा शरदां शतं समधिकं श्रीधंगपृथ्वीपतिः ॥
रुद्रं मुद्रितलोचनं स्वहृदये ध्यायञ्जपन् जान्हवी ।
कालिंद्याः सलिले [illegible] निर्वृतिम् ॥

made a grant in Benares (noted above Ind. Ant. XVI) which need not signify that he ruled as far as Benares; but that he was the most powerful of his line was certain. He was a devotee of Śiva his father being a devotee of Vishṇu. His inscription (Ep. Ind. XII. p. 210) begins with the words 'Om Namah Sivāya.' As stated already kings in those days were devotees of Śiva, Vishṇu, Sūrya or Devī without any bigoted feelings in favour of their own deity, intolerance coming on at a later stage only.

Coins have been found belonging to the Chandellas which resemble the coins of the Chedi kings, Durgā of the latter being substituted by Hanūman in those of the former. But, strangely enough,no coins of early kings even down to Dhanga have been found (see Ind. Ant. XXXVII wherein Smith has given the corrected information about the history of the Chandellas and their coins from the data available to 1908). Smith thinks that in the time of these kings people used Indo-Sassanian coins. It may, however, be surmised that people still used the coin of the Kanuaj empire viz., the Ādivarāha coin of Bhoja and other coins. It is only Gāngeyadeva of Chedi of the eleventh century who first struck special Chedi coins and probably the Chandellas imitating him struck coins of gold, silver and copper of their own substituting Durgā with Hanumān. Which king of the Chandellas was the devotee of Hanumān does not appear but this subject belongs to the period of history to be treated in our third volume. Here it may only be noted that the expression at the end of the Khajurāho inscription of Samvat V. E. 1011 (Ep. Ind. I, p. 123-35) "in the reign of Vināyakapāla" which Kielhorn is unable to explain may indicate that though Yaśovarman was independent he still acknowledged the nominal suzerainty of the emperor Vināyakapāla or Mahipāla who was then dead and his coins must have been current in the several states of India even though they were then independent as the Mogul coins were in the country of the Marathas.

Genealogy of the Chandellas with probable dates of accession as given by Smith in Ind. Ant. XXXVII p. 127.

I. Nannuka ac. 831 A.D.
|
II. Vākpati ac. 845 A.D.
|
III. Jayaśakti ac. 860. A.D.
|
IV. Vijayaśakti ac. 880. A.D.
|
V. Rāhila ac. 900 A.D.
|
VI. Harsha ac. 915 A.D.
|
VII. Yaśovarman ac. 930 A.D.
|
VIII. Dhanga ac. 950 A.D.
|
IX. Ganda ac. 1000 A.D.

The line continued to about 1287 A. D. in which year the last king Bhojavarman is said to have ascended the throne. This part of the line will be dealt with in our third volume.

NOTE.

SMITH'S WRONG VIEW ABOUT THE ORIGIN OF THE CHANDELLAS.

Sir Vincent Smith is nearly certain that the Chandellas are by origin Bhars or Gonds. In his Early History of India (2nd Edn.) he observes "The inference is fully justified that the Chandellas are originally Hinduised Bhars or Gonds," (p. 379). This inference has doubtless been suggested by the strange bias which has obsessed the views of almost all European scholars and induced them to believe that the Rajputs were foreigners and if not foreigners aborigines. Let us see what are the justifications for this inference. They are not given here by Smith but they appear from what he has written in his paper on the Chandels in Indian Antiquiry Vol. XXVII (p. 137). There he observes "I still hold the opinion (1908) that the Chandels sprang from an aboriginal stock, whether this stock was called Bhar or Gond, we cannot say." The first argument advanced is the 'silly legend' among the Chandels that they are born from the union of the moon with a Brahmin maiden. "The only significance of the myth is its implied admission that the pedigree of the clan required explanation which was best attained by including it in the moon-descended Rajputs and adding respectability by inventing a Brahmin ancestress. As a matter of fact the Chandels are regarded as a clan of impure descent." Secondly, Smith says that the indications are fairly distinct that the Chandel clan originated in the midst of the Gonds. The Chandel Zamindar of Mahoba claims to be autochthonous and traces his origin to Maniyagarh, the ancient ruined fortress on the Ken river. This tradition is confirmed by the fact that Maniya Dev (Devi) whose shrine exists at Maniyagarh was the tutelary deity of the Chandelas. When they occupied Mahoba in the beginning of the 9th century, they brought with them the worship of the goddess who appears to be akin to the Gond deities. The poet Chand associates Maniyagarh with a Gond chieftain so late as the 16th century." Thirdly, Smith states that the Chandel princess Durgāvati married the Gond chief of Mandala "The Gaharwars and the Haihayas of Chedi" finally adds Smith "came to the front in the same way as successful adventurers among some one or other of the aboriginal races who after attaining power claimed rank as Kshatriya, Rajput or Thakor as Gond chiefs do to this day." How flimsy all these arguments are will be apparent to every Hindu reader and they scarcely deserve any refutation; yet for the sake of European readers we proceed to make some observations on them.

The first argument is based on the "silly legend" about the origin of the Chandels current among them. Now it may be stated without fear of contradiction that such silly legends have been current in every age and country about heroes and heroic clans and that they lead to no inference whatever about their real origin. When the Greeks believed that Achilles was born of Apollo from Theatis, is it to be understood that this is a true story about his origin? Nay more, is it to be argued that this story was concocted in order to conceal the really base origin of Achilles? We have already said that such stories have been invented in India by poets and bards from Vedic times and that they have simply to be set aside as fancies, leading to no inference either as to the baseness or nobility of the hero's birth. Indeed when the Chandella bards invented this story about their patrons, in the usual fashion of what Kielhorn calls name-myths *i. e.*, myths suggested by names, they scarcely dreamt that the very story would be utilised by scholars for the purpose of debasing the ancestry of their favourite clan, instead of raising it in estimation. The name Chandella suggested that the originator of the family was the Moon himself and the mother assigned was the best that could be. But as we have said, these stories are simply to be ignored and we have only to infer that the Chandel clan was by public estimation assigned to the lunar race. What we have really to ascertain is whether the clan was at any time treated as non-Kshatriya. If so this claim of the Chandellas to Rajput descent would be invalid.

The really effective argument advanced by Smith, therefore, is that contained in the last sentence of Smith *viz.*, "as a matter of fact the Chandels are regarded as a clan of impure descent." Our reply to this is an emphatic denial and that this is not a fact. We have first the evidence of Chand himself (whom Smith subsequently quotes). Among the 36 Royal families enumerated by Chand the Chandels are among the very first. The name Chhand therein in the first verse stands for Chandella according to our view. And even if this were not so, we find that the Chandel is given by Tod in the Kumārapāla Sanskrit Mss. list incorporated by him in his table of lists giving the number of the traditional 36 Rajput families. The Chandels were then treated as good Rajputs in as far old times as the days of Kumārapālacharita. Then again in the long account given by Chand about the attack on Mahoba by Pṛithvirāja we do not find any statement which would lead us to believe that the Chandels were treated as of impure origin. Thirdly, epigraphic evidence shows that the Chandels married into good Rajput families, especially into the Haihaya family which has always been considered as of good Rajput blood, in spite of the doubt which Smith throws over its purity. Lastly, even at present the Mahārāja of Gidhaur who is the chief remaining representative of the family is considered to be a good Rajput and as he observes in a letter of his to us not only marriages into good Rajput families such as Chauhāns etc., but marriages from such families into the Chandel family take place constantly. It is, therefore, *not a fact* that the Chandels are or were regarded as of impure origin.

The third argument of Smith is equally unsound and illogical as the first though it is not based on incorrect information. For how does it follow that the Chandels are Gonds themselves, because the clan originated in the midst of the Gonds? We know from history that hundreds of Rajput families established small kingdoms among Gonds, Bhars, Bhils and other oboriginal tribes. In fact the instinct of the Rajput leads him to go into such wild regions inhabited by aborigines and carve out a small kingdom for himself if he has no room in the Aryan country. The Guhilots for instance lived among Bhils and founded a kingdom, but does that make the Guhilots Bhils? Even the British have established a vast kingdom among Hindus and Mahomedans, does that make them Hindus or Mahomedans? It is strange that historians cannot see how adventurous Kshatriyas went fron Aryan lands into Himalayan valleys, into the sands of Rajastan and the hilly regions of Mewad and Jaipur and established kingdoms for themselves. It does not, therefore, follow from the Chandels coming to sovereignty among Gonds that they are Gonds themselves. The Chandel Zamindar of Mahoba's belief that they are autochthonous need not be wondered at. When we know from history that the Chandels are there in Mahoba for nearly one thousand years it is not to be wondered at that the Zamindar believes that they have been there from the beginning of time. In fact the Chandels have been in Gond land at Manyagarh even from before their coming to Mahoba. When they came there we do not know; perhaps they came there during Kushan or Hun invasions of the Aryan land viz., the Panjab and the Gangetic valley. But as a matter of fact many well-read scholars still believe that the Indian Aryans are not foreigners and the Aryan ancient home was in India itself and not outside of India, neither in the Arctic region nor in the Volga region; why need we attach any importance to the view of the Chandel Zamindar that they are autochthonous to Bundelkhand and hence argue that the Chandels are Gonds?

The argument based on the Chandel deity Maniya Devi is equally absurd. It is well known that every Rajput family has its separate tutelary goddess and if we believe that the Chandel Rajputs when they first entered the Gond land established a kingdom about Maniyagarh, their first fortress, we may not be surprised that their tulelary deity is called Maniya Devi. The statement that the deity is akin to the Gond deities is vague and even if taken to mean that the Devi was adopted from the Gonds it does not prove that the Chandels are themselves Gonds. For as we have said elsewhere, the worships of Śivā and Durgā have apparently been borrowed by the Aryans from the aborigines and have been identified by them with certain Vedic deities' worship. It is, therefore, not strange if there is any thing common between the Chandel worship of Maniya Devi and the worship of Gond deities. Lastly the fact that in the sixteenth century Maniyagarh was associated with a Gond chief by Chand shows nothing as to the origin of the Chandellas. When these came to Mahoba and established from there a vast kingdom so early as the ninth century A.D., after their fall about 1200 A.D. that there was a Gond chief in Maniyagarh leads to no inference whatever.

It is strange that the story of Rāṇi Durgāvatī should have been distorted by Smith into proving what is exactly the opposite of what it shows. We quote below the account given in the Akbarnāmā of Abul Fazal (Beeveridge Vol. II p. 324) on which the inference of Smith is based apparently. "She (Durgāvatī) was the daughter of Raja Sālbāhan of Rath and Mahoba who was a Chandel by caste. The Raja gave her in marriage to Dalpat the son of Aman Das. Though he was not of a good family yet as he was wealthy and the Raja Sālbāhan was in bad circumstances the latter was compelled to make alliance." Further on it is stated " From old times the house of the ruler of Gadha was of high rank. Yet it had nothing beyond reverence. This Kharji took things under the denomination of peshkash " Lastly on page 326 we are told that Dalpat was in reality the son of Govind Das Kachhavāha and he was adopted by Sangram and named Dalpat and " Rani Durgāvatī was given in marriage to him." Now it is clear from the above that even Abul Fazal grants that the Chandels were pure Rajputs and that Durgāvatī was given to a Thakor of lower rank from compulsion. Best Rajput girls, we know from history, were often given in marriage to even Mahomedan kings. Does that make the Rajputs Mahomedans ? The Rajput instinct, as stated above, leads him to give his daughter to a king even though he may be a Mahomedan. But pride of caste prevents him from marrying from any but the best Rajput family. But the greatest wonder is that even Dalpat or his ancestors are not stated in this account to be Gonds; whence Smith treats them so is a puzzle. The family appears to be Rajput though it was of impure descent but rich and powerful and ruled in Gadha and the surrounding country. Finally it may be stated that Rāṇi Durgāvatī proved her true Rajput blood by fighting with the Moguls most stubbornly and when unfortunately defeated and wounded on the battlefield by stabbing herself to death with true Rajput courage and contempt of death in face of fear of dishonour. Is it not strange that the story of Rāṇi Durgāvatī which in fact proves the greatness and purity of the Chandella family should be destorted by Smith to prove the exact contrary ?

CHAPTER VIII.

THE KALACHURIS OF CHEDI.

The Haihayas are an ancient clan of Kshatriyas descended from Sahasrārjuna who is credited in the Purāṇas with having defeated the demon Rāvaṇa. They occupied the Nerbudda valley in very ancient times and are said to have fought with Sagara the solar race king of Oudh. They then obtained possession of South Kosala (Chattisgadh) and retained it down to the most recent times *viz.*, the days of the Marathas of Nagpore. In Volume I Chap. XV we have already given the history of these Haihayas of the Central Provinces and anticipated the history of the Kalachūris of Chedi who were undoubtedly a branch of these Haihayas of the Central Provinces. When the Kalachūris came to power and established their separate kingdom at Tripura (modern Jubbalpore) cannot be stated. Indeed the Kalachūris throughout their history down to the 14th century use an era of their own called the Chedi era and its commencement has been fixed by Kielhorn at 248 A.D. And this era is found to have been in use in even Western India *viz.*, Gujarat and Konkan and it is therefore probable that the Kalachūries enjoyed an extensive rule in centuries preceding even the Chālukyas of the Deccan. In fact it may be asserted that they succeeded to a great portion of the Āndhra empire of the the Śātavāhanas. They were certainly in possession of the almost impregnable stronghold of Kālanjara from a long time and had extended their sway up to the Jumna whence the name Chedi given to them.

Whatever this may be, it seems certain that the Kalachūris as a power came to notice in the mediæval period of Hindu India at about the middle of the ninth century. How they obtained the name Kalachūri need not detain us; for names of families and clans arise in a thousand unknown ways and as we have already observed, it as futile to inquire what Kalachūri means as to inquire what Haihaya means or Chālukya or Chāhamāna or Pratihāra and a score of other names mean (though poets and bards are fond of inventing legends to explain names which are fitly called etymological legends and which even though they may be found in the Ṛigveda are unfit to be seriously taken into consideration). It is undoubted that a king named Kokkalla belonging to the Kalachūri clan came to prominence at about 850 A.D. as may be gathered from the two earliest inscriptions of the Kalachūris edited by Kielhorn in Ep. Ind. Vol. I p. 255 and II p. 305 and called the Bilhauri stone inscription and the Benares copper plate inscription. The history of the Kalachuri line is given by Kielhorn from these records in Ep. Ind. Vol. II and we may still further summarise it as follows giving a few additional remarks of our own.

Kokkalladeva, the founder of the greatness of this family, is extolled in these inscriptions as having conquered the whole world and to have set up the two victory pillers in the North and the South *viz.,* Bhoja and Kṛishṇarāja. Now Bhoja is of course Mihira Bhoja of Kanauj whose dates are known as 862-76-82 A.D. while Kṛishṇarāja refers to the Rāshtrakūta Kṛishṇa II whose dates are known as 875-911 A.D. It is also stated that Kokkalla gave promise of security to Harsha of Chitrakūta a fact which we have already noticed. In another inscription Kokkalla is said to be Tri-Kaliṅgādhipati, the lord of Tri Kaliṅga. It is, however, difficult to believe that Kokkalla could have actually conquered all these powerful kings especially Bhoja and Kṛishṇa who were in fact the emperors of North and South India. It seems to be likely that the power of Kokkalla I, was recognised more owing to alliances than to actual conquests. We know that Kṛishṇa of the Rāshtrakūtas had married a daughter of Kokkalla and that he himself had Nattā sister of Chandella Harsha as his queen. It may be surmised that Bhoja of Kanauj was also connected with Kokkalla by marriage having probably married a daughter of his. The Haihayas were undoubtedly the best Kshatriyas and we know throughout mediæval history alliance with Haihayas was sought by all the Kshatriya families. The Deccan Chālukyas of the seventh and eighth centuries and later married Haihaya daughters and Pṛithvīrāja too of the twelfth century was connected with the Haihayas by marriage. It must, however, be admitted that Kokkalla was indeed a powerful king as he is mentioned in these records as the founder of the family. But the eulogy that he raised two victory pillers in the persons of Bhoja and Kṛishṇa in the north and south can be sustained, historically speaking, not on the basis of conquest but of alliance.

Kokkalla's son and successor was Mugdhatunga or Prasiddhadhavala (or simply Dhavala) who had two sons Bāla Harsha and Keyūravarsha. The former seems to have succeeded but had probably a short reign. The latter became king after him and had a queen named Nohalādevi born of a Chālukya Sāmanta or feudatory chief. The Bilhauri inscription gives the story of the first Chalūkya king springing from the handful of Drona of the Bhāradvāja gotra the importance of which legend we have already noticed. Nohalādevi had a temple built to Śiva called thence Nohaleśvara and the inscription records grant of villages to the temple and its worshipper. There appears to have been a reincarnation of Buddhist monks and monastaries, a continuation in Śaivaite monks and Mathas who professed the Śaivāgama of Lakulīśa and almost all Rajput kings who now came to prominence appear to be Śaivite and followers of the Āgama, a fact on which we will comment later on when taking a general religious survey of the country.

Keyūravarsha was also called Yuvarāja and he seems to have been defeated by a Chandella king as mentioned in a Chandella record. His son was Lakshmaṇa whose queen was Rāhadā. Their daughter Bonthādevī was the mother of the western Chālukya Tailapa of the second or later family whose certain date is 973 A.D. Lakshmaṇa was followed by Śaṅkaragaṇa and after him by his second son Yuvarāja II who was a contemporary of Munja (974, 979, 993 A.D). Yuvarāja's son and successor was Kokkalla-deva II whose son was the famous Gāngeyadeva of this family. His certain date from inscription is 1037 A.D. and his history naturally belongs to the third period of our history and will be dealt with in our third volume.

The Kalachūris, therefore, cannot be regarded as a new branch of Kshatriyas which came to the fore in the mediæval age ; but an *old* existing kingly line which attained prominence about 850 A.D. by alliance. Their greatest king Gāngeya and his successors belong to the period from 1000 to 1200 and they probably took advantage of the fall of the Kanauj empire caused by the shock of Mahmud's invasion. The line was always devoted to Śiva and it was also a pure well-known Kshatriya family. The dates are not quite certain but the genealogy of the family upto Gāngeyadeva may be given somewhat as follows :

I. Kokkalladeva 850 A.D. circ.
|
II. Mugdhatunga alias Prasiddhadhavala 900 A.D.
|
III. Bāla Harsha — IV. Keyūravarsha Yuvarāja m. Nohalādevī 925 A. D.
|
V. Lakshmaṇadeva 950 A.D.
|
VI. Śankaragana 970 A.D. — VII. Yuvarājadeva II. contemporary of Munja cir. 980 A.D.
|
VIII. Kokkalladeva 1000 A.D.
|
IX. Gāngeyadeva 1020 A. D.

CHAPTER IX.

THE PĀLAS OF BENGAL.

In the preceding chapters we have sketched the history of all the Rajput kingdoms which came to the fore in the second sub-period of the history of mediæval Hindu India *i. e.,* from about 800 to 1000 A.D. in what may be and is called the middle land comprising the modern U. P., Rajputana and Central India. These Rajput families were all orthodox Hindus, mostly devotees of Ṣiva and they first came to prominence owing to their offering successful resistance to Arab invasions from Sind. In the outlying provinces, similar Rajput kingdoms arose about the same time but not by the same causes. They arose in the usual way *viz.,* by the decadence of kingly families and the most important of these were the Pālas of Bengal and the Rāshtrakūtas of the Deccan.

It is interesting to note that India usually falls into the same divisions as those at present, owing to peculiarities of climate, soil, language and even the characteristics of the people. The present U. P. and Oudh formed then the empire of Kanauj. Oudh being directly held under it besides the Gangetic valley. Rajputana and Central India branch off into several kingdoms in the same way as now and is still distinct from U. P. Similarly, Bengal and the Deccan naturally constitute distinct kingdoms and so also the Madras Presidency usually tends to come under one rule either that of Chola or Pāndya. We need not, therefore, wonder that Bengal came to be one kingdom under the rule of the Pālas at about this period.

The rise of the Pālas is given in their documents in a manner which is. indeed, unique in Mediæval Hindu history, though it was a manner not uncommon in ancient times in India. We have seen in Volume I that after the fall of Harsha's empire

Bengal was divided into several small kingdoms which constantly quarrelled among themselves. During the empire of the Varmās and probably under Yaśovarman of Kanauj, Bengal nominally came under the suzerainty of Kanauj, the Gauda king being killed in fight with Yaśovarman. During the latter half of the eighth century, the central power of Kanauj becoming weak, the province became a prey to anarchy, called in the Khālimpur grant of Dharmapāla as a state of fishes eating one another. The people, consequently, by consent of all, elected Gopāla as the king of Bengal and he soon established a central government first at Pāṭaliputra and then at Monghyr or Mudgagiri which practically extended over the whole of Bengal including Magadha, Magadha and Bihar being often leagued with Bengal as they were a few years ago or separated from it as at present.

Gopāla was a Buddhist, Buddhism being still prevalent in Magadha and Gauda. There was, indeed, a reassertion of Hinduism against Buddhism in the time of Śaśānka of Karṇasuvarṇa or under Mādhavagupta of Magadha. But this part of the country was the birth-place and stronghold of Buddhism which naturally lasted here longer than in the rest of the country. Gopāla was, however, a Kshatriya being born of the Śuryavanśa as stated in Pāla records. The Varṇāśramadharma which Buddhism had flung away in the beginning was strong again and even the records of these Buddhist kings show that they were keen observers of it and kept Varṇa pure. They also respected Brahmins and made gifts to them. The rule of the Buddhist Gopāla was not, therefore, troublesome and his ministers and many of his subjects who were Hindus were not much offended. Gopāla is supposed by some to have belonged to the Pratihāra Pāla dynasty of Kanauj but it seems that there is no reason to suspect this. The name ending Pāla is taken by many Kshatriya families; in fact it is a suffix generally recommended for Kshatriyas who are required to take a suffix meaning protector and we consequently find Pāla and Gopa and Trātā as usual suffixes of Kshatriya names. Moreover, the rise of the Pāla dynasty did not follow the rise of the Pratihāra dynasty but was almost synchronous with it as will be presently seen.

Keilhorn has given the dynasty of the Pālas as follows in his paper on the Āmagācchi plates of Vigraharāja III putting together the inscriptions found till then. He has not assigned dates as unfortunately these inscriptions do not use any known era but give regnal years of kings. This is a great difficulty in fixing exact dates ; though this shows almost to a certainty that these were not open to influences which brought in the Vikrama era to the forefront in the rest of the country. We may, however, assign probable dates from contemporary events mentioned in these records of the Pāla dynasty.

The father and grandfather of Gopāla (Dayitavishṇu and Vāpyaṭa) may be omitted as we know that Gopāla was the first to obtain sovereignty by the choice of the people. He was the first king and appears to have fought with Vaṭsarāja of the west, Indrāyudha of the Varmā dynasty of Kanauj and the Rāshtrakūṭa king Govinda III as already mentioned. This gives for him a date about 780 to 800 A.D.

His son and successor was Dharmapāla who is said to have married a Rāshtrakūṭa lady. He conquered Indrarāja of Kanauj and replaced him by Chakrāyudha with the consent of many feudatory princes as stated in the oft-quoted two ślokas of the Khālimpur and Bhāgalpur grants. He thus may be placed from 800 A.D. to 825 A.D. It is well known that Nāgabhata, son of Vaṭsarāja defeated Chakrāyudha and thereafter deposing him became the king of Kanauj himself. He had, of course, to defeat this Dharmapāla before he could seize the empire. He was himself, however, defeated by Govinda III Rāshtrakūṭa but as already stated the defeat was not so serious as to oust him from Kanauj. This Govinda III appears to have been the father-in-law of Dharmapāla ; for the Bhāgalpur inscription (Ind. Ant. XXI p. 250) mentions that his wife was Rānnadevi, daughter of Parabala of the Rāshtrakūṭas and Parabala has been well identified by Keilhorn with Govinda III. It seems, therefore, consistent that Govinda III should have gone to his help against his enemy Nāgabhata who had defeated Dharmapāla and should have rested content with his defeat of Nāgabhata as it prevented the latter from encroaching further upon Bengal.

Dharmapāla was succeeded by Devapāla, his nephew and he may be assigned a reign from 825 to 850 A.D. He again was succeeded by his nephew Vigrahapāla I. It seems that both Dharmapāla and Devapāla were without sons and adopted their nephews as sons. This explains why Devapāla is in one grant called nephew of Dharmapāla and in another his mother is said to be Rānnadevi. Vigrahapāla married Lajjā, a Haihaya princess (see Bhāgalpur grant). He may be assigned a reign from 850 to 875 A.D. His son was Nārāyaṇapāladeva who made this oft-mentioned Bhāgalpur grant. The year is not certain as the date is mentioned in regnal years. Nārāyaṇapāla was succeeded by Rājyapāla who married Bhāgyadevī, daughter of Rāshtrakūṭa Tunga who is identified as Jaggattunga. He may be said to have reigned till 925 A.D. and was followed by his son Gopāla II (925-950) who was followed by Vigrahapāla II (950-976) and he was followed by his son Mahīpāla who issued the Sāranath grant which for the first time gives us a distinct date viz., 1083 V.E. or 1026 A.D. By assigning 25 years to each reign we come to Mahipāla's rule ending in 1000 A.D. and even if this inscription be supposed to belong to the last year of Mahīlpāla's reign we have a difference of about 26 years which, distributed over 9 reigns, gives a difference of about 3 years for each reign. This is really negligible and we may suppose some one of the kings to have had a long rule and probably Mahīpāla himself. This inscription mentions that Mahīpāla was driven from his position by enemies, but that he recovered his patrimony by his efforts. Who these enemies were and how the kingdom was regained are matters of great curiosity. Perhaps the shocks of Mahmud's invasions which India received at this time were responsible for this mishap for the effect of these shocks might have reached even distant Bengal. But this belongs to the third volume of our history and we close our notice of this Pāla dynasty here though it did not continue for long hereafter and it was succeeded by the power of the Senas in the eleventh century A. D. (Mahīpāla was succeeded by Nārāyaṇapāla and he was succeeded by Vigrahapāla III who made the Āmagāchhi grant on which Keilhorn has recorded his valuable note.)

The grants of these Pālas show that they were truly Kshatriyas though they were Buddhists, probably only in the beginning or in name. They had marriage relations with the Rāshtrakūṭas and the Haihayas of Chedi. They made grants to Śiva temples and ascetics of the Śivāgama sect (most probably Lakulīśa which was predominant at this time all over India). For Nārāyaṇapāla who made the Bhāgalpur grant does not call himself Ṣaugata, though he calls his father so and he expressly states that he had constructed a thousand temples to Śiva (svayam-kārita-sahasrāyatanasya). Then again these grants show that a distinct further advance had been made in the art of government and administration as will be noticed in detail in our chapter on administration in this volume. But one thing seems rather retrograde and tending towards the final ruin of the land viz., that the army seems to consist not of local levies but of merceneries from foreign races which are nearly the same as are now used by the British Government. The details of this will be found in our chapter on army in this volume.

The extent of Pāla rule appears to have comprised the whole of modern Bengal, Bihar and Assam and probably part of Orissa. The Bhāgalpur grant states that the Pālas had conquered Utkala and Prāgjyotisha or Assam. Magadha and Bihar were included in the very beginning as the Khālimpur grant is issued from Pāṭaliputra. Eastern Bengal, too, was included in their dominion; for we no longer read of two kings or kingly umbrellas in Bengal, a fact mentioned only in connection with Gopāla's rule.

The Pāla and Sena dynasties are both of them historical and have left contemporary records. Who was " Ādisura " and who the other kings whom tradition relates is a difficult problem to solve ; but records as yet have not proved their existence beyond the shadow of doubt and we, therefore, refrain from expressing any opinion on the subject.

THE GENEALOGY OF THE PĀLA KINGS OF BENGAL.

(The dates are all tentative).

Gopāla elected king of Bengal.
780–800 A.D.
|
Dharmapāla
800–825.
|
Devapāla———brother
(adopted nephew). |
825–850. |

Vigrahapāla I.
850–875.
|
Nārāyaṇapāla
875–900.
|
Rājyapāla
900–925.
|
Gopāla II.
925–950.
|
Vigrahapāla II.
950–976.
|
Mahīpāla
made a grant in V. E. 1083 or 1026 A.D.

CHAPTER X.

THE RĀSHTRAKUTAS OF THE DECCAN,

The Rāshtrakūṭas are represented as belonging to the race of Yadu. According to Wardha plates they belonged to the Sātyaki branch of the lunar race and were descendants of a princess named Rattā. Rattā is said to have had a son Rāshtrakūṭa after whom the family was named. But this is certainly a later theory and we already know that Rāshtrakūṭa, like modern Deshpande, is an official name. The first three princes of the Rāshtrakūṭa family given in grants hitherto discovered are Govinda I, Karka I, and Indra II (Dr. Bhandarkar mentions two earlier ones viz., Dantivarman and Indrarāja). Govinda, Karka and Indra II are noticed in only a few grants of the Rāshtrakūṭas and are described in general terms. The poets praise their bravery, their justice and their piety but nothing is said about them in particular.

Indra Rāja is said to have married a princess who was descended on her father's side from Śalikya (Chālukya) race and who was born in the Soma Anvaya (Samangada plates). With the state of relations during the succeeding reigns, matrimonial alliances between these two families were hardly possible. The Samangada plate which is the earliest grant of the Rāshtrakūṭas found upto this time gives us a clue to fix the dates of these kings (B. B. R. A. II p. 371). The grant is dated 675 Śaka *i. e.*, 753 A.D. and is given by Dantidurga the fourth king of the Rāshtrakūṭa family who first established his independence of the Chālukyas. Counting backward, therefore, and allowing 25 years for each generation the year 660 A.D. may be roughly assigned to Govinda I, 685 A.D. to Karka and 710 A.D. to Indra Rāja.

The fourth king Dantidurga the son of Indrarāja and his Chālukya queen was one of the greatest kings of the family. He is said to have acquired for his family the supreme sovereignty of Mahārāshtra the limits of which were the Narmadā on the north and the Tungabhadrā on the south. It is expressly stated in the Alās plate of Yuvarāja Govinda II (Ep. In. VI page 210) that he first conquered and conquered easily the Chālukya power, great as it was by its conquest of Kānchī, Kerala, Chola, Pāndya, Sriharsha and Vajrata (who the last is must be discovered).

The Sāmangad plate also attributes to Dantidurga this great exploit. He is said to have subdued without effort the Chālukya king Vallabha and to have obtained the title Rājādhirāja Parameśvara and he is said to have defeated with a few of his followers the whole army of Karnātaka which had been renowned for humiliation of Shriharsha (of course, the famous Kanauj Buddhist king). The king Vallabha above named must be the last Chālukya king Kīrtivarman II.

Dantidurga probably died a violent death at the hands of his paternal uncle and successor Krishnarāja. This is not borne out by many of the grants which make no reference to the event at all but the Baroda grant states that "Krishnarāja destroyed a relative who followed an evil course and assumed the sovereignty for the good of the race." If we take into consideration how anxious the court poets might be to avoid all references to internal dissentions in the families of their patrons we may accept this account as true even though mentioned in only one grant.

Krishnarāja carried on the work of Dantidurga and completely subjugated the Chālukyas. In the Rādhanpur plate he is said to have in short and swiftly torn the fortune of the Chālukya race. He it was who built the famous temple of Kailāsa at Elāpura (Verul or Ellorā). In the Wardha plates he is described as one "who protected the earth by the temples of Īśvara constructed by him by which the earth shines as by many Kailāsa mountains. The Baroda plates state a good deal alone about the beauty of this temple of Kailāsa: "When gods saw the temple," say the Baroda plates, "they were struck with wonder and said 'this temple of Śiva is self-existent, for such beauty is not to be found in a work of art'."

Krishnarāja was succeeded by his son Govinda II. Nothing particular is said about this king except the usual praise and the

Vani-Dindori, the Rādhanpur and the Baroda plates drop his name altogether. This shows that he was a negligible king. The Wardha plates state that "sensual" pleasures made him careless of the kingdom and entrusting fully the universal sovereignty to his younger brother Nirupama, he allowed his position as a sovereign to become loose. The Vani-Dindori and the Rādhanpur plates, however, seem to imply that he was dethroned by his younger brother Nirupama.

Dhruva, also known by the names, Nirupama and Dhora, was an able and warlike king. He conquered and imprisoned a prince named Ganga and also drove Vatsarāja the king of the west who was proud of having conquered Gauda to Maru land; and took from him the two umbrellas he had taken from Gauda (Rādhanpur grant Ep. Ind. VI p. 243). He also conquered a Pallava king in the south. It seems that this king Dhruva is referred to as reigning in the south, by the Jain Harivaṃśa written in 783 A.D.

The next king, Dhruva Nirupama's son, was Govind III. He is also called Jagattunga. The Vani-Dindori and Rādhanpur plates were issued by him in Śaka 730 *i. e.* in 808 A.D. Govind III was undoubtedly the greatest king of the Rāshtrakūta line. The Kāvi grant states that he was raised by his father to the supreme sovereignty for his great qualities which his brothers and enemies resented and a confederacy of 12 princes raised a rebellion against him. In such a condition Govind III seems to have acquitted himself bravely. He fought the confederacy and subdued it completely. After this he released king Ganga whom his father had imprisoned "from the prolonged pain of fetters" but Ganga remaining determined in his enmity Govinda subdued him again and again put him into confinement. He then undertook an expedition against the Gurjar king who fled when he heard of Govinda's approach and he probably took Kanauj. Next Govinda received submission of the king of Mālava, "who by this time had learnt to form a just estimate of his own powers." This was probably not a king of the famous Paramāra line. Then on his reaching the slopes of Vindhya hills, a king called Mārāśarva hastened to offer him presents. Then having passed the rainy season at Shrībhavana (Malkhed) he advanced with his army to the banks of the Tungabhadrā and again subdued the Pallavas whom his father had conquered already. Finally, he ordered the lord of Vengi into his presence and made him assist in building or fortifying a city. Govinda III's *biruda* ending in varsha was Prabhutavarsha "raining profusely". He has given the two grants mentioned above from Mayūrakhandi. This place has been identified with a hill-fort in Nasik territory of the name of Morakhand.

Govinda III was succeeded by his son known by the name of Amoghavarsha. This probably was one of his *birudas* but what his proper name was is not ascertained. In his grants he is also referred to as Atiśayadhavala and Lakshmīvallabha.

The date of the beginning of the reign of Amoghavarsha can be ascertained from the Nilagunda inscription (Ep. Ind. VI. p. 100). The inscription is dated Śaka 788 *i. e.*, 866 A.D. and the grant recorded in it is said to have been given in the 52nd year of the reign of the king. This shows that Amoghavarsha must have begun his reign in 814 or 815 A.D. The latest grant made by Amoghavarsha is recorded in a Kanheri inscription (Ind. Ant. XIII p. 135 No. 43) which is dated Śaka 799 *i. e.*, 877 A.D. This shows that the reign of Amoghavarsha came to a close at about 877 A.D. and extended over the unusally long period of sixty years.

In the Kharda grant, the city of Mānyakheta is spoken of as being very prosperous in Amoghavarsha's time and the question is whether it was this king who founded the city and made it his capital. The Wardha plates are clear on the point. In them Amoghavarsha is said to have founded Mānyakheta which laughed down the city of Indra, king of gods. Mānyakheta is identified with the present Malkhed in Nizam's territory. But we already have seen that Govinda, his father rested at Śrībhavana or Malkhed, and it seems that it was already chosen as capital by Amogha's father.

Amoghavarsha waged wars with the Chālukyas of Vengi and probably conquered some territory belonging to them. In the Kharepātan plate he is said to have marched against them and put several princes to death. The Nilagunda inscription represents him as being worshipped by Vanga, Anga, Magadha, Mālava and Vengi.

Amoghavarsha gave certain grants for the benefit of Jain sanctuaries. Dr. Bhandarkar in his history of the Rāshtrakūtas (Bombay Gaz. Vol. I. p. 11) alludes to two stanzas to be found in the historical appendix at the end of a Jain work entitled Uttarapurāṇa where Amoghvarsha is represented to have been a devoted worshipper of a holy Jain saint named Jinasena. In his note on Amoghavarsha as a patron of literature (Ind. Ant. XXXIII p. 197) Dr. Fleet refers to a small Sanskrit tract, containing about thirty verses consisting of questions and answers on moral subjects, entitled Ratnamālika or Praśnottaramālā. In the Digambara Jain recension of the work there is a stanza at the end which represents Amogravarsha as having abdicated the throne in consequence of the growth of the religious spirit in him. From this we may infer that Amoghavarsha was a patron of Digambara Jains, though we have no evidence to prove that he had accepted that faith. Amoghavarsha in the Deccan and Mihira Bhoja in the north seem to be contemporaneous powerful kings, a repetition, so to speak, of Harsha and Pulakeśin II of the seventh century A.D.

Amoghavarsha's son and successor was Akālavarsha. He married Mahādevī, daughter of Kokkala, a king belonging to the Sahasrārjuna (Haihaya) race. The proper name of this king was Kṛishṇa as is clear from the Wardha and Kardā plates.

The Wardha plates state that this king frightened Gurjara, destroyed the egregious pride of the arrogant Lāta king and deprived the people on the sea-coast of their sleep. Further, his command was obeyed by the Āndhra, Kalinga, Ganga and Magadha kings waiting at his gate.

The Navasari plates dated Śaka 836 give a description of Akālavarsha's wars with Gurjara as given by the old men of the time of the grant. This shows that the wars must have taken place about 25 or 30 years before this time *i. e.*, in about Śaka 811 or 806. According to Dr. Bhandarkar the date of this king ranges between Śaka 797 and 833 *i. e.*, between 875 and 911 A.D.

Akālvarsha's son was Jagattunga but his name is not given in the list of kings given in the Khārepātan grant. After Akālavarsha, the name of Indrarāja is mentioned who is spoken of as the grandson of Akālavarsha. The doubt is cleared by the Wardha plates which state that Jagattunga was taken to heaven by the creator without his having got the kingdom. Jagattunga married Laxmī, daughter of the son of Kokkala who is called Raṇavigraha in the Sangli and Navsari grants and Śankaragaṇa in the Kardā plates. From this union sprang Indra who succeeded his grandfather.

As stated above Indra III came to the throne after Akālavarsha. His title was Nityavarsha according to the Navasari grant. Nityavarsha is the donor of the Navasari grant. He is represented as residing at his capital Mānyakheta but as having gone to Kurunda on this occasion for his Pattabandhotsava. This must have been a ceremony in honour of his coronation. He is said to have weighed himself against gold on this day and is said to have given that gold to Brahmins. The grant is issued in Śaka 856 (934 A.D.) and Indra appears to have ascended the throne in that year. Dr. Fleet has published an inscription in Ind. Ant. XII p. 224 according to which Indra appears to be ruling in Śaka 838 *i. e.* in 916 A.D.

As regards the next king, there is some confusion in certain grants. The Sangli grant, however, is clear. It is recorded in these plates that Indra married Dvijāmbā (Vijayāmbā according to Dr. Bhandarkar) daughter of Anaṅgadeva who became by his virtue the son of Kokkala of the Haihaya race. By this wife Indra had a son named Govinda who is the donor of the Sangli grant. The Khārepātan plate, however, states that Govinda was the younger brother of a king named Amoghavarsha. The Wardha grant is more explicit. In this it is stated that Amoghavarsha died immediately after his father "as if through affection for him" and his younger brother Govindarāja ruled the kingdom.

This king as appears from the Wardha and Khārepātan plates was not a good ruler, the Khārepātan plate describes him as always surrounded by crowds of young damsels while the Wardha grant says "Fettered by the chains of the eyes of women, he displeased all beings by taking to vicious courses, and his limbs becoming enfeebled and the constituents of the (political) body becoming non-coherent, he met with destruction." The Sangli grant, however, which is issued by this king pours praises upon him.

The Sangli grant is issued in Śaka 855 *i. e.*, 933 A.D. In an inscription published by Dr. Fleet Govinda under the name Prabhūtavarsha is said to be reigning in Śaka 840 -41 *i. e.*, in 918-19 A.D. We have seen above that Indra ascended the throne in Śaka 836 so that it seems that Govinda had a short reign.

From the Khārepātan plate it appears that after Govinda IV, his paternal uncle and the second son of Jaggattunga came to the throne. The Wardha plates state that " after the death of Govinda IV king Amoghavarsha's son Jaggattunga being entreated by the feudatory chiefs to maintain the greatness of the sovereignty of the Rattas ascended the throne of heroes."

Amoghavarsha III was succeeded by his son Kṛishṇa ; the Wardha grant which is made by this king describes him in detail. The enemies who transgressed his commands were punished, he put to death Dantiga and Bappaṭa who had grown insolent. He thoroughly subdued the Ganga prince. Hearing of the ease with which he captured the strongholds in the south the Gurjara king who was preparing to take the fortresses of Kālanjara and Chitrakūṭa in the north had to give up the enterprise. All feudatory chiefs between the Himālayas and Simhala (Ceylon) paid obeisance to him. The Wardha grant is made by this king in the name of his younger brother Jagattungadeva and is dated, Ś. 862 *i. e.*, 940 A.D. He appears to be reigning in Śaka 873 (Ind. Ant. XII 256). From a statement at the end of a Jain work called Yaśastilaka Dr. Bhandarkar gathers that Kṛishṇa was the reigning monarch in Śaka 881. He thus seems to have ruled between 940 and 959 A.D.

Kṛishṇa III was succeeded by his younger brother Khottiga. The Kardā grant states " when the elder brother Kṛishṇarājadeva went to heaven, Khottigadeva, who was begotten by the king Amoghavarsha on Khandakādevī, the daughter of Yuvarāja, became king. " Kṛishṇa and Khottiga thus appear to be the sons of the same father but of different mothers. Khottika appears to be reigning in Śaka 893 (Ind. Ant. XII. p. 255).

Khottika was succeeded according to the Khārepātan grant by Kakkala, the son of his brother. The name of this brother according to the Kardā grant was Nirupama. From the Kardā grant Kakkala appears to be a brave soldier. He is stated to have conquered a numerous army of his foes in Gurjara and played and amused himself with Chola. He is said to be a constant protector of Hunavi prince and was dreaded exceedingly by the sovereign of Pāndya. Kakkala was, however, conquered in a battle by Tailapa who belonged to the Chālukya race and thus the sovereignty of the Deccan passed from the hands of the Rāshtrakūtas into those of the later Chālukyas about 974 A.D.

The Kardā grant was made in the reign of Kakkala and is dated Śaka 894 or A.D. 972 and another grant (Ind. Ant. Vol. XII. p. 270) represents him to be on the throne in Śaka 896 or 974 A.D. The Rāshtrakūtas were thus the supreme masters of the Deccan from about 750 A.D. to 974 A.D. An attempt was made to set up Indra IV a son of Krishṇa III by a western Ganga prince but it did not succeed and in an inscription (Ind. Ant. XXIII p. 124) it is said that Indra IV. starved himself to death by the performance of the sallekhana vow on 20th March 982 A.D. (Ep. Ind. VI. p. 182). *

---

* The kings of this line with dates of accession or death may be given together for the readers' benefit as follows (pedigree given separately).—

I. Dantidurga 753 A.D.
II. Krishṇa Akālāva. 773.
III. Dhruva Niru Dhārava. 783.
IV. Govinda III. Jagat. Pra. 808.
V. Śarva Nripat-Amoghav. 814-875.
VI. Krishṇa II Akālāva-Subhat. 875-911.
VII. Indra III Nityav, 914 grandson.
VIII. Amoghav. II.
IX. Govinda IV br. Suvarnav. d. 933.
X. Baddliga Amoghav. III uncle.
XI. Krishṇa III Akālāva. 940-961.
XII. Khottika Nityav 971.
XIII. Kakkala or Karka II. Amoghav. 972-974 ; lost the kingdom being conquered by Tailpaa Chālukya.

We will close this chapter with a few general observations about the Rāshtrakūtas of Mālkhed. They must be first distinguished from the Rāshtrakūtas or Rāthods of Rajputana. The former were lunar race Kshatriyas with probably Atri as their gotra, while the latter were and still claim to be Suryavaṁśi Kshatriyas with Gautama as their gotra. In this, the Rāshtrakūtas resemble their predecessors the Chālukyas. The Maratha Chālukyas with Mānavya as their gotra and probably solar-race Kshatriyas are distinct from the Rajput Chālukyas who are in inscriptions described as lunar race Kshatriyas with Bhāradvāja as their gotra. The identity of names should not mislead us. The same family name does sometimes recur, but the families are distinct. This is usually so where the name is a mere designation like Rāshtrakūta. The later inscriptions of these Rāshtrakūtas notwithstanding, as we have already shown in Vol. I, the word Rāshtrakūta meant the chief revenue officer of a province, Kūta or chief of Rāshtra or province. It is a revenue official designation like Deshmukh of modern times and it gradually became a surname. In the Maratha country the Deshmukh or head of a district is generally a Maratha and the Deshpande or the clerk of the district is generally a Brahmin. When the Maratha Aryas settled in Mahārāshtra they even then adopted this arrangement much like the Normans and distributed the head-ships of Rāshtras or districts (which is peculiarly a Mahārāshtra word) among the leading Maratha families who were thence designated Rāshtrakūtas. These Rāshtrakūtas were, therefore, pre-eminently Marathas and their empire in the Deccan from about 750 to 974 A.D. is the most glorious period of Maratha history.

The great danger of a Mahomedan invasion of Mahārāstra had already been averted by the prowess of a Maratha Chālukya chief of the Gujarat branch in 738 A.D. as the Navasari inscription indisputably proves. The greatness of this exploit is evidenced by the titles which the sovereign lord of the Deccan bestowed upon the Chief in Gujarat. He was given the title of the "repeller of the unrepellable" The Mahomedans had come onward in their career of conquest like a whirlwind having conquered Sindha, Kachha, Chāpotkata, Maurya, and others and had rushed southwards "to conquer the whole of the Deccan." They were met by their equals or superiors and annihilated by the sword of the Marathas. The danger of foreign conquest was thus averted from Mahārāṣhtra for five centuries more. The rise of the Rāshtrakūtas took place after this event and throughout their history the Arabs were their friends being the enemy of their common foe the Gurjaras, the kings of Kanauj.

The rise of the Rāshtrakūtas commenced with Dantidurga and his successor Krishṇa built or rather cut out the famous rock-cut temple of Elora which is, indeed, even now a wonder of the world. A whole temple of Śiva has been cut out of solid rock from a mountain and consists, so to speak, of one stupendous rock. The design is, indeed, sublime and the ornamentation is minute. It speaks volumes of the skill of the excavator engineer who must have carried the whole design in his head, plans and estimates being probably then unknown,. The Rāshtrakūtas have signalised their name for ever by this work though they appear to have left nothing more, Mānyakheta, their new capital, having in its delapidated condition nothing to boast of.

The Rāshtrakūta kings generally have simple names such as Krishṇa, Govinda and Indra a practice which continues down to this day in Mahārāshtra. But they too have birudas or titles of high sounding character. Besides the title Prithvivallabha or simply Vallabharai (Balhara of the Arabs) inherited from the Chālukyas, they took delight in special titles ending in varsha, such as Prabhūtavarsha, Amoghavarsha, Nityavarsha and so on and in tunga and the student of history is very often at a loss to remember what particular varsha or tunga each king is.

The Rāshtrakūta Marathas like their predecessors the Chālukyas and their modern representatives the Bhosles hold possession of Lāta or southern Gujarat especially Navasari which is still in possession of the Maratha Gaikwads. They also often held possession of Malwa. In the south they conquered up to Tanjore like their predecessors and successors. But the Rāshtrakūtas unlike the Chālukyas but like the modern Marathas went conquering north as far as Kanauj which as the seat of the Northern Empire, was the natural objective as much as Delhi the seat of the Mogul Empire was the objective of the modern Marathas. It does not appear that the Chālukyas had gone so far north. Pulakeśin had, no doubt, defeated Harsha and Vinayāditya had conquered Yaśovarman but that was probably in the Nerbudda region where the northerners had come and not in the heart of their own empire. The exploit of Indra is referred to with pride in the Cambay plates of Govind IV (Ep. Ind. VII p. 36) in crossing "the deep Jumna vying with the sea or the Indus" with cavalry swimming and storming and devastating Kanauj so that it truly became Kuśasthali or a plot overgrown with grass. The Jumna is broad and deep even now and must have been much more so in those days when it was not cut up by canals. And there were no bridges to cross it. The feat of cavalry swimming unfordable rivers is, indeed, not uncommon in history and the Marathas were then as now known for their horsemanship. These cavalry raids of the Marathas appear then to have been as effective as in modern history. Along with cavalry for which they were known the Rāshtrakūtas appear, however, to have kept up infantry also and a goodly elephant force (see Arab writers).

The Rāshtrakūta government was well regulated and what is strange they kept their army regularly paid as we shall presently see. They were by religion Śaivites but later kings appear to have an inclination towards Jainism and the spread of Jainism among the agricultural population of the Karnatic has to be specially noticed and may be thus explained. These Rāshtrakūtas of the Deccan had marriage relations with the Rajputs of the rorth, as we find Rāshtrakūtas marrying into the Pāla family of Bengal and the Haihaya family of Chedi. Then we are told in the Ātpurā inscription of Mewad that Allata's mother was a Rāshtrakūta princess; we are inclined to believe that she was a princess from the Deccan. There was then no Rāshtrakūta family of renown in the north and the special mention of the family of this princess here indicates that she came of a powerful family. The Nilagund inscription of Amoghavarsha I of 866 A.D. tells us that the Rāshtrakūtas had come into conflict with and defeated the people of Chitrakūta (Ep. Ind. VI. p. 106). Among the Rajputs conflicts and marriages follow one another without difficulty as in European history.

The same Nilagund inscription tells us that the Lānchhana (crest) of the Rāshtrakūtas was an eagle or Garuda. They appear to have used three white umbrellas (obtained by conquest), the Pāli Dhvaja of the previous Chālukyas and other ensigns of empire. The usual titles of emperors viz., Mahārājādhirāja Parameśvara and Bhattāraka they certainly use. It is strange that no comment has been made on the title Lattalūra-pura-Parameśvara by any writer. It appears to us that this indicates that before the founding of Malkhed the Rāshtrakūtas ruled in Lattalura ; where this town is has not yet been stated or discovered. Mr. Rājwade V. K. the well-known researcher in Maratha history thinks that it was a town in the Chedi country.

Genealogical Table of the Rāshtrakūta family.

- 1. Dantivarman.
  - 2. Indra I.
    - 3. Govinda I.
      - 4. Karka I.
        - 5. Indra II.
          - 6. Dantidurga conqu^red Chālukyas 753 A.D.
        - 7. Krishṇa I Akālavarsha 773 A.D.
          - 8. Govinda II Yuvaraj (grant Alās plate) 770 A.D.
          - 9. Dhruva Nirupama Dhārāvarsha 793 A.D. (m^ntioned in Jain Harivanśa of 783 A.D.
            - 10. Govinda III Jagattunga I Prabhūtavarsha 808 A.D,
              - 11. Śarva Nripatunga Amoghav. I 814—875 A.D.
                - 12. Krishṇa II Śubhatunga, Akālav. 875—911 A.D,
                  - Jagattimga (did not reign.)
                    - 13. Indra III Nityavarsha (914).
                      - 14. Amoghavarsha II.
                      - 15. Govinda IV Suvarṇavarsha (918—933 A.D.)
                    - 16, Baddiga Amoghav. VIII.
                      - 17, Krishṇa III Akālavarsha (940—968 A.D. Fleet in E. I. VI 180.)
                      - 18, Khoṭṭiga 971 A.D.)
                      - Nirupama
                        - 19, Kakkala or Karka II Amoghavarsha IV 972, 974, A,D, conquered by Tailapa Chālukya
                  - Dantivarmadeva (grant 867 A.D. E.I. VI 292.)
            - Indra.
              - Karka
              - Govinda.
                - Gujarat Branch.

CHAPTER XI.

THE OTHER KINGDOMS IN INDIA.

From 800 to 1000 A.D.

We have heretofore described the most important kingdoms in India which came into existence in the second sub-period of Mediæval Hindu Indian history (800-1000 A.D.), and will in this chapter notice the remaining kingdoms of India existing during this period. Many of them have already been noticed and described at length in our first volume and we shall name them here merely for the sake of completeness. Sind as far as Multan was under the Arabs, the governors being appointed from Baghdad by the Khalifas whose power gradually declined during this period and was finally supplanted by the Turks. Next we must notice the Shahi kings of Kabul already described at length in our first volume (p. 190-198). The Kshatriya Buddhist dynasty noticed by Hiuen Tsang ruled in Kabul till about 880 A.D. when the dynasty becoming effete was supplanted by a Brahmin Commander-in-Chief named Lalliya. He founded the Brahmin Shahi dynasty of Kabul which ruled from about 880 to 1021 A.D. when it was finally conquered by Mahmud of Ghazni. The kings of this dynasty are known from Alberuni as well as from coins and Rājataranginị (Vol. I p. 201) and were as follows—

1. Lalliya 880-900 A. D.
2. Sāmanta 900 -920 A.D.
3. Kamalu 920-940 A.D.
4. Bhīmadeva 940-960 A.D.
5. Jayapāla 960-980 A.D.
6. Ānandapāla 980-1000 A.D.
7. Trilochanapāla 1000-1021 A.D.

Shahi was the title of these kings from ancient times borrowed from Persia and even the previous Kshatriya dynasty kings bore the same title. The former dynasty was Buddhist but he latter was, as all over India, Hindu being worshippers of Śiva or Vishṇu.

As there was a Brahmin dynasty in Kabul, so there was a Kshatriya dynasty in Kandahar (see evidence of Arab travellers noted in next chapter) the history of which we will try to discover from Mahomedan records in our third volume. This dynasty probably belonged to the Bhatti clan of Rajputs and was overthrown by the Turks. In fact, Kabul and Kandahar were from ancient times parts of India; but since the invasions of the Turks they have been lost to India owing to the complete conversion of the population.

With these few remarks about the countries beyond the Indus we proceed to notice Kashmir the history of which has already been given in detail in our first volume. After Jayāpīda of the Karkota dynasty who ruled from 751 to 782 A.D. the kings of Kashmir rarely interfered in the concerns of the countries of India proper. This dynasty began thence to decline but it lived on till 855 A.D. when the vigorous rule of Avantivarman of the Utpala dynasty succeeded. But his dynasty soon became effete and came to end in 939 A.D. when there being no claimant, the people elected Yaśaskaradeva as king. His incapable son was set aside by Parvagupta of the Divira dynasty in 950 A.D. This dynasty, too, after two kings fell into the hands of the notorious Queen Diddā who practically ruled supreme and set up minor puppets on the throne one after another till her death about 1004 A.D. when her brother's son founded the Lohara dynasty of Kashmir. This dynasty produced many capable kings who prevented Kashmir falling like Kabul into the hands of the Turks. Kashmir, therefore, lived on as an independent Hindu kingdom during the third sub-period of our history (Vol. I p. 237) as we shall see again in our third volume.

Going on to the Panjab, we must notice first the Jālandhara or Kangrakota kingdom of Trigarta ruled by kings of the lunar race of Suśarman from the most ancient times. As stated in Vol. I p. 384 we have the mention of Jayachandra in an inscription which gives us a date 804 A.D. and Kalhana mentions a king Indrachandra in 1040 A.D. The dynasties in the Himalayan regions are all long-lived being free from molestation though the history of the fall of Kot Kangra before Mahmud forms an interesting episode in the history of Jālandhara which we shall have to relate in the account of Mahmud's invasions.

It is, indeed, difficult to determine what other kingdoms existed in the Punjab during this period. The Tekka kings, the Gujar Ālakhan, and Mihira Bhoja (Kanauj) are mentioned in the Rājtarangiṇi but we have no direct inscriptional evidence nor any continuous account. The history of Mahmud's invasions shows that there was a kingdom at Lahore which made strenuous efforts to resist Mahmud but we have only Mahomedan records to prove its existence. It is, therefore, a very difficult thing to determine the Panjab kingdoms of this period and we rest content here with this short notice of the Panjab.

At Delhi a new kingdom had been founded by this time by one Anaṅgapāla Tomara (Tuar) see Tod by Crorke Vol. I p. 104 where the Bardic tradition is given that Anaṅgapāla a descendant of the Pāndavas refounded the ancient Indraprastha in V.E. 848 (797 A.D.) which came to greater notice in the third sub-period of our history. We, however, find that even as early as about 913 A.D. the Chāhamāna king Chandana had to fight with a Tomara king named Rudreṇa. The fights between the Delhi Tomaras and the Sambhar Chāhamānas appear to have become hereditary and were natural as the Tomaras were the neighbours of the latter on the north. The king Tantrapāla defeated by the Chauhan Vākpati (943 A.D.) may be taken to be a Tomara king; and Vākpati's son Sinharāja is said distinctly to have defeated a Tomara king (name not given) in the Harsha stone inscription. We have very few inscriptions of the Tomaras of Delhi, then an insignificant town, which came into view only in the third sub-period of our history. These Tomaras of Delhi must have been subordinate to the Pratihāra empire of Kanauj as the Pehewa inscription (Ep. Ind. I p. 242-184) shows. This inscription is dated 882 A.D.

Passing on to the modern U. P. and Oudh we have already stated that these two provinces were then under the direct control of the emperors of Kanauj and there were no subordinate kingdoms in these parts.

In Nepal as stated in our first volume (p. 375-376) the Lichhavi dynasty came to end about this period and the Rajput dynasty of Nepal was established. This was, of course, in consonance with the trend of history in India generally. We have no inscriptional evidence relating to these kings; and we have to rely solely on local tradition and local Vamśāvalis. This dynasty founded an era of its own which runs from 879 A.D. and it was certainly not the first king of this line who founded this era. We may, therefore, state generally that a Rajput dynasty of kings ruled in Nepal from about 800 A.D. down to the end of our sub-period.

We have next to notice the kingdom of Kāmarūpa or Assam which seems to be still under the rule of the same Bhagadatta line of Bhāskaravarman. This kingdom was sometimes subordinate to the Pālas of Bengal but its continued existence cannot be doubted even as an independent kingdom. For Arab writers of the 9th and 10th centuries A.D. as shown elsewhere mention Kāmarūpa as an important kingdom of India to the east of Bengal.

Eastern and Western Bengal were during this period united under the Pālas of Monghyr and we, therefore, go on to notice the kingdom of Orissa, the history of which has already been given in detail in our first volume (p. 320-326). The Kesari line of kings continued to rule in Orissa during the second sub-period of our history and they were orthodox Hindu kings and worshippers of Śiva, the predominant deity of this period over the whole of India. Their rule according to the palm-leaf records of Jagannath lasted till 1132 A.D. when the modern Vishṇu worship of Jagannath was introduced, But this is not quite reliable, for other records show that a line of kings who were worshippers of the Sun intervened between them. When this Sun-worshipping line of kings was established we have no evidence of a contemporary character to show. The records which mention them are of much later date and give only probable information which may simply be noted here.

We have next to notice the Yavana kingdom in Āndhra ruled by Vindhya-Śakti and others called Kainkila Yavanas in the Vishṇu and Bhāgavata Purāṇas. The existence of Yavanas about 800 A.D. is proved by the Khālimpur grant of the Pālas where the Yavanas are described as subordinates of Kanauj. And in Kanauj records, too, we find mention of Āndhra being conquered. These Yavanas ruled till about 900 A. D. when their rule was subverted by a Vaishṇava dynasty which we shall notice in our third volume (see Vol. I p. 352-353).

In Kośala or Chattisgadh, the ancient Haihaya dynasty continued to rule during this sub-period. So also in Vengi the Eastern Chālukyas ruled. They were, indeed, fortunate as their rule lasted from 633 A.D. to about 1015 A. D. that is, about 400 years which is twice the average duration of a kingly dynasty. In what is modern Madras Presidency, many subordinate kings ruled but they were subject to the over-lordship of the Rāshtrakūtas of Malkhed. The Pallavas of Kanchi became effete about the same time as the early Chālukyas of Badāmi and the later Pallavas were subject to the Rāshtrakūtas, their king Dantivarman being defeated by the Rāshtrakūtas about 803 A.D. (Vol. I p. 293). These Pallavas were finally supplanted by the Cholas whose rise belongs to the third sub-period of our history as it took place after 1000 A.D. There were other minor kings like the Pāṇdyas and others, but the vigorous kingdoms of the south like those of the Cholas and the Hoysalas and the Gangas belong to the third period and we shall speak of these in detail in our third volume.

On the west coast and at Kolhapur ruled two important kingly families of the Śilāháras. They ruled from about 800 to 1200 A.D. They were certainly subordinate to the Rāshtrakūtas during this period and their greatness belongs to the third sub-period of our history and will, therefore, be treated of in our third volume.

CHAPTER XII.

CONTEMPORARY ARAB WRITERS.

Very interesting and corroborative information is found recorded in the accounts of travel of contemporary Arab writers and it deserves to be summarised in a special chapter. It is difficult to have access to the original writings of these writers as these are translated into French only ; but we can make use of the extracts given by Elliot in his most interesting history, Research in his time was in its infancy, and Elliot could not identify the names of kingdoms and towns, but now that the history of Mediæval Hindu India is much more explored, it is pleasant to note how the writings of these Arab travellers exactly represent the political, social and religious conditions of this period (800-1000 A.D.). We make, therefore, no apology to quote the relevant extracts here and to note their significance.

The first traveller noted by Elliot (Vol. I) is the merchant Sulaiman who made several voyages from the Persian Gulf to India and China and wrote his work in 857 A.D. He observes that the four great kings of the world are the kings of Babylon, of China, of the Greeks (Constantinople) and the Balhara who is the most eminent of the kings of India and is acknowledged as such by them. Elliot could not identify Balhara, nor his capital Mankir, but it is now well known that Balhara is the Arabic pronunciation of the word Vallabharai and Mankir is Mānyakheta, the capital of the Rāshtrakutas which is, no doubt, very distant from the sea. That the Rāshtrakūṭa king was the most powerful king in India at that time we have already seen and he was the over-lord of the whole of southern India. Sulaiman further says that " every prince in India is master in his own state but all pay homage to the Balhara ". We have always insisted upon the fact that ancient Indian Empire did not mean annexation. Each subject king was allowed to rule as before and had merely to pay homage on occasions to his over-lord. Unlike other kings the Balhara appears to have maintained a regular army and "this army was regularly paid as among the Arabs." "He has many horses and elephants." "The coins in use are the Tataria Dirhams and they are dated in the year in which the dynasty acquired the throne. They do not use any era like the Arabs." This is rather strange; for, the Rāshtrakūtas always use the Śaka era in their inscriptions; but possibly their coins had only regal years. "The Balhara is partial to the Arabs and his subjects follow his example." "Balhara is a title which is borne by all kings."

"The Balhara is always at war with the king of Jurz." The next important kingdom in India then was thus that of Jurz and Jurz or Gurjar is, undoubtedly, Kanauj as other Arab writers also testify. "This king of Jurz has most excellent cavalry. No other prince has so fine cavalry." "His camels and horses are numerous. He is unfriendly to the Arabs." "His territories form a tongue of land." This can be explained on the fact that the Kanauj empire extended into Kathiawar. "Exchange is carried on in this state by silver and gold dust." We know that Bhoja first struck coins called the Ādivarāha *dramma*. "No country in India is more safe from robbers." We have already quoted this certificate about the extremely well ordered administration of the empire of Kanauj which is valuable especially when we remember that the territories of modern Gwalior and Bundlekhand which were then under Kanauj have always been noted for dacoits.

The next kingdom mentioned by Sulaiman is Tafik which is a small state and where the "women are white and the most beautiful in India." Scholars are at a loss to identify this kingdom. It cannot, of course, be Aurangabad as Elliot thought. It may be located in the Himalayas as one Arab traveller actually states that it was in the mountains. If the name Tafik cannot be equated with any Indian name, it is, indeed, a misfortune but we think this kingdom may be identified with Jālandhara or part of the Panjab and the word Tak comes nearest to Tafik.

It is equally a misfortune that the next kingdom mentioned *viz.*, that of Rahmi cannot also be properly identified. "All these three kingdoms border on it and it is at war with Jurz;" would identify it with Bengal which seems most probable as from other Arab writers it appears that it extended up to the Bay of Bengal. " He has a great elephant force," exaggerated to 50,000. This is also well applicable to Magadha and Gauda in the jungles of which elephants abounded. " There is a stuff made in this country which is not found elsewhere, so fine and delicate that a dress made of it may pass through a signet ring. It is made of cotton and we have seen a piece of it." This clearly refers to the fine muslins made in Bengal and this testimony shows that Bengal was famous for its fine muslins even through the days of Mediæval Hindu India. This fact further identifies Rahmi with Bengal. But what is Rahmi? We have not yet found its Indian equivalent.

We have next three kingdoms mentioned viz., Kashbin (probably in the Himalayas with white people), Kiranj and Serendib (Ceylon) but these do not belong to India proper. The political condition reflected in this short description by Sulaiman of 850 A.D. shows as it really was at that period, the Rāshtrakūtas, the Pratihāras and the Pālas of the Deccan, the Gangetic valley and Bengal being the three most powerful kingdoms in India. We will refer to other statements recorded by Sulaiman in our notice of the social and religious conditions of the country.

II. Ibn Khurdadba who died about 912 A.D.

" The greatest king of India is the Balhara ; the other kings are Jabal (Java), Tafan, Jurz, Rahmi, Kamrun (Kamrupa). Between Rahmi and the other kings communication is kept by ships. He has 50,000 elephants. His country produces cotton cloth and Aloe wood." This amply identifies Rahmi with Bengal. This author describes the 7 castes of the people in a manner which requires special mention and these will be noticed separately.

III. Al Masudi, an acute Arab writer of 332 A. H. (953 A.D.) After describing some imaginary kings of ancient India he says, After Koresh (Sri Harsha) the country broke up into diverse nations and tribes such as Sind, Kanauj and Kashmir. The city of Mankir submitted to a king called Balhara. There prevails a difference of language and religion and they are frequently at war with one another. The greatest king is the Balhara of Mankir. Some kings have their territory in the mountains away from the sea as Kashmir, Tafan etc. The troops of the Balhara are innumerable including elephants but his troops are mostly infantry as his capital lies among mountains. One of the kings far from the sea is the Bautira who is the lord of the city of Kanauj. This is the title given to all the kings. He has armies on the west, the south, the east and the north."

Now this word Baunra offers a further puzzle which is yet unsolved. Foreigners twist Indian names into strange words. The Portuguese called the Adilshah of Bijapur Yadilcao. The word Baunra is repeated by other Arab travellers and historically applies to the Pratihāra Emperors of Kanauj. Ra is rai as in Balhara, but Baur leads to nothing unless one sees in it Pratihāra.

"The Mihran (Indus) comes from well-known sources in the highlands of Sind, and Kanauj and from Kashmir, Kandahar and Tafan." This shows first that the empire of Kanauj extended into the Panjab and secondly that the Tafan country lay in the Himalayas.

"The king of Kandahar is called Hāhaj a name common to all sovereigns. Kandahar is called the country of the Rahbut (Rajput). The king of Kashmir is called Rai. Kashmir forms part of Sind." What is Hāhaj is another riddle, but that there were Rajput kings in Kandahar at this period is clear from this. Kashmir forming part of Sind is an absurdity. Perhaps the Arabs of Sind laid claim to it in their vaunts.

"The Bauura king of Kanauj keeps four armies in the field in the four quarters. Each of these numbers 7 to 9 lakhs of men. The army of the north wars against the king of Multan and the Musalmans on the frontier and the army of the south fights against the Balhara king of Mankir." This is candid testimony to the power of the Kanauj emperors who kept the Arabs long confined to Multan and did not allow them to extend their conquest. The Rāstrakūtas of the south who were leagued with the Arabs were equally watched. The kings of Kanauj appear thus to be very rigid orthodox kings, powerful enough not to only check the Arabs but even to expel them from Multan. For this traveller further testifies that "whenever the unbelievers march against Multan and the faithful do not think themselves strong enough to oppose them, they threaten to break the sacred idol of the Sun and their armies immediately withdraw." What a strange testimony to the foolish superstitious beliefs of the Hindus of the 9th and 10th century!

Finally, Al Masudi speaks of the kingdom of Rahmi which he says "extends both along the sea and the continent." It is frequently at war with Juzr and with Balhara on whose kingdoms his dominions border. "It is bounded by an inland kingdom called Kaman "whose inhabitants are fair and have their ears pierced." This is plainly a reference to the kingdom of Kamrup or Assam the inhabitants of which we orthodox Hindus.

IV. Al Istakhri who wrote about 951 A.D. "From Kambaya to Saimur is the land of the Balhara." This distinctly shows that the Rāshtrakutas ruled in Gujarat, south and middle, and in Konkan. "And in it there are several Indian kings—" shows that there were subordinate kings under them. One of these was in Lāta or Gujarat itself. "It is a land of infidels; but there are Musalmans in the cities and none but Musalmans ruled over them on the part of the Balhara." This political arrangement resembles the modern capitulations of the Europeans in Egypt and elsewhere. "There are Juma Masjids in them." The Deccanies appear to be, from of old, tolerant and not very rigid Hindus, like the Hindus of the U. P. or Kanauj.

V. Ibn Haukal who seems to have finished his work in 976 A.D. "From Kambaya (Khambayat) to Saimur (Chaul) is the land of the Balhara and in it there are several kings. The city in which the Balhara resides is Mankir. From Kambaya to Saimur the villages lie close to one another and there is much land under cultivation." This shows that Gujarat and Konkan were in good flourishing condition under the rule of the Rāshtrakūtas.

BOOK V

GENERAL SURVEY.

CHAPTER I.

LANGUAGE.

Arab travellers record that there were diverse languages in India. This is, indeed, true of Mediæval Hindu India. But what languages were these? Were they the classical Prākṛits—Mahārāshṭrī, Śauraseni, Māgadhī and Paisachī which once were certainly spoken languages in the south, the middle, the east and the north-west respectively? We have some, yet not ample, Indian records to prove that the modern representatives of these, viz., the Marathi, the Hindi, the Bengali and the Panjabi had come into existence by this time. We exclude from our consideration the Non-Aryan languages of the extreme south viz., the Tamil, the Malyāli, the Kanarese and the Telagu of the eastern coast. Tamil was the oldest of these and, in fact, the parent of them all and these, too, appear to have come into existence about this time. We have observed in our first chapter that the second sub-period of Mediæval Hindu History viz., A.D. 800-1000 was characterised by the rise of modern languages. We believe that Marathi, Bengali, Hindi, and Panjabi came into existence about the same time and by about the same causes; and their rise cannot be traced further back than this period. Even the Kanarese, the Malyāli and the Telagu came into existence at this time by the operation of the same causes which we proceed to note.

When Buddhism was overthrown and Hinduism or Aryanism re-established, it was both a political and a religious revolution.

Buddhism was mainly professed by foreigners; even now foreigners are more in favour of Buddhism than Hinduism. The reason is plain. Hinduism is exclusive while Buddhism is not. Hinduism again believes in the revelation of the Vedas, Buddhism does not and hence has no connection with past India. When, therefore, Hinduism was established, ancient orthodox kingly families of Kshatriyas came to the front and the foreign ruling families or the Vaiśya and Śūdra ruling families disappeared. Naturally, Sanskṛit began to be studied by the Kshatriyas and by others to a greater extent and the Prākṛits which were taken up by Buddhism and Jainism for their sacred literature gradually fell into disuse. The infusion of Sanskṛit, therefore, began to operate on the spoken languages of the people and the modern vernaculars of India with their sterner character and stronger pronunciation began to be formed. The need of religion also assisted the process. New Hindu philosophy notably the philosophy of Śaṅkara arose about this time viz., about 800 A.D. and it was necessary to preach the new ideas to the people in their vernaculars. It was thus that the modern languages with their provincial peculiarities began to be formed in every province under both political and religious necessities. Thus under the influence of the same impulses by the infusion of Sanskṛit words and Sanskṛit sounds, the modern Sanskṛit-born and even Tamil-born languages arose about this time in the different provinces of India. What were these new languages named?

Al Masudi who describes the countries of the east and the west as they were in his age (332 A. H. or 943 A.D.) records that the inhabitants of Mankir which is the capital of Balhara speak the Kiriya language which has this name from Kira the place where it is spoken. On the coast as in Saimur, Subara, Thana and other towns a language called Lariya is spoken which has its name from the sea which washes these countries." (Elliot I p. 25.) Now here there is no mention of the name Marathi and Gujarati though the language spoken on the coast of Thana and Sopara and above the Ghats at Malkhed must have been the same. It seems that a language called Lādi did once exist in Lād or Lata country *i.e.*, modern southern Gujarat and that it it has now merged or changed into the Gujarati language. But Kiria must certainly be a name given to the new language of Mahārāshtra by the Arabs as it is expressly stated that the name was derived from Kir name of the place. The Arabs pronounce Indian names most strangely. Balhara is now known to be Vallabharai; while Mankir is Mānyakhet; and from Kir the second portion of Mankir the Arabs must have given the name Kiriya to the language. As the word Kiriya does not contain na, it does not seem that Kiriya is an abreviation of Kānari, nor can kā be changed into ki. It must, therefore, be held that Kiriya is the name coined by the Arabs for the Marathi language which then was being formed and was not a name actually in use in Mahārāshtra. Naturally at such a time there must have been strong differences in the speech of different localities. Under the influence of greater communication and of written grammar and vocabulary, the Marathi of modern days is nearly the same all over Mahārāshtra, Khandesh, Konkan, Baroda, Berar and Nagpore. But in the beginning there must have been greater local differences and the language of Thana, the capital of Northern Konkan must have been markedly different from the language of Mankir, the capital of the Ghat country; and hence the language of North Konkan must have struck the Arab traveller as different. Even at the present day, the language of the Mahomedans of Kalyan and Bhiwandi, though it is Marathi, is different from the language of the educated Hindus which again differs in some respects from the language of the villagers. The Marathi language of these North Konkan Mahomedans is again quite distinct from the language of the Southern Konkan Mahomedans; while the Konkani language of Goa is again distinct. These differences of Marathi require to be studied and they will show us how the present Marathi language emerged from the ancient Mahārāshtri Prakṛit.

That the Prakṛits were once spoken languages cannot be doubted. The rules of Sanskṛit dramaturgy require that certain characters should speak certain Prakṛits. For poetry and higher thought, Mahārāshtri is prescribed and for ordinary speech of women and other characters Śauraseni. For servants Māgadhi is to be used and for ruffians etc., the Paiśāchi. These rules show that occupations like provincial linguistic differences stick. The Pandits of the south were then as now learned men and servants came from the east; while soldiers and ruffians came from the north-west. It, therefore, cannot be denied that the Prakṛits were once spoken languages. But it canot also be denied that they ceased to be spoken languages in the 8th or 9th century A.D. They were then used in compositions by learned men only and had become as artificial as Sanskṛit. Thus, when Rājaśekhara wrote his play in Mahārāshtri and the same was acted at Kanauj it could not have been understood by the common people, but could have been appreciated only by the learned. How different modern Marathi is from the Mahārāshtri of Rājaśekhara will appear to any one who reads that work.

There it will appear that every Sanskṛit word is softened into the corresponding Mahārāshtri word by prescribed rules of softening the Sanskṛit forms and letters. The new vernaculars gave up this effeminate character, began to use Sanskṛit words without change, thus introducing Tatsama words in addition to Tadbhava and evolved new forms of inflexions and conjugations. These were, of course, different in different provinces but all were derived from Sanskṛit originals. Even the Non-Aryan languages began to use Sanskṛit words as they were and thus gave a different turn to themselves though inflexions and conjugations could not be copied from Sanskṛit and nouns and verbs were inflected and conjugated with Non-Aryan suffixes. It seems thus that the Kanarese language was formed about this time and spread in the Southern Maratha Country. How this country which is Maratha by race and which is properly called Southern Maratha Country even now, became Karnatik by language is a problem which has not been solved. That the people of this part spoke Mahārāshtri in centuries previous has already been shown by us in Vol. I page 317. Inscriptions of ancient times up to the 4th century A.D. undoubtedly prove that Mahārāshtri in a cultivated form was spoken in the country now the home of Kanarese. Why and how this change occurred we have not materials to discuss; but it is certain that this change had taken place by the end of the 8th century as we proceed to show.

The Alas Plate of Yuvarāja Govind II (Ep. Ind. VI. p. 260) states that Dantidurga "easily with a small force conquered Karnātaka which had humbled Kānchi, Kerala, Chola, Pāndya, Sriharsha and Vajrata." This is again repeated in the Paithan grant of Govind III dated 794 A.D. (Ep. Ind. III. p. 108) and is also mentioned in a grant of Krishṇarāja I (Ep. Ind. XVI. p. 121) of 772 A.D. It seems thus clear that in the latter half of the 8th century A.D., the Chālukya kingdom of Badāmi was looked upon as Karnātaka; while the Rāshtrakūtas from the north who conquered them from the north considered themselves as Marạthas or Rattas. It must be remembered that Hiuen Tsang in about 640 A.D. described Pulakeśin of Badāmi as ruler of Mahārāshtra; in fact, his Mahārāshtra extended from the Nerbudda down to the Tungabhadrā. A hundred and fifty years later Badāmi was Karnātaka, of course, by language and not race. The Kanarese language, it seems, like Northern Gaudian modern languages, had come into existence and had extended its influence up to the Kṛishṇā by this time.

The Eastern Chālukyas who were by race and origin Marathas had become by this time Andhras or Telagus. They were off-shoots from the Chālukyas of Badāmi and were nominally subject to their suzerainty. When the Rāshtrakūtas conquered Karnātaka Chālukya Empire, they laid claim to suzerainty over the Eastern Chālukyas and naturally had to establish it by the sword. The Alas plates speak of this conflict. The Eastern Chālukyas submitted and are shown to be subordinate to the Rāshtrakūtas in later grants and are described as Kalingas or Telagus. They had become so by language and by local marriage relations. They called themselves Chālukyas in their records; but were called Kalingas by outsiders. The Telagu language, too seems to have emerged into prominence at about this time.

We need not and cannot speak much of the Bengali which emerged out of the Māgadhi about this time with provincial peculiarities still the same ; nor of the Hindi, Eastern add Western. It is a subject of study by itself. But we give in the following note extracts from Dr. Grierson's Survey of Indian languages showing how far back the written literature in each important language goes back. These will support, to great degree, our theory that the modern vernaculars of India, whether Sanskṛit-born or Tamil-born began to flourish from the 9th century A. D.

NOTE.

Extracts from Dr. Grierson's survey of Iudian Languages relating to the dates of the oldest writings in each Indian Language.

(1) Kanarese :—The oldest works go back to at least the 10th century A.D. The origin of the Kanarese literature is due to the labours of the Jains and the first literary works are largely influenced by Sanskrit. Three periods are distinguished in Karnarese Literature (1) Ancient Kanarese from at least the 10th to the 13th. The principal productions are based on prosody and grammar based on Sanskrit originals, sectarian works and poetical works in a highly artificial style. This literature is in an old dialect which is said to be quite uniform and to show an extraordinary polish. It is full of Sanskrit loan words and differs from modern Kanarese in phonology and inflexional system ; e.g. Pampas Adipurana (941 A.D.) &c. (2) Mediæval Kanarese. The old rules of inflexion and syntax are no longer observed and new forms are introduced—13th to 15th centuries. (3) Modern Kanarese. Literature can be traced back to about the beginning of the 16th century. A large proportion of Vaishṇav poetry agrees with the dialect of the 2nd period.

(2) Telagu :—According to tradition the first Telagu writer was Kaṇva. His work is lost and the earliest extant work in Telagu belongs roughly to A.D. 1000. About that time King Vishṇuvardhana alias Raja—Rajanarendra (1022-1060) was a great patron of the Telagu literature and at his court lived Nannaya Bhatta, the author of the oldest extant Telagu grammar, and the principal author of the Telagu version of the Mahābhārata (p. 580 Vol. IV). Hiuen Tsang mentions that the Andhras had language of their own written in an alphabet which did not much differ from that of the north. Kumarila mentions the Andhra Dravida Bhasha (he mentions only the Dravida Bhasha) while the use of the same alphabet by Andhras noticed by Hieun Tsang is memorable.

(3) Bengali :—There is no doubt about the fact that it is from some eastern form of Magadhi that Bengali is directly derived. The very same incapacities of vocal organs exist with Bengali now that existed with their predecessors 800 years ago. A Bengali cannot pronounce kshm any more than they could. He cannot pronounce a clear s, but must make it sh. The compound letter hy beats him and instead he has to say jjh. In literature, one of the oldest poet is Chandidasa who flourished about the 14th century and wrote songs in praise of Krishṇa (page 15 Vol. V.)

(4) Eastern Hindi :—From earliest times Oudh has been the centre of literary activity and to describe the old literature would require a difficult study. But when Tulsidasa wrote his works in Hindi it sealed its fate altogether (he died in the year 1624) and every author writes in his manner Malik Mahommad Jaisi wrote the epic Padmavati before him (1540) which deals with the adventures of Ratnasing, king of Chitor and its siege and sack by Alauddin (Vo. VI. page 13.)

(5j Western Hindi :—Bhils, through Dravidians, of Rajputana and Khandesh have given up their language and speak a western Hindi dialect called Bhili.) Rajasthani and Marwadi have old literature which have not been studied. Prithviraj Rasa by Chand though the oldest extant work is of a suspicious character. Marwadi has an old literature which is called Diṅgal. The poems of Mirabai are in what is called the Braj Bhasha also called Piṅgala. (Vol. IX page 15.)

(6) Marathi :—Ramatarkavagiśa and Kramadiśvara mention Dākshiṇātya as a form of Mahārāshtra apabhranśa. The Sāhityadarpaṇa makes Dākshiṇātya identical with Vaidarbhika. Modern Marathi is so old that Dākshiṇātya and Vaidarbhika might well refer to it. The oldest Marathi inscription of which any thing is known goes back to about 1115 A.D. and an inscription of some extent is dated in 1207 A.D. Ep. India Vol. I page 343 and Vol. IX page 109 (Vol. VII page 15.)

CHAPTER II.

CASTE AND SOCIAL CONDITION.

We propose in this chapter to describe the social condition of India including caste (which is the most prominent feature of the Hindu society) during the second sub-period of our history. The materials for taking such a survey are not ample but nevertheless we can make an attempt from inscriptions as well as the writings of foreign (Arab) travellers whose evidence is always very important, for things striking strike foreigners more than they do ourselves. We have unfortunately no native writer like Bāṇa to assist us in this period ; but we propose to take some help from the later Smṛitis which were probably composed during this period though we can never be certain about their dates. We think a fairly accurate account of the social condition of the country can be presented from these materials. To begin with, the first observation to make is that caste was still not rigid as it is at present and that the ramification of the main castes into minor sub-castes had not yet begun. That is to say, the Brahmins, for instance, throughout India formed one caste without sub-divisions as at present based on provincial or other minor differences. Thus we do not find Brahmin donees in inscriptions described as Kanojia or Dravida. Indeed, the same method as prevailed in the preceding periods obtained of describing Brahmins by their gotra and by their Śākhā and the same practice in describing these continued viz., adding sa to the gotra name and the term Sabrahmachāri to the name of the Śākhā. Thus, for instance, the Vardhā grant of Rāshtrakūta Akālavarsha A.D. 940 (Ep. Ind. V) mentions the donee as नन्दिवर्धनविनिर्गत भारद्वाजसगोत्र वाजिकाण्वसब्रह्मचारिणे. In modern times the Brahmins have nearly forgotten their Śākhā or Sabrahmachāriship and if they remember their gotra they do not know that they have to add sa to it when mentioning it along with their name. It is not necessary to give many instances of this, for they occur in almost every grant. Brahmins were, therefore, then known and distinguished by their gotras and their Śākhā (or branches of Vedic ritual or Sūtras) and not known as Gujarati or Deccani though their place of residence is usually mentioned. Thus in the grant of Karkarāja dated 812 A.D. (J. Bengal VIII p. 292) चातुर्विद्यसामान्य वात्स्यायनसगोत्र माध्यंदिनसब्रम्हचारिणे is the description of the donee. A Brahmin from Valabhi in Kathiawad who had gone to the Rāshtrakūta king in Malkhed might well have been described as a Lāta or Saurāshtra Brahmin. So the donee in the Sangli grant (I. A. XII) is a Brahmin from Paundravardhana; but he is not called a Guad Brahmin, but is as usual described as कौशिकसगोत्र. वाजिकाण्वसब्रम्हचारि. It seems certain that the modern distinctions had not yet arisen and that the Brahmins of India formed one caste throughout India*. The same may be said of the second caste viz., the Kshatriyas. They too formed one caste without distinction of Khatri or Rajput, Bais or Maratha and freely intermarried throughout the whole country. The Kshatriyas no doubt ceased during this period to mention their gotras in their inscriptions. Whereas in the preceding centuries we find the Chālukyas of the Deccan taking pride in describing themselves as Mānavyasagotra and the Pallavas of Kānchi as Bhāradvājasagotra, the Rāshtrakūtas of Malkhed in the same Deccan nowhere mention their gotra in their records and the same may be said of the Kshatriya families of the north. Thus the inscriptions of the Pratihāras of Kanauj nowhere mention their gotra, nor those of the Guhilots of Mewad. The gotra of the Chāhamānas appears incidentally in their records while the Vasishtha gotra of the Paramāras also is not mentioned usually but only in the legend of the origin of the Paramāras. So also the gotra of the Chālukyas of the north is only incidentally mentioned in the legend of their origin. Probably the kula of the Kshatriyas became important from this time and began to assume importance which it holds to-day.

*We may here refer to the following śloka from Parāśara Smriti as showing that gotra and charaṇa were the only things that then differentiated Brahmins, न पृच्छेद्गोत्रचरणे न स्वाध्यायश्रुते तथा । (48·1) in connection with an Atithi.

In fact the kula began itself to be called gotra and in one inscription we find that the name of the kula is given as the Pratihāra-gotra (Buchk. Ins. E. I. IX. p. 199). So also the Naravāhana inscription of V. S. 1028 describes Bappaka as Guhilagotra-narendrachandra. This must be due to the fact that Vedic ritual and Vedic sacrifices were now not in vogue with the Kshatriyas and the worship of Puranic deities, especially of Śiva, became supreme. The former required the recital of gotra and Pravara, while the latter did not. Naturally gotra and Pravara lost importance with the Kshatriyas who, however, never lost respect for the Vedas and Vedic ordinary ritual not involving the killing of animals and hence have preserved the memory of their gotra and Pravara to this day, though they have ceased to count them of importance.

The Vaiśyas, too, may be presumed to form yet one caste throughout India, for we yet do not come across the names of their modern subdivisions Maheśri, Lād and so on. They, of course, had already lost touch with Vedic ritual, having turned Buddhists in far greater number than the higher two castes and hence they have not preserved the memory of their gotras. This must be placed even as early as the first spread of Buddhism under Aśoka, for we find that the Śrauta Sūtras in their Pravarādhyāyas treat Vaiśyas separately from Brahmins and Kshatriyas and assign to them only one gotra and Pravara *viz.*, Vatsapri. When the Vaiśyas returned to Hinduism they became mostly followers of Vaishṇavism for reasons which we will elucidate in our third volume.

These three castes were and are the most important ones, but there were many intermediate main castes also. These are not much mentioned in the inscriptions though the Kāyastha caste as writer of inscriptions often finds mention. These Kāyasthas, too, were apparently one caste throughout India, and had not yet split up into subdivisions as at present. The same may be predicated of other intermediate main castes.

The number of these main castes must have been even then large though not as large as it is at present. For, we have a description of Indian caste from an Arab traveller of the time and he counts the castes as seven only, much in the same way as

Megasthenes gave the number of Indian castes as seven. Ibn Khurdadba who wrote his book about 900 A.D. thus describes Indian castes :—" There are seven classes of the Hindus ; viz.. 1st Sabkutria who are men of highest caste from among whom kings are chosen. The people of the other classes do homage to this class only. 2nd, Brahmins who totally abstain from wine and fermented liquors. 3rd, Kataria who drink not more than three cups of wine. The daughters of the class of Brahmins are not given in marriage to this class, but the Brahmins take their daughters. 4th Sudaria who are by profession husbandmen ; 5th Baisura who are by profession artificers and domestics ; 6th Sandalia who perform menial services. 7th Lahud ; their women are fond of adornments and the men are fond of amusements and games of skill." This is a pretty correct description of caste as it existed in India in the 9th and 10th centuries and as it struck an outsider who though not acquainted with its intricacies can not but have marked the essential features of it. Strangely enough, in this list the Sabkutria who plainly form the class of the royal families of India (subsequently enumerated as 36) are placed even above the Brahmins. But that the Rajputs separated themselves from ordinary Kshatriyas is plain and they rightly deserved by their valour, their high morals and their indomitable spirit of opposition to Mahomedanism the first place assigned to them. The next class is plainly that of the Brahmins. The third are the ordinary Kshatriyas. The fourth can well be recognised as the Śudras who now formed the bulk of the agriculturists of the country. But they ought to have been placed below the fifth viz., the Baisura. These are the Vaiśyas. They had long given up agriculture which had belonged to them even according to the Bhagavadgīta and those who still practised it were as we have already shown in Vol. I, treated as Śudras. The Vaiśyas are described herein as artificers and domestics. They are not, strangely enough, described as traders who are nowhere mentioned. Probably this is an omission. But Megasthenes also includes merchants under artificers who again are usually treated as Vaiśyas in India. The sixth Sandalia are the Chāndālas and they performed all menial services. We saw in Bāṇa that the Chāndālas were employed as grooms in Harsha's army. Lastly; the Lahuds appear to be the ancesters of many of our wandering tribes from their description, viz., that their women are fond of ornaments and their men are fond of amusements and games of skill. All these names are identifiable, it must be lastly remarked, except the first and the last viz., the Sabkutria* and the Lahuda and their Sanskrit equivalents can not be guessed ; but from the description of their occupations these two castes are plainly the highest Rajputs and the lowest rope dancers and others.

Caste, as we have already explained elsewhere, has two aspects, the occupational and the matrimonial ; and in the above description of Khurdadba we have some hints as to the matrimonial aspects of caste also which we proceed to develop. First marriage appears to have been restricted generally to the caste itself. But Ibn Khurdadba marks, like Megasthenes, one exception viz., that the Brahmin could marry a daughter of a Kshatriya which was the fact. Probably, the Khsatriya also claimed a similar privilege and married Vaiśya wives. The provisions of later Smṛitis may be referred to here with advantage. The Vyāsa Smṛiti has the following interesting ślokas :—

ऊढायां हि सवर्णायामन्यां वा काममुद्वहेत् ।
तस्यामुत्पादितः पुत्रो न सवर्णात्प्रहीयते ॥
उद्वहेत् क्षत्रियां विप्रो वैश्यां च क्षत्रियो विशाम् ।
न तु शूद्रां द्विजः कश्चिन्नाधमः पूर्ववर्णजाम् ॥

Now this provision of law belongs somewhat to the previous period, but it represents the state of facts accurately even for this period with one exception. Formerly, by the Manu Smṛiti the Brahmin could marry Kshatriya, Vaiśya and Śūdra wives. Now the marriage of a Śūdra woman by a Brahmin or generally by the higher castes was prohibited. We have seen that Bāṇa had Pāraśava brothers and, therefore, such marriages were practised even as late as Bāṇa's father. Now the marriage of Śūdra women by all the three higher classes was prohibited. A Vaiśya could formerly marry a Vaiśya and a Śūdra wife, but now he had only one wife viz., his own caste woman. The Kshatriya could

* Is it possible that Sabkutria may be a distortion of Sukshatriya ?

marry still a Kshatriya and a Vaiśya woman, and a Brahmin could marry three. This is what is laid down by Vyāsa. But the remarkable thing is that the Smṛiti provides that a man must marry first a woman of his own caste and then marry a lower caste woman. Indeed, such seems to have been the general practice in this period which eventually led to the stoppage of marriage with other caste girls. Of course, among Brahmins, only those in affluent circumstances or in high position could get Kshatriya or Vaiśya wives. Ibn Khurdadba allows the privilege to Brahmins only who could marry a Kshatriya wife; but a Kshatriya also from the Smṛitis could marry a Vaiśya wife. The Brahmins could get Kshatriya wives as late as Rājaśekhara of the 10th century A.D. who had a Chāhamāna lady to wife. It may be noted that the Brahmin royal families of Kabul and Sind were, to all intent, Kshatriyas and were Brahmins still only in the fact that they could get Brahmin women still to wife, which the Kshatriyas could not. This privilege of marrying a woman of the lower caste in the Aryan varṇas could not but have had a wholsesome influence socially in bridging over the feeling of separateness caused by caste which did come over India in the next period when marriages became restricted to the same caste. Such marriages were feasible, it must be borne in mind, because the food of the three higher classes was still the same.

But the feeling of separateness must have begun to arise even then owing to the lower status that now began to be assigned to the progeny. The above quoted dictum of Vyāsa says that the progeny of the lower caste women was still of the higher caste. "A son born of her is not lower than a savarṇa." This was certainly the oldest law, a law which led to the present mixture of blood discernible in all classes. But the latest law prevailing in the 9th and 10th centuries was that progeny belonged to the caste of the mother. The intermediate step of assigning the progeny to a mixed caste which was neither that of the father, nor that of the mother must have led to many inconveniences and troubles. The progeny under the new rule would revert to the mother's caste and it would be cared for by the mother and her relations only.

This state of the altered status of the progeny, as has already been shown, is reflected in many inscriptions of the time.

Having described caste in its racial or matrimonial aspect we will now go on to describe caste in the 9th and 10th centuries in its occupational aspect. And here, as in marriage so in profession, Brahmins were at liberty to take to professions of the lower castes in addition to their own peculiar profession, viz., the priestly. They were particularly soldiers and government officers of high as well as low rank. The Brahmins, no doubt, still kept the van in the professions of learning. Thus the merchant Sulaiman, both in corroboration of and in addition to what Ibn Khurdadba has recorded says "in all these kingdoms the nobility is considered to form but one family. It is the same with learned men and physicians. They form a distinct caste and the profession never goes out of it." (Ell. I. p. 6). Abu Zaid says "There are men devoted to religion and science called Brahmins. They have also their poets who live at the court of their kings, astronomers, philosophers, diviners. Among them, are diviners and jugglers who perform most astonishing feats. These observations are specially applicable to Kanauj, a large country forming the empire of Jurz." (ditto p. 10). This shows that Brahmins followed the most varied professions of intellect and that Brahmins of Kanauj or rather Northern India were still ahead of the Brahmins of India as in the days of Bāṇa. Al-Masudi similarly records "Brahmins are honoured as the most illustrious and noble caste. Royalty is confined to one family. The positions of Vazir etc. are also hereditary." Thus Brahmins and Kshatriyas were usually proficient in letters and arms their respective professions. We may note, however, certain special features of the period. And first though religion and letters were the usual occupation of Brahmins and arms the occupation of Kshatriyas, there were many Kshatriyas who were devoted to letters. In as much as there was no objection to Kshatriyas studying the Vedas and the Śāstras, they often excelled in these branches of study and it is satisfactory to note that in all the leading Rajput kingly families there were found kings who were as expert in letters as in arms. Indeed, Mâharaj Amarsing of

Mewad was right when he said "it is only since the establishment of the British Raj that the Kshatriyas have forgotten both śastras and śāstras. The most famous instances of learned kings were, undoubtedly, those of Munja and Bhoja of the Paramāra dynasty; but instances of learned kings were not uncommon in other lines during this period. King Harsha of Kashmir and Vinayāditya of the Eastern Chālukyas who was a mathematician and hence called Guṇaka are instances in point. It may be generally stated that the Rajputs of those days, whether kings or not, were usually men of education, men who knew the Vedic mantras and had learned the śāstras as the Valabhi kings especially are in their inscriptions described. Secondly, it appears from the Parāśara Smriti which may be assigned to this period of Hindu history, that during this period many Brahmins and Kshatriyas took to agriculture. Indeed, whereas in the past only Vaiśyas were agriculturists, in the mediæval period, Vaiśyas ceased to be agriculturists altogether and Brahmins and Kshatriyas took to agriculture along with the Śūdras who now were the principal cultivators. According to Buddhist and Hindu sentiment, agriculture is sinful because it requires the cutting of the ground and thus involves the killing of various insects. The Vaiśyas, therefore, during the Buddhist period becoming Buddhists abstained from agriculture altogether and left it to Śūdras. When Buddhism was supplanted and Hinduism prevalent, Brahmins and Kshatriyas probably for want of occupation took to agriculture in place of Vaiśyas. They, no doubt, found it difficult to reconcile their occupation with their religious sentiment and the Parāśara Smṛiti came to their aid. The provisions of this Smṛiti in this respect are worth quoting here in detail. "I will detail hereafter the work and the duty of men in the Kali age, which is common and possible to all the four Varṇas. The Brahmin who performs the six duties assigned to him, may also do the work of cultivation; but he should not yoke a bullock when thirsty, hungry or tired. He should cultivate half the day and then bathe and then perform the sacrifices enjoined with corn produced by himself in his own field." In this manner the duties of Brahmins are reconciled with the occupation of agriculture. The sin of agriculture is admitted. For, it is stated "what sin a destroyer of fish commits in one year, a plougher with the iron—mouthed rafter commits in one day." But the sin can be atoned for by sacrifice and gifts. "The cultivator who cuts trees, tears land and destroys vermin and insects is freed from the sin incurred, by Khala-sacrifice i.e. gifts to Brahmins at the barn here also prescribed, indeed, to the extent mentioned in the Chachanama or history of Sind. "Having given ⅙ to the king and 1/20 to gods and 1/30 to Brahmins the agriculturist is freed from all sins of agriculture." We have seen in our first volume that in Sind the Brahmins used to get 3 p.c. of land produce in gift and that Mahomed Kasim confirmed the payment even under Mahomedan rule (Vol. I. p. 182). In this way the profession of agriculture was allowed by the Kaliyuga Hindu Śastra to Brahmins. The same permission was granted to the Kshatriyas also. "A Kshatriya may also, similarly, cultivate and worship gods and Brahmins. So also a Vaiśya and a Śūdra may follow either agriculture, trade or some handicraft." Agriculture became, in fact, permitted to all the four varṇas and during this period Brahmins and Kshatriyas did, as a matter of fact, cultivate. The Kshatriyas, probably, split up in consequence into two classes the Rajputs *i.e.*, the kings and rulers and ordinary Kshatriyas or cultivators and land-holders. This distinction is probably reflected in the enumeration of the seven castes, recorded by Ibn Khurdadba and, indeed, continues among the Marathas of the Deccan.

As the profession of agriculture which mainly belonged to the Śūdras was allowed now to Brahmins and Kshatriyas and was actually practised by them, so the profession of arms which mainly belonged to the Kshatriyas was allowed to be shared by the Brahmins and the Vaiśyas. The provision of Manu Smriti is explicit on this point. शस्त्रं द्विजातिभिर्ग्राह्यं धर्मो यत्रोपरुध्यते thus restricting the permission to occasions of danger to religion. But the Vasistha Smriti adds प्राणत्राणे वर्णसंकरे वा ब्राह्मणवैश्यौ शस्त्रमाददीयाताम् । क्षत्रियस्य तन्नित्यमेव रक्षणाधिकारात् ॥ (Chapter 3). Here the word Dvija of the Manu Smriti is expanded into Brahmins, Kshatriyas and Vaiśyas and the further object of self-protection is added for the taking up of arms. Probably, it will be remembered that in Sind history we read that Chacha did not allow the Jāts to carry swords or to ride horses. Under the Rajputs during the Hindu period, the same prohibition must have obtained ; for, the practice had sanction of the Hindu Śāstras also, the Vaśistha Smṛiti embodying to our mind the prevailing practice of the period.

Certain provisions with regard to the occupation of selling are worth noticing, when a Brahmin in adversity takes to the Vaiśya profession of trading. He is not to sell salt, tila unless produced in his own fields by his own labour, honey, liquor, flesh, milk and its products and other minor articles too numerous to mention, (an old provision of Smṛiti law). It is to be noted that the sale of liquor was prohibited even to the Vaiśyas and was allowed not even to good Śūdras. The sale of milk and its preparations was prohibited to the three higher classes probably because it was a good article and to sell it was as heinous as to sell bad articles like liquor. But the sale of milk and its products curds and whey was allowed to be done by good Śūdras though not liquor*.

We may close this disquisition on caste by the remark of Al-Masaudi that the Hindus are distinct from all black people such as the Zanjis and others in point of intellect, government, philosophy, strength of constitution and purity of colour.

Having described caste we go on to describe the food of the people and the first thing that strikes us is that the Indians were little addicted to drink. The Brahmins as of old were total

* The prohibition of the profession of usury to Brahmins and Kshatriyas was of old standing ; but it is interesting to note that Vaśishtha lays down certain limits such as Dām Duppat and Dhān Tippat. It is difficult to understand the following provision which regulates interest according to caste, Practically even now there is a difference of interest charged to Brahmins and Śūdras but this is due to the greater credit of the former. Vaśistha says " a man should take interest per cent per mensem, two, three, four and five from the different varṇas ". But the rate of five per thirty, per month per cent mentioned further on, is monstrous and inconceivable even though charged to Śūdras who pay at present, at the utmost two per cent per month. This made usury reprehensible and Brahmins were properly prohibited from practising usury.

abstainers from all intoxicating liquors but even the Kshatriyas especially kings are described as such by Arab travellers. Al Masaudi writes "The Hindus abstain from drinking wine and censure those who consume it. If it can be proved of one of their kings that he has drunk wine he forfeits the crown, for he is not considered able to rule as his mind is affected" (Elliot, I p. 20). Ibn Khurdadba makes the strange observation that "the kings and people of Hind regard fornication lawful and wine as unlawful." Whatever may be said of the first part of the observation, the second is indeed creditable to the Indians. The Kshatriyas are not bound by religious precept to abstain from wine but it is a fact that most of them abstained and do now abstain from wine like the Śisodias of Mewad. With regard to the Kshatriyas, however, Sulaiman's observation that they were allowed three cups is strange. The Vaiśyas, then as now, were total abstainers though there must have been many exceptions.

Secondly, abstention from flesh, as the result of the great efforts of Harsha, the last Buddhist Emperor mentioned in Vol. I p. 13, was gradually gaining ground over the country. The Brahmins were generally abstainers from flesh though not quite completely. When Al Masaudi remarks that "they (Brahmins) do not eat the flesh of any animal," he spoke more of the recluses both Hindu and Buddhist or Jain than of the Gṛihasthas or house-holders, for, he further observes that both women and men wear yellow threads suspended round their necks like a baldrick to distinguish them from the other castes of India" (Elliot Vol. I, p. 10). Now Brahmins put on a thread but it is not yellow; while Buddhist and Jain recluses put on yellow clothes, and not threads. Whatever the explanation, it is clear that some Northern Brahmin subcastes still eat flesh. The provisions of later Smṛitis show that the Brahmins were not in the habit of using flesh generally; but Vyāsa observes that Brahmins invited to a Śrāddha or sacrifice must eat flesh, otherwise they would fall into perdition* It seems that in

*नाश्नीयाद्ब्राह्मणो मांसमनियुक्तः कथंचन । कतौ श्राद्धे नियुक्तो वा अनश्नन् पतति द्विजः ॥

sacrifices which were becoming rare and in Śrāddhas which were still performed, flesh was necessarily served not only among Kshatriyas but among Brahmins and Vaiśyas also. The next following Śloka provides flesh in Śrāddhas even for Vaiśyas.† But for a Brahmin and even a Kshatriya or Vaiśya there was a general prohibition to kill or to eat flesh. "A dvija who eats flesh unconsecrated or kills animals except for proper ceremonies falls into everlasting perdition." The Brahmins were further not to drink the milk of any animal but cow and she-buffalo, nor to eat onions and other bad vegetables. Of course, the general prohibition against beef and the flesh of larger animals like tigers was imperative on all, Brahmins, Kshatriyas, Vaiśyas and Śudras. The Chāṇḍālas or out-casts alone did not observe this prohibition and hence were treated as out-casts. They were compelled to live outside towns and villages and were to walk in town streets so carefully as not only not to touch the other Hindus but not even to throw their shadows upon them as evidenced by the various precepts in the Smṛitis.

It may be further stated that the different higher castes had then no objection to take food at one another's house. And the privilege extended even to some higher grades of the Śūdra population. Not only is there no provision against a Brahmin eating with a Kshatriya or Vaiśya, but the Vyāsa Smṛiti specially allows such practice धर्मेणान्योन्यभोज्यान्ना द्विजास्तु विदितान्वयाः. The only condition here is one must know the family with whom one eats to be a Dvija family. And the Smṛiti allows the taking of food by Dvijas with the following Śūdras viz., barbers, friends of the family, coparceners, servants and cowherds. नापितान्वय-मित्रार्धसीरिणो दासगोपकाः । शूद्राणामप्यमीषां तु भुक्त्वान्नं नैव दुष्यति ॥ This free intercourse in food like the restricted intercourse in marriage among the different castes during the mediæval period can not but have had a good effect in strengthening the sense of unity in the different portions of the Hindu society Of course, the food of the people was still the same, flesh being

† मृगयोपार्जितं मांसमभ्यर्च्य पितृदेवताः । क्षत्रियो द्वादशोनं तत्क्रीत्वा वैश्योऽपि धर्मतः ॥

still allowed to be eaten by Brahmins and hence there was no hitch in this intercourse in food.

We now go on to describe the dress of the people of India; and on this point our informants are the Arab travellers alone; for we have no other material to rely upon except sculpture on ancient temples which it is difficult to interpret. But the writings of these travellers are detailed and afford reliable evidence and they tend to show that in Sind and in Multan and to the west-ward of these, under the influence of the Arab rulers dress had changed. Al Istakhari says that the dress of the people (in Mansura) is like that of the people of Irak, but the dress of their kings resembles that of the kings of India in respect of the hair and the tunic (Elliot I, p. 27), a statement repeated by Ibn Haukal who substitutes trousers for hair only. Regarding the people of the Balhara territory from Kambaya to Saimur, the latter states "the people both Hindu and Moslem wear the same dress and let their hair grow in the same fashion; they use fine muslin garments on account of heat. The men in Multan dress in the same way" (Elliot I, p. 39). Here the difference is not clear from the dress of people of Mansura (Sind): but apparently no trousers were worn and people in the Deccan and the Panjab continued the use of the two dhoties or pieces of cloth of ancient times. In Mekran (Persian border) all wear short tunics except the merchants who wear shirts and cloaks of cotton like the men of Irak and Persia" (Ditto).

With regard to ornaments the Indians were as fond of them as in previous centuries. The Arab travellers in particular were impressed by the ear ornaments of the kings. Abu Zaid says, "The kings of India are accustomed to wear ear-rings of precious stones mounted in gold." These certainly were worn in the lobes of the ears and were in use down to the days of the Peshwas, witness the large ear-rings shown in the ears of Nana Phadanavis in his picture. To put on golden ear-rings in the ear appears to have been prescribed to every Hindu householder (धारयेद्रुक्मकुंडले–वशिष्ठ) and the custom still prevails in the Panjab and elsewhere, "They also wear necklaces of great value formed of the most precious red and green stones." Big green stones necklaces may still be seen round the necks of

Indian princes. "Pearls, however, are held in the highest esteem and are greatly sought after" (Elliot I, p. 11), which is still true of Indian princes and rich merchants. Pearl necklaces were worn by both men and women. The story of a pearl necklace purchased by a Kanauj emperor of the previous Varmā dynasty, told in a drama of Rājaśekhara, is well known. We may record here finally our view that the nose ornament usually made of pearls worn by married Indian women, the natha, does not find mention in any work of the time and is according to our view an ornament borrowed from the Mahomedans hereafter.

It is indeed strange that Abu Zaid records "most of the princes of India when they hold a court allow their women to be seen by the men who attend it, whether they be natives or foreigners". (Elliot I, p. 11). This might have been true of the princes of Malabar and south, for there is and was no pardah with them. It can not be said to be true of the courts of northern kings, for pardah prevailed there from of old. Probably the traveller was misled by the presence of the female attendants of the kings who always attended upon him even in open court as described by Bāṇa. The king's wives and queens could not have appeared in open court in the north of India or even in Mahārāshtra. In other castes than Kshatriya, pardah is not so strict even in northern India, though it is partially observed at present even by them, except among the Śūdras. It is a mistake to suppose that pardah was introduced in India by the Mahomedans. For we find it recorded in the Rāmāyaṇa that the appearance of women in the open was not objectionable at the time of festivity, of sacrifice and of great calamity. This constituted the difference between the Indian and the Mahomedan pardah and there was then no absolute bar to women appearing in public in India.

Another popular misconception has to be noted here and that is that child marriages in India date from the time of the Mahomedan conquest. Women in India began to be married, it is believed, when quite young *i. e.,* of seven and eight years of age in order to prevent them from being seized by lustful Mahomedan conquerors. But the absurdity of this view would appear clear if one considers the fact that marriage could never have been a bar to the lust of conquerors; and young women could be seized whether they were married or unmarried. Historically considered, it appears that child marriages came into vogue in India during this second sub-period and not in Mahomedan times. We have already stated in Vol. I from the description of Rājyaśri's marriage by Bāṇa, that girls until the days of Harsha were grown up at the time of marriage. There is no direct evidence to show that early marriages began to be introduced thereafter. But this may be inferred from the fact that Smṛitis like those of Parāshara and Vyāsa which are undoubtedly later Smṛitis and belong to this period prescribe marriage for girls from 8 to 10 years of age. The text of Pārāśara is well known. विवाहयेदष्टवर्षामेवं धर्मो न हीयते ।. Vyāsa also recommends the marriage of girls who still wear lower cloth only *i. e.*, a girl at marriage should be so young that she has not yet taken the upper cloth to cover her shoulders. The very meaning of the word *Gauri* was changed. It meant according to Amarakosha a girl who is not yet matured, but according to Parāshara Gauri meant a girl of eight. It is, therefore, nearly certain that early marriages came into vogue about this period; why they did so it is somewhat difficult to explain. But as we have long ago stated elsewhere, this was a result of the revulsion of feeling against Buddhism and especially Buddhist nuns. A grown up unmarried girl had a right to become a nun according to the Buddhist canon. To effectually prevent women from becoming nuns, girls began to be married when they were 8 or 10 years old even in the north, a custom probably borrowed from the south, where among the Non-Aryans such marriages seem to have been a rule from ancient days. A comparison between the older Smṛitis together with the ancient Gṛihya Sūtras which prescribe consummation immediately after marriage and the later Smṛitis show that this change must have come over the Indian society after Bāṇa who describes that consummation took place in the case of Rājyaśri's marriage immediately after marriage. Whether the Kshatriyas adopted early marriages or not it is difficult to determine. We gather from poetical descriptions of Bilhaṇa and others that they did not; but from historical instances it appears that they too now and then married girls when very young. The marriage of girls before maturity began certainly to be insisted upon from this period. The Vyāsa Smṛiti lays down that the bestower of a matured girl incurs the sin of Bhrūṇahatyā. But it does not seem that in former times maturity was ever considered a defect in the girl. From Kālidāsa's poems or from the Gṛihya Sūtras girls at the time of marriage could not but have been matured. The Śakuntala described by Kālidāsa in his drama must have been a matured girl and her father Kaṇva Ṛishi never thought that he had been incurring the sin of Brūṇahatyā. But when this idea gained ground, marriage of girls even before the twelfth year must have been thought advisable for fear of girls becoming matured before marriage. The Parāśara Smṛiti even invented conventional maturity as opposed to real, when it laid down that a girl above 10 years of age was to be considered a rajasvalā or matured girl.

The enforced widow-hood of women among the higher castes was an ancient custom in India and must have been the rule during this period also when the Hindu religious feelings were even stronger. The combination of the two customs of early marriage and enforced widow-hood gives birth to that unfortunate class of beings the child-widows and these might have begun to increase now as child marriages spread, but the provision of the Smṛitis that child widows if unmatured might be remarried must have prevented the evil from being then felt. This provision was also abrogated later on in the third sub-period by a Kalivarja text.

The custom of Sati too is an old custom and it must have been in force during this period also. The custom of loyal servants of kings sacrificing their lives for their masters and burning themselves when they died noticed in Vol. I is also noticed by Arab travellers during this period. Abu Zaid records a peculiar custom. "Some of the kings of India when they ascend the throne have a quantity of rice cooked and served on banana leaves. When the king has eaten some of the rice, he gives it to some of his companions who join him of their own free will. Each in his turn approaches, takes a small quantity and eats it. When the king dies or is slain, all those who have taken rice with the king are expected to burn themselves on the very day of the king's decease."

The practice of men committing suicide in sacred places especially when they were old is noticed by Arab writers also during this period. We have already recorded the instance of king Dhanga drowning himself in the Ganges at Prayāga recorded in an inscription of the Chandellas. Abu Zaid records "When a person, either man or woman, becomes old and the senses are enfeebled, he begs some one of his family to throw him into fire or to drown him in water" (Elliot I, p. 10). "In the states of the Balhara and in other provinces of India one may see men burn themselves on a pyre. This arises from the faith of India in metempsychosis." The later Arab writers speak of the famous tree at Prayāg from the top of which people used to throw themselves into the Ganges which shows that the myth is as old at least as the 10th century A. D. Such instances, however, must be rare, and except in these circumstances, suicide even among the Hindus was considered to be sinful. In India the practice obtains and then obtained of burning the dead as Arab travellers have also recorded. The days of mourning and the practice of lamenting are also very old and have been mentioned by these writers*

It must lastly be mentioned that the Indians always bore a high character for probity with foreigners from the Greeks of the fourth century B.C. down to the Arabs of the 10th century A.D. Speaking of the people between Kambaya and Naharwala (modern Gujarat), Al Idrisi writes :—"The Indians are naturally inclined to justice and never depart from it in their actions; their good faith, honesty and fidelity to their engagements are well known and they are so famous that people flock to their country from every side and hence the country is flourishing."

---

* The people of India burn their dead and do not raise any tombs, The Mussalmans in Hind and Sind like Indians do not give way to long lamentations. (Elliol. I, p. 89).

We may also quote Al Idrisi on the food and kind-heartedness of the people of Gujarat typical of the character of people of other parts of India as well. " The inhabitants of Naharwala live upon rice, peas, beans, buricats, lentils, mash, fish and animals that have died a natural death ; for they never kill winged or other animals. They have a great veneration for oxen whom they inter after death. When their animals are enfeebled by age and are unable to walk they, free them from all labour and provide them with food without exacting any return."

NOTE.

SMRITI LAW OF ANULOMA MARRIAGE

It is necessary to show how different Smritis treated the progeny of marriages with lower caste women and thus to see how gradually its position declined eventually leading to the stoppage of Asavarṇa Anuloma marriages; of course, we are treating here of Anuloma marriages only which were allowed in historic times and were actually in vogue. To begin with Manu, we have the following provisions :—

स्त्रीष्वनन्तरजातासु द्विजैरुत्पादितान् सुतान् ।
सदृशानेव तानाहुर्मातृदोषविगर्हितान् ॥ ६–१०
अनन्तरासु जातानां विधिरेष सनातनः ।
द्व्येकान्तरासु जातानां धर्म्यं विद्यादिमं विधिम् ॥ ७, १०
ब्राह्मणाद्वैश्यकन्यायामम्बष्ठो नाम जायते ।
निषादः शूद्रकन्यायां यः पारशव उच्यते ॥ ८,१०

"From wives belonging to the immediately next Varṇa sons of Dvijas are treated as equal, though they are blemished by the defect of their mothers. This rule is of long standing with regard to sons born of immediately next Varṇa women. And the proper rule with regard to wives who are one or two Varṇas lower should be known as follows. The son of a Brahmin from a Vaiśya wife is Ambashṭha, while from a Śudra wife is a Nishada also called Pāraśava." This was the state of law with regard to progeny of mixed marriages in ancient times *i.e.*, down to the beginning of the Christian era. Let us see how it changed later on.

First with regard to Śudra wife, Yājñavalkya does not ban her but expresses his own opinion that a Śudra wife should not be taken. Such marriages presumably continued to take place, though rarely, down to the days of Bāṇa of 600 A.D. as he speaks of two Pāraśava brothers of himself. Later Smṛitis, however, entirely put a ban on the Śudra wife. Thus Vyāsa says—

उद्वहेत् क्षत्रियां विप्रो वैश्यां च क्षत्रियो विशाम् ।
न तु शूद्रां द्विजः कश्चिन्नाधमः पूर्ववर्णजाम् ॥

And the epithet 'husband of a Śudra wife' (वृषलीपति) became contemptuous in Smritis and he was treated as unfit to talk with or dine with; see Parāśara असंभाष्योऽह्यपांक्तेयः स विप्रो वृषलीपतिः ।

Secondly and principally, with regard to the Kshatriya wife married by Brahmins, we have seen such marriages down to the 10th century A.D. Rājaśekhara poet mentioning his own wife to be a Chāhamāna lady. The progeny of such marriages according to the Manu Smṛiti was a Brahmin. But Yājnavalkya treats it as 'Murdhāvasikta' a new word, not found in Manu, विप्रान्मूर्द्धावसिक्तो हि क्षत्रियायां विशः स्त्रियाम् । अम्बष्ठो शूद्रयां निषादो जातः पारशवोऽपि सः He does not recognise the Anantara and Ekāntara wife distinction. His first rule is सवर्णेभ्यः सवर्णासु जायन्ते हि सजातयः । That clearly says "only from the same caste women can same caste progeny be born."

Later on there is a distinct change in the Vyāsa Smṛiti "विप्रवद्विप्रविन्नासु क्षत्रविन्नासु क्षत्रवत् । जातकर्माणि कुर्वीत ततःशूद्रासु शूद्रवत् ॥ वैश्यासु विप्रक्षत्राभ्यां ततः शूद्रासु शूद्रवत् ॥ The meaning is not quite clear. The third line, however, makes it clear that the progeny of Brahmins and Kshatriyas from Vaiśya wives was treated alike. And hence it seems that the progeny of Kshatriya wives from Brahmins was treated not as Mūrdhāvasikta but as Kshatriya. This is 'no doubt' seemingly contradicted by the following further śloka of Vyāsa: ऊढायां हि सवर्णायामन्यां वा काममुद्वहेत् । तस्यामुत्पादितः पुत्रो न सवर्णात् प्रहीयते ॥ But this is conditional on the man marrying first a wife of his own caste. The Auśanasa Smriti which is solely concerned with this subject of mixture of caste, distinctly states:—नृपायां विधिना जातो विप्रान्नृप इति स्मृतः "A son born of a Kshatriya woman from a Brahmin by a legal marriage is a Kshatriya." A previous śloka mentions a new distinction which is worth mentioning but which cannot properly be understood. विधिना ब्राह्मणः प्राप्य नृपायां तु समन्त्रकम् । जातः सुवर्ण इत्युक्तः सानुलोमाद्विजः स्मृतः ॥ It seems that when a special rite was performed at the time of the marriage, the son born of a Kshatriya woman from a Brahmin was called a *Suvarna* Brahmin. What rites and ceremonies were preformed is not clear. But the professions assigned to the *Suvarna* Brahmin show him to be not a Brahmin. The next śloka in the Smṛiti gives his durties as follows:— अश्वं रथं हस्तिनं च वाहयेद्वा नृपाज्ञया । सेनापत्यं च भैषज्यं कुर्याज्जीवेच्च वृद्धिषु ॥ It may be taken that this Smriti reflects the latest phase of mixed marriages. And according to it the son of a Kshatriya wife from a Brahmin was generally a Kshatriya; and naturally the son of a Vaiśya wife from a Kshatriya was a Vaiśya, as expressly stated in the śloka नृपाज्जातोऽथ वैश्यायां गृह्यायां विधिना सुतः । वैश्यवृत्त्या हि जीवेत क्षत्रधर्मं न कारयेत् ॥

The marriage of a lower class woman to a higher class male was generally a luxury and Brahmins unless they were very learned men or great officers must rarely have got Kshatriya wives.

The marriage of a Kshatriya with a Vaiśya wife was, however, not uncommon. In fact, the rule prescribed by the Vyāsa Smriti "that after first marrying a wife of one's own caste one may for pleasure marry a lower caste wife" was generally observed among the Kshatriyas. Their first wife was always a Kshatriya but the second was generally a Vaiśya woman. I was told in Jaipur that the practice led to the second wife being called Gūjari. She was generally from the healthy and strong Jāt or Gūjar castes and these may be taken from this very fact to represent the real Vaiśyas in India to whom was entrusted the krishi and the gorakshya of the country.

CHAPTER III.

RELIGIOUS CONDITION.

"In India" says one Arab traveller of the 10th century "there are forty-two religions." Perhaps the word forty-two signifies only many. Al-Idrisi of the 11th century A.D. gives more details. "Among the principal nations of India there are forty-two sects. Some recognize the existence of a Creator but not of Prophets, while others deny the existence of both. Some acknowledge the intercessory powers of graven stones and others worship holy stones on which butter and oil is poured. Some pay adoration to fire and cast themselves into flames. Others adore the sun and consider it the creator and director of the world. Some worship trees; others pay adoration to serpents, which they keep in stables and feed, and consider this to be meritorious. Lastly, there are some who give themselves no trouble about any kind of devotion and deny everything." Such is the description of the religious state of the country given by Arab travellers who were the staunchest believers in one God and the severest unbelievers in idol worship.

It was natural for the Arabs to believe that there were many religions in India. But they all constituted the different modes of worship recognized by the one great religion which has been given the name of Hinduism. We must, therefore, say that the Arabs were wrongly impressed; for, there was no conflict or opposition in any of the different modes of worship enumerated above. Strangely enough, it can be said of this time than of any other time past or future that India was universally under one religion. Different gods such as Śiva, Vishṇu, Āditya, Devī and Gaṇesha were indeed worshipped, indeed even some trees and animals; yet all these kinds of worship were phases of one religion and had no ill-feeling or animosity among themselves. And the Vedic religion was considered supreme above all these and was supposed to sanction and countenance all these different worships. As a matter of fact, therefore, there was one religion in India at this time. For Buddhism had been supplanted and had vanished from the land except in Magadha, Jainism was yet a small religion and had not yet made extensive conquests though it was slowly spreading in the south. Hinduism flourished throughout the land and recognized every worship from the Agni worship of the Vedas down to the worship of stones and trees but specially of the five deities of modern Hinduism.

The Purāṇas now were re-edited and amplified and were devoted to the praise of some one of the five gods. Śiva, however, was a favourite deity with the rising kingly families; though as in olden times the son might change his deity and be a devotee of Vishṇu or the Sun. The genealogy of the Pratihāra emperors as given in their documents clearly brings this out and shows that the favourite deity changes almost at every step in the pedigree. While the first is Parama Vaishṇava, the next is Parama Māheshvara and the third is Bhagavatī-Bhakta and the fourth is Parama Āditya-Bhakta. It seems certain from this that there was no sectarian jealousy yet, between the devotees of the different gods and consequently among the gods themselves.

The kings and their queens, their ministers and their rich subjects delighted in building temples to their favourite deities. Such temples must have arisen over the whole country and the presents brought to these temples gradually accumulated riches in them which excited the cupidity of foreigners. Nay, even the Arabs of Multan allowed the worship of the famous Sun-god there for greed of the presents which the worship constantly brought from worshippers from over the whole of India. The Sun temple of Multan was famous and it is interesting to note that the powerful Pratihāra emperors of Kanauj could have very easily taken Multan which was, so to speak, an abutment on their territory, had it not been for the bigotry of the Hindus.

The Arabs when opposed by greater numbers, it is recorded by Arab writers, "threatened to break the idol and the Hindus retired." This speaks of the great reverence in which the idol of the Sun at Multan was held by the people of India.

The whole country was covered over with temples and idols. In fact, both Aryan and non-Aryan civilizations had joined hands in evolving this idolatry. Śiva, Vishṇu and Āditya were Aryan deities and Gaṇapati and Śaktī or Bhagawatī were probably non-Aryan deities. To these were added the worship of uncouth stones,. trees and serpents. And the idolatry was rampant not only among the Aryans but the non-Aryans down to the lowest strata of society. It is strange that the Hindus with their high philosophic minds did not penetrate to the essence of the principle of idol-worship which is allowed by Hinduism. As just stated, they believed in the inherent power of stones and trees and idols to do good or to do mischief. As stated in our Vol. I p. 102 an idol is after all an image of the highest Original and there can be no more absurd superstition than a belief in the supernatural power of idols, irrespective of man's devotion or high spiritual elevation. The deity is not in the idols but in man's own head and heart and an idol cannot effect wonders by itself. Idolatry is permitted in Hinduism on the principle that the idols help in the concentration of the devotional mind towards God. In fact, the ceremony of *Prāṇapratishṭha* by Vedic mantras is necessary for the invocation of the deity in the image. There is also a ceremony of Prāṇa-visarjana and by appropriate Vedic hymns the deity invoked may be sent back. It really strikes us, livng as we do in this different age, as pitiable ignorance of the Hindus of those days that they should have returned without seizing Multan for the fear that the idol of the Sun would be broken by the Moslems. The Hindus could have asked the priests of the idol to make Prāṇa-visarjana by appropriate mantras and then the image would not have been more than an ordinary stone or an ordinary block of wood. After conquering Multan and driving away the Moslems, a new idol could have been made and installed with the due ceremony of Pranapratishthā. Such ignorant feelings, however, continued to increase and how advantage of them was taken by the idol-breakers we shall have to relate at length in our third volume.

It is not necessary to mention all the famous idols of India of this day. The Skanda Purāṇa, Nāgara-khand, chapter 107, gives a list of 68 famous temples of the great god Śiva all over India including those of Nepal and Kālanjar, Prabhāsa and Ujjain. There were many Vishṇu temples also and the Sun-temple of Multan; the temple of Jwālāmukhi Devī in the Kangra valley and the Vindhyavāsinī at Ghazipur. Benares was the most sacred spot with the temple of Vishvanātha; (strangely enough, the Skanda Purāṇa list does not give this name for the Benares idol but merely calls it Mahādeva).

The worship of these different deities developed new rules and rituals and new philosophies and these were embodied in what were called Āgamas which gradually assumed precedence even over the Vedic rules and ritual. The growth of Āgamas probably led in future years to the rivalry between the different worships which so disfigures them in later centuries. The Śivāgama was most studied at this time and its professors were most respected as inscriptions testify. These professors were usually Śūdra ascetics. The Hindu mind, both Aryan and non-Aryan, is peculiarly susceptible to the feeling of admiration for asceticism. Where thousands run after the pleasures of life, the few who inflict upon themselves untold sufferings only for the sake of their merit are admired in India very highly. It is perhaps a cynical observation to make that the admiration of the people keeps up asceticism in India more than the real belief in the unseen merit of it. For, we actually find that in the present age when new enlightenment has permeated the Hindu mind, the admiration for asceticism has sensibly declined and the number of ascetics too, along with it. Whatever that may be, Tapas and Sanyāsa have always held a foremost place in the Hindu mind and Jainism and Buddhism too made Tapas and Sanyāsa their own but respectively. In the matter of Tapas and Sanyāsa the Aryans first tried to keep the non-Aryans out of them and the

Sūdras were not allowed to perform austerities or to become Sanyāsis. But the triumph of Buddhism and Jainism made the way easy for them. After the supplanting of Buddhism, Hindusim did not apparently stop them. The Vedic Tapas and Sanyāsa were indeed prohibited, but those prescribed by the Āgamas of the different deities were now freely open to them. The devotees of Śiva especially were probably generally non-Aryans and they lived in mathas built for them and performed austerities of various kinds. In fact, in the matter of physical suffering the non-Āryan Śūdra could easily beat the Āryan Brahmin bred in a more delicate way. These Tapasvis, therefore, multiplied and filled the land. They could be met with in cities and towns as well as in jungles. Sulaiman, the Arab traveller, mentions an ascetic who stood facing the Sun in the market of Multan for sixteen years in the same position without being 'melted by the heat.' He describes the jungle ascetics in this manner. "In India there are persons who according to their profession wander in the woods and mountains and rarely communicate with the rest of the mankind. Sometimes they have nothing to eat but herbs and fruits of the forest. Some of them go about naked" (Elliot I).

These tapasvis were ranged into different sects according to the Āgamas they followed. The Āgamas, at least the Pāncharātra Āgama, is as old as the Mahābhārata. But their growth and their greater sanctity belongs probably to this age. There was the Śivāgama and the Saurāgama also and the Vināyaka Āgama and the Devī Āgama while the Vaishṇava Āgama developed out of the Pāncharātra. It is necessary to study these different Āgamas to ascertain their age and their relative importance. But the subject is vast and we leave it here without going into further details.

The Vedic house-holder, sacrificing morning and evening to the house-hold fire, was still alive though his number was declining. The Brahmins and the Kshatriyas alone seem to have kept up this worship and we do find in Sulaiman's description the worship mentioned. Agnihotra, however, was too troublesome to be long practised and the worship of the holy stones representng Śiva and Vishṇu which gradually was now introduced into almost every household left the other worship neglected. The later Smṛitis still speak of the house-holder sacrificing in fire and the Kalivarjya prohibition which finally stopped Agnihotra belongs to the third sub-period.

Indeed, the sacrifice to fire with inanimate offerings had still the reverence and the sanctity which belonged to it from of old. Even the kings performed such sacrifices when solemn acts were to be performed. We find from inscriptions of this period that the kings often made the grant of a village with the ceremonies of bathing, worshipping Śiva and sacrificing to the holy fire. Strangely enough, when such grants are made to Jain temples, even then the donor king goes through these Vedic formalities. They were looked upon even by the Jains as useful in giving a greater binding force. Vedic religion thus was the religion of the Hindus at least in profession and was respected. The practices of idolatry under the different Āgamas, however, were in greater vogue and even the Brahmins and the Kshatriyas followed the general trend. The performance of the daily ablutions and of Sandhyā was probably still continued while Śrāddhas and other Vedic religious ceremonies were respectfully performed as before, with the difference that flesh was no longer served at Śrāddhas or served only at the houses of Khsatriyas.

The Arabs were struck with the firm belief of the Hindus in metempsychosis. In fact, this creed is peculiar to the Hindus and the wonder is that it has remained unshaken throughout all the changes in philosophical thought. That the soul is everlasting and that it migrates from body to body, even a vegetable body, has been believed in by the Vedic Aryas, the Buddhists, the Jainas and the Hindus too, whatever be the philosophical system they adhere to, Dvaita or Advaita ; and both the orthodox and the unorthodox, the Hindus and the Buddhists have utilised their belief in metempsychosis to inculcate high principles of morality. The punishment for sin and the reward for merits were sure to overtake the soul in the next life if not in this and this fear, it cannot but be said to the credit of it, made the Hindu society moral, even more moral than other societies in the world. We have already quoted the testimony of Arab writers which goes to prove the honesty, justice and truthftulness of the Hindus which made it so pleasant to deal with them.

The genarality of the people abstained from drink. The Brahmins were total abstainers and it is indeed creditable to Brahmins that they were total abstainers from the most ancient times and while the rest of the world was immersed in drink. The kingly family too abstained totally from drink, from the evidence of the Arab travellers supported by the known example of the Guhilots of Mewad. This is indeed still more creditable that being placed at the head of power the kings abstained from drink totally. Such self-abnegation in power is rarely witnessed in history. The ordinary Kshatriyas were temperate in drink and took *three* cups of wine only ! ! ! The Vaiśyas were probably total abstainers. The religious precept of the Smṛitis is that Brahmins, Kshatriyas and Vaiśyas should not drink liquor (तस्माद् ब्राह्मणराजन्यौ वैश्यश्च न सुरां पिबेत्). But the heinous sin or mahāpātaka of Surāpāna (liquor-drinking) was prescribed for the Brahmin only (नित्यं सुरा ब्राह्मणानाम्), and was visited with the most drastic punishment. Śūdras and others drank for we have evidence in inscriptions that liquor was manufactured and was a good source of revenue. But the example of the higher classes must have acted beneficially on the people generally and hence the drink habit in India was within reasonable bounds.

With regard to flesh-eating, the state of things was perhaps contrary to the above. The Vaiśyas and many Śūdras who had been Buddhists had abjured flesh; and many Brahmins and Kshatriyas under the influence of the revived doctrine of Ahiṁsā. But the Vedic religion did not generally prohibit flesh though it did certain kinds of it; and the performance of Śrāddhas which was a principal part of that religion and which under revived Vedic feeling of Hinduism were again performed with great respect (the Buddhists and the Jainas had derided Shrāddhas) required the preparation of flesh-food for the propitiation of the *pitṛis* (manes). Śrāddhas were, therefore, the opportunities when flesh was required to be eaten. A Smṛiti text declares that a Brahmin who declines to eat flesh at Shrāddhas will go to perdition. There are texts that Vaiśyas who had no way open to them of procuring flesh might buy it of Kshatriyas who could obtain it by hunting. Brahmins, except for sacrifices, could not kill animals. The result thus was that while the highest classes, Brahmins and Kshatriyas, who were orthodox followers of Vedic religion ate flesh, the Vaiśyas and many men of other castes totally abstained from flesh-eating. The Brahmins eventually, after the second sub-period, divided into two classes the flesh-eaters and the non-flesh-eaters ; and thus began the ramification of caste into sub-castes.

The influence of Ahiṁsā gathered strength by and by and the Jain religion which has put Ahiṁsā in the forefront of its principles seems to have gathered strength hereafter. In the second sub-period it was not, however, a progressing religion though we find, in Southern Māhārashtra, Jainism spreading not only among Vaiśyas who were always, for reasons inexplicable, prone to receive Ahiṁsā religions, but also among the agricultural population. Even some of the Rāshtrakūta kings were devotees of Jain saints. The Jain pandits now used the Sanskrit language itself for disputations and often defeated the followers of Pūrva-Mīṃānsā in them. This proficiency of the Jains in Sanskrit culminated, as we shall see in the third sub-period, when Hemachandra the greatest pandit of the Jainas became the Rajaguru of Kumārapāla. But it does not appear that Gujarat was yet under the influence of Jainism. Inscriptions in Gujarat still speak of the influence of Śiva worship which was the predominant worship of this period. A history of the spread of Jainism in the different parts of India will be very interesting but in the absence of it, the above seems to us to be the condition of that religion during this period. We speak with great hesitation, but we think that Jainism was spreading in Southern Maratha country at this time and thence it went in Gujarat into the third sub-period (1000 to 1200 A.D.) of our history.

Of course, Śiva worship was most predominant in those days. The Rajput families, almost all of them, which established powerful kingdoms at this time were worshippers of Śiva. We have seen that the Guhilots, the Chāhamānas, the Rāshtrakūtas were Śiva worshippers. The Chāvadas were also Śiva worshippers though Jains believe that they were followers of their religion. The Paramāras, the Haihayas and the Chandellas were also worshippers of Śiva and have left stupendous Śiva temples which still excite admiration. The Pālas of Bengal were known as Buddhists but they also built temples to Śiva. The Imperial Pratihāras alone are described as sometimes Parama Śaivas and Parama Vaishṇavas and even Parama Bhagavatī Bhaktas. Thus almost all the Rajput kingly families were worshippers of Śiva. Is Śiva worship more congenial to valour and the spirit of independence? It seems to be so. Śiva-worship compared with other worships seems to make people warlike and stubborn.

It would, indeed, be invidious to enter into the relative effects of the different systems of belief or worship comprized under Hinduism. It would, however, be necessary to remark that Śiva worship, absurd and even repulsive in its adoration of the linga, has been from ancient times connected with the highest religious philosophy, the Śvetāśvatara Upanishad identifying Śiva with Parabrahma. Consequently when the Hindus worship the god in its linga form, they never are conscious of any idea but of the deity being the highest god. Śiva woship originally in the Linga form was probably a non-Aryan worship; but the Aryans soon identified the god with the god Rudra of the Vedas and the Upanishads raised it to the position of the highest Parabrahma. It is no wonder thus that Śiva worship was and is more prevalent than any other worship. There was already, in the days of the Mahābhārata and the Vedantasūtra, a system of philosophy connected with the worship of Paśupati. When Lakulisa whose Śaiva philosophy seems to have been popular at this time flourished and preached we do not know. Śaṅkara has refuted his doctrines; but we do not find it on the wane at this time, Śaṅkara for himself was a real Vedantin and advocated all worships equally, though he refuted their special doctrines. But probably in response to the general sentiment, he appears to have worshipped the liṅga, a practice which his successors still follow. It is, hence, we believe, that

Śaṅkara's philosophy which was preached in the beginning of the ninth century had little influence on the prevalence of Śiva worship. As to Kumārila he was soon forgotten for he advocated Vedic sacrifices only. Yet he too in the sphere of the establishment of modern Hinduism had effected a great deal. It is necessary that our history should contain a short sketch of the life and preaching of both Kumārila and Śaṅkara, and though the materials are not very reliable, we treat this subject in the next chapter on the life and teaching of these great philosophers of the Mediæval Hindu age.

CHAPTER IV.

KUMĀRILA AND ŚANKARA.

A history of Mediæval Hindu India cannot be complete without a life of Kumārila and a life of Śaṅkara, the two great intellectual luminaries of the age who in fact laid the foundations and reared the superstructure respectively of modern Hinduism. Unfortunately we know so little about them that there is in fact nothing which can be said with certainty about their lives. Indeed even the fact is itself not undisputed that they belonged to this period since some place them in the centuries preceding the Chiristian era. We are, however, tolerably certain that they must have lived after Hiouen Tsang who makes no mention of them, and whose success as the most formidable exponent of Buddhism could not have happened after them. To add to the difficulty again they do not utter a word in their numerous writings about themselves; nor do they refer to any event, circumstances, or political entity of their time, so fully engrossed are they with the exposition of the respective doctrines of Jaimini and Bādarāyaṇa, in other words, of the Pūrva and Uttara Mīmānsā philosophies. Lastly, strangely engough, in spite of the fact that their writings and their labours wrought great changes in the ideas and feelings of the people yet no inscription, so far as we know, makes any mention of them, or their great triumphs in philosophical discussions during the tours which they are said to have, and which they most certainly must have, made throughout India. Handicapped as thus we are we will still make an attempt to place a few facts about their lives and their work before the curious reader from probabilities, from their writings and from traditions given in later works, most of which, however, are unreliable as history.

To commence with Kumārila then, his greatest achievement was that he established the sanctity of the Vedas and the efficacy of Vedic ritual, both of which were denied by Buddhism. In fact, he destroyed Buddhism in India by his philosophical writings. Even the Vedantists who subsequently triumphed under Śaṅkara admit this, for the Śāṅkaradigvijaya says that Śaṅkara, when he met Kumārila, as he was about to burn himself on a pyre, said "I know you are Guha or the god Kārtikeya incarnated on earth for the purpose of destroying the Buddhists who had opposed the religion of the Vedas".* There is a little sting even here by the Vedantist author. For he hints that as Śaṅkara was an incarnation of Śiva, the father of Guha, he could hence easily conquer the followers of Kumārila. One fact is, however, prominent from this verse. It is that it was Kumārila who finally conquered the Buddhists and not Śaṅkara as many suppose. As Harsha's rule was the last triumph of declining Buddhism, naturally the date of Kumārila falls about 50 years after Harsha and he is properly placed by most scholars about 700 A.D.

We may take this as the date of Kumārila burning himself on a pyre. We may take support in proof of this date the fact mentioned in our first volume that S. P. Pandit believed from the colophon in a manuscript of Uttararāmacharita that Kumārila was the teacher of Bhavabhūti who, as the Taranginị says, was a poet at the court of Yaśovarman of Kanauj. Yaśovarman's date falls about 700 A.D., and hence Kumārila must have lived before this period and died about 700 A.D. The meeting of Śaṅkara and Kumārila is a myth like the meeting of Kālidāsa and Bhavabhūti, or the supposed fight between Vikrama and Śātavāhana.

Having approximately settled Kumārila's date we will speak about his place of birth or at least his country. It is said somewhere that he was an Assamese and some believe him to be a Dravida Brahmin. It seems to us that he was a resident of the middle country or of Āryāvarta proper like Bāṇa whose uncles, as related by him in the Harshacharita, were great students of Mīmānsā. For he speaks in the Tantravārtika with great respect

---

* श्रुत्यर्थधर्मविमुखान् सुगतान् निहन्तुं ।
जातं गुहं भुवि भवन्तमहं नु जाने ॥

of Aryāvarta *and treats people outside as mlechha which he would not have done if had been an Assamese or a Dravida. He tries, no doubt, to show in one place that Dravida wordsare derived from Sanskṛit such as *chor* meaning corked rice, *tatar* road, or *vair* belly, yet this may have been owing to his communion with Dravida pandits. He certainly seems to have travelled much and known many languages. But if he had been a Dravida himself, he would not have treated the Dravida language as non-Aryan. We know that Dravida and Kanarese pandits of the time attempted to prove that these languages were derived from Sanskṛit. But Kumārila does not believe in it from this passage in the Tantravārtika (p. 157).

The non-Aryan languages which he mentions here are Pārasika, Barbara, Yavana and Romaka, exactly the languages which we have noticed in a note in Vol. I p. 354 which also supports the theory that Kumārila belonged to the 8th century. The Greek and Roman languages could not have been spoken in India later. It seems that during Buddhistic times, Buddhists from different countries beyond India came to India to study Buddhism or to visit holy places like Hiouen Tsang and hence people had occasion to speak here these languages. Kumārila indeed mentiones even interpreters or Dvaibhāshikas as he calls them (म्लेछैरवगतं पश्चादार्यैं द्वैभाषिकैः क्वचित्). He mentions the word Pīlu as meaning in Sanskrit a particular tree and in Mlechha language an elephant (यथापील्वादिशब्दानां वृक्षहस्त्यादिबोधने । समा विप्रतिपत्तिःस्यादार्यम्लेच्छादिबोधने). Now the word Phila in Persian really means an elephant. It seems, therefore, that Persian was really spoken and understood in India at that time*. We are thus led to believe in the truth of the tradition that Kumārila studied Buddhism under Buddhist masters themselves and thus came into contact with many and diverse foreigners. Of course, there was no treachery in this, as the tradition would make us believe. The Buddhists were not an exclusive people. They were indeed willing to teach intelligent Brahmin students if only they came to them. The

* हिमवद्विन्ध्यान्तरालकृष्णमृगचरणाद्युपलक्षित आर्यावर्तनिवासि-व्यतिरिक्त-बर्बरादिभाषागतम्लेच्छितत्वसमानाधिकरणापशब्द p. 198.

ranks of the Buddhists were constantly filled by recruits from Brahmins and Kshatriyas. And hence that Kumārila learned Buddhism by representing himself to be a Buddhist and thus practising deception upon his teachers need not be believed. He is supposed to have burnt himself in expiation of this sin viz. of deceiving his teachers. His manner of death was the usual manner of self-immolution with old devout Hindus of the time as we have already stated; and there was nothing strange in it when the practice of that age is considered. In later times, of course, this way of putting an end to one's own life became obsolete and people invented some explanation for this seemingly strange act of Kumārila.*

There is good reason to believe that Kumārila was not a Dākshinātya which was then the word used for a Māhārāshtra. For, he derides in a way the Māhārashtra practice of marrying one's own maternal uncles's daughter. That this unorthodox practice belonged to Mahārāshtra' is most certain. Nay, it comes from the Chandravansi Yādavas themselves whose descendants the Marathas are. But if Kumārila had been a Māhārāshtra, he would not have railed at the practice though he might have mentioned it. He would not have used the word तुष्यति in the line स्वमातुलसुतां प्राप्य दाक्षिणात्यस्तु तुष्यति (p. 129 ditto).

There is another observation which marks him as a Northern Central Indian man. The observation अन्तरीयोत्तरीये हि योषितामिव वाससी shows that he looks upon female dress as consisting ordinarily of the nether piece of cloth and of the upper one. Now the Deccan or more southern women always used and now use one long piece of cloth only which serves the purposes of both.

Lastly, he belongs to a state of society wherein Brahmins freely and willingly ate flesh. The remark पशुहिंसादसंबंधे यज्ञे तुष्यन्ति हि द्विजाः । तेभ्य एव हि यज्ञेभ्यः शाक्याः क्रुद्ध्यन्ति पीडया ॥. "Brahmins are glad when they get a sacrifice where animals are killed, while the same enrages and pains the Buddhists" shows

* It is curious to note that the instances of mlechha words in use in Sanskrit given by S'abara and also by Kumarila are *pika* (cuckoo), *nem* (half), *tāmarasa* (a lotus) and *sata* (a wooden pot). We recognise *nem* or *nim* as Persian for half but to what language do the other words belong? And *pika* and *tāmarasa* seemed to be original Sanskrit words !!!

that Brahmins were then glad to get opportunities of eating flesh. The Deccan and Southern Brahmins seem from Buddhist times to have disliked animal sacrifices, at least flesh-eating and hence the subsequent division of Brahmins into northern and southern or rather flesh-eaters and flesh-abstainers. Kumārila seems to have belonged to the former class.

These are the few straws which we have gathered in the sea of disquisition on Mīmāṅsā topics written by Kumārila in which a historian vainly seeks for some personal remarks or a remark that throws light on the social or political condition of the time. We will close with the one political observation which we came across. The question is being discussed whether the word Rājā in the Śruti dictum Rājā Rājasūyena Yajeta means a Kshatriya king only or any king *de facto*. Of course, the reply is that the provision applies to a Kshatriya king only as Kshatriyas alone have a right to rule. Kumārila says that the doubt arises from the fact that all the four castes are seen ruling in different kingdoms. (तच्च राज्यमविशेषेण चत्वारोऽपि वर्णाः कुर्वाणा दृश्यन्ते). दृश्यंते "are seen" is in the present tense and this shows that Kumārila lived in times when kingdoms were actually ruled by kings belonging to all castes. Now we can describe such a time. Up to the days of the Nandas the old rule obtained viz., that Kshatriyas alone should rule. Chandragupta was the first to break through this custom and hence the remark of the Purāṇas नन्दान्तं क्षत्रियकुलम्. From 300 B.C. up to Harsha and his immediate successors kings belonged to diverse castes. We know from Hiuen Tsang that in his days Harsha was a Vaiśya king, there were Kshatriya kings in Bhinmal, Valabhi, Mahārāshtra and Kānchi; Brahmin kings in Ujjain, Chichīto, and Maheśvarapura and a Śūdra king in Sind. We also find that from the days of Bappā Rāwal and other Rajput new dynasty founders, the old rule was revived and Rajputs alone were thought competent to rule. In the second sub-period of our history we find Rājputs alone ruling every where. Perhaps this Mimānsa controversy itself led to the assertion of this right by the Rājputs. The fact is noted by even Arab travellers. It seems, therefore, clear that Kumārila must have lived at least before 750 *i.e.*,650 to 750, as we have already supposed. He may have lived at an earlier period when even mlechhas ruled in India. But he does not mention such rulers. Indeed, our point here is that he could not have lived later. That he could not have lived before Hiouen Tsang we have already shown.

There is a further interesting remark of Kumārila here in which he differs from or explains away the Bhāshya and which we have not been able to understand, Śabara remarks on this point; ननु जनपदपुररक्षणमनुपजीवत्यपि क्षत्रिये राजशब्दमान्ध्राः प्रयुञ्जन्ते. "The Āndhras use the word king even with respect to a Kshatriya who does not rule." Now Kumārila observes here दाक्षिणात्य सामान्येनान्ध्राणामिति भाष्यकारेणोक्तम् "The Bhāshyakāra speaks of the Āndhras here as they are the same with Dākshinātyas". Now this probably means that in Kumārila's time it was the custom with the Dākshinātyas *i. e.*, Māhārāshtras to use the word Rāja with respect to a Kshatriya who is not ruling; and that he thinks that Śabara has spoken of the Āndhras inadvertently when he should have spoken of the Dākshinātyas. It is, indeed, difficult to know what the practice was in Mahārāshtra and what in Āndhra in the days of Śabara and those of Kumārila. In the latter country we know that there were Yavana kings at this time.

Such, then, is the little that can be or has been gathered by us from Kumārila's Tantravartika alone. It is possible that an industrious perusal of all his works might yield some more information. But the patience required is so great that the task is almost prohibitive. So far then we have been able to show that Kumārila must have worked from about 650 to 700 A.D. It is not possible to hold that he might have flourished in the second century B.C. for he quotes a verse from Kālidāsa himself सतां हि संदेहपदेषु वस्तुषु प्रमाणमन्तःकरणप्रवृत्तयः—(p. 133). Even if Kālidāsa be held to belong to 57 B.C., Kumārila can not go to the second century B. C. Kumārila belonged to the middle country or Āryāvarta. He studied Buddhism under Buddhist teachers. He had an acquaintance with several non-Aryan languages, Indian and foreign. He was a great dialectician and his greatest achievement was that he conquered the Buddhists in controversy and established the shaken belief in the revelation of the Vedas. In very old age, he probably burned himself on a pyre as a religious meritorious act.

Between Kumārila and Śaṅkara there must be supposed a pretty long period, a hundred years at least, to have elapsed. The greater renown and the greater success achieved by Śaṅkara was due to the fact that he appealed to some of the most pressing demands of the people. To be in union with the most absorbing sentiment of the time is the usual key to the success and highest popularity of new leaders of thought. Śaṅkara is often said by his opponents to be a Prachhanna Bauddha; *i.e.*, a Buddhist in disguise. This is probably said in reference to the Māyāvāda preached by him which was somewhat like the Vijṅanavāda or Nihilism of the Buddhists. Whatever may be said of his philosophical views, in two points, we think, Śaṅkara responded to the returned Buddistic feelings of the people. The Mīmāṅsā doctrines of Kumārila, no doubt, triumphed but they could not entirely remove the sentiment of the people against animal sacrifices; nor suppress the tendencies of the people towards Sanyāsa or renunciation of the world; a tendency which had characterised the Indian Aryans from the Upanishad times *i.e.*, for at least three thousand years. Kumārila established the revealed character of the Vedas; but at the same time his philosophy was entirely antagonistic to Sanyāsa and his method of worship was by Agnihotra and animal sacrifices. To a *Karmatha* the sacred fire was everything. A Sanyāsi was a nuisance, a sight offensive to him. It was, therefore, impossible that the popular sentiment should not return again in favour of Sanyāsa. It was impossible that people should again generally take to Agnihotra giving up their usual Puranic deities viz., Śiva, Vishṇu and Āditya and even Devī and Gaṇesha. The rebound of feeling against animal sacrifice was still greater. as Ahiṁsā was a doctrine which had been preached even by Aryanism or Vedantism before it was taken up by Buddhism and Jainism. And especially among those people who had given up flesh-eating, the doctrines of Kumārila could not have been popular. And a preacher arose from among such people viz., the Brahmins of the south who had given up flesh-eating for centuries before, a preacher of remarkable power of controversy and graceful diction and of great common sense, and political shrewdness who preached a new doctrine based on the Vedas themselves and the old Vedanta sūtras and who thus appealed to the people strongly because he advocated Sanyāsa and deprecated Agnihotra and animal sacrifices, who further, though he did not give it the highest place, sanctioned the worship of idols, of Śiva and Vishṇu, Āditya and Devī. This is the way in which Śaṅkara may be said to have revived Buddhism except its doctrine repugnant to Aryan feeling viz., denial of the sanctity of the Vedas and denial of caste distinctions. Śaṅkara may be said to have thus raised the whole super-structure of modern Hindustan on the foundations of the Veda laid by Kumārila. This is the reason why a pandit of the south gained renown and why he may be called in a sense a Buddhist in disguise.

The date of Śaṅkara and his native place are more certain than those of Kumārila. He is generally believed to have belonged to Kerala or Malabar and he was born in a family of Nambudri Brahmins. His birth-place is said to be Kāladi where a great temple has recently been raised to his memory. The date of his birth is traditionally given as Śaka 710 or 788 A.D. and this is extremely probable as his sphere of activity falls about a hundred years after the death of Kumārila. Some place both Kumārila and Śaṅkara in centuries preceding the Christian era and even carry them to about the 5th century B. C. taking Buddha himself again several centuries before his accepted date. We think all such theories upset the course of Indian history already settled with tolerable certainty, the sheet-anchor being Chandragupta's date fixed in conformity with Greek history at about 312 B. C. We shall, therefore, not try to refute such theories at any length and content ourselves with making the above observation.

The details of his life given in the several *digvijayas* may be taken to be generally historical. Having lost his father in early life, he was fondly brought up by his mother. Owing to his phenomenal intelligence, he mastered the Vedas and the Vedic literature even in his boyhood. The mother then began as usual to form plans of marrying him. But Śaṅkara being without a father to check him, had already formed his own plan of leading a life of Śanyāsa. Perhaps, he had already vivid glimpses of his mission in life viz., that of establishing Śanyāsa against the doctrines of the Mīmāṅsā philosophers. His extraordinary plan of roving about as a Sanyāsi shattered to pieces the fond mother's simple plain ideal of a household life with grand-children moving about and she was sorely grieved; but Śaṅkara eventually succeeded in inducing his mother to give him permission to be a Sanyāsi; and promising to return to his native place when his mother would call him, he set out on his first journey in his itinerant life.

In the Vindhya region he found a teacher to his heart's satisfaction and he received regular ordination as a Sanyāsi from Govinda Guru who was himself a disciple of a famous teacher viz., Gaudapāda who has left a commentary on the Śānkhya Kārikā. Having for some years studied under Govinda Guru, Saṅkara went to Benares, the most prominent seat of learning in India and the accepted touch-stone of all new doctrines from ancient days-even from the days of Buddha. There, in Benares, Śaṅkara published his new doctrine of Vedanta and convinced the Pandits of Benares of its truth. He wrote, it is said, his commentaries on the Prasthānatrayī there and this has become traditional with later teachers viz., to write commentaries on the ten Upanishads, the Bhagvadgītā and the Vedanta Sūtras of Bādarāyaṇa. He also composed several minor works and poems. The literary excellence of Śaṅkara's writings has been recognised by all, even Western scholars and his Bhāshya on the Vedanta Sūtras stands supreme as a high specimen of both literary finish and polemic power.

Having reduced his doctrines to writing and established the truth of his views among the Pandits of Benares, he left Benares on an extended tour throughout India. The account of his controversies is not all historical, but the one he had with Maṇdana Miśra, the renowned teacher of Mīmāṅsā must be taken to be a fact. For, the latter was eventually defeated, his own wife being represented as the umpire between the two; and as the wager was, he became a Sanyāsi himself and a disciple of Śaṅkara. He was, as Sanyāsi, named Sureshvarāchārya and he is mentioned as the first successor of Śaṅkarāchārya on the gaddi of the math he founded at Śṛingeri. He, in fact, is the St. Peter of India's popes. Śaṅkara is said to have visited Ujjain which was also then a seat of learning in India and vanquished in argument a Pāsupatāchārya, Ujjain being a famous holy place distinguished for worship of Mahākāla. Śaṅkara is said to have also visited Assam which again is represented as a seat of learning. He, of course, visited Kashmir which has all along been famous for the learning of its pandits. And he is said to have opened the forbidden gate of the temple of Śāradā which he alone could do who would defy the whole world of Pandits. Śaṅkara is, of course, represented as having defeated all his adversaries. He finally went on a pilgrimage to Badarikāśrama in the Himalayas and established a math there also.

We have already said that Śaṅkara was a man of remarkable common sense and great political tact. Moreover, his equable temper and love for all without any undue favour, his *samatva buddhi*, in short, properly secured to him the respect of all shades of opinion in the country. The title *Jagadguru* given to him was properly bestowed on him and he was rightly looked upon as a teacher of the whole world so much so that the word Śaṅkarāchārya has now become a common noun meaning pope or head priest of any sect. Thus they speak even of a Jain Śaṅkarāchārya. He saw that for the permanent preaching of his doctrine and for its continued hold over the whole country, certain premanent institutions were necessary and he founded four sees in the four directions in India, sees which still carry his apostolic succession down to this day. The chief of them is the Śṛingeri math in the south of India founded in the country of his birth. The other three are the sees of Dwarka in the west, Puri in the east and Badari Kedāra in the north.

Śaṅkara, it is said, carried out his promise to revisit his mother whenever she thought it imperatively necessary. When she fell ill she called for him and Śaṅkara came and was present at her death-bed. Carried by filial love, he desired to perform her funeral obsequies himself though he as a Sanyasi could not do so. His relatives opposed him in his design and would not come to assist him in the funeral. Śaṅkara, therefore, had to burn his mother's body in the compound of his own house, a practice which commencing from that time is still observed in Kāladi, his birth-place in Kerala. It is difficult to imagine that Śankara would insist upon doing a thing prohibited by the Śāstras or that he who had conquered the whole world and himself would be so carried away by filial love as to do a wrong act. There must be some other explanation of this practice and Śankara must have burnt his deceased mother in his compound according to an already existing custom. Or the whole story may be a myth, the custom having arisen in times of Mahomeden religious oppression.

Śankara again went on his religious tour, being an itinerent Sanyāsi and with a purpose, a mission before him. He moved throughout India. As stated above, it is really strange that we do not possess any contemporary record referring to Śankara or his great work. There is one single exception, however, which we have already noticed in Vol. I. In the native historical records of Nepal there is a reference to the visit of Śankara to that country. It is stated he came to see whether the rules prescribed by a former Śankarāchārya a thousand years before regarding the worship of Paśupati, the national deity of Nepal were duly observed. It cannot be said that this is a contemporary record, but it is an old one. And it proves that Śankara visited Nepal's god Paśupati and made certain regulations for his worship. It is pertinent to remark here that the worshippers of Paśupati in Nepal are from old times Mahārāshtra Brahmins ; others, it is believed, will not do. Nepal Brahmins are flesh-eaters and perhaps not learned in the Vedas ; while Mahārashtra Brahmins are the reverse. Whether this rule was introduced by Śankara cannot be determined though it is generally believed that in the temple of Kedāranātha in the Himalayas, supposed to be built by Śankara, the practice from his days is that the worshippers must be Kerala Brahmins. This preference given in two places in the Himalayas to Southern Brahmins may be solely attributed to Śankara, for Brahmins learned in the Vedas and proficient in Śiva worship could have been obtained in those days without difficulty in the north, though in later centuries under Mahomedan oppression, most probably northern Brahmins are now mostly devoid of Vedic learning almost devoid of the knowledge of even a single Vedic Mantra.

Śaṅkara, it is said, in one place died at a very early age, some say at the age of 32, while Macdonell in his history of Sanskṛit literature says "Śaṅkara was born in 788 A.D., he became an ascetic in 820 and probably lived to an advanced age." Here 820 is taken as the date of Śaṅkara's ordination by adding 32 to 788. We do not know the authority for this statement as also for the last statement that he lived long. He is said to have died at Badarikaśrama and it may be that he retired to that holy place in the Himalayas at the age of 32 and ever afterwards remained absorbed in holy contemplation till his death, whenever it may have happened.

Śaṅkara's reputation as a great metaphysical philosopher will always stand high among the philosophers of the world. His Māyāvāda or theory of cosmic illusion is, indeed, the greatest stretch of human imagination to pry into the mystery of the world. Whether this theory of illusion has anything to do with the political capacities of the people, whether Śaṅkara's upholding of Sanyāsa had any evil influence on the tendencies of the people and whether finally his sanctioning or at least encouraging the worship of images of Puranic gods, either made by hand and established in temple, or nature-made in the form of certain small stones exhibiting certain signs such as Śālagrāma worshipped in almost every household, led to the fostering of superstitions of the people, we shall have to discuss in our next volume, though this is, indeed, a subject which is both delicate and subtle and admits the possibility of the most diverse and conflicting opinions.

NOTE.

DATE OF ŚANKARA.

The various dates suggested for Śaṅkara with their authorities have been given by Mr. K. K. Lele in a Marathi paper published by him in "Achārya" of 13th May 1916. He favours the date we have adopted; viz., Śaka 710 or 788 A.D. which was first urged by Prof. Pathak on several authorities. These are 1 Śaṅkara-Mandara-Saurabha of Nīlakantha, 2. Kudalagi Matha tradition :—Nidhināgebhavanhyabde vibhave Saṅkarodayah" i. e., 'Śaṅkara was born in Kali year 389.' 3. In the Śṛingeri Pītha tradition the same date is given in a stotra. 4. This the chief Matha founded by Śaṅkara is believed in the Matha to have been founded in the Kali year 3909 'Kalyabde nidhikhānkāgni Sesha Samvatsare matham Samsthāpya bhāratīpītham &c. 5. In the traditional stotras of the same Matha Śaṅkara's entering a guhā 'cave' in the Himalayas is placed in Kali year 3921. 6. Kudali Matha in Shimoga, Mysore, gives the same dates.

In support of these outside authorities, Prof. Pathak adduces the following chief arguments from internal evidence. 1. The Chinese traveller Itsing states in his travels that the famous grammarian Bhartṛihari died in 650 A.D. Kumārila has repeated one statement of Bhartṛihari; hence Kumārila and, therefore, Śaṅkara must have flourished after this date. 2. Sureśvara a pupil of Śaṅkara in his Vārtika on the Bṛihadāranya has repeated a statement of the Buddhist Dharmakīrti by name. Now the Chinese traveller Fa-hian states that Dharmakīrti was his contemporary in 695 A.D. Hence Śaṅkara and his pupil Sureśvara cannot be taken back before 695 A. D. 3. Jain Pandit Akalankadeva flourished in the reign of the Rāshtrakūṭa Dantidurga Sāhasatunga of the 8th century A.D. Śaṅkara refutes his opinion in his works, and therefore his date must be later than that of Akalankadeva. 4. The Kāsikāvriti on the sūtras of Pāṇini was written in the 7th century A.D. Śaṅkara quotes some of its sentences. All these arguments conclusively prove that Śaṅkara cannot go back before 700 A.D. The opposite tradition of the Kāmakoti Matha is not valuable as compared with that of Śṛingeri. And the manner in which the first tries to reconcile itself with the latter by supposing that there were two Śaṅkaras, one before the Christian era and the other in the 8th century A.D., is, to say the least, suspicious.

Mr. C. V. P. Aiyar, Astronomer of Cochin, has shown that the planetary positions given by Vidyāraṇya at the time of Saṅkara's birth indicate that date to be Śaka 728 or A.D. 806 which again has been reiterated by S. V. Venkateśvara in a paper published in R. A. S. 1915 (Jan.) and he further shows that the date of Śaṅkara's death must be taken 60 years later than the usual one viz., A. D. 820. Both these views are according to our opinion not correct; for, the astronomical data given by Vidyāraṇya 500 years after Śaṅkara cannot be reliabe. Moreover, when Saṅkara was born he was an unknown person and the exact time of his birth can not have been marked or remembered. We know how, when a man becomes celebrated, a horoscope with uchcha grahas is invented for him. The tradition of the Sṛingeri Matha about its foundation is the most reliable of all. Lastly, that Saṅkara lived up to the 85th year of his age cannot be accepted on the basis of a line in a stotra supposed to have been composed by Śaṅkara himself. It is likely that some one of his successors who are all called Śaṅkaracharyas like Cœsar may have composed it and spoken of himself therein as 85 years old. And men of extraordinary intellect and energy who finished their brilliant career at 32 are not historically impossible in this world of ours.

CHAPTER IV.

POLITICAL CONDITION.

We have explained at length in our first Volume Chapter VII (pp. 115-127) how the development of political ideas in the east and the west have been divergent and how in India the sentiment of nationality never came into existence. The idea that the state was the people never gained root in this country although in the beginning the people not only formed the state but gave the name to it. The inclusion of a large aboriginal population as Śūdras in the state having no or very few political rights gradually concentrated political power in a few of the leading spirits among the Brahmins and the Kshatriyas and finally in the kingly family. And while the king, as a matter of fact, possesses political power because of the consent of the people, the latter were gradually forgotten and the king's power was supposed to be drawn from the favour of gods extended in recompense for performance of severe austerities in former lives. Under such a view of kingly power the sentiment of nationality was naturally absent as also the feeling of patriotism. The sentiment of loyalty generally and steadfast attachment to a particular kingly family are alone developed. They are, of course, often cancelled by contrary tendencies born of treason and ambition; and as the people were believed to have nothing to do with the choice of the king, usurpers often succeeded in founding new royal families by the help of treacherous officials. We must also remember that kingly families tend to deteriorate in kingly virtues and become old and rotten like every thing in this world and do require to be uprooted now and then. The founding, therefore, of new vigorous kingly families is not always an evil; and such we actually find to be the case in India about the beginning of the 9th century A.D. The new Rajput families that were founded about this time were all despotic kingly families and did maintain themselves in power no by the consent of the people but by their own energies and the support of the bhaibands as they are called in Rajput history. Such a state of political philosophy is, no doubt, favourable to the establishment of any ruling dynasties if they are only strong and fortunate. And yet the testimony of Arab writers shows that the people of India did, in fact, exercise some choice in the matter of their giving allegiance to rulers. This indicates that the Indian people had yet some life left in them.

This evidence is afforded by almost all Arab writers who, perhaps, copy statements from one source. Sulaiman, the earliest traveller, records "The Indians sometimes go to war for conquest but the occasions are rare. I have never seen *the people of one country submit to the authority of another* except in the case of that country which comes next to the country of pepper (Malabar). When a King subdues a neighbouring state, he places over it a man belonging to the family of the fallen prince who carries on the government in the name of the conqueror. *The inhabitants would not suffer it to be otherwise.*" (Elliot I. p. 7). We have often laid emphasis on the fact that in Ancient or Mediæval Hindu India empires never meant annexation. The conquered king was allowed to rule or some one belonging to his family as before, subject only to payment of some tribute. Thus within the Kanauj empire of the Pratihāras we find from inscriptions that there were many subordinate kingdoms like the Chāvotakas of Wadhwan or the Chālukyas of Bhārapa. And in the same way, under the Rāshṭrakūṭas there were many subordinate kings as even Arab writers state. The further clear statement, however, of Sulaiman that "The inhabitants would not suffer it otherwise" shows that there was some life, some consciousness of power, yet in the people. Strangely enough, Sulaiman mentions an exception and that of the state which adjoined the country of pepper. This seems to indicate that the non-Aryan Dravidian kingdoms which existed in the south of India were not alive even to this modicum of the sentiment of nationality. We are of the opinion that this sentiment of nationality is strong in the Aryan and next to it in the Mongolian race which, indeed, are the two advanced races of the world, but that the Dravidian and the

Negro are so undeveloped yet that they are not susceptible to this sentiment. They do not even now exhibit that strong antipathy to foreign rule which characterises the white and the yellow peoples of the world. In the rest of India too, which is half Aryan and half non-Aryan, nationality is barely existent and this is one of the root causes why India has almost permanently been enslaved by foreign domination. There was no such force alive in India as is described in the short sentence of Sulaiman "The inhabitants would not suffer it otherwise," when the Mahomedans under Ghori finally conquered India.

There were thus, in India, during the Mediæval period as before, many kingdoms, some of which were large and were, in fact, empires having many subordinate kingdoms under them. And these were often at war not for conquest but to prevent conquest of one by another as we see from the struggle going on during this period between the Pratihāras of Kanauj and the Rāshṭrakūṭas of Malkhed as also between either of these and the Pālas of Bengal. These kingdoms were all governed by Rajput families, the Kshatriya Rajputs alone now being considered to be entitled to exercise sovereignty by divine law. And the people exercised their power by sometimes electing or rather accepting kings as founders of new families as Bappā Rāwal was chosen in place of the effete or rather defunct Mori dynasty or as Gopāla was elected in Bengal.

The right of descendants alone of such founders to rule was recognised by the customs and the sentiment of the peoples as in Europe of this or even later period. The hereditary rights of the kingly families, nay, their even divine right, was acknowledged in Europe. It is, therefore, no wonder that in India such right should have been conceded and religiously respected at this period.

But the people in the west asserted their right to guide and control the state affairs through popular assemblies while in Inda such assemblies never came into being. How did then the people assert their semi-recognized right of accepting or refusing a king? This difficult question is solved if we take into consideration the further statements of Sulaiman. "The troops of the kings of India are numerous; but they do not receive pay. The king assembles them only in case of a religious war. They then come out and maintain themselves without receiving anything from the king" (Elliot I. p. 7.). This state of things in India was also similar to that in Europe at this time. Generally, there were no standing armies paid regularly in India as in Europe at this time. Certain classes of Kshatriyas and chiefly Bhaibands (kulaputras) and others were bound in their enjoyment of land by the obligation of military service and they provided the necessary volunteers whenever required. They were not paid by the state but they maintained themselves out of their own income and probably by plunder also. Such armies having interest in the land and not paid by the state in cash must have had a great power in times of change of dynasties and could withold their allegiance from new masters if they chose. And hence the statement of Sulaiman that the people always insisted on a scion of the old reigning family being allowed to rule.

We must note, however, a few exceptions to the rule that there were no standing regularly paid armies in India; and these are recorded by Arab writers themselves. The Balhara or the king of the Rāshṭrakūṭas maintained a standing army and it was *regularly paid*. It is refreshing to note that the Marathas of the 9th century could pay their army regularly which fact was found impossible by their modern representatives the Marathas of the 18th century. But it seems that armies were kept in this way by the Pratihāras of Kanauj also and by the Pālas of Bengal. In fact, the example set by Harsha was followed in this respect by all the Hindu *empires*. Harsha, indeed, acquired and kept under subjection a vast empire by means of a well equipped regularly paid army and the same practice was followed by the successive imperial dynasties of Kanauj and also by the Rāshṭrakūṭas and Pālas as they were also in a sense Imperial kings having kingdoms subordinate to them. In Kanauj it is recorded that four armies were regularly posted east, south, west and north, and chiefly in the west for the empire was confronted there by the rule of the Arabs in Multan and Sind who were ever ready to rush on Hind as they called it. The army in the south was posted against the Balhara who was a friend of the Arabs. There was not much work for the army in the east and the north though danger was always apprehended in these directions also from Bengal and Kashmir and it is recorded by the Arabs that these two armies constantly moved from place to place. We further glean from Arab writers that the army of Kanauj consisted chiefly of cavalry while that of the Rāshṭrakūṭas consisted of all the three arms, foot, horse and elephant. Bengal was strong in elephants which abounded in its jungles though the number of elephants has been exaggerated to 50,000 by these Arab writers.

It is natural that inscriptions do not assist us in this matter, these being generally recorded to commemorate gifts to Brahmins and temples and we are really indebted to Arab travellers for this valuable information. But from the Bhāgalpur inscription we come to know that the army in Bengal consisted of many foreigners such as Mālava, Khasa, Hūṇa, Karnāta and Lāta (Ind. Ant. XV. p. 305). It must be noted here that a standing army consisting of foreigners is always dangerous to the sovereignty of the state. Whenever a people resign to foreigners the task of protecting them or even of aggrandizement abroad they soon lose their martial nature and slide downwards on the path of enslavement. The kingly family, too, becomes an instrument of oppression and plunder in the hands of a foreign army. This was experienced even in the modern history of the Marathas at Poona and of the Moguls at Delhi or the Turks at Constantinople, as at Rome by Romans in ancient times and at Bagdad in the middle ages by the Arabs. It is, therefore, pertinent to enquire of what material the standing armies in India at this time were composed. The army of the Rāshṭrakūṭas probably consisted of Marathas and that of Kanauj, Pratihāras or Rajputs of Marwar. The army of Bengal appears, however, to have consisted of foreign military castes such as Khasas etc., as the inscription records and this need not be wondered at as the kings were Buddhists and the people also generally Buddhists just converted to Hinduism. It seems that in Bengal the long prevalence of Buddhism and its still continuing influence made the people effete and unfit for military service. Yet Magadha in ancient Hindu times for nearly 800 years from Chandragupta 300 B. C. to Budhagupta 500 A. D. had by its own armies held almost the whole of India under subjection

The despotic character of the rule in Indian kingdoms had, however, one relieving feature viz., that according to the Indian political view kings had no power to promulgate new laws. The sacred Smṛitis contained all the laws that were required for human guidance and no human institution had any authority to change the laws prescribed by Brahmā in the beginning of the world for the guidance of Manu, the first king. However absurd the story, the theory was correct that despotic government had no legislative powers. Despotic as the rulers were they were bound by the Smṛiti-made law and could not thus add to the evils of despotic administration the evils of despotic legislation. The Smṛiti law may be defective in many respects but was practically the law prescribed by good conscience and the experience of wise men and hence was always conducive to the happiness of society. The expenses of government were limited and no state or king ever thought of taxing the subjects more than the prescribed $\frac{1}{6}$th of land produce and $\frac{1}{50}$th of trade profits. And when the kings paid their greatest attention to the suppression of robbery, the chief duty of the state (as the Pratihāras did during the period), the Indian states with even autocratic kings were well governed and happy.

The several states of India were often at war with one another and did not form a league or confederacy. This was not an evil according to our view though it is sometimes thought that India fell before the Mahomedans because of the constant wars among the kings and because of their not forming a confederacy. We have already answered these arguments in our first volume and will here add some further observations on the subject. Constant wars may be an evil, but occasional wars are necessary for the progress of humanity. Such wars keep up the martial qualities of the people and lead them onward in intellectual progress. In fact, Europe progresses by its occasional wars and so did India in the Mediæval period. And even if the Rāshṭrakūṭas took the help of the Arabs in their wars against the Pratihāras of Kanauj, this did not interfere with the solidity of the latter kingdom or of the whole country. As pointed out in our first Volume, Chapter VII, France under Francis I took the help of the Mahomedan Turks in its wars against their own Christian brethren, the Germans. But neither the French, nor the Germans have fallen before the Turks. Why the states of Europe were able to stand against the Saracens or the Turks can be explained only on the ground of the intense feeling of nationality which animates the people of these states. In India during the Mediæval period although the different kingdoms fought among themselves, and some sometimes even sought the help of foreigners they were still strong states, for, the sentiment of nationality was alive, to some extent, as noted by the Arab writer Sulaiman in his pithy sentence " the people would not suffer it otherwise."

According to our view the normal political condition of India was and has been that there were different kingdoms in the country and their coming under one empire occasionally as under Aśoka or Harsha was its abnormal condition. Differences of languages, of nature, of climate, of tradition and provincial capacities must lead to the foundation of different kingdoms and nations in India. Although India as a whole has naturally marked boundaries, while the different kingdoms in it have not, strong natural boundaries are not a *sine qua non* of a state. The boundaries of Holland and Belgium are almost threads as against Germany and France and yet they have maintained their independence through a thousand years against repeated attacks by the latter. The boundaries of such kingdoms in India as Sind, Panjab, U. P. with Oudh, and Bengal are not very marked or strong and yet these kingdoms which flourished in the Mediæval period might have remained strong and invulnerable if but they could have produced and developed the sentiment of a strong nationality.

The sentiment of nationality is developing under the unification of the country under British rule which extends over the whole country and transgresses provincial boundaries. Under the operation of this sentiment India as a whole can become one state or at least a confederacy of states like the United States of America. There are many factors which make for the whole country being one state. But India in the Mediæval age resembled Europe under the Holy Roman Empire in many essential points. The people of India were one by race like those of Europe viz., Aryans with, no doubt, an admixture of Dravidian blood. Though there was a diversity of languages as in Europe they professed one faith viz., Hinduism with its belief in the revelation of the Vedas and the worship of the Puranic gods chiefly Śiva and Vishṇu, just as Europe under the Holy Roman Empire professed the Roman Catholic faith with the Bible as its revelation and the worship of many saints. The different kingdoms in India recognized the same laws viz., the Smṛiti prescribed laws just as Europe was governed by and recognized the same Roman law. The boundaries of the different states in India were again as fragile as the boundaries of European states and their number was as great as in Europe. And yet as Europe under the Holy Roman Empire could not be consolidated into one state, India in the 10th century could not, because the provincial sentiment of nationality was too strong to be overcome and the different kingdoms in India did not and could not merge into one state. But as we have said, this was not an evil either in India or in Europe, had the provincial sentiment of nationality been developed here as in Europe. Unfortunately it declined as we shall try to elucidate in our third volume and India finally fell before the Afghans and the Turks at the end of the twelfth century. Not that the Indian kingdoms did not attempt combination against foreign domination and foreign faith. Such attempt was twice made as Europe attempted to combine against the onslaught of the Mahomedan Arabs and Turks. The difference only is that while Europe has succeeded, India failed ignominously.

Such combination was possible because in this period of Mediæval history the several kingdoms of India were all ruled by Rajput families who, indeed, formed one clan or separate caste as the Arab writers state. From Kabul to Kāmarūpā and from

Kashmir to Konkan all kingdoms were under Rajputs and these in a sense constituted a confederacy of 36 Royal families. This number seems to have become traditional long before Chand first mentioned it, for as stated before, we find it mentioned in the Rājataranginī of Kalhaṇa who wrote his work in 1148 A.D. This was also as in Europe where almost all royal families were connected with each other by marriage.

CHAPTER VII.

CIVIL AND MILITARY ADMINISTRATION.

(*A*) CIVIL.

In our first volume we have detailed at length the civil and military administration of the countries of India in the seventh century A.D. and it needs no stretch of the imagination to conceive that in the ninth and tenth centuries the form of the administration remained practically the same. We get glimpses of the system of administration in the inscriptions of the period which are usually grants to temples or Brahmin donees by kings. And we are assisted in this inquiry, as in the previous century by the writings of Hiouen-Tsang, so in these centuries by the writings of Arab travellers. We propose in this chapter to give a short description of the system of civil and military administration as disclosed in the writings of the period.

The whole country was parcelled into several tens of kingdoms which were called Deśa and which were ruled by despotic kings. Some of these kingdoms were empires, so to speak, but empires in the old sense, subordinate kingdoms being allowed to be ruled independently, rendering nominal allegiance to the emperor. Such empires were the three kingdoms of Kanauj in the north, Mahārāshtra or Malkhed in the south and Bengal or Monghyr in the east. These empires and these kingdoms were usually well governed, though ruled despotically. As stated in our first volume, (p. 128) according to the Hindu view of a state, the state or the king had no legislative power and hence the chief root-cause of mal-administration *viz.*, the promulgation of pernicious arbitrary laws was absent. The laws were already there, being divinely ordained and the kings had merely to execute them. Those kings who set at naught the divine made laws naturally incurred the disapprobation of the people and of the religious heads and hence could not long continue on their thrones. Examples of such kings are, indeed, not wanting, as for instance, Śaṅkaravarman of Kashmir; but generally the kings from very religious fear observed the Smṛiti-made laws scrupulously and thus inspite of the despotic nature of the rule, the kingdoms of India were usually well-governed and happy.

The kings took $\frac{1}{6}$ th of the land produce and $\frac{1}{50}$th of the profits of trade according to the Smṛiti laws from the people as taxes and in return protected them from the evils of foreign invasion and the oppression of internal marauders. How well this duty was performed by the Pratihāra emperors of Kanauj has already been noticed from the observations of an Arab traveller who states that the country of the Gurjaras was the most immune from robberies and dacoities. Other countries, too, must have been usually free from these evils.

For purposes of civil administration, the country was usually divided, as in previous centuries, into districts and Tahsils, that is, into Bhuktis and Vishayas as appears from the grants of the several kingdoms during this period. Thus, for instance, the Pratihāra empire grant of DighwaDuboli by Mahendrapāla dated 951 V. E. describes the village granted as "the village Pāniyaka situated in the Vālayika Vishaya or Tahsil falling under the Śrāvasti maṇḍala in the Śravasti Bhukti or district" (I. A. XV. p. 113). There is a mention of maṇḍala in this between the Bhukti and the Vishaya and it means in modern language a sub-division. The word maṇḍala was already in use in the south concurrent with Bhukti but it appears that it began to be used in the north also about this period. The word Maṇḍalapati still survives as Mandaloi in Malwa and other parts of the country.

Some variations may be noticed which appear in the grants of the different kingdoms. The Rāshṭrakūṭas of Mahārāshtra mention often in their grants the Vishaya only e. g. the Alas plates of Govinda II of Śaka 692 or 770 A.D. mention only the Alaktaka Vishaya without mentioning the Bhukti. The particulars of the officers, too, and the dues to be derived from the village are also not detailed. In the grants relating to Karnātaka and Konkan, the word Vishaya is often substituted by the number of villages in it as also the Bhukti or Maṇḍala. Thus in the record of Dhruva at Naregal, Banavasi is described as Banavasi 12000 (E.I.VI.p.161) and in the plates of Dantivarman of Gujarat the village granted is described as situated in the 42 of Lāta country; so in the Nilgund plates Belvola is described as Belvola 300 and a small portion of it as Mulgunda 12 (E.I. VI pp. 287 and 107). These appear to be the special features of grants in Karnātaka, Lāta, Konkan and countries furhter south and these numbers still survive in such names as Sāshti (Thana) and others. In the Rādhanpur plates of Govinda III (E. I. VI. p. 245) only the Bhukti is mentioned (Rasiyāna Bhukti). This grant relates to a village in Gujarat. So also in the Paiṭhan grant of the early Rāshṭrakūṭas of 794 A. D. Pratishthāna Bhukti alone is mentioned (E. I. III. p. 108).

The nature of the administration and the names of the several officers appear from many grants in details which are very interesting. The Kanauj grants are, from the days of Harsha, as already noted, terse and concise and address themselves to the officers *concerned* (यथास्थाननियुक्तान्) but the Bhāgalpur grant of Nārāyaṇapāla exhibiting the usual propensity of the Bengalee to verbosity noticed by even Bāṇa (गौडेष्वक्षरडम्बरः) fortunately gives us details which are very useful for the information they convey. The officers who are concerned with the grant of a village are enumerated therein as follows:—(the officers' designations are not translated by the writer in I. A XV, but we shall try to translate them though with diffidence) 1 Rājarājānaka (feudatory chiefs) 2 Rājputra (Kshatriya warriors related to the kings) 3 Rājāmātya (ministers of the king) 4 Mahāsandhivigrahika (the state officer for peace and war *i.e* foreign minister) 5 Mahākshapatalika (chief revenue officer) 6 Mahāsāmanta (the chief officer over the Sardars) 7 Mahāsenādhipati (the Commander-in-chief) 8 Mahāpratihāra (the chief usher or Lord Chamberlain) 9 Mahākārtāntika (not recognisable) 10 Mahādausādhyasādhanika (the chief officer for military engines) 11 Mahādaṇḍanāyaka (The chief Justice). 12 Mahākumārāmātya (the chief officer over kings' sons).,

These are all chief officers of the state. Then come the representatives of the king in districts viz., 13 Rājasthānīyoparika (chief district officer) 14 Daśāparādhika (magistrate entrusted with the punishment of the ten offences), 15 Chauroddharaṇika (the officer entrusted with the pursuit of robbers), 16 Dāṇḍika (jailor), 17 Daṇḍapāshika (Executor of punishments), 18 Śaulkika (collector of customs), 19 Gaulmika (Heads of Police thanas), 20 Kshetrapa (protector of fields or agriculture), 21 Prāntapāla (protector of prānta *i. e.*, boundaries of the state), 22 Koṭṭapāla (custodian of forts), 23 Khandarakshaka (not recognisable), 24 and their Āyuktaka and Niyuktaka (agents and clerks). Then follow details of military officers viz. 25 officers of the forces of elephants, horses, foot-soldiers and boats, 26 The superintendents of foals (horses), cows, bullocks and sheep. 27 Dūtapreshaṇika (spies), 28 Gamāgamika (not recognisable) 29 Abhitvaramāṇa (ditto), 30, The chief of the Tahsil, 31 The chief of the village and 32 policemen and soldiers (chāṭā bhata) belonging to Lāta, Karnāta Kulika, Hūṇa, Khaśa, Mālava and Gauda countries. These details are numerous enough and yet the verbose writer of the inscription adds "And other officers not mentioned." It is conceivable how all these officers are concerned with the grant of a village and we may liken the list to the list of officers to whom under the British Government gazetted orders are addressed. Thus the usual condition attached to such grants viz., that the village is not to be entered by policemen or soldiers requires that the order should be communicated to all military officers as well as to the Police and to judicial officers also. These details show that the civil and military administration of the countries of India at that time was well advanced and included almost all the departments of a civilised government. Though these officers' names are recited with respect to the kingdom of Bengal, such officers must have existed in all other states with insignificant variations. We have already in our first volume enumerated the officers existing under the Valabhī administration and the details now presented are not very different.

Though the forms of grants in different kingdoms are different there is no reason to suppose that the form of administration was also different. A few differences may, however, be noticed. The Rāshṭrakūṭa grants are addressed to all officers concerned such as Rāshṭrapati, Vishayapati, Grāmakūṭa, and Āyuktaka Niyuktaka officers with. Mahattaras. Now Rāshṭrapati was a peculiar officer in the Deccan. We have often said that the word Rāshṭra for a division was peculiar to Mahārāshṭra and each division had a chief officer or Rāshṭrapati (named Subadar in Mahomedan times) and Vishayapati was the Tahsil or Taluka officer under him (E. I. VI. p. 245). The Mahattara is the headman of the village, a word still surviving as Mhātre in the Konkan. The plates of Dantivarman of Gujarat add the word Vāsāpaka to those already mentioned which has not been translated by any one and which it is difficult to understand. The Sangli grant of 933 A.D. (I. A. XII) repeats the usual formula राष्ट्रपति विषयपति ग्रामकूट महत्तर आयुक्तक नियुक्तकाधिकारान् and describes the village as situate in Rāmpuri 700 as this village belongs to Karnātaka. So also the Kardā grant of 972 A.D. mentions the same officers and describes the village as situate in Uppalika 300, Vavvutalla 12 (I. A. XII. p. 263).

It is interesting to note the different ways in which the villagers are described in these grants. The Bengal grants, of course, give the most detailed description. The inhabitants are led by Brahmins the Mahattama, Uttama (leading merchants) and come down to Medas and Chāndālas who are probably scavengers and hangmen (I. A. XV. p. 385). The Rāshṭrakūṭa grants mention only Mahattara and others. The word Mahattara has survived in the Konkan but strangely enough not above the Ghats in the Deccan. The Mālwa grants under the Paramāra Vākpati and Bhoja ,contain the expression प्रतिवासिनः पट्टकिल जनपद दींश्च बोधयति "The king informs the inhabitants, Pattakila (Patel), Janapada (Villagers) and others." The word Pattakila which occurs here for the first time in Malwa grants of about 1000 A.D. has spread all over India and is now the designation of the headman of a village from the Panjab down to Mahārāshṭra in the modern form Patel which is plainly derived from it. But whence comes Pattakila and what is its meaning? It seems to us that it is a contracted form of Akshapatalika which we saw was in use in Harsha's time (see Vol. I p. 131) and Patalika was changed into Pattakila by transposition of letters and this again into Patel.

The items of revenue, land tax and other dues, paid by the villagers are described in almost the same words as in previous centuries, the Inām villages being usually described as granted सोद्रंग, सोपरिकर, सदशापराध, सभूतवातप्रत्याय, सोत्पद्यमानविष्टिक, सधान्य हिरण्योदय (see Paithan plates of Govinda III dated 794 A.D.). The Bhagalpur grant of Bengal describes the gift as ' स्वसीमातृण-यूति गोचरपर्यन्तः सतलः सोद्देशः साभ्रमधूकः सगर्ताधरः सोपरिकरः सदशापचारः सचौरोद्धरणः अचाटभट प्रवेशः समस्तभाग भोग कर हिरण्य विप्रत्यायय समेतः These two descriptions come to nearly the same thing. The Udranga was the chief tax on land viz. ⅙th of its produce, and Uparikara was a minor tax. Bhoga is often substituted for Udranga and Hiranya means probably taxes paid in cash and levied on profits of trade etc. at $\frac{1}{50}$th. The other epithets describe the privileges of owners of Inām villages viz., that the village was not to be entered by policemen or soldiers, it had the right to try its own cases of ten offences, it had the privilege of grazing its cattle up to its limits, it had a right to its mango trees (साभ्र should be read as साम्र) and Madhūka or Mahua trees (which were probably very valuable in Bengal). This means that the state forest department could not enter such villages by reserving valuable trees or grazing lands. The village was granted together with the low lands also (Tala and Gartādhara) which in Bengal would be numerous and valuable and which in ordinary villages would be government property. So also mango and Mahua trees when not specially planted and owned by individuals would belong in ordinary villages in Bengal to the state and not the villagers. It must further be mentioned that the state had a right to Vishti or forced labour up to a certain limit in every village and each labourer was obliged to work for the state a certain number of days in the year and this right to Vishti in Inām villages was transferred by the state to the Ināmdār by the expression Sotpadyamānavishtika in almost all grants. The description in Mālwa grants is similar viz. स्वसीमातृण

काष्ठ गोचरपर्यन्तः सवृक्षमालाकुलः सहिरण्य भागभोगः सोपरिकरः सर्वादायसमेतः. We find Kāshtha added here to the Gochara or gurcharan of modern days and all trees whether valuable or not in the precincts of the village were granted to the Inamdar. All grants are careful to add " with the exception of what has already been granted to gods and Brahmins " an exception usually made in modern sanads also. It is lastly difficult to find out what Bhutavāṭapratyādeya meant which is often mentioned as granted in these sanads of this period as also of the past.

The revenue officers in the villages were hereditary but the heads of Tahsils and of the Bhuktis or districts (the Mālwa grants under the Paramāras introduce a new name for Bhukti viz. Pathaka which is further sub-divided into southern, eastern etc.) were certainly appointed by the king and removable at pleasure. We find mention of such appointments in the inscriptions of the period. Thus from the Siyadoni inscription (E. I. I) we get the information that that province was under Mahārāja Durlabha in 912 A.D. and under Mahārāja Nishkalanka in 960 A.D. Nay, we find from the Gwalior Vallabha Swāmi inscription (ditto p. 157) that a Nagar* Brahmin from Ānandapura in Gujarat (called Latamandala in this inscription) named Alla was appointed keeper of the Gwalior fort by Ādivarāha *i. e.*, emperor Bhoja of Kanauj in recognition of his merits श्रीमदादि वराहेण त्रैलोक्य-विजिगीषुणा । तद्गुणान्यः परिज्ञाय कृतो गोपाद्रिपालने ॥० His father was also an officer under Rāmabhadra, Bhoja's father. We find thus that Gujarat and Gwalior were both under Kanauj and that an inhabitant of the former could be a great officer in the latter. There is a mention in inscriptions of officers appointed in Gujarat from Kanauj. Similarly, under the Rāshṭrakūṭas there were officers appointed in Karnātaka from Mahārāshṭra as at Belvoli. The district officers were generally invested with full powers and were in fact miniature kings in

* The word Nāgara may be treated here as indicative of caste though such sub-caste names had not yet arisen. We find, however, the word Nāgarabhatt-kumāra treated as one name here and not divided into two parts Nāgara and Bhattakumāra. In the 13th century A.D., the word Nāgara had become the name of a subcaste as we find the word Nāgara-Jnātibhājā in the Chitorgadh inscription

their districts. They were invested with the five royal sounding instruments (Samadhigata-panchamahāśabda) such as the conch, the drum and so on. They could even make valid religious gifts like the Subadars in Mogul and Maratha times. These officers though not hereditary often times became so and eventually became Sāmantas or Sardārs. How they were paid does not appear from the inscriptions. Perhaps the Manusmṛiti law of paying them by the assignment of the revenue of one whole town or even a Tahsil may have still obtained. That they were very rich may be conceived as Alla could build a temple in the name of his wife at Gwalior and have certain endowments made to it. Lastly, it seems that while the chief officer of the district had great powers, the military was not under him but under a separate officer as we find in the Gwalior second inscription (E. I. I. p. 159) the same Alla keeper of the fortress mentioned but the name of the military officer is given separately. The whole line in this connection is worth quoting here from this private inscription; परमेश्वरश्रिभोजदेवे तदधिकृत कोट्टपालअल्ले बलाधिकृत तत्तके स्थानाधिकृत श्रेष्ठी वव्वियाके । "when the emperor was Śribhojadeva and the fortress-keeper appointed by him was Alla, the officer of the army being Tattaka and the local (municipal) officer being merchant Vavviyāka."

The last statement furnishes us with the information that towns were under municipal officers who were local influencial men. Probably there were municipal bodies also which controlled the affairs of the towns and these were called Mahājans or boards of great men of the place and they appointed their head such as the above named merchant Vavviyāka at Gwalior. The important markets of the towns were under the control of these Mahājans, as inscriptions actually make mention of new markets or Hattas (modern Hāts) and the formation of new Mahājans. These town municipalities and these markets often times imposed taxes for religious gifts to temples and inscriptions recording such voluntary taxation are very numerous in this period. The most important of such records is the Siyādoni inscription found near Lalitpur in Gwalior territory. This inscription forms a study by itself (E. I. I. p. 174). It records various gifts made in several years, in favour of a Vishṇu temple built by a merchant, both by himself and others. The object is to create what is usually called an Akshayanīmika or a perpetual purse for the use of the temple. Several vīthikās are dedicated to the temple in this way. What vīthikā means is not quite clear, but it seems that it means a seat or a stall in the market which a man owns or has purchased and the rent of such stall is assigned to the temple. Houses are also assigned but that is not strange, But what is strange is that in two places the Kalals or manufacturers of liquor have imposed upon themselves a tax or a Tali of ½ dramma or rupee on each pot of liquor that may be ready and go out of the shop. The words here are समस्त कल्लपालानां मध्ये यस्य यस्य सत्कमद्यभाण्डं निष्पद्यते विक्रयं याति स चाचंद्रार्कं यावद् विग्रहपाल सत्क द्रम्मार्धिका ताली दातव्या . What an irony on the futility of human wishes and arrangements! Here is an arrangement made designed to last as long as the sun and the moon last, for the payment of ½ dramma on each pot of liquor as it goes out for sale from the Kalal's shop—an arrangement which perhaps lasted for some years only after it was recorded on stone and then fell into disuse, the stone lying unknown for centuries till discovered by some curious European researcher. The temple is no more nor the tax! What is strange, however, to discover is that Kalals (a word which is derived from the Sanskrit word Kallapāla used here) manufactured liquor in the tenth century A.D. in India as they did till recently and a tax was imposed on the manufacture voluntarily for the benefit of a Vishṇu temple. A second mention of a similar tax has been misinterpreted, we think, into a statement that a certain fixed quantity of liquor went into the Vishṇu temple as tax; but this seems absurd. Of course, money realised from tax on sale of liquor was not objectionable then as now. Even potters were to pay some taxes. The Pehewa inscription again mentions a tax imposed by horse-dealers on the sale of horses for the benefit of three temples built in Kanauj and a fourth built at Pehewa or Pṛithūdaka on the river Sarasvatī in the Panjab to be divided in certain fixed proportions among them.

The chief need of temples was oil and flowers. When kerosine was not known nor electricity either, the importance of the oil-extractor was supreme. In India in every village and town there were Telis or oil-men who were leading personages in the place and they often accepted investments and promised, out of the interest, to give every day a certain number of palikās (measures) of oil to temples per ghānaka or oil press. The inscriptions frequently speak of such daily supplies of oil. Besides the above named Siyadoni inscription, we may refer to the Bilhauri Chedi inscription (E.I. 1 p. 263) in this connection. The line herein on the subject cannot be well understood; पत्तनमण्डपिकायां लवणस्य खाण्डिकायां शोडाशिका घाणके च शोडाशिका तैलस्य मासि मासि दिनमनु च युगायुगे च पौरस्तु. The Mandapikā mentioned here is mentioned in other inscriptions also and means the government toll-office of the town. There and on the bazar of salt a Shodaśikā tax was imposed as also on each oil press. The oilmen paid the tax willingly, of course, but there was apparently an organisation which bound the whole community of oilmen. In fact, every trade appears to have had its guild and no man could offend the guild with impunity.

The Māli or flowerman was also an important personage in villages and towns and gave flowers daily to the temples. The temples were also provided with Inām plots of land as flower gardens by pious donors (See Siyadoni and Gwalior inscriptions above noted).

It seems that the Dharmādāyas to temples and Brahmins were assessed on other portions of the community also such as tradesmen and merchants and even extended to the most important portion viz., the agriculturist. There is no reference to this in the inscriptions as yet found but the following śloka in the Parāśara Smṛiti which appertains to the present Kali age mentions it;

राज्ञे दत्त्वा तु षड्भागं देवानां चैव विंशकं ।
विप्राणां त्रिंशकं चैव सर्वपापैः प्रमुच्यते ॥

"Having given to the king ⅙th and to temples 1/20th and to Brahmins 1/30th, the agriculturist is freed from all sins (of agriculture)." The mention of this 1/30th part of produce given to Brahmins in this Smriti is corroborated by what we saw was prevalent in Sind. Three parts out of every hundred were there paid to Brahmins in Dahar's days and the practice was continued even during Mahomedan times by Mahomed Kasim. No corroboration of this voluntary payment was found until we came across the above text in the Parāśara Smṛiti and the attention of the reader is specially drawn to it in this place showing that it was a general well-recognised practice in India.

The minute and circumspect nature of the revenue administration is evidenced by the Daulatpura grant of Bhoja, Pratihāra emperor of Kanauj (E. I. V.). The grant recites that the grand-father of Bhoja, Vatsarāja, had given an Agrahāra (Inām to Brahmins) to the grand-father of the donee named Vāsudevabhatta who had enjoyment of the same, that 1/6th part of it was given by Vasudevabhatta by a deed of gift to Bhattavishṇu and the same was sanctioned by Mahārāja Nāgabhatta ; and that the deed of gift and the letter of sanction by government being lost, this new order had been issued after ascertainment of the deed and the sanction and also of subsequent enjoyment. This recital shows that deeds of gifts were passed among the people and that sanctions were obtained from government which could be subsequently ascertained from government records and finally that documents together with actual enjoyment as necessaries in every legal transaction were carefully looked into. It would thus appear that revenue records were regularly kept and the ordinary principles of law and revenue administration were minutely observed in the Imperial government of Kanauj.

It is interesting to know whether these records were on paper or on any other material. As the word patra is usually used in connection with documents some paper must probably have been used ; but this is not necessary as in the north patra might have been an actual leaf viz., of a Bhūrja tree and in the south it must have been a palm leaf and sanads were issued first on such papers or leaves and copies on copper plates were then made for securing permanence. The circumspect nature of revenue administration is further apparent from the following verse in a Śilāhāra grant dated Śaka 930 (1008 A.D.)

मुद्राशुद्धं क्रियाशुद्धं भुक्तिशुद्धं सचिन्हकम् ।
राज्ञः स्वहस्तशुद्धं च शुद्धिमायाति शासनम् ॥

"A document embodying an order of Government is correct if it bears the Government seal, is properly drawn up, is followed by possession, bears the proper mark and has the signature of the king." The last condition makes it necessary that such documents should be originally drawn up on paper or leaf. We find copper plates in this period (though not in the Gupta period) conforming to this rule and bearing always the signature of the king who made the grant and also his seal affixed on the ring and the village or land granted is always put into the possession of the donee on the spot by some royal officer mentioned in the grant. What chinha or sign means is not, however, clear.

Land was always measured as shown in our first volume (p. 133) and there was a land measure of government. The ancient measure was Nivartana (bigha being Mahomedan and acre English) but sometimes small plots were measured by cubits. We have the mention of such measurement in the Gwalior second inscription (E. I., I, p. 159) where the Imperial cubit (Pārameśvarīya Hasta) is mentioned as 217 long by 187 broad. Two pieces of land are further on mentioned where no measurements are given but where the seed required for the fields is mentioned as 11 Dronas. This way of describing the extent of the field was in vogue in some parts of the Konkan down to the beginning of the British rule. Again fields have names and are always mentioned in grants with their boundaries the word for which is Āghāta. Villages also are described by their boundaries. We see from the Smṛitis that the boundaries of villages were always defined and fixed and boundary disputes were of special importance.

The chief revenue was collected in kind and the grain so collected was stored in every town and city under Government control. The pay of civil servants was in chief part always paid in kind and only partially in money. The taxes on trade brought in money but we may at once see that under such arrangements money circulation in every state must have been very limited. Even trade transactions were chiefly carried on by barter, grain being the ordinary medium. We have already seen this in Kashmir (Vol. I. p. 238) and practically the same was the condition prevalent throughout Indian history even up to British times in every part of India.

Much coin not being needed we may take it that there were very few mints in India and coin was struck not very often. We do not know any particulars on this subject from inscriptions of the period but we may mention here such scraps of information as can be gathered from them. The Siyadoni inscription (E. I. I) speaks of many coins which are worth noticing here. The chief coin which it mentions is the dramma evidently a foreign word and two kinds of drammas are mentioned; the Śrimadādivarāha dramma and the Vigrahapālīya dramma. Adivarāha is, of course, the great Pratihāra emperor Bhoja of Kanauj. He must have struck coin which was in use in the days of his son and grand-son. It does not appear that coin was struck in the time of every king though we have seen it was so in Kashmir and for formality a few coins must have been struck on the accession of each king in every state, but not sufficient for circulation. The Ādivarāha dramma appears to have been in circulation nearly a hundred years after it was struck. It is difficult to determine who Vigrahapāla was whose dramma is constantly mentioned. It seems that foreign coin was no-where banned. Coins struck in foreign countries whether in India or outside appear to have been current everywhere. The Vigrahapālīya dramma was plentiful in the neighbourhood of Siyādoni. Even in the times of the Peshwas different rupees were in circulation; while the Marathas or the Peshwas had no coin specially their own. The Chandodi and the Haliśikka were, indeed, numerous but there were other Śikkas also current at the same time.

And here we may go into a little digression. The art of coining money appears to have been a foreign art in India. It was, of course, introduced in very ancient times and probably from the Greeks whether of the days of Alexander or before him. The Arthaśāstra of the time of Chandragupta by Kauṭilya gives special detailed rules about the mint. The old Sanskṛit name for the chief coin was the Niskha which was neglected in the days of the Greek and Śaka dominions and the word and coin dīnāra came into use. This word is certainly of foreign origin. Later on during the Hindu period we have the word dramma in use which is also foreign. We find in one place the use of the word rūpaka in this period द्रम्ममेकं करी दद्यात् तुरगो रूपकद्वयम् (Bhav. In. p. 68. V. E. 1010). This indicates that Rūpaka was almost one-fourth of a dramma. The word rupee came into general use in Mahomedan times. We may infer that the art of coining was a foreign importation. It is, in fact, allied to chemistry and Natural Sciences were not much studied in India. Moreover, the legend on the coin and the face of the reigning monarch are difficult to impress and the Haliśikka of the Peshwas contented itself with copying Mahomedan legends and the clumsy addition of a distinguishing letter betokening the state where the coin was struck.

The minor coins that are mentioned are the half dramma and the Viṁśopaka, presumably the 20th part of a dramma and the Kapardika, Kākinī and Varātaka. What relation the last three bore to the dramma cannot be found. The present arrangement by which a rupee is divided into sixteen annas was probably not then in existence* and the dramma appears to have been divided into 20 parts, unless we interpret shodaśikā above mentioned as 1/16th part or anna. The Viśvanśa was in vogue in Mahomedan times also. Kapardika seems to have been the lowest coin.

(B) Military.

We will now go on to describe the military administration of the countries of India during this period. In the first place, the forces in each country were generally levies supplied by the nobility and the gentry. It does not appear that there were standing armies in most countries; for, the Arab writers mention the Balhara alone as entertaining a standing army and what is more creditable as paying it regularly, an achievement which his latest representatives the Marathas except in Śivaji's times could not accomplish. But it seems to us that the two other

* Perhaps Shoḍaśikā mentioned before may be 1/16th of a dramma like the modern anna.

empires of the period also kept standing armies viz., the Pratihāras of Kanauj and the Pālas of Bengal and these too must have regularly paid their forces.

These forces consisted now of the three arms foot, horse and elephant. The fourth arm the Ratha or car had fallen into disuse. The Pālas of Bengal, however, from the Bhāgalpur inscription (I. A. XV p. 305) had a fourth arm, so to speak, viz. the navy. The country was full of big rivers and distances could easily be traversed by boats. Moreover, fighting on the rivers was often necessary as much commerce was carried on by water and brigandage on rivers was frequent.

But each of these three empires was specially strong in one arm. The Kanauj forces were known for their excellent cavalry, the Bengal forces for their elephants and the Deccan forces for their infantry. It is strange that an Arab writer says that the Balhara has to keep much infantry because his capital lies among mountains. We think, however, that the Rāshṭrakūṭas had not only many elephants but had much and excellent cavalry also. In fact, infantry did not then possess that importance which it possesses now. And elephants could be had in plenty in the jungles of Malabar and Karwar and even of Aparānta or the Thana district. For the Mahābhārata even, in one place, praises an elephant as born in Aparānta. Bengal, of course, had plenty of elephants from the jungles of the Eastern Vindhyas and of the Mahendra mountains. But it had no horses and it is curious to note that the Bhāgalpur inscription states that the cavalry consisted of horses presented by northern kings. Both the Deccan and Marwad produced excellent horses fit for cavalry and the Panjab and Afghanistan also supplied horses. Hence could large cavalries be maintained by the Pratihāras and the Rāshṭrakūṭas. Yet foreign horses were, no doubt, superior in popular estimation as well as in fact and there was a very large trade in the import of Persian aud Arabian horses carried on by Arabs who for this reason had always easy access to the courts of the several kingdoms in India.

Where the army consisted of local levies there was no danger of disloyalty affecting it ; for such forces fight for their own country. But standing armies are prone to enlist foreign mercenaries and these often prove most dangerous as has already been stated. It seems that the armies of the Pratihāra and the Rāshṭrakūṭa kings consisted mainly of men from their own countries. In fact, the Rajputs and the Marāthas have always been martial peoples and therefore there was plenty of material at home for enlistment in their armies. In Bengal the case seems to have been different. The detailed Bhāgalpur grant shows that in the army of Bengal there were soldiers from foreign countries such as Khaśa, Mālava, Hūṇa, Kulika, Karnāta and Lāta besides Gauda itself. There is no mention here of Rajputs and Marāthas and these apparently had enough employment in their own countries. The other people mentioned here seem to be martial people who sought employment abroad though one is surprised to find the names of Lāta and Mālava in the list. For the people of Mālava and Lāta or south Gujarat have never been known as martial people. Perhaps the inscription writer takes delight in lengthening details and mentions names without reference to reality. Or it may be that the nature of peoples changes even in historic times. The people of Mālwa and of south Gujarat may have lost their martial character for various reasons by Mahomedan times. Nay, it is pertinent to point out that even though this inscription itself shows that the people of Bengal are generally not martial from ancient times, yet recent events show that the Bengalees too will one day establish a reputation for valour and will be counted as a martial people.

There were the usual officers in each arm and a commander-in-chief. The Bhāgalpur grant calls him the great commander-in-chief (Mahāsenāpati) and mentions him separately. He was thus the chief military officer over all the arms and in immediate communication with the king, while there were Senāpatis under him for each arm. What the Dauhsādhya-sādhanika was it is difficult to imagine, but as we have translated the word he was probably an officer entrusted with the work of using catapults and other military engines used in assaulting unassailable places. All the soldiers were paid out of the treasury monthly cash wages and from government graneries monthly allotments of grain. As to officers they must have also been paid similarly or like the chief civil officers given assignments of land. This is only a surmise as there is no contemporary record to determine the nature of payment.

There were, of course, the necessary complementary departments such as transport, commissariat, espionage etc. We found an officer mentioned in Kāshmir history called Mahāsādhanika (see Vol. I p. 209) though we do not find him mentioned in the Bhāgalpur inscription. We have the mention therein of an officer entrusted with the breeding of horses and cattle and an officer of spies. What is Gamāgamika who is distinctly connected with the military administration we have not been able to discover; as also Abhipratāpa who is next mentioned in the Bhāgalpur grant.

The army on the field was almost always led by the reigning king in person. In fact, in ancient times that was considered the chief duty of a king and the tradition survived down to modern times when the Peshwas, almost all of them except the last, led armies in person on the battle-field. And the kings were usually in the van as they were expected to set an example to their soldiers. In modern warfare the value of a commander-in-chief has increased a hundred-fold and it is his duty to protect himself and to remain in the rear.

It is difficult to understand the manner of fighting in vogue in those days when the gun had no existence. The bowmen were the most important and usually began the fighting. The king usually rode an elephant and fought with his bow. The most terrible fighting was that with the elephant force and the inscriptions of the times almost always extol the kings' valour in attacking black masses of elephants and breaking open their temples with the blows of their swords "thus spilling on the ground pearls stored therein" a poetic' 'fancy'!! The art of fighting with elephants had, indeed, developed in India to a remarkable extent and the fight tested the valour and physical strength of the fighters. The elephant force was, in fact, the artillery of ancient times. But we wonder how the elephant arm could not have been nullified by the ancient Indians ere this, by the use of firework. Of this we shall have to speak later on in our third volume.

The death of the king or the commander on the battle-field almost always led to the defeat and the running away of his army. This would perhaps suggest that there was no regular military gradation of officers by which command would descend. But the true explanation of this strange demeanour of Indian armies lies, in our opinion, not in defect of administration but in the total lack of the feeling of self-interest in the soldiers in the success of the battle. We have already seen how patriotism or even the feeling of nationality had no existence in those days. The kingdom was the king's and since the king for whom they were fighting was dead, where was the use of continuing the struggle? Such thoughts must always have damped the ardour of the soldiers of a defeated or dead king and hence the peculiar phenomenon in Indian history of armies, often strong and unbeaten, not offering tough and dogged resistance till the end.

CHAPTER VIII.

THE NINTH AND TENTH CENTURIES, A.D—THE HAPPIEST PERIOD IN INDIAN HISTORY.

In our Marathi edition of this history we have styled it the history of the rise, the *prosperity* and the fall of Hindu kingdoms. The second sub-period of our history is thus there considered the period of the prosperity of Hindu kingdoms. We are certainly of the opinion that during the 9th and the 10th centuries of the Christian Era, India undoubtedly enjoyed greater happiness than in any century of her known history whether previous or subsequent, of course, omitting out of consideration the hoary past. In this chapter we propose to describe the various aspects of the country's situation which contributed towards this its happiest condition.

The first and the foremost aspect is that India was during these centuries under one religion. The conflict of religions and the consequent animosities and estrangements leading sometimes to the dangerous desire in the followers of one religion to overthrow those of another, socially and even politically, was conspicious by its absence. Mahomedanism had taken hold of Sind, no doubt, but in the rest of the country in stern opposition to it the people of India had in a way rallied and gathered strength in Hinduism or rather juvinated Aryanism. The deplorable condition of later and modern days in which in every town and even village there are Mahomedans and Hindus ready to quarrel with one another on the slightest religious occasion and even to fly at one another's throat had not come into existence. There were no mosques in India then raising high their minarets along side with temples and proclaiming from high the everlasting disunion of the people into which dread destiny has for ever thrown India. On the other hand Buddhism had been entirely supplanted. The great philosophers, Kumārila and Śaṅkara, had established the Vedic religion on a firm though new basis both ritually and spiritually. And the wonder is that no Buddhistic temples remained in the land though there were thousands when Hiuen Tsang visited India, if we except the cave temples and the colossal images of Buddha hewn out of hill sides. How these Buddhistic temples disappeared is a mystery, for the Hindus have never been iconoclasts. The Mahomedans in the time of Mahmud of Ghazni and later destroyed temples by thousands, but they were apparently all Hindu temples. Although we have no record of the fact, it seems that Buddhist temples generally fell into ruins by sheer desertion being mostly built of wood. And perhaps stone temples were converted into Hindu temples by the substitution of Hindu idols. Jainism was, no doubt, yet alive but was confined only to detached places. It had not yet succeeded in capturing Gujarat and Southern Mahārāshtra nor the Panjab or Rājputana. Imagine, therefore, the whole country following one religion viz., the Hindu religion, worshipping in temples of Śiva and Vishṇu, Bhagavatī and Āditya or Gaṇeśa without any bias or ill-feeling; for the philosophy of Ś..ṅkara which was preached in the beginning of this sub-period had taken away all animosity from the worship of these different deities, if such had existed at any time before.

And finally we must add that within that Hinduism itself the great gulf which now divides Śaivism from Vaishṇavism and Advaita from Dvaita had not yet come into existence. The great teachers of Vaishṇavism, Rāmānuja and Madhva, had yet to be born and the days when there were to be most pitiable wranglings between Śiva worshippers and Vishṇu worshippers, between the preachers of monism and dualism and the most wretched bickerings between their followers had yet to come. The disunion caused by these differences of worship and philosophy is not less deep than that caused by the animosities between the followers of Hinduism and Mahomedanism. Fortunately both these disunions had yet to arise and the one cause of disunion which existed in previous times viz., the struggle between Hinduism and Buddhism had disappeared.

Perhaps it may be objected that Hinduism though then the sole religion of the people was not of such a high character as to ensure complete happiness of the people. Hinduism of those days was, indeed, in many respects defective but what we chiefly lay stress on is the fact that there was unity of religious belief in the people, a great factor leading to their happiness. We are not going to enter into the merits of any religion here; for we believe that all religions are equally good and perhaps equally bad or absurd. It is the differences of religious beliefs causing deep-seated animosities that contribute more to the evil condition of a society than the tenets or the philosophy of any particular religion. It is for this reason we say that the condition of India during these two centuries was unique and as a matter of history we draw the curious reader's attention to this unique condition of the country during the ninth and the tenth centuries A.D.

And further, it must be remarked that some of the most objectionable features of modern Hinduism had no existence in those days. In particular, the evils which spring from the division of Indian society into numerous hard-bound castes did not then exist. In the first place there were no sub-castes then as now. Brahmins thus all over India were then one caste and the thousand and one sub-castes (speaking literally) which to-day go to form that caste had no existence. So were the Kshatriyas and Vaiśyas all over India undivided into sub-castes. There was no interdiction on marriage or food between the Rajputs of Northern India and the Maratha Kshatriyas of the south as we have already shown. Even the 36 Kulis of Rajputs had not yet been enumerated. What a great source of strength and happiness to the people when there were no Kanojia Brahmins to hate the Srimāli Brahmins and both to hate the Deccanis or the Karnatics to hate the Deccanis and both to hate the Tamils! What a great source of strength and happiness to the country when the Rajputs did not look down upon the Khatris or the Marathas or both upon the Bengal and Madras Kshatriyas!!!

In the second place, there was no enmity or envy between the Brahmin and the Kshatriya or between the Kshatriya and the Vaiśya. For, Anuloma marriage among those three higher castes was still practised. They had, no doubt, ceased to take Śūdra wives as in past centuries. According to our view this was beneficial and not harmful. For, the Śūdra represented the Dravidian race and the three higher castes represented the Aryan race. A mixture of races is always harmful and the ancient Rishis were right in declaiming against Varṇa-saṅkara. But there was no such harmful racial mixture in the Anuloma marriages among the three higher castes which were more classes than castes. A Brahmin could marry a Kshatriya wife and a Vaiśya wife, their progeny being treated as Kshatriya and Vaiśya (this was also a good feature as the assignment of the progeny to intermediate castes in previous centuries naturally created jealousies and tended to increase the number of subcastes). Imagine then the condition of the higher Hindu society of that period when in the same family there were Brahmins, Kshatriyas and Vaiśyas. All partook of the same food which did not put a ban on flesh (with the exception of certain kinds such as beef which were prohibited to all), drinking out of the same pot of water and freely touching each other without any idea of polution, learning the same Vedas and performing the same Vedic rites ! ! ! The Brahmin could not then have been hated inwardly and respected outwardly as he is to-day by Kshatriyas and Vaiśyas. The Brahmin's untouchable lota could not have been an object of inward contempt, his untouchable sacred dhoti, an object of hatred, his learning the Vedas to the exclusion of others as at present, a matter for both envy and hatred. Thus members of the Aryan society were more firmly bound one to another by sentiments of affection and unity than it is now. Even to the other half or non-Aryan part of the people viz., the Śūdras, the three higher castes were bound by greater ties of affection than at present. Though there was no inter-marriage, yet there was no ban still on inter-dining; omitting, of course, out of consideration the great class of outcastes or Panchamas. This statement might perhaps startle many a reader, but this is a fact which cannot be gainsaid. Although we have no reference to this in the inscriptions of the period, we have the Smṛitis themselves to rely upon on this subject. The later Smṛitis even, not to speak of the older, distinctly allow such inter-dining. Of course, interdining was freely allowed among the three higher castes and a Brahmin could take food with Kshatriyas and Vaiśyas without any fear of losing caste; but he could do so even with certain classes of the Śūdras as the provisions of the Smṛitis distinctly declare. We have studied the Smṛitis with this object carefully and we find many things allowed by the Smṛitis then which in these days are prohibited by caste rules and which if practised to-day would involve loss of caste. In the Appendix we have culled together all such provisions of the different Smṛitis and the reader will be interested therein to find many things which he could not have dreamt of. Here it will suffice to notice the Smṛiti provisions which allow interdining with Śūdras. The Vyāsa Smṛiti which seems to be the latest says that a Brahmin taking food with a barber, a friend of the family, a coparcener in cultivation, a servant, a cowherd, even though these be Śūdras, incurs no sin.* Now these Śūdras were considered fit to be dined with, because they were more cleanly and had more claims on the friendship of the Brahmins. Indeed, it may be added that the above really reflects the condition of society in the second sub-period of our history. For, the Parāśara Smṛiti which is specially intended for the Kali age declares that it is allowable for Brahmins and Kshatriyas to take to cultivation and still observe their own Vedic ritual. This shows how the present condition of society observable now in Northern India has arisen, wherein among the agriculturists there is a large percentage of Brahmins and Kshatriyas and in the Deccan where Marātha Kshatriyas have mostly taken to agriculture. Now under such condition of society, the Brahmin and Kshatriya agriculturists would be thrown into contact with good Śūdras who may be either Ardha-sīrīs (parceners) or servants and these are declared to be fit to be taken food with; thus binding even the Śūdras with bonds of sympathy with the Aryans. The Vaiśyas were already agriculturists but the agricultural Vaiśyas had, as stated before, lost social estimation and had begun to be classed with Śūdras. This was also another reason why Śūdras occupying a higher status were treated as fit for

---

* नापितान्वयमित्रार्द्धसीरिणो दासगोपकाः ।
शूद्राणामप्यमीषां तु भुक्त्वान्नं नैव दुष्यति ॥

inter-dining. In fact the Atri Smṛiti and others allow even Srādha and other rites to be performed by Śūdras and naturally on such occasions Brahmins were expected to dine with them. The Atri Smṛiti declares, " The Śūdra is of two classes, one who can perform Śrāddha and the other who can not. The first class of Śūdra viz. Śrāddhi is fit to be dined with, though the other is not."* Here is a condition of society portrayed entirely differing from that of the present day, wherein no Śūdra and even no Vaiśya and no Kshatriya is considered fit by the Brahmin even to take water from, not to speak of taking food with ! ! ! Naturally disunion with consequent hatred and ill feeling is more rampant now than it could have been in the 9th and 10th centuries when interdining was freely allowed between all these classes.

How in later centuries interdining ceased, we will discuss in the third volume, but here we may remark that the result has been curious. Brahmins, instead of gaining anything, have rather sunk in position. Brahmins alone are now looked upon as fit for supplying water to Kshatriyas and Vaiśyas owing to their alleged greater purity and altogether the best for cooking. Naturally well-to-do Kshatriyas and rich Vaiśyas employ Brahmins as cooks and water bearers and it is thus the word Brahmin means now as stated before a priest, a cook, a waterman and a beggar. It is, indeed, a most ludicrous situation and sight..a Brahmin cook preparing food for his Vaiśya master and serving him too, yet keeping his higher caste purity unsullied by prohibiting any person even his master's family from entering the *chowka* or the sacred ring round the cooking hearth ! !

We now go on to describe the third aspect of society which must have contributed to the happy condition of the country viz., the absence of begging bands. One of the great defects of Buddhism was unquestionably its sanction of begging, nay, in fact, its organising beggary. When it allowed anybody to become a Bhikshu *i. e.* a begging monk and

---

* शूद्रोऽपि द्विविधो ज्ञेयो श्राद्धी चैवेतरस्तथा ।
श्राद्धी भोज्यस्तयोरुक्तो अभोज्यास्त्वितरः स्मृतः ॥

provided sumptuous dwellings for the residence of Bhikshus, the number of Bhikshu beggars naturally increased and idleness flocked to the Buddhist monasteries. This eventually proved, no doubt, its own disease and death, much in the same way as with the Christian monasteries of the west. In Buddhistic times these Bhikshus numbering several hundreds in each band would issue from monasteries and beg in towns and villages. The people, indeed, gave alms to them willingly but beggary and especially organised beggary is a nuisance and a cause of demoralisation. The remnant of this Buddhist Sanyāsa is still to be seen in the Panjab and U.P. where Sādhus roam and beg and even exact. Moreover, all castes were allowed to join the ranks of these shaven-headed beggars and naturally Śūdras formed the majority; the few Brahmins and Kshatriyas who joined the society did so from ambitious motives such as the desire to be the head of a monastery and so on. When Buddhism was supplanted entirely, these bands of beggars naturally disappeared owing to popular contempt. But the evil practice was too long in vogue to die finally. It revived again in the form of Śaiva and Vaishṇava ascetics called Gosavis and Bairagis who apparently led an unmarried life and lived on begging. But for a time begging was banned and Sādhu beggars did not exist. It is the privilege of the Brahmin to beg or to accept alms, but this is in consideration of his devoting himself to the performance of his religious duties. Ignorant Brahmins have no right to beg and during this sub-period such Brahmins were not allowed to beg. We find it laid down in a Smṛiti that the king should punish *the village* which gives alms to Brahmins who are neither learned nor religiously engaged. The reason given is that such almsgiving is supporting thieves. Brahmins in those days, therefore, were almost compelled to follow primarily their own priestly profession and they might follow the profession of Kshatriyas viz., that of arms and lastly the profession of Vaiśyas viz., agriculture. It seems thus very probable that the social condition of Mediæval Hindu India discouraged beggary even by Brahmins and necessarily by other castes.

While this evil arising from Buddhism was absent, the two great good results which Buddhism had achieved remained in their full force and added to the happiness of the people. In the first place, Buddhism laid the strongest emphasis on a moral life (so also did Jainism) and used the doctrine of metempsychosis with the allied doctrine of Karma for this purpose. No doubt, these two doctrines were taken from the ancient Aryan religion; but there can be no question that Buddhism succeeded in making them strongly impressed on the minds of the mass of the people and made them morally strong as described in the chapter on Religious condition. The high truthfulness and honesty of the people of India have, as noted already, struck foreigners who visited India during these two centuries and even later. It requires no detailed argument to show that a high moral tone prevailing among the people is a great factor in contributing to the happy condition of the society. In the second place, Buddhism had expelled animal sacrifice from the land finally. As already stated, respect for the Vedas had been re-established by the Mimānsā philosophy; but animal sacrifices were not revived. One can imagine how this factor also contributed to the happiness of the people. Ordinary Agnihotra is not a matter involving much trouble. But animal sacrifices which usually are of a higher order require a deal of expenditure of physical and pecuniary energy, as we actually know from present day experiences of such sacrifices which, though very rarely indeed, are still sometimes performed. Such energy was naturally applied to other purposes and generally useful purposes. Moreover, the highest animal sacrifices could be performed by kings and rich merchants or grandees only and these spent lakh of rupees on those useless ceremonies. Lastly the Aśvamedha and the Rājsūya performed by kings of kings only always led to devastating wars and their stoppage was, indeed, a blessing and a source of happiness to the people.

Having heretofore explained how the religious condition of the country during the 9th and 10th centuries contribu-ted to the happiness of the people, by the absence of all religious feuds, there being only one religion in the country, by the absence of caste jealousies, caste being still loose and interdining being still allowed between all the castes, by the absence of beggary, of moral depravity and of animal sacrifices, we will turn next to the economical condition of the country. This could not but have been most prosperous, because there was no foreign domination in the country either external or internal. We will take it as an established fact of history that where there is foreign domination especially of an external alien race, there is a constant drain out of the country in the form of tribute and the emoluments of higher officials civil and military and the exploitation of the country by foreign traders and capitalists. Every thing that is best, nay, even good, goes out of the country and benefits the dominant foreigner. Even internal foreign domination leads to similar though less spoilation. Mauryas ruling south from the north or Āndhrabhrityas ruling north from south were an evil. The political condition of the country in the ninth and tenth centuries was ideally good. There was no foreign domination (except in Sind) either external or internal. The three great empires of Kanauj, Malkhed and Monghyr were ruled by entirely local ruling dynasties. There was no domination of either the Marātha over the Bengali or of the Bengali over the Assamese. The Kanauj rule in Kathiawar and north Gujarat might have partaken of the evils of foreign domination and it actually led to the establishment of the local Chavda kingdom in Gujarat. But elsewhere the Kanuj empire must not have been felt as foreign. Similarly, the Rāsṭrakūṭas properly ruled in the Deccan and S. M. country. They were over-lords, no doubt, of kingdoms further south; but as often stated before such over-lordship was never felt where local kings were allowed to rule almost independently in their own lands. In fact, an Arab traveller has in effect recorded that in India people were ruled every where by their own kings. Under such a political condition there could not have been the economic drain so well described by Dadabhai Nowroji and the condition of the country economically must have been every where prosperous. We get glimpses of this in the writings of Arab travellers though few and far between. One writer, for instance, has stated (as mentioned already) that the country from Kambāyā to Saimur was thickly populated and well cultivated.

The system of civil administration has a great influence on the happiness of the people and on this score too we hold that there was very little to be desired. When revenue was paid in kind and at the rate of 6 the cultivator was saved almost all bother. The revenue automatically adjusted itself to the actual produce. When there was no produce owing to famine there was no revenue to be paid. Cash payment is convenient to the government; while payment in kind was convenient to the cultivators. Secondly, as already explained there were very few or no other taxes, the expenses of government being limited and Abkari and forest were practically unknown. There was vishti or forced labour, no doubt, but it fell very lightly especially on the cultivators. And lastly, internal foes viz., banditti and robbers were most rigorously dealt with and suppressed. As noted by an Arab traveller, the kingdom of Kanauj was particularly free from robbers and we think the other empires of the south and the east were also equally rigorous in the suppression of robbery and brigandage.

The sufferings which are inflicted by invasions of foreign foes on a nation are almost always the bitterest that it can undergo. Fortunately, destiny had so arranged events that India was absolutely free from foreign invasions during the centuries we are dealing with. The Arabs had been checked and they themselves had deteriorated. The Turks had yet to arise or rather to leave their Central Asian steppes to overrun and devastate the rest of Asia. The people of India had constantly suffered from such foreign inroads in her history. The Greeks, the Śakas, the Kushāṇs, the Mundas, the Tibetans, the Hūṇas, the Arabs, had over-run India before. The Turks, the Moguls, the Persians and the Afghans had yet to come. This intervening period of the ninth and the tenth centuries was a breathing period and thus peculiarly happy. It may be objected that there was constant waging of war between the Juzr and the Balhāra, between the Deccani and the Bengali. These wars were not with foreigners, but between native kingdoms and were consequently not waged with that ferocity with which the foreigners fought with the Indians. There were many considerations which impelled civilized and humane treatment and as we actually see, the kingdoms were never sought to be subverted. Even if Kanauj was sometimes seized by Rattas or Malkhed by Parmāras, the seizure was only temporary, the kings were always restored and the kingdoms always remained intact. In fact, such wars might be compared with wars which were waged in the fifteenth century and later between England, France, Germany and Spain. They were wars waged between peoples of the same race, the same religion, and the same civilization and were never carried on with racial animosity or motives of seizure of territory. No doubt, the rules of warfare which were in vogue in India in the days of the Mahābhārata or even down to the coming of the Greeks were not now observed ; when cultivators securely sowed or reaped while hostile armies passed. And the Indians had learnt the method of devastating an enemy's country in order to weaken him ; for we find from an inscription that the Rāsṭrakūṭa Govinda when he took Kanauj devastated it and made it not only in name but in reality Kuśasthalī or ground overgrown with Kuśa grass. The evil, however, was always restricted in time and not as extensively spread as in Mahomedan wars and we may take it that the wars between the several Hindu kingdoms did not much interfere with the general prosperity or happiness of the people.

On the contrary, in our view these wars contributed in their own way to increase the happiness of the people. Wars are a necessary evil and distinctly work towards the good of humanity, when not waged with ferocity, by keeping up the martial spirit of the people, by fostering martial virtues such as courage, valour and patriotism and by increasing the stock of human knowledge by means of inventions. They prevent the people from becoming effete and effeminate ; and they aid the progress of humanity on its onward march in civilization. We have already stated that India need not and could not be one state ; its division in consequence of physical peculiarities and the different development of the people in language and in customs into four or five large states was natural. Thus the ninth and tenth centuries in many ways formed the happiest period for the people of India. How in the next century it fell a prey to the sword of Mahmud of Ghazni and how its strength was found unequal to cope with the evil of foreign invasion we shall have to elucidate in our next volume.

[THE END.]

APPENDIX

I.—THE SOLAR AND LUNAR KSHATRIYA RACES OF INDIA IN THE VEDAS.

[We have said at p. 12 Chap. 3 Book III that the idea of the Solar and Lunar races of Kshatriyas goes so far back as the Vedas themselves. It would not be out of place, therefore, to show in this appendix how the idea of the Solar and Lunar races can clearly be traced back to the Vedas and we make no apology for giving here in extenso a paper read by us on this subject before the Bombay Branch of the Royal Asiatic Society in 1914 and published in its journal for that year. Indeed this subject is intimately connected with the question of the claim of the Rajputs to be treated as the descendants of Vedic Aryans and it would be interesting to the reader to know that the theory of Solar and Lunar descent of Kshatriyas is as old as the Vedas and that the genealogies of the two races given in the Purāṇas are not imaginary but have a historical background of unquestioned authenticity behind them. With these introductory remarks we give the aforesaid paper below without any change.]

It would be proper to state at the outset that I was led to study this subject in my own way on reading Mr. Pargiter's most valuable paper on the Earliest Traditional History of India published in this year's April number of the Journal of the R. A. S. of Great Britain and Ireland. Mr. Pargiter has devoted himself so zealously to the otherwise uninteresting study of the Purāṇas that he has been able to extract from them interesting information regarding the ancient history of India. His contention that the Purāṇic genealogies can afford material for constructing that history nobody can now deny and he has shown how that material can be so utilised. A few of his conclusions, however, will not be acceptable to many, especially his idea that the Solar dynasty of Indian Kshatriyas was Dravidian or that the Lunar Kshatriyas had their original kingdom at Allahabad or Prayāga. Indeed, according to my view, Mr. Pargiter has attached too much weight to the Purāṇas and has consequently arrived at conclusions which will not be readily acceptable to all. I set myself to study the materials, therefore, in my own way. Having already studied the Mahābhārata and the Rāmāyaṇa I was able to do so very easily. I looked into the principal Purāṇas and co-ordinated the facts according to my own light. But I more particularly looked into the Vedic Literature for the study of which Macdonell's Vedic Index proved to be a most invaluable book. In fact, the historical material from the Vedas is already collected there and you have only to study it carefully. On this material I have come to certain conclusions of my own which I take the liberty of placing before this learned Society with the hope that they will be found interesting and will be carefully considered.

In two important matters my way of looking at things differs from that of Mr. Pargiter and it is necessary to describe this difference of standpoint in detail. In the first place, I make no difference between Brahmin tradition and Kshatriya tradition as Mr. Pargiter does. In fact, it is because Mr. Pargiter looks upon the Purāṇas as Kshatriya tradition and consequently as more reliable that he attaches so much more value to the Purāṇas than they deserve. Brahmin tradition is usually looked at askance by European scholars who have an inexplicable bias against the writings of the Brahmins. But I do not take my stand upon this aspect of the matter. What I urge here is that no difference need be made between Brahmin tradition and Kshatriya tradition in this study. The Brahmins and the Kshatriyas were, in ancient times, except on very rare occasions, friends and even accomplices of one another. They came from the same race and even family as appears clear from the genealogies themselves. They stood to each other in the same relation as the Teutonic noblemen in the middle ages, the elder of whom became the prince and the younger the prelate. They were equally interested in exaggerating the glories of one another and were thus not antagonistic. The Kshatriyas extolled the holiness of the Brahmins and the Brahmins extolled the prowess and liberality of the Kshatriyas. In short, there is very little discrimination to be made in the reliability of Brahmin or Kshatriya traditions. And I would urge that both of them should be viewed with the same searching scrutiny, neither more nor less than any other human traditions. The Brahmins or the Kshatriyas were certainly not more culpable in exaggerating matters than other peoples of the ancient world. Nay, if anything, I would accord Brahmin tradition greater weight than any other tradition. It is a phenomenon nowhere to be met with in the world that the Brahmins have preserved to this date what their ancient Ṛishis composed in the shape of hymn or dissertation thousands of years ago, without the addition or alteration of a single word. The Vedic literature knows no different readings and no different recensions. It has come down to us without any tampering and hence whatever exaggeration or untruth may have been used in the original composition, we feel sure that no subsequent colouring or emendation or omission has taken place in the course of thousands of years (5,000 at least according to my view). The world must, therefore, be thankful to the Brahmins for preserving almost hermetically sealed what the Indo-Aryan Ṛishis said or thought. This difficult task they have accomplished by making it the chief duty of their caste. They have, by several rules, ensured the maintenance of those who make the reciting of the Vedas their sole occupation in life and thus secured the preservation untampered of the Vedic literature. It must be noted here that a similar provision was also made for preserving Kshatriya tradition. In my view if the Vedas recorded Brahmin tradition, the Itihāsa-Purāṇa recorded Kshatriya tradition. Itihāsa was the account of particular kings or events and Purāṇa was genealogies. Genealogies were preserved in India as scrupulously as they were in Egypt, Chaldæa, or Palestine. Their recitation was made the caste-duty of the Sūtas, or sons born of Brahmin women by Kshatriya fathers. Itihāsa-Purāṇa was a branch of study even for Brahmins themselves. Mr. Pargiter seems to be incorrect when he says in a foot-note that the Brahmins did not care to learn Kshatriya tradition. In the Chhāndogya Upanishad we have the Nārada-Sanatkumāra dialogue wherein Sanatkumāra asks Nārada "What have you studied?" "I have studied the

Ṛigveda" answered Nārad "the Yajurveda, the Sāmaveda, the Atharva, the Itihāsa-Purāṇa, grammar, arithmetic, astronomy, the science of war" and so on. This clearly shows that even Brahmins studied Itihāsa-Purāṇa. But it was the special duty of Sūtas and the reputed reciters of the Purāṇas, *viz.*, Lomaharshaṇa and his son were Sūtas. Even now modern Kshatriya genealogies are preserved by Bhātas who enjoy equal respect with Brahmins in all Rajput States. The natural desire for preserving genealogies is so great in the Hindu community of the north that even Chamars have their Bhātas who preserve their genealogies and recite them at the time of marriage festivals. In short, the Indo-Aryans had made sufficient provision in their caste-system for the preservation of Kshatriya tradition; a provision which still subsists. My idea is that this system fell into abeyance for some centuries during the rise and progress of Buddhism when the caste-system was convulsed or when Non-Kshatriya kings during Buddhist or Greek or Śaka times had no interest in preserving Kshatriya genealogies. During several centuries, therefore, say from about 300 B. C. to 300 A. D. these genealogies became neglected and mutilated and when the Brahmins again asserted themselves under the Guptas and reconstructed the Purāṇas, the materials before them were meagre and incoherent. Hence while the Brahmins have preserved their Vedic traditions intact, the Kshatriya traditions presented in the Purāṇas are incomplete, conflicting and generally untrustworthy.

This brings me to the second point of difference in my standpoint of view. I look upon the Purāṇas as the last in the list of our authorities in this study. The information they give is, no doubt, very valuable; but that information is garbled, is unconnected and incomplete, and is distorted so as to suit new ideas. Hence it must be admitted very cautiously. In fact, I may arrange the authorities in this study in the following order, an order which is at once their proper order in point of priority of time as well as priority of value. For, it will be easily conceded that whatever is more ancient is also more reliable. To speak in Indian form पूर्व-पूर्व-प्रामाण्य should be the rule. The authorities for the construction of ancient or pre-Buddhistic history may, therefore, be arranged as follows :—

(1) *The Ṛigveda.*—It is almost contemporaneous evidence and as preserved untampered with, is very valuable and naturally stands first in this list.

(2) *Yajurveda and Sāmaveda.*—These are somewhat later in date. I do not bring in the Atharvaveda whose date is so very uncertain.

(3) *The Brāhmaṇas.*—As coming next after the Mantras, their evidence is of great value. They are the utterances of those who have some remembrance of the Vedic times and can speak with authority about them better than any later books.

(4) *The Vedāṅgas.*—By their time the Vedic traditions had become hoary and a matter of speculation as with us. For their own times, they are valuable. They are also valuable as coming in date after the Brāhmaṇas. Vedāṅgas include Yāska, Pāṇini, Lagadha and the Kalpa or Śrauta Sūtras.

(5) The later Sūtras, *viz.*, Gṛihya and Dharma.

(6) Megasthenes, Arrian and other Greek writers about the time of Alexander or Seleucus come in here in point of time. The information which they have recorded from personal observation and hearsay is very valuable and must be co-ordinated.

(7) *The Mahābhārata.*—The date of the last or present edition of the Mahābhārata according to my view is about 250-200 B.C. and hence its evidence is of less value than that of the Greek writers.

(8) *The Harivaṁśha.*—Ditto.

(9) *The Rāmāyaṇa of Vālmiki.*—The date of the present form of the poem is about 100 B.C.

(10) *The Purāṇas.*—Their dates range from 300 to 900 A.C. and they naturally come last in the list of our authorities.

This is the order of our authorities and we must try to combine all the historical information they afford. Where statements are conflicting, greater weight must be attached to the older of the statements. That is the only way in which the vagaries of the Purāṇas can be checked and one is thus alone able to find some rule for rejecting, as often we shall have to do, the exaggerated, mutilated or emended accounts of the Purāṇas.

But this does not exhaust the list of our authorities. There are two important new sciences the conclusions of which must be respected and co-ordinated in this study. They are ethnology and philology. The inferences derived from considerations of features and of language with regard to the history of races are very valuable and in recent times these sciences have much advanced. They have been applied to the people of this country by noted scientists of the west and I think the conclusions which they have arrived at are of great value to us in the inquiry into the racial problems of India. They are, therefore, fit to be included in the list of our authorities and the value to be attached to their conclusions transcends the value of all other evidence.

I must lastly notice another piece of evidence which will be found to be of great value to us in this inquiry by way of analogy if not directly. I think the ancient history of India resembles, to a very large extent, the modern history of the discovery and colonization of America. India was a vast unknown continent covered with forests and inhabited by people very much inferior in civilization, when the Indo-Aryans first discovered the land. The migration of Aryans from some unknown country in the north to several countries is spoken of in the Vendidad, I think, and it is stated therein that the Aryans came to Sapta-Sindhu but Aingra Mainyu visited that land with serpents and heat. In this we have sure evidence that one branch of the Aryans came to India and settled there. Their history must naturally very greatly resemble the history of the colonization of America with its oft-recurring struggles with the native races but sometimes with the co-operation and willing consent of the milder peoples thereof; and with its internecine strife between the different settlers themselves. The history of America during the first stages, therefore, in my view, has much importance by way of analogy and we may often consult it in our inquiry with advantage.

Having so far stated the materials on which I base my conclusions and the respective value to be attached to them I proceed to sketch some important points in the history of the Solar and Lunar races of Kshatriyas of India in the following pages.

The first fact of importance which we have to notice is that there were two invasions of India by the Aryans. To put it in a different way two hordes of Aryans came into India, of course, from the north-west, by different routes and at different times. This fact is disclosed both by ethnology and philology and is supported by tradition. It was perhaps Dr. Hoernle first to point this out and Dr. Grierson has accepted the theory from a consideration of the modern Sanskrit-born vernaculars of India (see *Imperial Gazetteer*, Vol. I, page 358). The following extract from the last Census Report of India is relevant in this connection.

"These languages, according to Dr. Hoernle, were brought to India by two successive hordes of invaders. After the first horde had settled in the plains of northern India, a fresh horde came in and penetrated the original mass like a wedge, blotting out the language in the centre and extending from Ambala in the north to beyond Jubbulpore in the south and from Kathiawar in the south-west to Nepal in the north-east. Western Hindi is the modern representative of the languages of these peoples of the second invasion; while that of the earlier invaders covers Rajastani, Punjabi, western and eastern Pahadi and eastern Hindi" (page 325).

This conclusion suggested by a comparison of the several Sanskrit-born vernaculars of northern India is very strongly corroborated by the conclusions arrived at from ethnological considerations. Sir Henry Risley took ethnological measurements at the time of the Census of 1901 and found that the people of the Punjab and Rajastan were undoubted Aryans with long heads and prominent noses. In the United Provinces he found medium heads and tolerably prominent noses and he looked upon their people as a mixture of Aryans and Dravidians. Now the Aryans who mixed with the Dravidians of the United

Provinces must have been Aryans of a different type. They must have been broad-headed Aryans so that their mixture with the long-headed Dravidians has resulted in the medium heads of the present population of the United Provinces speaking generally. We thus find from ethnological considerations also that there were two hordes of Aryans who came into India, the first long-headed and the second broad-headed. The first occupied the Punjab and Rajastan and extended as far east as Mithila and the second came in subsequently like a wedge and mixed with the native Dravidians of the United Provinces now form the chief population of this vast tract. Now this conclusion deduced from both philology and ethnology is supposed by tradition. These two Aryan hordes in my view were the two races which are known as the Solar and Lunar races of Kshatriyas from Mahābhārata onwards. We have a distinct reference to them in the Mahābhārata in a speech of Śhrikṛishṇa. This is what he says to Yudhishṭhira in the Sabhāparva when the latter proposes the performance of Rājasūya sacrifice. "Of the two races of Kshatriyas born from the sun and the moon there are at present in India 101 families and of these families the Bhojas of the Lunar race are the most numerous and occupy the middle land." This shows that the Kshatriya families of India in Epic times ranged themselves under two chief races, the Solar and the Lunar, and that the Lunar race, occupying the middle land, had at that time thrown the Solar race into shade. Thus we are fortified in believing that the first race of Aryan invaders was what was subsequently called the Solar race, that it occupied the Punjab and extended onwards along the foot of the Himalayas as far east as Mithila and that the second race of Kshatriyas which came into India subsequently and which was later on called the Lunar race came through Kashmir and like a wedge shoved itself through the territory of the Sarasvati or Ambala downwards as far south as Kathiawar and Jubbulpore or even further south, covering many Bhoja kingdoms especially the Śauraseni, Chedi, Magadha and Vidarbha kingdoms and Yādava kingdom of Dwarka. We shall try to see how far this conclusion finds support in the Ṛigveda about the time, of which, of course, these invasions must have taken place.

The chief people of whom the Ṛigveda frequently speaks are, as is perhaps well-known, the Bharatas. Now it is a misconception of many scholars, native as well as European, that these Bharatas were the descendants of Bharata, the son of Dushyanta, who is a well-known king of the Lunar race. According to my theory, the Lunar race which came later and mixed with the aboriginal population of the United Provinces forms the people who at present speak Western Hindi. The difficulty thus presented to me was, however, solved accidentally in my study and in a proper manner. I found that this Bharata was an entirely different king from the Daushyanti Bharata of later days. I accidentally came across the following ślokas in the Bhāgavata and was struck to see that the idea commonly entertained on the subject was erroneous. Bhāgavata, 11th Skandha, Chapter 2, says :—

प्रियव्रतो नाम सुतो मनोः स्वायंभुवस्य यः ।
तस्याग्नीध्रस्ततो नाभिर्ऋषभस्य सुतः स्मृतः ॥ १५
तमाहुर्वासुदेवांशं मोक्षधर्मविवक्षया ।
अवतीर्णं सुतशतं तस्यासीद् ब्रह्मपारगम् ॥ १६ ॥
तेषां वै भरतो ज्येष्ठो नारायणपरायणः ।
विख्यातं वर्षमेतद्यन्नाम्ना भारतमुत्तमम् ॥ १७ ॥

Transl. " Priyavrata was a son of the first Manu called Svāyambhuva. His son was Agnīdhra and his son was Nābhi and his son was Ṛishabha who is believed to have been born of the essence of Vāsudeva. He had a hundred sons all well-versed in the Vedas. The eldest of them was Bharata after whom this land is called Bhāratavarsha." In Skandha 5, chapter 7, the same thing has already been stated; अजनाभं नामैतद्वर्षं भारतमिति यत आरभ्य व्यपदिशन्ति. This clearly shows that India is called भारतवर्ष from Bharata who was a great-grandson of the first Manu. This tradition recorded in the Bhāgavata is also found in the Vāyu Purāṇa where the line of Svāyambhuva Manu is described in detail. Priyavrata divided the world of seven Dvīpas among his seven sons. Agnīdhra got Jambudvīpa and divided it among his sons. Nābhi got a portion of it and his son, Ṛishabha gave Bharata, his son, land to the south of the Himalayas. Says Vāyu chap. 33.

हिमाद्रेर्दक्षिणं वर्षं भरताय न्यवेदयेत् ।
तस्मात्तं भारतं वर्षं तस्य नाम्ना विदुर्बुधाः ॥ ५२ ॥

Thus the tradition of this country being called Bhāratavarsha refers to Bharata, a descendant of the first Manu and not to Bharata, the son of Dushyanta.

Another derivation of this name भारतवर्ष is given in the same Vāyu Purāṇa wherein Bharata is identified with Manu himself.

वर्षं यद्भारतं नाम यत्रेयं भारती प्रजा ।
भरणाच्च प्रजानां वै मनुर्भरत उच्यते ॥
निरुक्तवचनाच्चैवं वर्षं तद्भारतं स्मृतम् ॥ ७६ ॥

The Matsya Purāṇa gives the same story and repeats this very śloka. This shows that Bharata was also identified with Manu in later tradition. But he never is, we must remember, दौष्यन्ति भरत. The king whose name the land now bears is never thought to be Bharata, the son of Dushyanta and Śakuntalā, but is always another king much earlier who was born of the first Manu or was Manu himself. In the Nirukta to which reference is given in the Purāṇa ślokas I found that Yāska interprets Bharata as Āditya or the Sun himself (अ० २ पा० १० भरत आदित्यस्तस्य भारती). This then is the tradition of the Nirukta and the Purāṇas. We shall find that the Ṛigvedic tradition is also the same and that it frequently speaks of this Bharata and not the later Daushyanti Bharata as I will presently show.

The difficulty then which naturally presents itself is solved. India is called भारतवर्ष not from a king of the later Lunar Kshatriya race but from a king of the earliest Kshatriyas who entered India. Here we have an analogy from American history. America was discovered and colonized by two hordes of people and in different directions just as it happened in India. The Spaniards, the Portuguese, the Italians and the French were the pioneers of discoverers of America. They were all of the Latin race. The subsequent discoverers were the Dutch and the English who naturally went northwards and came to Northern America. They were of the Teutonic race. The whole hemisphere is, however, called America from one Amerigo, an Italian discoverer, who first set his foot on the Southern Continent and the name has generally been adopted. He was almost a contemporary of Columbus who had only discovered some islands. The honour of discovering the main continent belongs to Amerigo and his name was properly given to the land and has cordially been accepted by all people. The case was exactly similar in India. Bharata was a famous king of the first Kshatriyas who came to India and his name has been given to the country. The descendants of this Bharata who were subsequently known in Epic times as the Solar race Kshatriyas gradually overspread the land from the Indus to the Gandakī or Sadānīrā, the boundary of the kingdom of Mithila. This is exactly what appears from the Ṛigveda, our eldest and best authority, as I now proceed to show.

The following information is given under the word Bharata in Vedic Index Vol. II page 95. " Bharata is the name of a people of great importance in the Ṛigveda, where they appear prominently in the third and seventh Mandalas in connection with Sudāsa and Tritsus, while in the sixth Maṇdala they are associated with Divodāsa." Now I looked into the Ṛigveda hymns mentioned here in the original and found that very interesting information could be gathered therefrom. The first thing apparent is that the Vasishṭhas were the Purohitas of the Bharatas. Now according to later trradition the Vasishṭhas were never the Purohitas of the Lunar race but served the Solar race throughout. Here is a confirmation of the view that these Bharatas were the people who subsequently were called the Solar Kshatriyas and the Vasishṭhas who appear also to be called Tritsus were their hereditary priests. The seventh Mandala of the Ṛigveda consists solely of hymns composed by the Vasishṭhas and it is but natural that the Bharatas should predominate therein. Ṛigveda vii, 33, is very interesting in this connection. It says that in the fight with the ten kings called दाशराज्ञ, the Bharatas became afraid and defenceless like sticks asunder but Vasishṭha by his strength and prayer became their leader and made them victorious. (दण्डा इवेद्गो अजनास आसन् परिच्छिन्ना भरता अर्भकासः । अभवच्च पुर एता वसिष्ठ आदित्तृत्सूनां विशो अप्रथन्त ॥ ६ ॥) In this hymn the birth of Vasishṭha from the dual god Maitrā-Varuna and the Apsaras Urvaśi is also mentioned. Vasishṭha is thus already a mythical person and born of gods. He saved the Bharatas in their difficulty. Secondly, Bharata's fire is frequently spoken of in different places in the Ṛigveda. The Aryans were worshippers of fire in contrast with the Dāsas or aborigines and hence Bharata's fire must have become a favourite name as typifying the Aryan religion. In Ṛigveda vii, 8 this Bharata's fire is mentioned as also the original king Bharata (प्र प्रायमग्निर्भरतस्य शृण्वे । अभि यः पूरुं पृतनासु तस्थौ ॥ ४ ॥). " This is Bharata's own fire, he who defeated Pūru in battle." In this sentence we have a distinct reference to king Bharata and his exploit is said to be that he defeated Pūru. Under the word Pūru Macdonnell refers to this hymn and seems to interpret Pūru as the well-known king of the Lunar race, an ancestor of Dushyanta, who is one of the five sons of Yayāti and whose descendants are also frequently mentioned in the Ṛigveda as Pūrus. But the Śatapatha Brāhmaṇa explains in one place that Pūru in this hymn is the name of an Asura. On this Macdonell remarks that the Pūrus had been forgotten so far in the days of the Śatapatha that Pūru had become an Asura-Rākshasa. I have already said that the authority of the Brāhmaṇas as coming immediately after the Mantras and as the utterances of Ṛishis who had some touch with the Vedic times ought to be given greater weight than all later authorities. In my opinion the Śatapatha Brāhmaṇa is here correct and this Pūru whom Bharata defeated must have been some aboriginal king. He cannot be the Pūru who was a son of Yayāti and an ancestor of Dushyanta. As shown above this Pūru could not have been a contemporary of Bharata who was a king of the earliest Kshatriyas who came to India. The Lunar Pūru came into India later and the Pūru in this hymn whom Bharata conquered cannot have been that Pūru but some Asura or Rākshasa. One thing is at least apparent from this that if you take by Pūru, the

Pūru of the Lunar race, this Bharata assuredly is not his descendant दौष्यन्ति भरत. Thus Bharata whose Agni is spoken of so frequently in the Ṛigveda is entirely a different and a much earlier king of a different race who fought with Pūru.

This is a digression, but an important and necessary digression. To return to our subject, Vasishṭha's hymns (vii, 33 and 8) show that Bharata is the name of a king in the Ṛigveda, that his Agni is often spoken of and that his descendants were Bharatas whose Purohita was Vasishṭha. The next most frequently mentioned subsequent king of the Bharatas is Sudāsa whose battle with the ten kings on the banks of the Parushṇī is spoken of in detail in another hymn of Vasishṭha, *viz.*, Ṛigveda vii, 83 as also in vii, 18. I will speak of this battle further on. But Sudāsa in hymn vii, 83, is the same king who fought the battle with the ten kings or दाशराज्ञ expressly mentioned therein and the Bharatas are also mentioned in vii, 83 as dejected in दाशराज्ञ or the battle with the ten kings. Other important kings presumably Bharatas whom Vasishṭha speaks of (Ṛigveda vii, 19), are Purukutsa and Trasadasyu as I shall show later on. I shall now proceed to a consideration of the hymns in Maṇḍala iii wherein also the Bharatas are mentioned expressly and by a Ṛishi whose name is very inportant.

This third Maṇḍala consists of hymns entirely composed by Viśvāmitra as Maṇḍala vii consists of hymns by Vasishṭha or his descendants. The first relevent hymn in the third Maṇḍala is 23. This hymn is, however, said to be composed by Devaśravas and Devavāta, two Bharata kings. "The Bharatas lighted or rubbed Agni, *viz.*, Devaśravas and Devavāta on the banks of the Drishadvatî and Āpayā and Sarasvatī." This clearly shows that the Bharatas extended their occupation of the land as far as the Sarasvatī in the time of these two kings. The next hymn is iii. 33. It is a very eloquent hymn addressed by Viśvāmitra to the two rivers Vipāśā and Śatadru (Bias and Sutlej) combined. Probably the Bharatas had arrived at the confluence of these two rivers in some expedition and finding the swift rivers unfordable

Viśvāmitra prayed to the rivers to become fordable and they became so and the Bharatas were allowed to cross over, the water not touching even the axles of their carts (अधो अक्षः सिन्धवः स्रोत्याभिः). "As soon as the Bharatas have passed over, let your streams flow on in rapid motion." (यदङ्ग त्वा भरताः सन्तरेयुः गव्यन्ग्राम इषित इन्द्रजूतः ।). The third interesting hymn is iii. 53. In this hymn Viśvāmitra is represented to have assisted Sudāsa by his prayers to Indra, (विश्वामित्रो यदवह-त्सुदासमप्रियायत कुशिकेभिरिन्द्र), He even says that his prayer it was which saved the Bharata people. (विश्वामित्रस्य रक्षति ब्रह्मेदं भारतं जनम्). Three or four things, therefore, appear clear from this hymn. First, the Bharata people had already become very numerous, they being called भारत जन. (We have almost an echo here of the present भारतवर्ष). Secondly, their king was Sudāsa and that Viśvāmitra of the Kuśikas saved him and his people by his prayers to Indra. Here we have a confirmation of the chief points in the later Puranic tradition about Viśvāmitra. He was born of the Kuśikas (whether they were Kshatriyas is not here apparent). Viśvāmitra acted as priest to the same Sudāsa whose family priest has already been shown to be Vasishṭha. Vasishṭha and Viśvāmitra must, therefore, have sometimes become enemies. Later tradition of Rāma brings in both Vasishṭha and Viśvāmitra as his friends. Viśvāmitra always comes in in the stories of the Solar race kings such as Sudāsa and Rāma and Hariśchandra who, according to Vedic tradition, purchased Śunahśepa to redeem his son Rohita from a vow to Varuṇa. Viśvāmitra saved this Śunahśepa by praying to Varuṇa and adopted him as Devarata or given by the gods. Śunahśepa's hymns are to be found in Ṛigveda Maṇḍala I, and they plainly refer to this story of the Brāhmaṇas. Viśvāmitra is a person who figures in the history of the Bharatas in the Vedas and also in that of the Solar Kshatriyas of the Epic days and thus we are fortified in our conclusion that they are the same people. Sudāsa is a Bharata king in the Vedas and he is a Solar king in the Purāṇas. His story is given in the Rāmāyaṇa Uttarakāṇḍa Chap. 65, where Vālmīki tells Śhatrughna that Sudāsa was one of his ancestors and that his grand-son quarrelled with his Guru Vasishṭha and became कल्माषपाद who again appears to have been assisted by Viśvāmitra. Thus the rivalry between Vasishṭha and Viśvāmitra continues throughout the Vedic and the Epic tradition. Vasishṭha assists Sudāsa in the battle with the ten kings on the banks of the Parushṇi and Viśvāmitra assists him in his eastern progress and enables him by his prayer to ford over the Vipāśa and the Sutlej. I may add, Viśvāmitra always figures in the Bharata or Solar race history, but he does not do so, to my knowledge, in the history of the Lunar race, a fact on which I will comment later on.

The next Maṇḍala which mentions the Bharata people is the sixth wherein their king Divodāsa is mentioned. This Maṇḍala again consists of hymns principally or almost solely composed by Bharadvāja Bārhaspatya or Bharadvāja, son of Bṛihaspati. The principal hymn which we have to refer to here is vi, 16. It is a long hymn and mentions Bharata, the Bhārata people, the Agni of Bharata and king Divodāsa more than once. It also mentions Bharadvāja himself. (त्वमिमा वार्या पुरु दिवोदासाय सुन्वते। भरद्वाजाय दाशुषे । 5, आग्निरगामि भारतो वृत्रहा पुरुचेतनः । दिवोदासस्य सत्पतिः । 19, प्र देवं देववीतये भरता वसुवित्तमम् । आ स्वे योनौ निषीदतु । 41.) Surprise is expressed by some scholars (see Vedic Index) that Divodāsa who is always spoken of in the Ṛigveda as the father of Sudāsa should be associated with Bharadvāja while his son is always spoken of with Vasishṭha and Viśvāmitra. But I do not think there is matter here for surprise. The Vasishṭhas were undoubtedly the Purohitas of the Bharatas. They plainly appear so from the Ṛigveda itself. But that does not prevent other Ṛishis coming in religious relations with the Bharatas. Viśvāmitra does so admittedly with Sudāsa and so might Bharadvāja come in contact with his father Divodāsa. It is curious to see that the contact of Bharadvāja with the Solar race people appears also in the Rāmāyaṇa wherein the same Ṛishi or his descendant comes in in the story with his affection for Rāma and Bharata and his friendship with their father.

Such then are the coincidences which make it almost certain that the Bharatas of the Ṛigveda are the oldest Aryans who came to India and spread over the land from the Indus eastward as far as the Sarayu which is mentioned in three Ṛigvedic hymns. Their Ṛishis were Vasishṭha and Viśvāmita and Bharadvāja, actors in the story of the Rāmāyaṇa also and other legends of the kings of the Solar race. The kings of the Bharatas mentioned in the Ṛigveda are Bharata, Divodāsa, Sudāsa, Devaśravā and Devavāta and probably Purukutsa and Trasadasyu ; and Ikshvāku ; and finally, we find, in one hymn of the tenth Maṇḍala Rāma himself. Now Bharata, according to the Nirukta, is the Sun and he is also Manu and again a king of the first Kshatriyas who came to India, of the first Manu's race according to the Purāṇas. Sudāsa is a Solar race king, as per Chapter 65 Uttarakāṇḍa already noticed, wherein the son of Sudāsa's story is related. He was about to curse Vasishṭha, but was prevented by his wife who implored him to remember that Vasishṭha was their family priest. The śloka in the Rāmāyaṇa is as follows :—

युष्माकं पूर्वजो राजा सौदासस्तस्य भूपतेः ।
पुत्रा वीर्यसहो नाम वीर्यवानतिधार्मिकः ॥

In this वीर्यसह who became कल्माषपाद, with feet blackened by the water taken for the curse, is said to be a son of Saudāsa, who again is said to be an ancestor of Śhatrughna. And a Sudāsa is actually found in the Puranic genealogy of the Solar race with his son Kalmāshapada though his father is not Divodāsa of the Vedas. I am of opinion that the Puranic genealogy must be considered to be here incorrect and must give precedence to the Ṛigvedic tradition which makes Sudāsa a son of Divodāsa and a grandson of Pijavana. Divodāsa and Sudāsa are found in Lunar race genealogies also, but the Ṛigvedic Sudāsa is undoubtedly a Solar king ; for his Purohita is Vasishṭha both according to the Ṛigveda and the Rāmāyaṇa. And hence Sudāsa's father Divodāsa must also be treated as a Solar king. Next Purukutsa and Trasadasyu are Solar race kings in the Purāṇa genealogies and they are found nowhere else. And we have a confirmation of the same in the statement of the Śatapatha

Brāhmaṇa (see Vedic Index) that they were Aikshvāka kings or kings of the race of Ikshvāku. Thus the names of the original Bharata and later kings as identified by the Brāhmaṇa and Purāṇa traditions coupled with their association with the Purohita Vasishṭha make it almost convincingly clear that the Bharatas of the Ṛigveda are the Solar race Kshatriyas of the Epics. These Bharatas appear to have spread from the Panjab as far east as Ayodhyā even in the times of the Ṛigveda. I had formerly been of opinion that the Ṛigvedic Aryans had not gone much beyond the Ganges. But the fact now found that the Sarayu* the river of Ayodhyā is mentioned thrice in the Ṛigveda, makes it clear that they had already spread that far. The mention of Rāma, the illustrious hero of Ayodhyā, in the tenth Maṇḍala of the Ṛigveda, becomes thus consistent and proper. The Aryans might even have gone still eastward as far as Mithila which though not mentioned in the Ṛigveda is associated with Gotama; for Gotama is represented to be the Purohita of the Mithila Kshatriyas, as Vasishṭha is of the Kośala Kshatriyas and Gotama, the husband of Ahalyā, is a Vedic Ṛishi and the composer of Vedic hymns. Such is then the history of the progress of the first Aryan invaders of India, *viz.*, the Bharatas later called the Solar Kshatriyas and hence we see why their languages at both ends, *viz.*, the Eastern Hindi and the Panjabi, are allied to each other.

Having so far spoken of the Bharatas or the Solar Kshatriyas with their first famous king Bharata who gave his name to the whole country, *viz.*, Bhāratavarsha and their subsequent kings

* The Sarayu is mentioned in three Vedic hymns (Vedic Index). In the note on Sarayu Macdonnel thinks that it is the Ayodhya river; but he refers to the opinion of some Vedic scholars that it is the Kramu or Kurrum of Afghanistan. In v. 64, it seems to be an Afghanistan river. But in x, 64, it is associated with सरस्वती and सिन्धु and must be a large river like these. In iv. 30, it is apparently a large river and seems also to be the river of Ayodhya. It may be stated here that Haraivaity and Harayu are also rivers of the Zend people. These probably are old Aryan names which the Indo-Aryans in their new settlement in India assigned to Indian rivers, much as they did in America and elsewhere.

Divodāsa and Sudāsa, Purukutsa and Trasadasyu and their Rishis, Vasishtha and Viśvāmitra, Gotama and Bharadvāja, we will go on to consider the history of the advent and progress of the second horde of Aryan invaders, *viz.*, the Lunar Kshatriyas. They are also a Rigvedic people but they evidently appear to be a later one, although of the same race, language and religion. Their history resembles very much the history of the advent and progress of the Dutch and the English settlers in America. These, unlike their predecessors the Spaniards and the French, lived generally in friendly relations with the aborigines. Nay, they had regular treaties with what were called the Five Nations. They eventually came into conflict with the earlier settlers and their fights with them were often long and bloody. They were assisted in these fights by their aboriginal allies. Finally they conquered the Spaniards and the French and appropriated the whole of the northern portion of America, which has now become Teutonic America. Central and South America remained in the hands of the Latin races or the first invaders and is often now appropriately styled Latin America. Their religion, though Christian, was and still is different from the religion of the subsequent invaders, *viz.*, the English and the Dutch. This short sketch of the history of the colonization of America by the Teutonic and Latin Aryans of the west will show how strongly it corresponds with the history of the colonization of the continent of India by the Indo-Aryans of the east.

The first Aryans who came to India were the Bharatas of the Rigveda and we have identified them on strong grounds with the Solar race Kshatriyas of the Epics. The identification of the second horde of Aryan settlers with the Lunar Kshatriyas of the Epics and the Purāṇas is still more certain and complete. The first fact which deserves to be mentioned is, what was almost a revelation to me, that the Yadus, the Turvaśas, the Anus, the Druhyus and the Pūrus are mentioned in the Rigveda very frequently and often together. The first two are mentioned together still oftener. They were, therefore, clearly allied races and the first two were particularly allied. They are mentioned sometimes in the singular and sometimes in the plural which shows that

Yadu and Turvaśa and Anu, Druhyu and Pūru were individual kings who gave their names to the races sprung from them. Ḥere there is a clear coincidence with and confirmation of the Epic and Puranic version according to which they were the five sons of Yayāti, an ancient king of the Lunar race. Yadu and Turvaśa were Yayati's sons by his first wife Devayāni, the daughter of Śukra and the other three were his sons by his second wife Śarmishṭha, the daughter of the Asura or Persian king Vrishaparvan. Hence, while sometimes all are mentioned together, we see why sometimes Yadu and Turvaśa only are spoken of together in the Ṛigveda. The Purāṇas and the Epics give the name Turvaśa of the Ṛigveda as Turvasu; but, I think, they do so to bring it in consonance with the other four names which end in u. The identification is otherwise complete and this little difference cannot count. The second fact of importance is that the Ṛigvedic hymns sometimes speak of these people with abhorrence, as people who should be killed or suppressed, and sometimes they speak of them with respect and affection. The Vedic Ṛishis sometimes invoke the blessings of their gods on them and implore them to give them power and prosperity, but they often ask their gods to destroy or defeat them. This clearly indicates that these people came later and were for some time intruders and therefore hated as enemies by the first settlers. They, however, eventually settled in certain lands and were then invoked blessings upon, being Aryans and professors of the same religion as the first settlers with certain differences only. This also explains the Puranic tradition that the Lunar Kshatriyas many times fought with the Solar Kshatriyas and eventually became supreme lords of the middle land. I will now proceed to set forth detailed proofs of these statements from the Ṛigvedic hymns and trace the history of the advent and progress of this second race of Kshatriyas.

The ancient ancestor of these Kshatriyas was, according to the Purāṇas, Purūravas. Now Purūravas is also a Ṛigvedic name. He is even there a mythical person. He probably lived in the Himalayas and married the heavenly nymph Urvaśī. He learned from the Gandharvas how to produce fire and worshipped it. This clearly indicates that he was also a fire worshipping Aryan like the first race of invaders. He lived in the Himalayas about the Gandhamādhana mountain and among the Uttara Kurus so to speak, according to the Purāṇas, as also according to the Brāhmaṇas. This shows that the ancestors of these Lunar Kshatriyas lived beyond the Himalayas and thus these people must have come from thence. Purūrvas' son was Ayu and his son was Nahusha, names of which mention is also made in Ṛigvedic hymns. His son was Yayāti who married two wives, Devayānī and Śarmishthā according to the Purāṇas and had two sons by the first wife and three by the second, a circumstance which finds support from the Ṛigveda as already stated. This Yayāti is also mentioned as a fire-worshipper in the Ṛigveda. He appears to have still been beyond the Himalayas and it was his sons who came to India and settled, like a wedge in the previous Aryan settlement, about the region of the Sarasvatī or as we might say Ambala.

It must here be stated that the story of the Purāṇas, that Yayāti ruled in Prayāga and divided the land of India among his five sons in a certain manner must be rejected as a later theory started by the last editors of the Purāṇas. Mr. Pargiter seems to accept it; but it appears to me that this story conflicts with the inferences derivable from the Ṛigvedic references; and I think that the now generally accepted belief that the Aryans both of the first and the second race of invaders came from the north-west and gradually spread themselves over the land is more probable. As I have already said, where the Purāṇas and Ṛigveda conflict, greater credence ought to be given to the Ṛigvedic version. Now in the Ṛigveda we have a distinct mention that Pūru was settled on both the banks of the Sarasvatī (Ṛigveda vii, 96). Pūru, therefore, could not have got the middle land about Allahabad according to the Purāṇas. And how could he come to occupy the banks of the Sarasvatī? For the other portions of India were also, according to the Purāṇas, given to his four brothers. The Purāṇic version must have become current about 300 A.D. naturally enough. By that time the Indians had lost all memory of the Aryans having come from beyond the Himalayas and their land from the beginning was what they had occupied so long. The centre of their land was at Prayāga in

Puranic days. They saw that Rāma, their greatest hero, was at Ayodhyā, also in the centre and they thought Ayodhyā was the first and oldest kingdom of the Solar Kshatriyas founded by Manu himself. Though Krishṇa belonged to Mathurā, the greatest line of the Lunar race was that of the Pauravas and the last Paurava king of fame, Udayana (immortalised together with his minister Yaugandharāyaṇa by Guṇādhya in his Bṛihat-kathā), belonged to Prayaga or Kaushambi more correctly. Hence they represented Prayāga as the centre and origin of the Lunar race. The Puranic division of Bhāratavarsha among the sons of Yayāti does not again represent history but the state of things that existed in the time of the Purāṇas or the time nearest to them. As Mr. Pargiter has himself shown (see. page 273, J. R. A. S., 1914), Pūru got the middle kingdom according to the Puranic version of Yayāti's division of India and the Pauravas were then supreme about Allahabad. Yadu got the south-west and they were in the south-west at that time occupying Kathiawar and Mahārāshtra and Ujjain. Turvasu got south-east and, according to the Purāṇas, the Pāndya, Chola and other kingdoms of the south belonged to Turvasu's line. Druhyu got the west and Anu the north. The Ānavas were according to the Purāṇas the ancestors of some of the Pūnjab kings, while Druhyu, according to them, was the ancestor of the Gāndhāra and other western people. Mr. Pargiter himself hereafter observes: "These positions agree with the subsequent notice of the Yādavas and the Ānvas" (page 274). In my opinion it is the subsequent position of these and Pūrus and Turvaśas which misled the last editors of the Purāṇa's into this story of Yayāti ruling in Prayāga and dividing the Indian enmpire among his sons in the particular manner. The last positions of the Solar and Lunar races, *viz.*, Ayodhya and Prayāga, were taken to be their first positions by these last editors of the Purāṇas, because they had no idea whatever of the real course of history, *viz.*, that the Aryans spread from the north-west to the south-east and south. But Purūrava, even according to the Purāṇas, was north of the Himalayas about Gandhamādana, the region assigned subsequently to the Uttara Kurus and his son and grandson were probably still there. Yayāti's sons came to

India and Pūru probably first occupied the Sarasvatī tract and it is from hence that the Lunar race spread south-east and south which were not occupied by the Aryans and also tried to oust the first settled Aryans in the east and the west, *i. e.*, in the Panjab and in Oudh. I think Dr. Grierson's theory based on language that the population of the U. P. expanded from its original seat near the Upper Doab and the sacred river Sarasvatī seems to be supported by the oldest evidence of the Ṛigveda and is more probable than the last Puranic version that it spread from Allahabad westward towards Kurukshetra.

This is a digression no doubt but again a necessary and important one. I should reject the Puranic version on this point and accept the story of the occupation of the region of the Sarasvatī first by the Pūrus as evidenced by Ṛigveda vii, 96 (उभे यत्ते महिना शुभ्रे अन्धसी अधिक्षियन्ति पूरवः) a hymn to Sarasvatī. Here they became strong and firmly settled. Here the Lunar race evolved its civilization. Here came to be the most sacred land in India, *viz.*, the region of the Sarasvatī. Here the later Aryans flourished in Kurukshetra. Here was the language most pure. Here the Lunar people appear to have come from beyond the Himalayas by Gilgit and Chitral and perhaps from about the Mānasa lake and not by the usual pass in the north-west, *viz.*, the Khyber. For it appears even from the Brāhmaṇas that the speech of the Uttara Kurus and the Kuru Panchala was similar and was considered specially pure. (See Vedic Index under Kuru.) Dr. Grierson remarks that even now in the language about Gilgit and Chitral " words are still in everyday use which are almost identical with the forms they assumed in the Vedic hymns and which survive only in a corrupted state in the plains of India." (*Imp. Gaz.* Vol. I, page 356). The evidence of the Ṛigveda, the Brāhmaṇas and the actual present state of the Himalayan languages lead one to believe that the Lunar people of the second Aryan invasion descended first into the region about the Sarasvatī or modern Sirhind through Himalayan passes and thence spread elsewhere. Taking this fact as our basis we will now proceed to discuss the history of these Lunar races as disclosed by the Ṛigvedic hymns.

The first and most important hymn to which I have to refer is Ṛigveda i, 108. This is addressed to the two gods, Indra and Agni, and says in verse 8, " Oh Indra and Agni, even if you be among the Yadus and the Turvaśas, the Druhyus, the Anus, and the Pūrus, you come here and drink the Soma juice prepared for you."

यदिंद्राग्नी यदुषु तुर्वशेषु यद्द्रुह्युष्वनुषु पूरुषु स्थः ।
अतः परि वृषणा वा हि यातमथा सोमस्य पिबतं सुतस्य ॥ ८ ॥

Now this verse uses the words in the plural and shows that the Yadus, Turvaśas, Druhyus, Anus and Pūrus had become peoples. Secondly, they are also allied peoples and among themselves formed two sets, the first two and the other three. Thirdly, they were Aryans, and worshipped the same gods as the other Vedic Aryans, *viz.*, Indra and Agni. Thus all the chief points in connection with the Lunar Kshatriyas are apparent in this one verse of the Ṛigveda. It must also be noted that the Ṛishi or composer of this hymn is Kutsa Āṅgirasa, the relevancy of which fact I will explain later on.

The next point of importance is that these allied races of the Aryans came into conflict with the Bharatas or the earlier settled Kshatriyas in different regions. The first king of the Bharatas with whom they fought appear to be the same Divodāsa who was of so great a fame among the Vedic Ṛishis as a generous donor. His favourite appellation in the Ṛigveda is Atithigva or one to whom Atithis or guests go. The first hymn to be noticed on this point is Ṛigveda ix, 61 verse 2. " Indra broke the castles and towns of Śambara for the sake of Divodāsa and then smote Yadu and Turvaśa " (I usually take the meaning given by Arnold) पुरः सद्य इत्थाधिये दिवोदासाय शम्बरम् । अध त्यं तुर्वशं यदुम् ॥ Here is a reference to the aid of Indra given to Divodāsa to conquer his aboriginal enemy Śambara and then his Aryan enemies Turvaśa and Yadu. There is another reference to a fight between Aryan Bharata kings with Yadu and Turvaśa about the river Sarayu in which the Bharata kings are said to have been killed, a hymn already noticed, *viz.*, Ṛigveda iv, 30 (उत त्या तुर्वशायदू अस्नातारा शचीपतिः । इन्द्रो विद्वाँ

अपारयत् ॥ १७ ॥ उत त्या सद्य आर्या सरयोरिन्द्र पारतः । अर्णाचित्ररथावधीः ॥ १८ ॥). But the most important fight between the Bharatas and the later Aryans was the fight called दाशराज्ञ or fight with the ten kings. It is noticed in three hymns composed by Vashishṭha and given in his Maṇḍala, *viz.*, the seventh. It was fought between Sudāsa, the Bharata king, assisted by his Purohita Vashishṭha and five aboriginal kings and the five Aryan peoples, Yadu, Turvaśa, Anu, Druhyu and Pūru. It was fought on the banks of the Parushṇi or the modern Ravi of the Panjab. The first hymn to be noticed is vii, 18. The Vedic hymns are, of course, always composed in praise of certain deities and cannot ordinarily be expected to contain historical information. But even the Vedic Ṛishis in their hymns to their gods could not avoid mentioning prominent past or contemporaneous events and hence it is that we are enabled to glean some historical information about these hoary times in the past. The hymn vii, 18, is an eloquent hymn by Vashishṭha and contains a vivid description of the battle of Sudāsa with his ten opponent kings. The hymn is not fully intelligible but it appears certaln to most Vedic scholars that Sudāsa in this battle conquered the ten kings leagued against him on the banks of the Parushṇi, which, while he forded easily and safely by the aid of Vashishṭha's praise of Indra, drowned his enemies and many of these were killed. Sudāsa was first in a difficult plight and the ten kings hoped to plunder him but after all, the river suddenly submerged them as they were trying to divert its stream and it was Sudāsa eventually who got great plunder. Six thousand Anus and Druhyus who were taking cattle, says the hymn, slept on the battlefield. This is what can be gathered about this fight from this important hymn. The Aryan kings were, of course, Turvaśa, Yadu, Anu, Druhyu and Pūru. Yadu is not specially mentioned but he must be taken to be included in Turvaśa. The aboriginal tribes mentioned are Pakhtas, Bhalanas, Bhanantalins, Vishaṇins and Śivas. A great deal of conjectural information can be derived from these names; for instance, the Pakhtas are some modern Afghan tribes among whom the name Pashtu is still pronounced according to Dr. Grierson as Pakhta. Or that the

Vishaṇins might be some aboriginal people who tied to their heads pairs of horns like some modern rude races of America, But that there were Aryan and non-Aryan kings leagued against Sudāsa in this fight is not a matter of conjecture but is what is expressly mentioned in another hymn which I next proceed to notice. It is hymn vii, 83, by Vashishṭha also, wherein he says that the gods Indra and Varuṇa assisted king Sudāsa when he was opposed by his Aryan and Dāsa enemies (दासा च वृत्रा हतमार्याणि च सुदासमिंद्रा वरुणावसावतम्.) "You smote and slew his Dāsa and Aryan enemies and helped Sudāsa with favour" —Arnold's Translation. There is a further clear reference in the hymn to ten kings attacking Sudāsa. (यत्र राजभिर्दशभिर्निबाधितं प्र सुदासमावतं तृत्सुभिः सह). "You protected Sudāsa with the Tritsus when he was oppressed by the ten kings." It thus appears clear that there were in this battle ten kings, five Aryans and five non-Aryans, whose names we have already given. It seems to be a great effort by all new Aryan invaders with their aboriginal friends to suppress the first settled Aryans, *viz.*, the Bharatas. But in this they failed and Sudāsa with Vashishṭha's help prevailed. The five aboriginal peoples correspond curiously enough to the five Nations of American history leagued with the English in their fights against the French; and we have thus one of those many curious analogies in history which suggest and support the saying "History repeats itself." And, as in American history, although Sudāsa, the older Aryan king, prevailed in this battle, his race was eventually overshadowed by the later invaders as I now proceed to show.

In hymn vii, 19, Vashishṭha appears to speak of the Pūrus in a favourable manner though he still refers therein to the defeat of Yadu and Turvaśa by Divodāsa. This hymn seems to give ground to some Vedic scholars to think that Purukutsa was a Pūru king and hence I think it proper to give a detailed translation of two of its verses. (त्वं धृष्णो धृषता वीतहव्यं प्रावो विश्वाभिरूतिभिः सुदासम् । प्र पौरुकुत्सिं त्रसदस्युमावः क्षेत्रसाता वृत्रहत्येषु पूरुम् ॥) "You, Oh valiant Indra, protected, by all your protection, Vītahavya and Sudāsa and Trasadasyu, Purukutsa's son and

Pūru in his fight with the Vṛittra (or aboriginies)." In this verse many kings are mentioned and I would take each separately and thus Pūru as different from the preceding Trasadasyu. In fact, as I have already said, the authority of the Brāhmaṇas is supreme in this matter and Purukutsa and Trasadasyu being, according to the Śatapatha, Aikshvāka or descendants of Ikshvāku, cannot be Pūrus or descendants of Pūru. There are other kings also mentioned in this hymn, *viz.*, Kutsa (verse 2) and Dabhīti who killed the aboriginal (दस्यु) enemies, Chumuri and Dhuni (verse 4). And in verse 8, we have a mention of the Atithigva (*i.e.*, of course, Divodāsa) for whose sake Indra killed Yadu and Turvaśa (नि तुर्वशं नि याद्वं शिशीह्यतिथिग्वाय शंस्यं करिष्यन्). Thus then it appears that at the time of this hymn composed by some Vashishṭha, the Pūrus had become settled and popular while the Yadus and Turvaśas were still considered the enemies of the Aryans. Other hymns show that even the Yadu and Turvaśas became eventually settled in the country and reconciled with the first Aryans and are mentioned favourably by composers of hymns. In many hymns the blessings of Vedic deities are invoked on even Yadus and Turvaśas. These hymns are principally to be found in Maṇḍala viii, which consists of hymns chiefly composed by the descendants of Kaṇva. They are (as shown in the Vedic Index) 4, 7, 9, 10, and 45 of this eighth Maṇḍala. Hymn 4 is by देवातिथि काण्व and mentions the Kaṇvas often and also Turvaśa and Yadu, and Kaṇva is said to have taken 6,000 cows from a Turvaśa king. Hymn 7 is by पुनर्वत्स काण्व and praises the favour of Maruts shown to Yadu, Turvaśa and Kaṇva. (येनाव तुर्वशं यदुं येन कण्वं. धनस्पृतम् । राये सुतस्य धीमहि). In hymn 9 Śaśakarṇa-Kāṇva (शशकर्ण काण्व) invokes the favour of the Aśvins on Yadu and Turvaśa and Kaṇva (इमे सोमासो अधि तुर्वशे यदाविमे काण्वेषु वामथ ॥ १४ ॥) Hymn 10 is by प्रगाथ काण्व to the Aśvins whose favour is invoked on Anu, Druhyu, Yadu and Turvaśa in different directions (see verse 5). Lastly, in hymn 45, त्रिशोक काण्व the Ṛishi praises Indra and Agni and says that undeniable strength was given by them to Yadu and Turvaśa. (सत्यं तत्तुर्वशे यदौ विदानो अन्हवाय्यम् । २७ ।). All these different notices of Yadu and Turvaśa and even of Aṇu and Druhyu are favourable and found in hymns by Ṛishis of the Kaṇva family. The natural inference from this is that they had established themselves by this time and that their Ṛishis were the Kāṇvas or persons born in the Kaṇva family. A remarkable confirmation of this fact is found in the Purāṇa and also Brāhmaṇa tradition in that the Purohita of Daushyanti Bharata was Kaṇva and Dushyanta got Śakuntalā from Kaṇva's Āshrama. Thus Vedic and Puranic traditions lead us to believe that the Purohitas of the Lunar race or rather of the Yadus and Turvaśas were Kaṇva and his descendants. The same idea is, I think expressly supported by a hymn in the first Maṇḍala which I proceed to notice. Hymn i, 36, is by Ghaura Ṛishi and is in praise of Agni. In this hymn Kaṇva is frequently mentioned and along with him Turvaśa and Yadu. See verses 17 and 18. (अग्निर्वव्रे सुवीर्यमग्निः कण्वाय सौभगम् । अग्निः प्रावान्मित्रोत मेध्यातिथिमग्निः साता उपस्तुतम् ॥ १७ ॥ अग्निना तुर्वशं यदुं परावत उग्रादेवं हवामहे ॥) I think we shall not be far wrong if, from all the hymns of the Kaṇvas relating to Yadu-Turvaśa in the eighth Maṇḍala and this in the first by Ghaura, we infer that Kaṇva stood in the same relation to Yadu-Turvarśas or the Lunar race Kshatriyas as Vashishṭha stood to the Bharatas or Solar race Kshatriyas. It may here be mentioned that the Puraṇic genealogy derives Kaṇva from the family of Pūru himself *i.e.*, from मतिनार, tenth descendant of Pūru and some fourth ancestor of Bharata . (See Harivaṁśa I Ch. 32.)

The next hymns to be noticed mentioning Yadu-Turvaśas favourably are Ṛigv. i. 54, by Savya Āngirasa to Indra, verse 6 त्वमाविथ नर्यं तुर्वशं यदुं त्वं तुर्वीतिं वय्यं शतक्रतो, ।) and i, 108, already noticed by Kutsa Āngirasa in which all the five Yadu, Turvaśa, Anu, Druhyu, and Pūru are mentioned together. I said before in noticing this hymn that I would explain the relevancy of its Ṛishi later on. This is the place to record the remark that the Āngirasas appear to be other Ṛishis who are connected with the Lunar Kshatriyas. The Ṛishi of i, 36, is Ghora and he appears to be an Āngirasa, and of i, 54 is Savya Āngirasa, so that in all the three hymns of the first Maṇḍala, *viz.*, 36, 54 and 108 in which the Yadu Turvaśas are favourably mentioned, the Ṛishis are Angirasas (Ghora, Savya and Kutsa). Now in the Chhāndogya Upanishad it is mentioned that one Ghora Āngirasa taught a certain Vedantic doctrine to Krishṇa Devakīputra who is presumably the Yādava Śri-Krishṇa of the Mahābhārata. The Āngirasas, therefore, also appear to be the favourite Ṛishis of the Lunar race in addition to the Kāṇvas as Viśvāmitra was of the Solar race in addition to Vashishṭha.

The remaining hymns in favour of the Yadu Turvaśas are i, 174, by Agastya to Indra, iv. 30, by Vāmadeva (about Sarayu already mentioned), v, 31, by Avasyu Ātreya, vi, 45, by Śamyu Bārhaspatya x, 49, by Indra Vaikuntha in which Nahusha is also mentioned ; see verse 8 (अहं सप्तहा नहुषो नहुष्टरः प्राश्रावयं शवसा तुर्वशं यदुम्). The first of these hymns must be specially noticed as the reference therein to Samudra is somewhat strange if interpreted literally as is done by Arnold. The verse is त्वं धुनिरिन्द्र धुनिमतीर्ऋणोरपः सीरा न स्रवन्तीः । प्र यत्समुद्रमति शूर पर्षि पारया तुर्वशं यदुं स्वस्ति ॥. If this line means that Indra should take Yadu and Turvaśa safely over the sea, Yadu and Turvaśa must be taken to have crossed it like Bhujyu, the favourite seafaring king of the Ṛigveda whom the Aśvins are said to have safely brought over the sea in their own boat. Had the Yadus and Turvaśas progressed as far as the sea in the days of the Ṛigvedic Ṛishis? Some Aryans had undoubtedly done so, as for instance, the above-mentioned Bhujyu and it may perhaps be that the Yadus had also travelled so far in those days. The word Samudra in the hymn has, however, been taken to mean the sky where the heavenly waters burst. In v, 35, above-mentioned, Indra is also said to have stilled the flooded waters of the Sudughā for Yadu and Turvaśa who were beyond these waters. Thus the progress of the Yadus and Turvaśas across rivers and even upto the sea may be taken to be indicated in these hymns.

Having spoken so far of the five allied races, Yadu, Turvaśa, Anu, Druhu, and Pūru I will now proceed to note the progress of each individually as evidenced by the Vedas. The Yadus are not mentioned in the Yajus and Sama, nor are they apparently mentioned in any of the several Brāhmaṇas. (Of course, I speak as usual on the authority of the Vedic Index). They, therefore, may be taken after their defeat in the Panjab to have moved south, south-east and south-west in which regions they are actually found in Epic times. In these directions there was plenty of room for expansion as the first Aryans had only occupied the Panjab and the region eastward along the Himalayas. The Yadus do not appear to have founded kingdoms of their own and hence perhaps the tradition that they were under a curse by Yayāti. They lived under the Bhojas in Śaurasena about Mathurā. This Mathurā, according to Epic tradition, originally belonged to the Rākshasa or aboriginal king Madhu from whom it was first conquered by Śatrughana, Rāma's brother, and after the decline of his descendants it was taken possession of by the Bhojas and Yādavas. Mr. Pargiter thinks that Madhu was not a Rākshasa but was actually the Yādava chief Madhu from whom his descendants were called Mādhavas. I do not, however, think it proper to abandon here the version of the Harivaṁśa and the Rāmāyaṇa. For it is more consistent with the course of history as sketched above that this region of the Yamuna should first be in the possession of the Rākshasas, then that of the first Aryan or Solar race and then of the Lunar race which, as we have seen, endeavoured in different directions to oust the first settled Kshatriyas. Instead of this Mr. Pargiter would first have the Lunar Aryans, then the Rākshasas and then the solar race. This is by the by. The Yādavas settled in Mathurā and perhaps thence went south-west as far as Dvaraka on the sea. The only indirect reference to the Yādavas in the Brāhmaṇas is that to Kṛishṇa Devakīputra in the Chhāndogya Upanishad who, as stated before, learned Vedantic doctrines from Ghora Āngirasa. Were it not for Śrikrishṇa, the Yādavas would have been entirely forgotten in the later Vedas and Brahmaṇas and even the Epics. It was he who raised them to immortal renown by his Bhagavadgīta and by his prominent part in the Mahābhārata fight which probably falls in time between the final compilation of the Rigveda and the composition of the Brāhmaṇas. The latter naturally thus mention persons taking part in the Bhārata fight and hence the reference in the Chhāndogya to Kṛishṇa Devakiputra may properly be taken to apply to Śrīkrishṇa of the Yadavas, the great counsellor of the Pāṇḍavas in the Bhārata fight.

We will next consider the progress of the Turvaśas. These entirely disappear so to speak in the later Vedic times. But there is one important reference to them in the Brāhmaṇas which discloses their fate. They became merged in the Pānchāla people according to a statement in the Śatapatha Brāhmaṇa. Of these Pānchālas I shall speak later on. Before proceeding further I might mention here that the Purāṇas, especially Harivaṃśa (I. chap. 32), represent Pāndya, Chola, Kerala and Kola as descendants in this Turvaśa's line. This is clearly a later theory of the Purāṇas. We must remember that one great incentive to the later editors of the Purāṇas to make additions to genealogies must have been the desire to connect the famous lines of kings in their time with some heroes or persons mentioned in the Vedas and the Epics and thus secure to them venerated antiquity of connection much as the Romans loved to connect themselves with Homeric heroes. Now the Pāndya, Chola and Kerala people were outside the pale of Aryanism for a long time. They were Dravidas and non-Aryans like the Angas and the Vangas, and even according to the Vedas residence in their country led to fall from Brahmanism. Yet in later Puraṇic times the Hindus went into and settled in these lands and then attempted to connect kings in them with Vedic and Epic lines of Kshatriyas. This descent of the south-east kings may properly be treated as imaginary and being opposed to the statement of the Śatapatha that the Turvaśas merged into the Pānchālas, the later Puraṇic version may be rejected as a tradition not worthy to be accepted.

Coming next to the other set of the three races, *viz.*, Anus, Druhyus and Pūrus, we find that the Pūrus became by far the most important people both in later Vedic times and in Epic days. This explains the story of the blessing of Yayāti to his son Pūru for obeying his wishes. "Pūru," thus runs the boon "would be the king of the ancestral land and would be very prosperous. In fact, the Pūrus would be so numerous that they would overspread the whole country. Nay, the earth may be divested of the Sun and the Moon but never of the Pūru people." (अपौरवा तु हि मही न कदाचिद्भविष्यति।). Now the Pūrus first settled, as already stated, in the region of the Sarasvatī, having ousted the originally settled Kshatriyas from there. They extended thence their conquests east, west and south by and by till they became the lords of the whole of India in the days of the Pâṇḍavas. The contests of the Pūrus with aboriginal kings are mentioned in many Ṛigvedic hymns. They are, as given in the Vedic Index, i, 59, 131 and 174, iv, 21 and 28, vi, 20 and vii, 5 and 19. Looking into these references we find i, 59 is a hymn to Agni by Gautama Nodha in which he says " Agni whom the Pūrus follow as the slayer of Vṛitra or aborigines." (यं पूरवा वृत्रहणं सचन्ते ।); i, (131 is a hymn to Indra by Paruchchhepa in which he says (विदुष्टे अस्य वीर्यस्य पूरवः पुरो). " Pūrus of old have known of this power"; iv, 21, is by Vāmadeva to Indra (हंता वृत्रं वरिवः पूरवे कः) " who gave freedom to Pūru by slaying Vṛitra ?" (iv, 28, as also i, 174, are, I think, wrongly included here as they contain no mention of Pūru). vi, 20, is addressed to Indra by Bhāradvâja (प्र पूरवः स्तुवन्त एना यज्ञैः). " The Pūrus laud thee, oh Indra, that thou destroyedst seven castles of the Dāsas for Purukutsa." vii, 5, is by Vasishṭha to Agni (वैश्वानरे पूरवे शोशुचानः पुरो यदग्ने दरयन्न दीदेः) " Oh Agni, for Puru thou lightest up and rendest their castles "; and lastly vii, 19, already noticed, where Vasishṭha says to Indra (प्र पौरुकुत्सिं त्रसदस्युमावः क्षेत्रसातौ वृत्रहत्येषु पूरुम्) " Thou protectest Trasadasyu and Pūru in their fights with Vṛitras." On these hymns two or three observations have to be made. Vṛitra usually stands in Vedic verses for Dāsa enemies and they have castles or forts or fortified villages which have to be carried. Secondly, vii, 19 and more particularly vi, 20, give ground for supposing that Purukutsa and Trasadasyu were of the Pūru line. But as I have already stated, on this point the authority of the Brâhmaṇas should be respected and as the Śatapatha says that they were Aikshvākas and as they are also found in Purāṇic genealogies among the descendants of Ikshvāku alone and nowhere else, here Brāhmaṇa and Purāṇa traditions combine to prove that they were Aikshvāka or Solar race kings. In vii. 19, the line plainly means Trasadaşyu *and* Pūru, while in vi, 20 we may say that the Pūrus in their prayer to Indra give example of Indra's aid to Purukutsa not as a king of their own people but of another people, Purukutsa being well-known as a favourite king of Indra. Thirdly, Pūrus became eventually so numerous that according to later authorities (of course, not later than Yāska), the word Pūrus stands generally for men. In some of the above verses the word has been so interpreted by commentators, but as Prof. Macdonell has observed, Pūrus may be translated as Pūrus without difficulty in all these cases.

The historical inference from these and previous verses is that after several fights with non-Aryans Pūru established himself firmly in the region of the Sarasvatī. His later or previous contests with the Aryan enemies of the Solar race, especially with Sudāsa on the Parushṇī in his or his race's progress westward in the Punjab also appear. His line flourished both at home and abroad. The first known king in his line was Ajamīdha, the Ājamīdhas being spoken of in the Ṛigveda also. The next is Bharata, son of Dushyanta, who is not mentioned in the Ṛigveda but is mentioned in the Brāhmaṇas and who performed sacrifices on the Sarasvatī, Yamunā and the Ganges which shows that he extended his dominion eastward. The Bharatas mentioned in the Brāhmaṇas are his descendants and not the Bharatas of the Ṛigveda as the Śatapatha clearly introduces them by first mentioning Daushyanti Bharata. The epithet Daushyanti appears to be purposely used in the Brāhmaṇa to discriminate the two Bharatas. The next famous king was Kuru who became so famous that the ancient land of the Pūrus came to be called Kurukshetra. Now this Kuru is also not to be found in the Ṛigveda. This non-mention, of course, does not prove that the compilation of the Ṛigveda preceded him, but we may take it that his fame had not become exaggerated in the time of the Ṛigveda. The Bharatas and still more the Kurus, however, became famous in the Brāhmaṇa literature. The Kurus are always mentioned therein with the Pānchālas and they were one people, it seems, in their time. This probably indicates that the Mahābhārata fight had been fought before this and, all the Pānchāla princes being dead, the Pāṇḍavas and especially their great-grandson Janamejaya Pārikshita became their king. This Janamejaya Pārikshita is also a favourite king with the Brāhmaṇas. Thus then the chief people of the Pūru race were the Kuru-Pānchālas in later Vedic times.

I must speak of the Pānchālas here in more detail. According to the Purāṇic genealogies the Pānchālas were the descendants of a younger branch of the Pūrus. Their first great king was Sṛinjaya, even according to the genealogies and this Sṛinjaya gave his name to his descendants. The Sṛinjayas are mentioned in the Ṛigveda also. The first mention is in Ṛigv. vi, 27, where Sṛinjaya is said to be a son of Devavāta. (स सृंजयाय तुर्वशं परादाद्वृचीवतो दैववाताय शिक्षन्) "He who gave Turvaśa to Sṛinjaya, the son of Devavāta and the Richīvats." This is looked upon as identifying Ṛichīvat with Turvaśa. The next mention is still more important. It is Rigveda iv. 15, which shows that his Agni is also mentioned and thus invests him with greatness. अयं यः सृंजये पुरो दैववाते समिध्यते । "This is the fire which is enkindled in the eastern altar of Sṛinjaya, the son of Devavāta." The last four verses of this hymn mention Somaka the young son of Sahadeva who gave donations to the Ṛishi or composer of this hymn, *viz.*, Vāmadeva and he invokes blessings on him. (एवं वां देवावश्विना कुमारः साहदेव्यः । दीर्घायुरस्तु सोमकः). This Sahadeva and Somaka were most probably born in the line of Sṛinjaya and hence they are mentioned in this hymn. Sṛinjaya, Sahadeva and Somaka are actually found in the Pānchāla genealogy and Somaka is the fourth ancestor of Drupada. He performed a Rājasuya and became renowned as is mentioned in the Aitareya Brāhmaṇa. The Pānchālas were thus Sṛinjayas in Ṛigvedic times and their name Pānchāla became famous in the times of the Brāhmaṇas. The Mahābhārata uses both the names Sṛinjayas and Pānchālas and even Somakas from their famous king Somaka. Somaka must have been later than Kuru. The Pānchālas were settled to the south-east of the Kurus between the Ganges and the Yamunā. The name Pānchāla is derived by Harivaṃśa and the Purāṇas from the five sons of a king (who were thought to be enough for the world, पंच अलम्), but this is a quibble. Probably they were so called because composed of five peoples. The merging of different peoples into one people is not an unfrequent event in history and I believe this merging means that one people elect the sovereigns of another people as their kings and thus mingle with them. This happened either because they were conquered or the family of their kings became extinct. The Kuru-Pānchālas became one people in this second way after the Mahābhārata fight. The Pānchālas themselves must have been composed of five peoples in some such way. We have a distinct mention of the mingling of three peoples, *viz.*, Sṛinjayas, Turvaśas and Kṛivis, the first in the Ṛigvedic hymn vi, 27, and the second in the Śatapatha Brāhmaṇa. These three and two more peoples probably went to form the Pānchālas, so famous in the times of Brāhmaṇas and the Epics for their learning as well as their valour.

The people who thus most predominate in the later Vedic times are people of the second Aryan invasion especially of the line of Pūru and in this line again the peoples more prominent than the rest were the Kurus and the Pānchālas or Sṛinjayas. But the Solar race preople were not entirely extinct in later Vedic times. In the Punjab they were probably over-shadowed by the Lunar people. The general population there must doubtless have remained Solar but the kings were genera ja y of the Pūru line. It is hence why a Poros is found in the Pun is b in the days of Alexander. It is sometimes surmised that th finding of a Poros on the Hydaspes in the Punjab shows that the Pūrus came from the north-west and extended eastward. But, according to the course of history we have sketched above, the Pūrus first came into India about the region of the Sarasvatī and thence extended west. We find a confirmation of this latter idea in the Mahābhārata where Janamejaya is said to have conquered Takshaśilā in the Punjab after he was installed in the kingdom of the Kurus at Hastināpura. After the Mahābhārata fight the Kurus became the overlords of India, and perhaps Takshaśilā still remained defiant and hence it was that Janamejaya found it necessary to go and conquer that land. The founding of Takshaśilā by the Solar Aryans is indicated in the Rāmāyaṇa story of Bharata having conquered the land from the Gandharvas. This is probably a restatement of the real fact that the older Bharata and his people, the Solar Kshatriyas, settled in that country originally. Whatever that may be, in the Punjab the kings generally appear to have been Lunar race Kshatriyas in the days of the Brāhmaṇas and the Epics. But the Solar race people had their kingdoms in the east and they were the Kosala-Videhas of Brāhmaṇa fame. The Brāhmaṇas love to speak of the Kosala-Videhas as much as they love to speak of the Kuru-Pānchālas. The Kosala-Videhas were plainly a different people from the latter. Macdonnell accepts the opinion of Dr. Grierson and others based on language, *viz.*, the affinity of eastern Hindi with Punjabi rather than with western Hindi, and says under the word Kuru that these Kosala-Videhas must have been shoved onward by the Kurus when the latter took possession of the land about the Sarasvatī. I may even say that they may have come eastward even before the coming in of the Kurus, *i. e.*, when the whole land from the Punjab eastward up to Mithila was occupied by the Solar race people. Professor Macdonell, however, expresses some doubt about this in a foot-note on the word Kuru and refers to the narrative given in the Śatapatha of the progress of Agni from the Sarasvatī to the Sadānīrā, the eastern boundary of the Videha kingdom and thinks that it may be argued from the story that the Kosala-Videhas were of the same race as the Kurus. But I do not think that any such inference is necessary. The Aryan fire went from the Sarasvatī no doubt, but no mention is made of the Kurus in this story and hence the Agni may have gone forth eastward even before the days or the Kurus, of even Pūrus. Moreover the story in the Śhatapatha (IV. 1, 10) is that Videgha Māthavya took fire in his mouth and went eastward up to the Sadānīrā where he had to take it out and lay it on the ground in consequence of a question by Gotama Rahūgaṇa, his priest. Hence, says the Brāhmaṇa, no Brahmin crosses the Sadānīrā. Now this name of Gotama tallies with the later Epic story that the priests of the Videhas were Gotamas, as I have already mentioned. It seems to me then very probable that these Kosala-Videhas were of the Solar race and had their differences in religious matters from the Kuru-Pānchālas, the representatives of the Lunar race people. The Kosala-Videhas were more famous in the days of the Brāhmaṇas for their philosophic tendencies than their ritual purity and their great king Janaka had disputations with Yājñavalkya on philosophy which have been preserved in the immortal Upanishads. This laxity in ritual also connects the Kosala-Videhas with the people of the Punjab who are said to be also lax in this matter, as much as the affinity of language ; and the remarks of Prof. Macdonnell on this head under Kosala and Kāshi in the Vedic Index should be interpreted in this way to support their affinity with the eastern Aryans than with the Kuru-Pānchālas.

We have lastly to see what became of the Anus and the Druhyus. The latter are mentioned separately in two Vedic hymns viii, 10 and vi, 46. The first has already been noticed. The second mentions Druhyu and Pūru, two only, together. What subsequently became of the Druhyus does not appear either in the Ṛigveda or the later Vedic literature. Perhaps, they were the fourth people who merged in the Pānchālas. Puraṇic tradition makes the Gāndhāras their descendants. The Gāndhāras are mentioned in the Chhāndogya. The Anus probably became a great people even in the days of the Ṛigveda ; for, in one hymn their Agni is mentioned specially, see viii, 74 (आगन्म वृत्रहन्तमं ज्येष्ठमग्निमानवम्). But there is no mention of them in the later Vedic literature. The Purāṇas state that they gave rise to several dynasties in the Punjab, especially to the Śibi dynasty whose famous king was Śibi, son of Uśīnara, mentioned among the sixteen great performers of Aśvamedha sacrifice in the Mahābhārata. I am not quite sure if the Purāṇas are correct here ; but I think this is not the place to discuss that point. This completes our list of the Vedic references to the Lunar people whose five branches, the यदु, तुर्वश, अनु, द्रुह्यु, and पूरु are famous even in the Ṛigveda.

To take a rēsume, the conclusions of ethnology and philology as applied to India by Sir H. Risley and Dr. Grierson quoting

Dr. Hœrnle show that there were two Aryan races which invaded India at different times and settled in this country. The first long-headed Aryans, settled in the Punjab and in Rajputana and are found there even now, with offshoots about Ayodhya and Mithila whose present language, Eastern Hindi, is allied to the Punjabi and Rajastani. The second race of Aryans which was broad-headed and mixed with the Dravidian original population of the country is now found in the large tract from Ambala in the north, to Kathiawar in the south-west and Jubbulpore in the south-east and Nepal in the north-east. The present language of these people is Western Hindi. Now tradition also represents that there are two races of Aryans in India, *viz.*, the Solar race of Kshatriyas and the Lunar. This naturally suggests that the first race of Kshatriyas who came to India must be identified with the Solar race and the second with the Lunar race. And we find that this inference is strongly fortified by references in the Vedic literature, especially in the Ṛigveda, our oldest and most trustworthy authority. The Ṛigveda frequently mentions a people called the Bharatas. Now it is almost a riddle to Vedic scholars who these people were and what became of them. As stated by Prof. Macdonnell under the word Kuru the general opinion is that these Bharatas merged in the Kurus. Now my suggestion, based on conclusions derived from ethnology, philology and tradition, is that these Bharatas being the older Aryans should be identified with the Solar race Kshatriyas of the Epics and the Purāṇas. Strong grounds for this identification are not wanting. The first is that their Purohitas were the Vasishṭhas, also called Tritsus in the Ṛigveda. Now the Vasishṭhas are in Epic and Purāṇic tradition inseparably connected with the Solar race. Secondly, the famous king Sudāsa of these Bharatas is found in the Rāmāyaṇa as an ancestor of Rāma and Śatrughna. Sudāsa is found in the Purāṇic genealogies also in the Solar line, but his father is not Divodāsa as in the Ṛigveda. I think Purāṇic genealogy ought to give way in this matter. Sudāsa, (Pijavana), Divodāsa and Vadhryaśva form the ascending line according to the Ṛigveda. It may be noted here that names ending in aśva are found mostly in the Solar race and Vadhryaśva (Ṛg. vi, 61 and x, 19) seems to be a Solar race king. Thirdly, Viśvāmitra in the Ṛigveda is also a Ṛishi of the Bharatas and according to Epic and Purāṇa tradition also, Viśvāmitra is chiefly connected with the history of the Solar race.* Fourthly, the names of Purukutsa and Trasadasyu† are to be found in the line of Ikshvāku only, in the Purāṇas and they are Aikshvāka also according to the Brāhmaṇas. For all these reasons I identify the Bharatas as the Solar race people of the Epics. They are usually taken for the later Bharatas, *viz*, the descendants of Daushyanti Bharata, but wherever this Bharata is mentioned in the Brāhmaṇas the epithet Daushyanti is found added and he is not mentioned in the Ṛigveda at all. This mixing up of the two has led to the popular notion that India is called Bhāratavarsha from the second Bharata. But tradition, even Purāṇic tradition, plainly contradices this idea and states that India is called Bhāratavarsha from Bharata, a grandson of the first Svāyambhuva Manu. According to another Purāṇa, Bharata who gave the name to this country is Manu himself or even the Sun. Hence, we have a further confirmation of the Bharatas being Kshatriyas of the Solar race.

---

* The Purāṇas derive Viśvāmitra from the Lunar line, but there is a contradiction here between the Purāṇas and the Rāmānyaṇa and there is a contradiction among the Purāṇas themselves. Rāmāyaṇa, Bālakāṇda, Chapter 51, gives the ancestry of Viśvāmitra as Prājāpati and then Kuśka at once in whose family of course Viśvāmitra was born even according to the Ṛigveda. He is hence neither Solar nor Lunar according to the Rāmāyaṇa but he is plainly a person of the older race of Kshatriyas. The Purāṇas derive Viśvāmitra in the Lunar line in two ways. Harivaṁśa derives him from Amavasu, another son of Purūravas than Ayu whose son was Nahusha; while in another place it derives him from Ajamīdha and Janhu. I think the Purāṇic genealogy ought to give way here to the Rāmāyaṇa which makes Viśvāmitra born in the oldest line of Kshatriyas. Curiously enough this uncertainty of descent still remains attached to their modern Kshatriya representatives, *v.z.*, the Rathods who are derived differently in the Solar and the Lunar lines.

† Kuruśravaṇa, a king in the Trasadasyu family is supposed to be a Kuru, but I do not see why he should be so. In the Rigvedic hymns he is expressly said to be a Trāsadaśyava and not a Kuru. The beginning word Kuru cannot make him a Kuru in race in the same way as Divodāsa cannot be a Dāsa or non-Aryan as actually suggested by a German Vedic scholar.

These Bharatas became so numerous that Bharata in one place in the Aitareya Brāhmaṇa stands for warrior generally.* In the Nirukta in one place Bharatas are said to mean priests also along with Kurus. The reason why Bharatas may be substituted for Kurus in sacrificial formulas as mentioned in Vedic Index under Kuru, is not because they were identical with Kurus but because they were a different people with equal reuown, and wherever they were meant their name was to be substituted in the sacrificial formulas. In fine, there are very strong reasons to identify the Bharatas with the Solar race people of the later, *viz.*, Epic days. Their representatives in the days of the Brāhmaṇas were the Kosala-Videhas the undoubted Solar race Kshatriyas of the Epics and the Purāṇas.

The identification of the Lunar race Kshatriyas in the Vedas is not a matter of any difficulty. They are, of course, the Yadus, the Turvaśas, the Anus, the Druhyus and the Pūrus, so frequently mentioned in the Ṛigveda. Of these the Pūrus became numerous and supreme and in their line came the Kuru-Pānchālas of Epic and Puraṇic fame. The Yadus also became famous and were the progenitors of the Yādavas amongst whom was born Krishṇa referred to in the Chhāndogya. The Anus are supposed to give rise to several Punjab kings, *e.g.*, the Śibis and the Madras who had their counterpart beyond the Himalayas, the Uttara Madras as the Kurus had theirs, the Uttara Kurus. All this is so plain that later Epic and Purāṇa tradition may be said to find complete support in the Ṛigvedic and Brāhmaṇa references. And in my opinion the five races, Yadus and others, had for their ancestor Yayāti though this is doubted by Prof. Macdonell under the word Yayāti in the Vedic Index. Purūravas, Ayu, Nahusha and Yayāti are all mentioned in the Ṛig-

* Macdonell says under Kuru that Bharatas in this passage (ii, 25) means the Daushyanti Bharatas and they attacked the Satvantas. Sāyana, however, translates Bharatas by warriors and Satvantas by charioteers. This interpretation seems correct though the derivation of Bharata given by Sāyana is fanciful. I think the word Bharatas became subsequently a synonym for warriors and even for priests as stated further.

veda and form, so to speak, the starting line of the Lunar race. There is, of course, no express mention in the Ṛigveda of this connection between Yayāti and the five peoples, Yadu and others, but some such conneetion may be inferred from hymn 1. 31, where Yayāti is mentioned. This hymn is composed by Hiraṇyastūpa Āṅgirasa and the Āṅgirasas are connected, as we have already seen, with these five peoples. Moreover, the fourth verse in this hymn may almost be taken to contain the confirmation of the later traditional genealogies of the Purāṇas, as it shows that (besides the Ṛishi Āṅgirasa) Agni was revealed. originally to two persons, Manu and Purūravas (त्वमग्ने मनवे द्यामवाशयः पुरूरवसे सुकृते सुकृत्तरः ।) followed by verse 17 (मनुष्वदग्ने अंगिरस्वदङ्गिरो-ययातिवत्सदने पूर्ववच्छुचे) in which ययाति is plainly substituted for पुरूरवस् as his representative. Thus, the Purāṇa tradition, supported by these references in the Ṛigveda, cannot be fairly ignored. I think, therefore, that the Lunar race kings from Purūravas down to Ajamīdha are mentioned in the Ṛigveda, and from Bharata to Kuru and Janamejaya even, in the Brāhmaṇas. In short, the Lunar race Kshatriyas are undoubtedly a Vedic people identifiable with Pūruravas and his descendants, Yadu, Turvaśa and others.

Before concluding this paper I must advert to a very important question which arises at this stage and it is this: if the Solar and Lunar origins of the two races are not expressly mentioned in the Vedic literature, how did the idea arise in Epic days? The idea of the descent of all races from one ancestor is not a fancy of the Indo-Aryans only but of many peoples; and the birth of heroes or great men from gods is also a myth which many peoples have believed in. Not only did the Greeks in ancient times make their heroes the sons of gods, but even in later history we find the Mexican Aztecs looking upon the Spaniards as the children of the Sun. The notion, therefore, that certain races were born from the Sun and the Moon was not an unnatural one with the Epic and Purāṇa writers. But some reason must have influenced the selection of these gods as the ancestors of the two races of Kshatriyas and we may try to see what this reason may have been. Manu is even in the Rigveda the son of Vivasvat, or the Sun. It is not an idea of the later Indo-Aryans but even of the Vedic Ṛishis and the word Bharata which was the origin of the name of the ancient Ṛigvedic people the Bharatas, is explained by the Nirukta to mean the Sun. The idea, therefore, that the first race of Kshatriyas was descended from the Sun was inherited by the Epic writers from the Ṛigveda itself. The birth of the other race of Kshatriyas from the Moon was a natural idea as opposed to the Sun and hence they must have been looked upon as descendants of the Moon. Or perhaps, these people coming from the north may have been called descendants of the Moon for Soma is the lord of the north. We may add that the first race of Kshatriyas, being in Epic days in the east, may have been looked upon as descendants of the Sun. Lastly, it is also possible to explain this idea on a difference between these races in their observance of the year which is plainly discernible in the story of the Mahābhārata fight. The Pāndavas had to pass twelve years of exile and one of incognito according to the covenant at their gambling game. Now the Kurus argued, when the Pāndavas appeared in Virāta's fight, that they were discovered before their time, but the Pāndavas replied that they had kept their word truly and fully. Bhīshma decided the point in favour of the Pāndavas and held that they had kept their word by the Lunar year of 354 days. This decision would undoubtedly be strange if the Pāndavas observed the Lunar year only for the purpose of this covenant. I think this phase of the question has not sufficiently attracted the attention of scholars. I hold that this decision clearly proves that the Pāndavas generally followed the Lunar year like the Mahomedans of the present day. In the Taittirīya Saṁhitā you have clear references to different years observed by the Aryans, *viz.*, the Civil year of 360 days, the Solar year of 365 days and the Lunar year of 354 days. Of course, later Aryans observed the Solar year only and these differences have now disappeared entirely. But in ancient times the Pāndavas the latest branch of the Lunar race people, must have observed the Lunar year in much the same way as they observed polyandry so common among the Himalayan people; while the Kurus or rather the Dhārtarāshtras as older people must have observed the solar year generally in vogue among the older Kshatriyas. The people of the Punjab and of Ayodhyā and the other eastern people seem to have observed the Solar year and they were all on the side of the Dhārtarāshtras, while on the side of the Pāndavas were all southern Aryans chiefly of the Lunar race, *viz.*, the Pānchālas, who were apparently polyandrous still and the Yādavas and the Chedis and the Magadhas. In my opinion the different peoples ranged on either side observed different years and they were, so to speak, people of the old tradition and the new tradition. The former observed the Solar year and the latter the Lunar year. Hence might also arise the idea that the Pāndavas, Pānchālas, etc., were the desendants of the Moon. It is true that some peoples of this race were observers of the Solar year as the Dhārtarāshtras themselves and the Madras, etc., but they were all inhabitants of the Punjab and must have adopted the year of the first settled Aryans there. I put forward this theory with some diffidence, but I think it to be of sufficient importance to find a record here. I have already given expression to this view in another place and detailed the whole theory as it appears from the story of the Mahābhārata. I touch it here in bare outline and I put it forward only as an alternative to account for the Epic names assigned to these two most famous races of Kshatriyas, *viz.*, the Solar and the Lunar races who have so gloriously distinguished themselves not only in the Vedic, the Epic and the Puranic days, but also in the modern history of India commencing with Mahomedan times.

APPENDIX II

SOME INSCRIPTIONS IN THE ORIGINAL.

(1) Āṭpurā inscription of Śaktikumāra relating to the Guhilots of Mewād.

(*Indian Antiquary* XXXIX *of* 1910 *p.* 191)

संवत्सरशतेषु दशसु चतुस्त्रिंशत्यधिकेषु वैशाख शुक्ल प्रतिपदि संवत् १०३४ वैशाखशुक्लप्रतिपदातयौ श्रीनानिगस्वामिदेवायतनं कारापितं ॥ आनंदपुरविनिर्गतविप्रकुलानंन्दनो महीदेवः । जयति श्रीगुहदत्त प्रभवः श्रीगुहिलवंशस्य । यस्यान्वये जगति भोजमहेन्द्रनागशीलापराजितमहेन्द्र-जायतैक वीरः ॥ जातैर्यथार्कसमशोभितकालभोज खोम्माण—नृपैः सह भर्तृपट्टैः ॥ २ ॥ सिंहोऽभवत् तदनु तद्भृतीपि जज्ञे खोम्माण इत्यथ सुतोस्य महायकोऽभूत् । खोम्माणमात्मजमवाप स चाथ तस्मात् लोकत्रयैकतिलको जाने भर्तृपट्टः ॥ ३ ॥ राष्ट्रकूटकुलोद्भूता महालक्ष्मीरितिप्रिया । अभूद् यस्याभवत् तस्यां तनयः श्रीमद्दल्लटः ॥ ४ ॥ स भूपतिः प्रिया यस्य हूण-क्षोणीशवंशजा दरीयदेवी यशो यस्या भाति हर्षपुराव्हयम् ॥ अविकलकला-धारो धीरः स्फुरद्विलसत्करो विजयवसतिः क्षत्रक्षेत्रं क्षताहृतिसंहतिः समजनि-जना—प्रतापतरूद्भृतो विभवभवनं विद्यावेदी नृपो नरवाहनः ॥ ६ ॥ चाहमानान्वयोद्भूता श्रीजेजयनृपात्मजा राजा जयति शालिवाहनः इति ख्यातप्रतापस्ततः ॥ ८ ॥ ततः शक्तिकुमारोऽभूत् सुतः शक्तित्रयोर्जितः भर्तृपट्टाभिधाश्रीश्चप्राप राष्ट्रमधापयत् ॥ ९ ॥ श्रीमदाटपुर—युतालयं यस्य वास इति संपदां पदं यत्र सन्ति नृपपुंगवाः समं कल्पपादपपदात-गामिनः ॥ १० ॥ &c.

(2) Harsha Stone Inscription relating to the Chāhamānas of Sāmbar.

(*Ep. Indica* Vol. II. p. 121).

आद्यः श्रीगूवकाख्याप्रथितनरपतिश्चाहमानान्वयोभूत्
श्रीमन्नागा (वा ?) लोकप्रवरनृपसभाल (ब्ध) वीरप्रतिष्ठः ।
यस्य श्रीहर्षदेवे ऽवरभवनमयी भौतली कीर्तिमूर्त्ति—
ह्लोंके द्यापि स्थिरैषा प्रतपति परमैः—७—७–[गै ?] :—
॥ १३ ॥

पुत्रः श्रीचंद्रराजो भवदमलयशास्तस्य तीव्रप्रतापः
सूनुस्तस्याथ भूपः प्रथम इव पुनर्गूवकाख्यः प्रतापी ।
तस्माच्छ्रीचंदनोभूत्क्षितिपति भयदस्तोमरेशंसदर्पं
हत्वा युद्धेन भूपं समर [भुवि] [ब] लाद्ये [न लब्धा]
जयश्रीः ॥ १४ ॥

ततः परमतेजस्वी सदा समरजित्वरः ।
श्रीमान्वाक्पतिराजाख्यो महाराजो भवत्सुतः ॥ १५ ॥

येनादैन्यं स्वसैन्यं कथमपि दधता वाजिवल्गा मुमुक्षु
प्रागेव त्रासितेभः सरासिक [रि] रटड्डिंडिमौड्डिं ५
यन्दक्ष्माभर्तुराज्ञां समदमभि [व] हन्नागतोनंतपार्श्वं—
क्ष्मापालस्तंत्रपालो दिशि दिशि गमितो द्रागनिषण्णः प्रसण्ण
(न्न) ॥ १६ ॥

शूरस्येदं ।
लोकैर्यो हि महीतले ननु हरिश्चंद्रोपमो गीयते
त्यागैश्व [र्य] त्रयेषु की [र्त्ति] [र] मला धर्मश्च
यस्योज्व [ल्व] लः ।
येनादायि हराय मंदिरकृते भक्त्या प्रभूतं वसु
श्रीमद्वाक्पतिराजसूनुरसमः श्रीसिंहराजोभवत् ॥ १७ ॥

हैममारोपितं येन शिवस्य भवनोपरि ।
पूर्णं चंद्रोपमं स्वीयं मूर्त्तं य [श] ~ [पि ?] डक
[म्] ॥ १८ ॥

— — । तोमरनायकं सलषणं सैन्याधिपत्योध्दतं
युद्धे येन नरेश्वराः प्रतिदिशं निर्न्ना (ण्णा) सिता जिष्णुना ।
कारावेश्मनि भूरयश्च विधृतास्तावध्दि यावद्गृहे
तन्मुक्त्यर्थमुपागतो रघुकुले भूचक्रवर्ति स्वयम् ॥ १९ ॥

[न्वि] ग्रहराजो भुत्तत्सुतो वासवोपमः ।
वंगलक्ष्मीर्जयश्रीश्च येनैते विधुरोध्दृते ॥ २० ॥

श्रीसिंहराजरहिता किल चिंतयंती भीतेव संप्रति विभुर्ननु को
ममेति । येनास्मबा (वा) हुयुगले चिरसन्निवासं संधी
रितेति ददता निज [रा] जलक्ष्मीः ॥ २१ ॥

येन दुष्टदमनेन सर्वतः साधिताखिलमही स्व (बा) हुभिः ।
लीलयैव वश्यवर्तिनी कृता किंकरीव निजपादयोस्तले ॥ २२ ॥

यस्य चारुचरितं सतां सदा शृण्वतां जगति कीर्तितं जनैः ।
हृष्टिजातघनरोमकं –आयते तनुरलं महुर्म्मुहु ॥ २३

मुक्ताहारैः सुतारैः प्रतरलतुरगैश्चारुवस्त्रैश्च शस्त्रैः
कर्प्पूरैः पूगपूरैर्म्मलयतरुवरैर्हेमभारैरपारैः ।
उद्यद्दानैः समानैश्चलकुलगिरिभिर्दन्तिवारैः सदारै–
र्निव्याजै प्रातिर ~~ भिरितिभृतैः प्राभृतैर्यः सिषेवे ॥ २४ ॥

छत्रधारी वरग्रामो द्वीतियिः शंकराणकः
तेनेमौ हर्षनाथाय [याय] [भ] क्त्या दत्तौ सशासनौ ॥ २५ ॥

श्रीमद्दुर्लभराजेन योनुजेन विभूषितः
लक्ष्मणेनैव काकुत्स्थो विष्णुनेव हलायुधः ॥ २६ ॥

[महा] राजावली चासौ शंभुभक्तिगुणोदया
श्रीहर्षः कुलदेवोस्यास्तमाद्दिव्यः कुलक्रमः ॥ २७ ॥

अनंत गोचरे श्रीमाद् पण्डित औत्तरेः श्व (स्व) रः ।
पंचार्थलाकुलाम्नाये विश्वरूपो भवद्गुरुः ॥ २८ ॥

(3) Gwalior Bhoja praśasti, relating to the Imperial Prātihāras of Kanauj p. 290

Archäölogical Survey of India 1903—04, p. 280.

L 1 ओम् नमो विष्णवे ॥
शेषादितल्प धवला धरभागभाक्षि-
वक्षःस्थलोल्लसित कौस्तुभकान्तिशोणं ।
श्यामं वपु शशिविरोचनविम्बचुम्बि-
व्योमप्रकाशमवतान्नरकद्विषो वः ॥ १ ॥
आत्मारामफलादुपार्ज्य विजरं देवेन दैत्यद्विषा

L 2 ज्योतिर्बीजमकृत्रिमे
गुणवति क्षेत्रे यदुप्तं पुरा
श्रेयः कन्दवपुस्ततस्समभवद्भास्वानतश्चानरे
मन्विक्ष्वाकुककुस्थमूलपृथवः क्ष्मापालकल्पद्रुमाः ॥ २ ॥
तेषां वंशे सुजन्मा क्रमनिहितपदे धाम्नि वज्रेषु घोरं
रामः पौलस्त्यहिंस्रं क्षतविहितसमित्कर्म्म चक्रे पलाशैः ।

श्लाघ्य-

L 3 स्तस्यानुजोसौ मघवमदमुषो मेघनादस्य संख्ये
सौमित्रिस्तीव्रदण्डः प्रतिहरणविधेर्यः प्रतीहार आसीत् ॥३॥
तद्वंशे प्रतिहारकेतनभृति त्रैलोक्यरक्षास्पदे
देवो नागभटः पुरातनमुनेर्मुर्तिर्ब्बभूवाद्भुतं ।
येनासौ सुकृतप्रमाथिबलनम्लेच्छा-

L 4 धिपाक्षौहिणीः
क्षुन्दानस्फुरदुग्रहेतिरुचिरैर्दोर्भिश्चतुर्भिर्ब्बभौ ॥ ४ ॥
भ्रातुस्तस्यात्मजोभूत्कलितकुलयशाः ख्यातकाकुस्थनामा
लोके गीतः प्रतीरु पृथुवचनतया कक्कुकः क्ष्माभृदीशः ।
श्रीमानस्यानुजन्मा कुलिशधरधरामृद्वहन्देवराजो
यश्चे च्छिन्नोरुपक्षक्षपितग-

L 5 तिकुलं भूभृतां धनियन्वा ॥ ५ ॥
तत्सूनुः प्राप्य राज्यं निजमुदयगिरिस्पर्धि भास्वत्प्रतापः
क्ष्मापालः प्रादुरासीन्नतसकलजगद्वत्सलो वत्सराजः ।
यस्यैतास्सम्पदश्च द्विरदमदसुरास्वाद सान्द्र प्रमोदाः
पद्माक्षीराक्षिपन्त्यः प्रणयिजनपरिष्वंग कान्ताविरेजुः ॥ ६ ॥
ख्या (ताद्) भण्डि

L 6 कुलान्मदोत्कटकरि प्राकार दुर्लङ्घतो
यः साम्राज्यमधिज्यकार्मुकसखा संख्ये हटादग्रहीत् ।
एकः क्षत्रियपुङ्गवेषु च यशोगुर्व्वीन्धुरं प्रोद्वह-
न्निक्ष्वाकोः कुलमुन्नतं सुचरितैश्चक्रे स्वनामाङ्कितं ॥ ७ ॥
आद्यः पुमान्पुनरपि स्फुटकीर्तिरस्मा-
ज्जातस्स एव किल नागभटस्तदाख्यः ।

यत्रा—

L 7 न्ध्र सैन्धव विदर्भ कलिङ्ग भूपैः
कौमारधामनि पतङ्गसमैरपाति ॥ ८ ॥
त्र्य्यास्पदस्य सुकृतस्य समृद्धिमिच्छु-
र्यः क्षत्रधामविधिबद्धबलिप्रबन्धः ।
जित्वा पराश्रयकृतस्फुटनीचभावं
चक्रायुधं विनयनम्रवपुर्व्यराजत् ॥ ९ ॥
दुर्व्वारवैरि वर वारण वाजिवार-
याणौघसंघट-

L 8 न घोरघनान्धकारं ।
निर्जित्य वङ्गपतिमाविरभूद्विवस्वा
नुद्यन्निव त्रिजगदेकविकास कोषः ॥ १० ॥
आनर्त्त मालव किरात तुरुष्कवत्स-
मत्स्यादि राजगिरिदुर्ग्गहटापहारैः ।
यस्यात्मवैभवमतीन्द्रियमाकुमार-
माविर्ब्बभूव भुवि विश्वजनीनवृत्तेः ॥ ११ ॥
तज्जन्मा राम

नामा प्रवरहरिबलन्यस्तभूभृत्प्रबन्धे—
रावधून्वाहिनीनां प्रसभमधिपतीनुद्धत क्रूरसत्वान् ।
पापाचारान्तरायप्रमथनरुचिरः सङ्गतः कीर्त्तिदारै-
स्त्राता धर्मस्य तैस्तैस्समुचितचरितैः पूर्व्ववन्निर्ब्बभासे ॥१२।
अनन्य साधनाधीन प्रतापाक्रान्तदि—

L 10 ङ्मुखः ।

उपायैस्सम्पदां स्वामी य सव्रीडमुपास्यत ॥ १३ ॥
अर्थिभिर्व्विनियुक्तानां सम्पदां जन्म केवलं ।
यस्याभूत्कृतिनः प्रीत्यै नात्मेच्छाविनियोगतः ॥ १४ ॥

जगद्वितृष्णुः स विशुद्धसत्वः ।
प्रजापतित्वं विनियोक्तुकामः ।
सुतं रहस्यव्रतसुप्रसन्ना—
स्सूर्यादवा-

L 11 पन्मिहिराभिधानं ॥ १५ ॥

उपरोधैकसंरुद्ध विन्ध्यवृद्धेरगस्त्यतः
आक्रम्य भूभृतां भोक्ता यः प्रभुर्भोज इत्यभात् ॥ १६ ॥
यशस्वी शान्तात्मा जगदहितविच्छेद निपुणः
परिष्वक्तो लक्ष्म्या न च मदकलंकेन कलितः ।
बभूव प्रेमार्द्रो गुणिषु विषयः सूनृत-

L 12 गिरा—

मसौ रामो बाग्रे स्वकृतिगणनायामिहविधेः ॥ १७ ॥
यस्याभूत्कुलभूमिभृत्प्रमथनव्यस्तान्यसैन्याम्बुधे-
र्व्यूढावस्फुटितारिलाजनि वहान्हुत्वा प्रतापानले
गुप्ता वृद्धगुणैरनन्यगातिभिः शान्तैस्सुधोद्भासिभि-
र्धर्म्मापत्ययशः प्रभूतिरपरा लक्ष्मीः पुनर्भू-

L 13 र्न्न या ॥ १८ ॥

प्रीतैः पालनया तपोधनकुलैः स्नेहाद्गुरूणां गणै-
र्भक्त्या भृत्यजनेन नीतिनिपुणैर्वृन्दैररीणां पुनः ।
विश्वेनापि यदीयमायुरमितं कर्तुं स्वजीवैषिणा
तन्निम्ना विदधे विधातरि यथा सम्पत्परार्द्धाश्रये ॥ १९ ॥

अवितथमिदं यावद्दिवं श्रुते-

L 14 रनुशासना-
भवति फलभाक्कर्ता नेशः क्षितीन्द्रशतेष्वपि ।
अघरितकलेः कीर्त्तेर्भर्तुस्समतां सुकृतैरभू-
द्विघुरितधियां सम्पद्बुद्धिर्यदस्य तदद्भुतं । २० ॥
यस्य वैरिवृहद्वङ्गान्दहतः कोपवन्हिना
प्रतापादर्ण्णसां राशी न्पातुर्व्वैतृष्णमाबभौ ॥ २१ ॥
कुमार इव विद्यानां

L 15 वृन्देनाद्भुतकर्मणा ।
यः शशासासुरान्घोरान्स्त्रैणेनास्त्रैक वृत्तिना ॥ २२ ॥
यस्याक्षपटले राज्ञः प्रभुत्वाद्विश्वसम्पदः ।
लिलेख मुखमालोक्य प्रातिलेख्यकरो विधिः ॥ २३ ॥
उद्दामतेजः प्रसरप्रसूता
शिखेव कीर्त्तिर्द्युमणिं विजित्य ।
जाया जगद्भर्तु-

L 16 रियाय यस्य
चित्रं त्विदं यज्जलधिस्ततार ॥ २४ ॥
राज्ञा तेन स्वदेवीनां यशःपुण्याभिवृद्धये ।
अन्तःपुरपुरं नाम्ना व्यधायि नरकद्विषः ॥ २५
यावन्नभः सुरसरित्पसरोत्तरीयं
यावत्सुदुश्चरतपः प्रभवः प्रभावः ।
सत्यञ्च यावदुपरिस्थमवस्यशेषं
तावत्पु—

L 17 नातु जगतीमियमस्य कीर्त्तिः ॥ २६ ॥
पातुर्व्विश्वस्य सम्यकरमग्रुनिमतश्रेयसस्तम्विधाना-
दन्तर्वृत्तिर्व्विवेकः स्थित इव पुरतो भोजदेवस्य राज्ञः
विद्वद्वृन्दार्जितानां फलमिव तपसां भट्टभव्वेक सूनु-
र्व्वालादित्यः प्रशस्तेः कविरिह जगता साक (?) माकल्पमूह्येः
॥ २७ ॥

APPENDIX III.

Extracts from important Smṛitis (Manu and Yājñavalkya excepted) showing the freer social condition of India in the Ninth and Tenth Centuries A.D.)

अत्रिः—

१ राजन्यैः श्वपचैर्वापि बलाद्विचालितो द्विजः ।
पुनः कुर्वीत संस्कारं पश्चात्कृच्छ्रत्रयं चरेत् ।

२ (यतिः) चरन्माधुकरीं वृत्तिमथ म्लेच्छकुलादपि ।
एकान्नं नैव भोक्तव्यं बृहस्पतिसमो यदि ॥

३ गोकुले कन्दुशालायां तैलयन्त्रेक्षुयन्त्रयोः ।
अमीमांस्यानि शौचानि स्त्रीणां च व्याधितस्य च ॥

४ देवयात्राविवाहेषु यज्ञप्रकरणेषु च ।
उत्सवेषु च सर्वेषु स्पृष्टास्पृष्टिर्न विद्यते ॥

५ आरनालं तथा क्षीरं कन्दुकं दधिसक्तु च ।
स्नेहपक्वं च तक्रं च शूद्रस्यापि न दुष्यति ॥

६ आर्द्रमांसं घृतं तैलं स्नेहाश्च फलसंभवाः
अन्त्यभाण्डस्थिता ह्येते निष्क्रान्ताःशुचिमाप्नुयुः ॥

विष्णुः—

१ परिणीय तु षण्मासान् वत्सरं वा न संविशेत् ।
औदुम्बरायणो नाम ब्रह्मचारी गृहे गृहे ॥

२ शूद्रोपि द्विविधो ज्ञेयः श्राद्धी चैवेतरस्तथा ।
श्राद्धी भोज्यस्तयोरुक्तो अभोज्यस्त्वितरो मतः ॥

३ त्रिदण्डलिङ्गमाश्रित्य जीवन्ति बहवो द्विजाः ।
न तेषामपवर्गोस्ति लिङ्गमालोपजीविनाम् ॥

उशनाः—

१ विधिना ब्राह्मणः प्राप्य नृपायां तु समन्त्रकम् ।
जातः सुवर्ण इत्युक्तः सानुलोमद्विजःस्मृतः ॥

२ नृपायां विधिना विप्राज्जातो नृप इति स्मृतः ॥

आपस्तम्बः—

१ ब्राह्मण्या सह योऽश्नीयादुच्छिष्टं वा कदाचन ।
न तत्र दोषं मन्यन्ते नित्यमेव मनीषिणः ॥

२ उच्छिष्टमितरस्त्रीणामश्नीयात्स्पृशतेपि वा ।
प्राजापत्येन शुद्धिः स्याद्भगवानङ्गिरोऽब्रवीत् ॥

३ ब्राह्मणस्य सदा भुंक्ते क्षत्रियस्य तु पर्वणि ।
वैश्यस्य यज्ञदीक्षायां शूद्रस्य न कदाचन ॥

४ आममांसं मधु घृतं धानाः क्षीरं तथैव च ।
गुडस्तक्रं रसा ग्राह्या निवृत्तेनापि शूद्रतः

५ शाकं मांसं मृणालानि तुम्बुरुः सक्तवस्तिलाः ।
रसाः फलानि पिण्याकं प्रतिग्राह्या हि सर्वतः ॥

संवर्तः—

१ तस्माद्विवाहयेत्कन्यां यावन्नर्तुमती भवेत् ।
विवाहोष्टमवर्षायाः कन्यायास्तु प्रशस्यते ॥

कात्यायनः—

१ अजातव्यंञ्जनालोम्नी न तया सह संविशेत् ।
अयुगूः काकवन्ध्याया जाता तां न विवाहयेत् ॥

बृहस्पतिः—

[बहुभिर्वसुधा दत्ता &c. दशहस्तेनदण्डेन त्रिंशद्दण्डान्निवर्तनम् ।
दश तान्येव विस्तारो गोचर्मैतन्महाफलम् (निवर्तन=३०० हस्त and गोचर्म=३००० हस्त)]

२ वीरासनं वीरशय्या वीरस्थानमुपाश्रितः ।
अक्षय्यास्तस्य लोकाः स्युः सर्वकामगमास्तथा ॥

पराशरः—

१ अव्रता ह्यनधीयाना यत्र भैक्ष्यचरा द्विजाः ।
तं ग्रामं दण्डयेद्राजा चोरभक्तप्रदो हि सः ॥

२ षट्कर्मसहितो विप्रः कृषिकर्म च कारयेत् ।
क्षुधितं तृषितं श्रान्तं बलीवर्दं न योजयेत् ॥

३ राज्ञे दत्वा तु षड्भागं देवानां चैवविंशकम् '
विप्राणां त्रिंशकं भागं सर्वपापैः प्रमुच्यते ॥

४ क्षत्रियोपि कृषिं कृत्वा देवान् विप्रांश्च तोषयेत् ।
वैश्यः शूद्रस्तथा कुर्यात् कृषिवाणिज्यशिल्पकम् ॥

व्यासः—

१ ब्राह्मणक्षत्रियविशस्त्रयो वर्णा द्विजातयः।
श्रुतिस्मृतिपुराणोक्तधर्मयोग्यास्तु नेतरे॥

२ शूद्रो वर्णश्चतुर्थस्तु वर्णत्वाद्धर्ममर्हति।
वेदमन्त्रस्वधास्वाहावषट्कारादिभिर्विना॥

३ वर्धकिर्नापितो गोपः आशायः कुम्भकारकः।
वणिक्किरातकायस्थमालाकारकुटम्बिनः॥ भोज्यान्नाः

४ ऊढायां हि सवर्णायामन्यां वा काममुद्वहेत्।
तस्यामुत्पादितः पुत्रो न सवर्णात्प्रहीयते॥

५ उद्वहेत्क्षत्रियां विप्रो वैश्यां च क्षत्रियो विशाम्।
न तु शूद्रां द्विजः कश्चिन्नाधमः पूर्ववर्णजाम्॥

३ नापितान्वयमित्रार्द्धसीरिणो दासगोपकाः।
शूद्राणामप्यमीषां तु भुक्त्वान्नं नैव दुष्यति॥

४ नाश्नीयाद्ब्राह्मणो मांसमनियुक्तः कथंचन।
क्रतौ श्राद्धे नियुक्तो वा अनश्नन्पतति द्विजः॥

५ मृगयोपार्जितं मांसमभ्यर्च्य पितृदेवताः।
क्षत्रियो द्वादशोनं तत्क्रीत्वा वैश्योपि धर्मतः॥

शंखः—

१ आपद्यपि न कर्तव्या शूद्रा भार्या कथंचन।
तस्यां तस्य प्रसूतस्य निष्कृतिर्न विधीयते॥

दक्षः—

१ एको भिक्षुर्यथोक्तस्तु द्वौ चैव मिथुनं स्मृतम्।
त्रयो ग्रामः समाख्याता ऊर्ध्वं तु नगरायते॥

२ नगरं नैव कर्तव्यं ग्रामो वा मिथुनं तथा।
एतत्त्रयं तु कुर्वाणः स्वधर्माच्च्यवते यतिः॥

३ नीरुजश्च युवा चैव भिक्षुर्नावसथार्हणः।
स दूषयति तत्स्थानं वृद्धादीन्पीडयत्यपि॥

गोतमः—

१ व्यवहारप्रासेन सार्ववर्णिकं भिक्षाचर्यमाभिशस्तं पतितवर्जम्।

२ राज्ञे बलिदानं कर्षकैर्दशममष्टमं षष्ठं वा पशुहिरण्ययोरप्येके पञ्चाशद्भागं विंशतिभागः शुल्कः पण्ये मूले फलमधुमांसपुष्पौषधतृणेन्धनानां षष्ठं तद्रक्षणधर्मित्वात्तेषु तु नित्ययुक्तः स्यात्॥

३ प्रशस्तानां स्वकर्मसु द्विजातीनां ब्राह्मणो भुञ्जीत प्रति-
गृह्णीयात् ॥

४ वृत्तिश्चेन्नान्तरेण शूद्रात् पशुपालक्षेत्रकर्षककुलसंगत-
कारयितृपरिचारका भोज्यान्ना वणिक् चाशिल्पी

वसिष्ठः—

१ आत्मत्राणे वर्णसंकरे वा ब्राह्मणवैश्यौ शस्त्रमाददीयाताम।
क्षत्रियस्य तु नित्यमेव रक्षणाधिकारात् ॥

२ अष्टौ ग्रासा मुनेर्भक्तं वानप्रस्थस्य षोडश ।
द्वात्रिंशच्च गृहस्थस्य अमितं ब्रह्मचारिणः ॥

३ न मृगयोरिषुचारिणः परिवर्जमन्नम् ।
विज्ञायते ह्यगस्त्यो वर्षसाहस्त्रिके सत्रे मृगयां चचार तस्या-
संस्तु रसमयाः पुरोडाशा मृगपक्षिणां प्रशस्तानामपि ह्यन्नः ।

४ राजा सह नागरैश्च कार्याणि कुर्यात् ।

५ पाणिग्राहे मृते बाला केवलं मंत्रसंस्कृता ।
सा चेदक्षतयोनिः स्यात्पुनः संस्कारमर्हति ॥

APPENDIX IV.

GENESIS OF THE DICTUM ‘कलावाद्यन्तयोः स्थितिः’

We have not yet been able to trace the above dictum, meaning that there would be only two varṇas (Brahmins and Śūdras) in the Kali age, to its original source. We find it quoted by Kamalākara Bhatta of Benares in his work Śūdrakamalākara but he did not plainly believe in it as we shall presently show and hence perhaps he merely says "In some Purāṇa" (Purāṇāntare) when he quotes it. We have not yet been able to fix upon the Purāṇa which contains this oft quoted line. It is most probably an imaginary line first quoted by the above Pandit of Benares who cannot, however, have been its originator. Kinjavadekar Śastri of Poona a well-known scholar and particularly versed in Mīmānsā pointed out to us another interesting place where a similar verse is quoted and we make no apology for giving the whole quotation. In his Mahābhāshya or commentary on the Sūtras of Pānini Patanjali says "ब्राह्मणेन निष्कारणो धर्मः षडङ्गो वेदोऽध्येयो ज्ञेयश्च" meaning a Brahmin even though without necessity should learn the Veda with its six Aṅgas and understand it. On this line of the Bhāshya (circa. 150 B.C.) of Patañjali, there is no comment in the gloss of Kaiyyata (who wrote his work about 600 A.D.). Nāgojibhatta of the 14th century A.D. in his commentary named Udyota says here "ब्राह्मणेनेत्युक्तेरन्यस्यैव-मध्ययनं काम्यमेवेति सूचयतीति कश्चित्" "Some one says that in using the word Brahmin the Bhāshyakāra intends to suggest that this learning the Vedas is optional with others." Vaidyanātha Mahādeva Pāyagunde of the 16th century, who has written a Chhāyā on the Udyota remarks on this "अत्रारुचिबीजम्। तयोर्नित्याध्ययनाविधायकस्मृत्यन्तरादिविरोधापत्तिरिति। तस्माद्ब्राह्मणपदं त्रैवर्णिकोपलक्षणमिति बोध्यम्। क्षत्रियस्य च वैश्यस्य च साङ्गवेदाध्ययनं ज्ञानं चेत्यर्थः।

वस्तुतस्तु कलौ क्षत्रियस्याभावं सूचयितुं तथोक्तमिति यथाश्रुतमेव तत्साधु । तथा च "कलौ न क्षत्रियाः सन्ति कलौ नो वैश्यजातयः । ब्राह्मणश्चैव शूद्रश्च कलौ वर्णद्वयं स्मृतम्" इति स्मृतिरिति तत्त्वम् । Translation. The writer of Udyota expresses his disapprobation of the opinion in using the word kaschit some one for this reason viz., that the two (varṇas) Kshatriyas and Vaiśyas are expressly enjoined by the Smṛitis to study the Veda and hence the opinion that its study is optional with them is contradictory of the Smṛiti injunction. Therefore (in the opinion of the Udyotakāra), the word Brahmin in the Bhāshya sentence should be taken to include all the three varṇas by upalakshaṇa (suggested inclusion) and therefore the sentence means also that Kshatriyas and Vaiśyas have to study and understand the Veda. But (we think) the sentence is proper and mentions Brahmins only in order to indicate that in the Kali age there are no Kshatriyas nor Vaiśyas. For a Smṛiti says " In the Kali age there are no Kshatriyas and no Vaiśya castes. There are in Kali only two Varṇas *viz.*, Brahmins and Śūdras " The editor Śivadatta who publishes the Udyota with the Chhāyā of Pāyaguṇḍe tacks on the remark श्रुतीनां कलियुगपरत्वकल्पनमसमञ्जसमिति त्रैवर्णिकानामुपलक्षणमित्येव युक्तम् । "To suppose that the Veda (study) is regulated by Kaliyuga is not sensible and hence the word Brahmin includes by upalakshaṇa the three Varṇas."

The above is a curious illustration how views based on the same original text change and toss from one side to another as times change. We will add the following historical comment on this. Originally, that is before Buddhism arose and spread, the Dharmaśāstra properly laid down the rule that all the three Varṇas should study and understand the Veda and such indeed was the practice in those days. This rule is naturally embodied in Manu and other Smṛitis. When Patañjali wrote his Bhāshya after the general spread of Buddhism in about 150 B.C. Kshatriyas and Vaiśyas had mostly become Buddhists and had given up the study of the Veda. Many Brahmins also were doing the same and Patañjali thought that it was the duty of Brahmins even without necessity to study the Veda. He, therefore, wrote the sentence above quoted with reference to the actual state of the country, Brahmins now being responsible for the preservation of the Veda. Kaiyyata lived about 600 A.D., when Buddhism was still supreme and naturally thought no comment was necessary. In the days of Nāgojibhaṭṭa of about 1300 A.D. things had entirely changed, Buddhism had gone out of India for centuries and Rajputs—orthodox Rajputs-had established their right to study the Vedas though the study was taken up by some only. Hence Nāgojibhaṭṭa found room to record the opinion of *some one* that the study of the Vedas for Kshatriyas and Vaiśyas was optional according to Patañjali. Pāyagunde of Wai wrote his work after the Mahomedans had long established their sway over the whole of India including the south and after the Kshatriyas, especially the Marathas of the south, had given up learning the Vedas, took occasion to express the opinion that the Bhāshyakāra had properly restricted his statement to Brahmins, as there were no Kshatriyas in the Kali age according to the above quoted dictum which probably must have come into existence in the interval, reflecting the actual state of the country of the time. Lastly, under the present awakening of the country and the effort of the Kshatriyas and Marathas to re-establish their right and status, Śivadatta like ourselves denies the correctness of the view of Pāyagunde that the study of the Veda can be subject to any Kaliyuga rule and reverts to the oldest state of law that all the three varṇas have to study and understand the Veda.

From the above discussion it will be apparent that the dictum "कलावाद्यन्तयोः स्थितिः" arose sometime between 1300 and 1600 A. D. If the belief had arisen before the time of Nāgojibhaṭṭa he would certainly have taken the line of argument adopted by Pāyagunde later and justified the statement of Patañjali by the simpler method *viz.*, that Patañjali intended to convey that there were no Kshatriyas and Vaiśyas in the Kali age. It is hence extremely probable that the idea arose later than Nāgojibhaṭṭa.

It is, however, possible to suggest that Najogibhaṭṭa knew the dictum but did not support it. For we know that Kamalākarbhaṭṭa, one of the descendants of Nāgojibhaṭṭa only quotes the dictum in order to refute it. This is what he states at the end of his Śūdrakamalākara—

" ननु कलौ क्षत्रियाभाव उक्तो भागवते नवमस्कन्धे.........द्वादश-स्कन्धे देवापिः शन्तनोर्भ्राता मरुश्चेक्ष्वाकुवंशजः । कलापग्राममासाते महा-योगबलान्वितौ ॥ ताविहेत्य कलेरन्ते वासुदेवानुशिक्षितौ वर्णाश्रमयुतं धर्मं पूर्ववत् प्रथयिष्यतः ॥ विष्णुपुराणेपि महापद्मपतिर्नाम नन्दः क्षत्रविनाश-कृत् ।......पुराणान्तरेपि ब्राह्मणाः क्षत्रिया वैश्या शूद्रा वर्णास्त्रयो द्विजः । युगे युगे स्थिताः सर्वे कलावाद्यन्तयोः स्थितिः ॥ अतः कथं द्विजसंकरजा उक्ताः । मैवं कलौ तु बीजभूताश्च केचित्तिष्ठन्ति भूतले इति विष्णुस्मरणात्-ब्रह्मक्षत्रविशः शूद्रा बीजार्थे य इह स्थिताः । कृते युगे तु तैः सार्धं निर्विशेषा स्तदाभवन् । इति मत्स्योक्तेश्च प्रच्छन्नरूपा स्वकर्मभ्रष्टाः क्षत्रियवैश्याः सन्त्येव क्वचिदित्यस्मत्पितृचरणाः ॥ "

Transl. : " But in Bhāgavata Purāṇa 9th Skandha the absence of Kshatriyas in the Kali age is declared as also in the 12th Skandha in the verse " Devāpi, brother of Śantanu and Maru born of the race of Ikshvāku will live in the village of Kalāpa endowed with great yogic power. These two, at the end of Kali, will again promulgate the Dharma of Varṇa and Āśrama by the command of Vāsudeva." Again in the Viśhṇu Pūraṇa also (it is stated that) a Nanda named Mahāpadmapati will destroy the Kshatriya people. Again in another Purāṇa (it is said) "Brahmins, Kshatriyas, Vaiśyas and Śūdras are the four varṇas the first three of which are Dvijas. All these exist in every age but in the Kali age only the first and the last remain. " How then can you speak of subcastes born of mixture with Dvijas ? The answer is : this doubt is not correct for Vishṇu says "In the Kali age some remain as seed " and in the Matsya Purāṇa it is stated "Those Brahmins, Khatriyas, Vaiśyas and Śūdras who will, remain as seed (at the end of Kali) will become mingled with these in the beginning of Kṛita Yuga." From these two authorities our respected father holds the opinion that there are Kshatriyas and Vaiśyas in the Kali age though their appearance is concealed and their Karma or mode of life is defiled." It must be pointed out that the author, Kamalākarbhaṭṭa, belongs to the famous Bhaṭṭa family of learned men and Dharma-Śāstris of Benares to which belonged Gāgābhaṭṭa also who crowned Śivaji with Vedic rites, believing him to be a good Kshatriya. To the same family belonged Nājogibhaṭṭa and it is possible to explain his silence on this question by supposing him to be unwilling to enter into this question of Dharmaśāstra in a work on grammar.

But whether this dictum had or had not arisen in the days of Nāgojibhaṭṭa it had certainly no existence before 1200 A.D. as we proceed to show. In the time of Kumārila (Circa 650-700 A.D), there was no such idea in the mind of any writer on Dharmaśāstra that there were no Kshatriyas nor Vaiśyas in the Kali age. For Kumārila distinctly says in his disquisition on the word Rājā in his Vārtika (p. 587 Calc. Edn.) that there were in his time kings of all the four castes reigning (तच्च राज्यमविशेषेण चत्वारोऽपि वर्णाः कुर्वाणा दृश्यन्ते). The question was whether the word Rājā in the sūtra राजा राजसूयेन यजेत meant a Kshatriya and the eventual answer given by him after discussion is that the word meant a Kshatriya. Now this clearly establishes that he not only believes that there were actually Kshatriya and Vaiśya kings in his days (a fact historically true, as stated already) but that there would be Kshatriyas in times to come and that Kshatriya kings alone could perform the Rājasūya sacrifice. It is, therefore, certain that the dictum 'Kalāvādyantayoh sthitih' had not arisen in the days of Kumārila. In inscriptions of the Rāshṭrakūṭas, the Śilāhāras and the Yādavas, they are certainly represented as Kshatriyas; but perhaps these are documents drawn up in praise of kings by royal orders. But we find Vijnāneśvara an authoritative writer on Dharmaśāstra not doubting that there were Kshatriyas in his days. He would certainly have stated so in his commentary where he discusses the question of the gotra of Kshatriya by adding that the question was not important in the Kali age. Vijnāneśvara's commentary belongs to the 12th century. Then again Hemādri, also an athoritative writer on Dharmaśāstra, does not desist from describing the Yādavas as descendants of Śri Kṛishṇa and therefore Kshatriyas. No doubt, it may be objected that he was a minister to the Yādava king Rāmchandra. But this eulogy of the Yādavas is not in a State document but in his work on Dharmaśastra. And the famous saint and poet of Mahārāshtra, Jnāneśvara, also describes Rāmachandrarao Yādava as Kshatriya. He was a man of great learning and saint as he was, he had no reason or motive to flatter any person. We, therefore, feel sure that this dictum had not arisen yet, when Jnāneśvara wrote his poem in Śaka 1212 or 1290 A.D. All these considerations, therefore, in our view point to the conclusion that this dictum arose about after 1300 in Mahomedan times, in the east and the south, where Pāyagundes and Kamalākar lived.

APPENDIX VI

THE RULING FAMILIES OF THE DECCAN IN THIS PERIOD WERE MARATHA KSHATRIYAS.

Mr. V. K. Rājavāde, the well-known historical researcher of the Deccan, in his learned preface in Marathi to the Rādhā Mādhava-Vilāsa-Champu, a poem composed by a Marathi poet named Jayarāma Pindye, a contemporary of Śahāji, which he has recently discovered remarks that the Marathas who settled in Mahārāshtra in ancient times (according to him after the time of Buddha) were of lower capacities and civilisation and hence were subject to foreign rule from about 250 B.C. down to 1600 A.D His contention that the Marathas of the Deccan were ruled by Kshatriya kingly families from the north from time to time in effect means that the Chālukyas and the Rāshṭrakūṭas and the Yādavas whose brilliant rule has been and will be described in the volumes of this history were not Maratha but Northern Kshatriya families. As this opinion is opposed to the view propounded in this work, it is necessary that this theory put forth by Mr. Rājavāde should be carefully examined in this appendix.

It may be stated at the outset that this theory coming as it does from Mr. Rājavāde is really surprising. In fact, Mr. Rājavāde himself observes "Our readers will be astonished to find us calling the Chālukyas and others foreigners." We may go further and add that the readers will not only be surprised but painfully surprised ; for none, not even Dr. Sir Bhandarkar had yet formulated the theory that these Chālukyas and others were not Marathas but foreigners. Indeed, we frequently hear it propounded that they were Marathas but not Kshatriyas and here we find Mr. Rājavāde going to the opposite extreme and holding the opinion that they were Kshatriyas but not Marathas.

Mr. Rājavāde calls the Chālukyas and others, Kshatriyas from the north. But all Marathas whether Brahmins, Kshatriyas or Vaiśyas are Aryans, come into Mahārāshtra from the north. The question really is, did these kingly families come into Mahārāshtra at a much later time than the other Marathas and did they live here as foreigners? A foreign rule is a rule maintained by a foreign people who do not permanently reside in the country ruled and whose military and civil power is exercised by a constant influx of men from a foreign country, men who eventually return to that country after their work is done, who, in fact, never intend to settle in the country ruled. The English rule in India is a perfectly foreign rule of this kind. British soldiers and military officers and British civil administrators who hold this country in subjection always return to their country after they have worked for a definite period in this country which they never intend to make their permanent habitation. Mahomedan rule in the south or in the north in past times was also practically a foreign rule; for, there was a constant supply of soldiers and officers from outside from Irān and Khurāsān, from Syria and Arabia. And even though Mahomedan rulers and many Sardars resided permanently in India, the majority of the foreigners coming to India eventually returned to their own country and thus there was a constant drain from India which, as Dadabhai Nowroji has shown, is the root cause of the evils of a foreign rule. Even in India itself the Maurya rule over the Deccan (Circa 250 B.C.) or the Andhrabhṛitya rule over Magadha must be considered as a foreign rule. The Maratha rule of the Peshwas in modern times must also be treated as foreign; for, the soldiers of the army and the officers of civil administration who kept the north under subjection were Marathas from the Deccan and these never made Northern India their home but always returned to the Deccan to enjoy their earnings. But the present rule of Scindia, Holkar or Gaikwad cannot be looked upon as foreign though it is in parts of the country outside Mahārāshtra. For, their civil and military administration is carried on mostly by local men and the few Marathas who are found chiefly among clerks and officers are recruited not from the Deccan but from locally residing

Maratha families. And what is more important, these ruling families have made the respective territories ruled by them their home and they never think of returning to the Deccan although their marriage relations are usually contracted with the Maratha families of the Deccan. This examination of the essentials of a foreign rule will enable us to determine whether the Chālukyas, the Rāshṭrakūṭas and the Yādavas can be considered foreign rulers in Mahārāshtra.

Looked at from the above stand-point, in no way can the Chālukya, Rāshṭrakūṭa and Yādava rule in Mahārāshtra be treated as a foreign rule. There is nothing to show in the records of their time that their civil and military administration was maintained by an influx of foreigners into Mahārāshtra. Then again these ruling families had made the Deccan their home and their eyes never turned towards the north whence they are supposed to have come. Nay more, unlike the modern ruling families in Gwalior, Indore and Baroda, their marriage relations too, did not principally take place with northern Kshatriya families. Sometimes, no doubt, we find such marriages mentioned but therein there was no consciousness of the idea that these ruling families of the Deccan were foreigners in that land and that they had to continue their marriage affinities with their Kshatriya kinsmen in the north. In short, there is nothing in their rule or their family connections which would suggest, much less prove that their rule in the Deccan was a foreign rule.

But it may be urged that these families were, as a matter of fact, Kshatriya families come into the south from the north and though they may have eventually considered themselves as natives of Mahārāshtra and mingled their blood with its people, yet their inherent capacities of mind and body, their political instincts and their love of independence were those of the northern Kshatriyas whose civilisation was higher than that of the people of the Deccan. In other words, they were fresh incomers from the north into Mahārāshtra and had not yet lost their higher feelings and capacities. Probably Mr. Rājavāde calls these ruling families of the Deccan foreigners from this point of view. But properly considered this view also is not historically correct. The Aryan settlement of the Deccan took place according to our opinion and that of Mr. Rajavade also, after Pāṇini and before Kātyāyana *i. e.*, after 900 B. C. and before 300 B. C. The only point of difference between us is that while Mr. Rajavade thinks that this settlement took place after Buddha *i. e.*, after 500 B. C. we think it must have taken place before Buddha's time (following as we do the opinion of Dr. Sir Bhandarkar) *i. e.*, about the 7th century B. C. (see Vol. I. p. 79). But whether the Aryans of Mahārāshṭra came to it before or after Buddha does not concern us here. The question here is: Did the early Chālukyas whose rule in the Deccan began about 500 A. D. come to it a little before that time or did they belong to the general stock of the Marāṭhā Aryans settled there for centuries? Similarly did the Rāshṭrakūṭas whose rule began about 750 A. D. and the Yādavas whose rule began about 1100 A.D. come to the Deccan a little before their rules began? We think Mr. Rajavade's apparent view that these families were fresh-comers is wrong and we proceed to show in detail how it is so.

Let us first take the case of the early Chālukyas, Pulakeśin and others. Mr. Rajavade says that they were Kshatriyas from Ayodhyā. This fact though indeed mentioned in the inscriptions of the Eastern Chālukyas is not mentioned in any inscriptional record of the early Chālukyas themselves who ruled from about 500 to 750 A.D. And even in the grants of the Eastern Chālukyas of Vengi it appears so late as about 1011 A.D (See Ranastipundi grant E. I. Vol. VI p. 357). When after the new editions of the Purāṇas notably after the Bhāgavata of about the 10th century A.D. had come into popular favour and every ruling family in India wished to assign itself to either of the Purāṇic solar and lunar Kshatriya Vaṁśas it is very probable that the Eastern Chālukyas promulgated the view that they belonged to the lunar Vaṁśa and that they originally ruled in Ayodhyā. The most famous family of this Vaṁśa was of the Pāṇḍavas and Udayana was the last famous historical king of this family who ruled in Kauśāmbi about 600 B. C. After about 59 generations from him, it is alleged, had ruled in Ayodhyā, a king of the family came to the Deccan. This no doubt brings the first Chālukya king to the Deccan about 500 A. D. as shown by us in Vol. I. p. 262. But this is according to our view a subsequent story, for it is not even hinted at in the records of the early Chālukyas (who were then appae rently believed to be solar Kshatriyas). As this story is given o- late as 1000 A. D. it is not historical and from the records of the early Chālukyas they appear to be, as we have already recordas our opinion (Vol. I p. 269), true Marāṭhā Kshatriyas of the Māndvya gotra, the gotra of the northern Chālukyas being Bhāradvāja. Their marriage relations appear from their grants to be generally contracted with Pallavas, Rāshṭrakūṭas and Sendrakas who were undoubtedly Marāṭhā families represented by the modern Marāṭhā families of Pālave Raṭakute and Sinde.

The case of the Rāshṭrakūṭas is still clearer. Their rule began about 750 A. D. and they were certainly not fresh-comers at that time; for it can be clearly proved that they were then a well-known old Marāṭhā family. The early inscriptions of the Chālukyas state that they wrested the sovereignty of the Deccan from the Rāsṭrakūṭas. And the early records of the Rāshṭrakūṭas themselves state that in seizing the sovereignty from the Chālukyas they got back what had been lost. In an inscription of Nityavarsha dated Śaka 834 (912 A.D.), we find it stated that Dantidurga the first Rāshṭrakūṭa king recovered back the Lakshmī or regal splendour of the Raṭṭa kingdom which had been drowned in the ocean of Chālukya power, like Nārāyaṇa who brought up the earth sunk in the ocean. (निमग्नयश्चलुक्याब्धौ रटराज्यश्रियं पुनः। पृथ्वीमिवोद्धरन् धीरो वीरनारायणोऽभवत्॥) J. Bom. Br.R.A.S. XVIII p. 260). This shows that the Rāshṭrakūṭas always believed that they were the rightful kings of the Deccan even during Chālukya supremacy from 500 to 750 A.D. It is, therefore, clear from Chālukya as well as Rāshṭrakūṭa records that the latter were kings of the Deccan in about 400 A. D. *i. e.* about 350 years before their Imperial rule began about 750 A. D.

The Rāshṭrakūṭa records no doubt describe them as Laṭṭalūrapurādhiśvara or kings of the town of Laṭṭalūra and we have already stated that no body has yet ascertained the whereabouts of this town. It is possible to suppose that this was some town in the Deccan itself but Mr. Rajavade suggests that this was the town of Ratnapura in the Chedi country in the north, on what ground it is not stated. We think that writers of Sanskṛit inscriptions could easily have given the Sanskṛit name instead of the Prākṛit Laṭṭalūra in their records just as they give the Sanskṛit form Mānnyakheta instead of the Marathi name Malkhed of the capital of the Rāshṭrakūṭas . But even granting that Mr. Rajavade is right in identifying Laṭṭalūra with Ratnapura in the Chedi country, the really pertinent question is when did the Rāshṭrakūṭas come to the Deccan from Ratnapura ? Did they come about the time of the establishment of their rule in about 750 A.D. in other words were they then fresh-comers into the Deccan from the north ? As we have shown above, they were not, as from records their rule about 400 A.D. in the Deccan is undoubted and thus they were at least 350 years old in Māhārāshṭra when they became masters of it.

But we believe they were far older inhabitants of Mahārāshṭra, being as old as the days of Aśoka (250 B.C). These Rāshṭrakūṭas are the same people as the Rāshṭrikas mentioned in the inscriptions of Aśoka. The word Rāshṭrakūṭa, as we have already stated, means chief among the Raṭṭas. Indeed this truth lies embedded in the subsequent bardic concept contained in Rāshṭrakūṭa records that in the vaṁśa of the Yādava Sātyaki there was a king named Raṭṭa whose son was Rāshṭrakūṭa who gave his name to the family. The Rāshṭrakūṭas were, therefore, Raṭṭas, in fact the original people who gave their name to the country and the kingdom of the Rāshṭrakūṭas is described in their records and even in the Purāṇas as Raṭarājya. It seems, therefore, that the rule of the Rāshṭrakūṭas was par excellence Marāṭhā rule and they were emphatically a Marāṭhā family. For the Chālukyas of Badāmi had latterly become so to speak a Karnātaka family and their kingdom is in Rāshṭrakūṭa records spoken of as the kingdom of the Karnātakas (see p. 145). It may be mentioned here that while Karnātaka scholars try to represent the Chālukyas as southern or Karnātaka Kshatriyas and not Marāṭhās, Mr. Rajavade tries to prove that they were northern Kshatriyas and we try to prove that they were Marāṭhā Kshatriyas of the Deccan. These different views are practically one and the same for the Chālukyas, Rāshṭrakūṭas and Yādavas originally all came from the north, Marāṭhās and Karnātakas being local names of the same Aryan people from the north. What is, however, necessary to point out here is that these people were not fresh-comers into the Deccan or Karnātaka about the establishment of their rule and particularly the Rāshṭrakūṭas were unquestionably one of the oldest and truest Marāṭhā Kshatriya families of Mahārāshṭra.

Lastly, the Yādavas who established their rule over Mahārāshṭra about 1100 A.D cannot also be proved to be Kshatriyas recently come from the north. They are undoubtedly Kshatriyas belonging to the Yādava Vaṁśa as their name indicates, believed to be descended from Śri Kṛishṇa as stated in a Praśasti of Hemādri; and from the same Praśasti it seems clear that they were long established in the Deccan; (Bombay Gazetteer Vol. I part I. p. 270). "They all originally belonged to Mathurā; from the time of Kṛishṇa they were lords of Dvārakā. From the son of Subāhu these heroes of Yādava vaṁśa ruled in the south." The intermediate steps between Subāhu and Seuṇa who gave his name to the country are many and we can well see that when the Yādavas rose to eminence they were not fresh-comers. They were connected by marriage relations with Chālukyas and other Marāṭhā families of the Deccan and not with Kshatriya families of the north and were, therefore, as completely Marāṭhās as other Marāṭhā families.

But if Mr. Rajavade looks upon the Chālukyas, the Rāshṭrakūṭas and the Yādavas as foreigners and treats their rule as foreign in the Deccan, the Bhosales of Śivaji were more certainly foreigners and yet he does not consider their rule as foreign. Śivaji unquestionably belonged to the

Northern Rajput family of the Śisodias. It is sometimes thought that this myth was created by Chitnis and other flatterers of Śivaji at the time of his coronation. But Mr. Rajvade by the discovery of this poem composed by a contemporary poet in the court of Śahāji has set at rest all such doubts and has shown that the belief prevailed even in the time of Śivaji's father. We have always accepted the truth of this pedigree for other reasons and chiefly for the fact that in lists of Marāṭhā family names belonging to pre-Śivaji time which we have come across, the Bhosales are not mentioned at all. This discovery by Mr. Rajavade has confirmed our view, a view which we have already recorded at page 5 of this volume. Perhaps, it may be objected by some that Śivaji's gotra is given as Kauśika in sanads issued by the family while that of the Śisodias is Baijavāpa. There is no doubt this discrepancy exists; but we think that it is due to the mistaken notion of the Paṇḍits of the Deccan recorded in Vijñāneśvara's dictum that Kshatriyas have no gotras of their own but have to take the gotras of their Purohitas. When the Bhosale family settled in the Deccan they probably took up the Kauśika gotra from their new Purohitas. In fact it may be contended that if this fiction had been set up by Chitnis at the time of Śivaji's coronation he would certainly have established the Baijavāpa gotra of the Śisodias for his patron's family. It, therefore, seems probable that the pedigree from the Udaipur family believed in Śahāji's time is true and believable. But that question apart, what we are concerned with here is since the Bhosales were undoubtedly Kshatriyas from the north even according to Mr. Rajavaḍe, why does he not look upon their rule as foreign? In fact on this theory the foreign domination of Mahārāshṭra comes down to our own day without intermission over 22 hunded years. For the Peshwas too were foreign to the Deccan coming as they did from Konkan and even to Konkan from Persia according to a theory of Mr. Rajavade. But historically speaking the Bhosales though belonging to a Śisodia northern Kshatriya family cannot be treated as foreigners, for they had settled in the Deccan nearly 300 years before their rise; secondly their marriage relations were all with Marāṭhā families of the Deccan; thirdly they never looked back to Chitore nor even wished to return to the north and fourthly and lastly the soldiers and officers of the Bhosale rule were all men of the Deccan, the very first soldiers assisting Śivaji in his struggle for independence being the Mavala Marāṭhās of the Poona district. In short, even Śivaji's rule and the rule of the succeeding Bhosale kings, Śisodias though they were, was not foreign in Mahārāshṭra.

But it may still be contended that although the Bhosale family in consequence of the mixing of blood with Marāṭhās for 300 years was practically a Marāṭhā family and although it was assisted in its rule by Marāṭhās yet the spirit of independence and the genius for organisation exhibited by Śivaji the founder of Marāṭhā rule, was his own inherited from the higher civilisation and capacities of northern Kshatriyas. There may be some truth in this contention which, however, is practically valueless. For the ancient Marāṭhās cannot really be considered to be lower in civilisation. They were a blend of the Aryan with the Nāga vaṁśa. To which race the Nāgas belonged is a root question; but even if we concede that they were not Aryans, they appear to be men of a higher capacity than the ordinary Dravidian people. From the Mahābhārata we know that the Nāgas offered a most stubborn resistance to the Pāṇḍavas and were their hereditary enemies for three generations. In the Sarpasatra of Janamejaya which was in effect a war of extermination waged against them, many Nāgas perished but many were saved by Āstika and some of the names of these Nāgas recorded in the Mahābhārata are to be found, as Mr. Rajāvade has himself pointed out, among Marāṭhā families of the Deccan. The Nāgas were a very powerful ruling race in India from Takshaśilā in the Panjab down to the Pāṇḍya country in the south as can be gathered not only from the Mahābhārata but also from ancient Tamil poems of the south. The Marāṭhās, therefore, from ancient times must have been a virile race with higher political capacities and Marāṭhā history shows that it is not only Śivāji of the Śisodiya Rajput clan who exhibited extraordinary political insight and military genius but even men from undoubted ancient Marāṭhā families whose coming from the north has not yet been hinted, such as Rāṇoji Scindia and Malhārarao Holkar can be described as great soldiers and politicians. Indeed Mahadji Scindia's fame as warrior and statesman, as an organisor of armies and a founder of empire, stands unquestioned by any. In fine, the theory of Mr. Rājavade that the Marāṭhās of the Deccan were lower in civilisation than the Kshatriyas of the north is itself mistaken and is at the root of his mistaken view about the Chālukyas and Rāshṭrakūṭās being foreign peoples in the Deccan.

And why should the Marāṭhās of the Deccan be treated as of lower civilisation and of less vigour than the Kshatriyas of the north ? Ethnologically the Marāṭhās may be considered to be a mixture of Aryan and Dravidian people but such mixture of blood must be presumed to have taken palce even in the north as can be gathered from the accounts of the birth of the Pāṇḍavas and other heroes of the Mahābhārata and the Purāṇas. We have stated elsewhere that the lunar race Kshatriyas appear to have had a greater admixture of Dravidian blood not only from their accounts but from the physical charactersitics of the people of the United Provinces though it is true that the Rajputs of Rājputāna and the Panjab exhibit more distinct Aryan physical characteristics and are purer Aryans than those of U. P. to Mahārāshṭra. But as we have shown above, history does not show that the Marāṭhās have suffered to any appreciable extent in racial vigour and intellectual capacities. And if the Marāṭhās could not stand against the Afghans, Turks, and Moguls, equally the Kshatriyas of the north could not and north and south were eventually equally subjected to the foreign domination of Mahomedans. Before the Western Aryans of the present day too both have equally bent their necks. If any thing, it was in Mahārāshṭra alone that a successful struggle was made against the domination of foreign Mahomedans. And the credit for this success under Śivāji must be shared if it is to be shared, equally between the Kshatriyas of the north and the Marāṭhās of the south speaking ethnologycally as well as historically. To look upon the Marāṭhās of the Deccan as lower in civilisation and capacities is, therefore, not correct from any stand-point.

That in the first and second sub-periods of Mediæval Hindu History the Marāṭhās were looked upon as Kshatriyas and of equal status by the Kshatriyas of the north we have already shown. But we may further add here that just as Kshatriya families of the north are in historical times known to have come to the south we have historical evidence to show that at least one Marāṭhā Kshatriya family went from the south to the north, settled there and obtained not only renown but full recognition as a Rajput family. We are here anticipating matters which will be elucidated in our third Volume but we may state here succinctly that the traditions of the Rāṭhods of the north who are in Indian history one of the most valiant Rajaput clans declare that they came originally from the Deccan and its name was Rāshṭrakūṭa which by the usual rules of Prākṛit transformation has become Rāṭhoda. Of course this family is not the same as the Rāshṭrakūṭa family we have described in this volume for the present Rāṭhods of the north are a solar race family and its gotra is Gautama. We mention this fact here, however, simply to show that in the tenth century A.D. the Marāṭhās were as vigorous as the Kshatriyas of the north and founded a Rajput family which is now included among the 36 Rajput families of the present day. There is, therefore, no reason whatever to distinguish between the capacities mental and moral of the Kshatriyas of the north and the the Kshatriyas of the south;

We may thus conclude that the Chālukya or Rāshṭrakūṭa rule in the Deccan was not a foreign rule like that of William the Conquerer over England who came to England as a foreigner conquered it with the aid of his foreign Normans and held it in subjection by the aid of the same foreign warriors. The founders of the Chālukya and Rāshṭrakūṭa rule had been established in the Deccan for centuries and they founded and maintained their rule not by the aid of foreign peoples but by the help of the people of the Deccan itself. They were thus in effect Marāṭhā Kshatriyas and the theory of Mr. Rajavade that they were northern foreign Kshatriyas is, to say the least, not well founded.

Before concluding it will be convenient to bring here in one place all the available evidence in disproof of the opposite theory that these ruling families of the Deccan were Marāthās but not Kshatriyas. We have shown that the first proof we have goes so far back as the 1st century A.D. A Nasik cave inscription of Gotamīputra Śātakarṇi describes him as "Khatiya—Dapamāna—Damanassa" *i. e.* restrainer of the pride of Kshatriyas. The opinion of Cunningham that the Kshatriyas mentioned here are those of Rajaputana is untenable as, firstly there were no or very few Kshatriyas then in Rajaputana and secondly Gotamīputra never went to Rajaputana; in fact his conquests never extended beyond the Nerbudda. The Kshatriyas referred to here are, therefore, the Kshatriyas of Mahārāshtra itself such as the Rāshtrakūtas, the Aśmakas and others mentioned in the inscriptions of Aśoka. Next we have the evidence of Śabarasvāmin author of the Bhāshya on the Mīmānsā Sūtras of Jaimini, who may be placed in about 400 A. D. He mentions that the Kshatriyas of Āndhra call themselves Rājās even though they may not actually be doing the work of a Rājā *viz.*, protecting town and country. This clearly admits the existence of Kshatriyas in the south. Again Kumārila who belongs to about 700 A.D. and who wrote his famous commentary on the Bhāshya of Śabara remarks that this statement about the Āndhras was made by the Bhāshyakāra in common with the Dākshiṇātyas which means that the practice of Kshatriyas calling themselves Rājās was really prevalent among the Marāthas of the Deccan. The word Dākshiṇātya in ancient Sanskrit writings always means Marāthā the latter word being indeed a later and a Prākṛit word. This is a most reliable piece of evidence to hold that the Marāthās of the Deccan were in the 7th and 8th centuries considered by the orthodox and learned Brahmins of the time to be Kshatriyas. And the practice of even ordinary (not ruling) Marāthā families styling themselves Rājās still prevails in the Deccan. We have the support of Hiuen Tsang for this statement of Kumārila as in 640 A. D. he calls Pulakeśin king of Mahārāshtra a Kshatriya. Fourthly the Rāshtrakūtas were considered to be descendants of Sātyaki a lunar race Kshatriya. And the Yādavas were considered to be

42

descendants of Śri Kṛishṇa himself by Hemādri, a great Brahmin writer on Dharma-Śāstra belonging to the 12th century A.D. Even Jñāneśvara, the famous saint and Marāthi poet, describes Rāmadeorao Yādava in the thirteenth century as a lunar race king at the end of his Marāthi commentary on the Bhagavadgītā. This continuous chain of evidence, extending over twelve centuries, of Brahmin writers on Dharma-Śāstra is in our view conclusive and shows that the Marāthās were all along treated as Kshatriyas. The theory that there are no Kshatriyas or Vaiśyas in the Kali age came into existence hereafter as shown in Appendix IV. and notably found expression in the works of Dharma-Śāstra writers of the Deccan. The Marāthās in Mahomedan times apparently lost touch with Vedic rites and the gotra system was probably not properly kept up by them owing to the wrong theory of Vijñāneśvara that Kshatriyas have no gotras of their own. The Marāthās as Kshatriyas had certainly their own gotras as testified to by the inscriptions of Pulakeśin and others; but the records drawn up by the Rāshtrakūta and Yādava governments do not unaccountably mention their gotras though this fact is in consonance with the practice also followed by the northern Kshatriyas of the time; for we do not find mention of gotras in the records of the Pratihāras and other Rajput kingly families. This circumstance encouraged the neglect of the gotra system by the Marāthās. There is, however, reason to believe that like the Kshatriyas of the north the Marāthas also kept up some memory of their gotras in their bardic records and vaṁśāvalis, though marriage relations as among the Rajputs of the north were now regulated by the clan-system and not the gotra system. The gradual neglect of Vedic rites and of the gotra system led to their being ranked in Mahomedan times as Śūdras. It would be most interesting if these ancient vaṁśāvalis of Marāthās of pre-Śivaji days were found in the diligent search going on in the Deccan for old documents. But whether such vaṁśāvalis be discovered or not and inspite of some discrepancies to be noticed in their gotra system as at present known, it will be conceded that the Marāthas must be treated as Kshatriyas from the long chain of evidence sketched above.

We will close this Appendix by noting certain authenticated gotras of Marātha Kshatriya families from published and unpublished ancient records. The gotra of the Bhosale family is Kauśika while that of Nimbalkars (Paramāras) is Vasishtha. The gotra of the Pātankars and of Dubals of Karhad is Bhāradvāja which is the gotra given in ancient records of the northern Chālukyas from whom they claim to be descended. The gotra of the Māne family of Mhasvad is Atri, their clan being Gaura. The gotra of Palaves or Pallavas is Bhāradvāja as mentioned in stone inscriptions from the fourth century A. D. and of Kadams and Chālkes is Mānavya mentioned in records of the sixth and seventh centuries A.D. and even earlier. Lastly, the gotra of the Gaikwad family of Baroda is mentioned in their state records to be Bhārgava.

APPENDIX VI.

NOTE.

RAI BAHADUR GAURISHANKAR OJHA ON BAPPĀ RĀWAL.

It is fortunate that before this book has been finally printed we have been placed in possession of the views of Rai Bahadur Gaurishankar Ojha on the several disputed topics in connection with Bappā Rāwal, embodied by him in a recent brochure in Hindi published in the Nagari Pracharini Patrika Part I No. 3. This brochure is written in elucidation of a golden coin of Bappā which the learned Pandit has recently obtained; and contains a full discussion of all the topics with detailed references to the authorities relied upon. Rai Bahdur Gaurishankar Ojha's intimate acquintance with the ancient inscriptions of Rajputana, nay of the whole of India, is so well known that his views would always be entitled to the highest respect. It is, therefore, but meet that this volume should contain his views on Bappā Rāwal, although they may differ in some particulars from the views adopted in this volume. We, therefore, in this note in the Appendix will try to set forth Pandit Gaurishankar's views together with the authorities on which he relies and will also explain where necessary why we still adhere to the view advocated in this volume.

1 Was Bappa a Brahmin ?

Firstly then with regard to the question whether Bappā was a Brahmin or a Kshatriya, it is gratifying to find that Rai Bahadur Gaurishnakr distinctly and emphatically is of opinion that he was a Khsatriya and not a Brahmin, and that he was a solar race Kshatriya. For this view, he firstly relies on the disc of the sun impressed on the obverse of the golden coin of Bappā recently found, which he has minutely described in his paper. But this is not the only piece of evidence on which he relics. It is no doubt true, he observes, that the Ātpura Inscription of V.E. 1034 begins with a verse in which the word Mahīdeva occurs which can be translated as Brahmin, though it can also mean a king; it is also true that the two inscriptions next in date found at Abu and at Chitod distinctly state in the beginning that Bappā was a Brahmin (Vipra). Yet the matter is settled he thinks by the expression Raghuvaṁśa-kirtipiśunāḥ applied to the ascetics of Ekalinga by the Naravāhana inscription which is earlier than the first named inscription at Ātpura and is dated V. E. 1028. This inscription is republished by Dr. D. R. Bhandarkar himself in B.B. R. A. S. Vol. XXII p. 167. Pandit Gaurishankar Ojha thinks that

Dr. D. R. Bhandarkar has wrongly omitted these words from consideration in the purport of the inscription which he has given in the beginning of his notice of the inscription where he says (p. 152) that "the fame of the ascetics had spread from the Himalayas to Rāma's bridge"* whereas in reality the expression means that "these ascetics had spread the fame of Raghuvaṁśa from the Himalayas to the bridge of Rāma or Cape Comorin." Dr. D. R. Bhandarkar has no doubt knowingly or unknowingly omitted to take into consideration the word Raghuvaṁśa. This inscription, we have already shown, makes the earliest mention of Bappā Rāwal and states that he was the very moon to the Guhila gotra kings. It clearly follows that these ascetics of Ekalinga who were their Gurus were instrumental in spreading the fame of the Guhilavaṁśa kings. The word piśuna means displaying (see Apte's Dic.); the epithet could not have been interpreted as meaning being famed. It is, therefore, clear that as early as the Naravāhana inscription of V. E. 1028 or A.D. 971, Bappā was not only famed as the greatest king and even the founder of the Guhila Vaṁśa but the vaṁśa was also known as Raghuvaṁśa. Pandit Gaurishankar Ojha has certainly the credit of distinctly pointing out this old authority for believing that Bappā was considered to be a solar race Kshatriya both from this inscription and also Bappa's coin (p. 260).

The word Mahīdeva in the Ātpura inscription recorded only 6 years after this Naravāhana inscription should, therefore, be translated as king and not Brahmin. But how do the Chitod and Abu inscriptions say that Bappā was a Vipra or Brahmin as they distinctly do? Gaurishankar rightly says that they do so by mistake but he has not given an explanation as to how this mistake must have arisen. We have explained in the body of this book (p. 87) how the word Mahīdeva in the Ātpura incription being misleading was found useful, when later bards were in search of an explanation for the Brahmin gotras of Rajputs. They generally invented new origins for the Rajput families and assigned Brahmins of their gotras as their first ancestors. Thus we have seen that the Chāhamānas who were all along reputed to be solar race Kshatriyas were said to be born from a Brahmin of the Vatsa gotra, nay one tradition represents the first Chāhamāna as born from a tear of the Vatsa Rishi himself. Similarly the Paramāras whose gotra is Vasishtha are said to have been born from Vasishtha's sacrificial fire; and the Chālukyas who are of the Bharadvāja gotra are said to have been born from the chuluka or handful of water in the hands of Droṇa Bhāradvāja. We have clearly explained in our chapter on gotra and Pravara how Brahmins and Kshatriyas have the same gotras (see pp. 56-63) but mediæval bards who did not probably sufficiently know Vedic Sūtra literature invented new stories

---

* The wording is योगिनः । शापानुग्रहभूमयो हिमशिलाबन्धोज्वलादाविरे-रासेतो रघुवंशकीर्तिपिशुनास्तीव्रं तपः...(तेपिरे) p. 167.

for the founders of Kshatriya families in which they are represented as Brahmins. Even the Pratihāras who were also known as Solar race Kshatriyas are said in one inscription to have been born from a Brahmin father and a Kshatriya mother. During an interval of three hundred years this new theory of Bappā being a Brahmin may thus have arisen and found expression in the Chitod and Abu inscriptions dated 1331 and 1342. But as in the case of the Agnikula theory based on a wrong interpretation of a verse in Prithvirāj Rāsā and now exploded from more ancient inscriptions, we have also to abandon this theory of a Brahmin origin for Guhilots given in these later inscriptions, on the strength of an earlier inscription and the golden coin. All later records copy the Chitod tradition including the Ekalinga Purāṇa and must be disregarded in this matter at least; just as Vaṁśa Bhāshasa of the Chauhans must be disregarded on the basis of ancient inscriptions of the Chauhans themselves. The story of Bappā being given when an infant to a Brahmin to rear must also be similarly set aside and the Naravāhana inscription as the oldest record on this subject followed.

We must refer here in detail to the Chātsu inscription two words in which Dr. D. R. Bhandarkar has wrongly interpreted in order to find a support to the theory of a Brahmin extraction for the Guhilots first propounded if not started by him. Pandit Gaurishankar has referred to this inscription but on another point (p. 283). He has not marked the wrong interpretation of two words by Dr. D. R. Bhandarkar and has, therefore, not pointed out how the interpretation is wrong. The Chātsu inscription was found at Chātsu a Tahsil town of Jaipur state lying to the south of Jaipur city. It relates to a Guhila family no doubt; but it is not certain that it is the same as the Udaipur Guhil family and hence it may be urged that the inscription is irrelevant. But it is not unlikely that the two families are one and we will, therefore, notice this inscription further in this connection. The inscription is not dated though the word Samvat appears at the end but without any figures or words following it. The inscription gives a genealogy extending over 12 kings from one Bhatripatta of the family of Guhila. This first king is described as the equal of Rāma and Dr. D. R. Bhandarkar says at page 11 (E. I. XII) "Rāma here referred to is, of course, Paraśurāma and what the verse intends saying is that as Paraśurāma was a Brahmin by caste, but did the duties of a Kshatriya, Bhatripatta also was a Brahmin by extraction and displayed martial energy; in other words Bhatripatta was a Brahmakshatra, *i. e.*, what is now known as Brahmakshatra." This clearly shows how Dr. D. R. Bhandarkar is obsessed by the theory of the Brahmin extraction of Guhilots. For the theory represents Bappā alone as a Brahmin and not every king in the Guhila family as a Brahmin. Bhatripatta is nowhere represented as a Brahmin; and he could not be so as we shall presently show. Nor can he be represented to be a Brahmin, because he is likened to Parśurāma. For one must always remember the definition of Upamā given by Mammata viz., that there can be a simile only when there is a resemblance in some points and a difference in others. In order, therefore, that Bhatripatta may be taken to be a Brahmin, it ought to have been distinctly stated that he was a Brahmin. And further Dr. D. R. Bhandarkar has here also ignored the word 'asame' which to our mind refers to the different character of the families of the two.*

The second word which has similarly been misinterpreted is the word dvija used in connection with king Sri Harsharaja born from Śankaragaṇa, a descendant of Bhatripatta, on which Dr. D. R. Bhandarkar observes at p. 12 " In inscriptions of this period, so far as my knowledge goes, this word denotes a Brahmin only. " Now it is well known that the word dvija means also a person belonging to any of the three higher castes and as an adjective it means twice-born. The word means, so far as we can judge, no more than 'twice born' in this verse taken in conjunction with the previous verse†. In the previous verse, Śankaragaṇa is said to have married one Yajjā who was like Pārvati, because she was the daughter of a great Mahibhrit (the word being double meaning) and because her mind was pleased with Śiva (ditto). Now in the verse in dispute the son of Sankargaṇa and Yajjā (who were like Śankara and Pārvati) is naturally likened to Skanda ; and each epithet is double meaning and applicable to both. Now dvija seems to us to mean, therefore, in this connection, twice-born, as Skanda was born twice through Śikhi or fire. The expression 'Śikhinah parigrihatayā' is not quite clear, but it refers in our view to Skanda being taken up gladly by fire. But whatever this may be where was the necessity or the propriety of the poet's stating with regard to this king alone out of the 12 descendants given that he was a Brahmin ? And unless it was stated that Śankaragaṇa was a Brahmin and Yajjā was also a Brahmin woman, their son could not have been a Brahmin. Yajjā is merely described as daughter of a great king and taking into consideration, the condition of the caste system as it existed at this period, Srīharsharāja could not have been called a Brahmin.

It is necessary to state here that a good deal of misconception would be avoided if the social fabric obtaining at this period, differing as it did

---

*The verse is as follows; अस्त्रग्रामोपदेशैरवनतनृपतीन् भूतलं भूरिभूत्या । भूदेवान् भूमिदानैस्त्रिदिवमपि मखैर्नन्दयन्नन्दितात्मा ॥ ब्रह्मक्षत्रान्वितोस्मिन्सम-भवदसमे रामतुल्यो विशल्यो शौर्याढ्यो भर्तृपट्टः रिपुभटविटपिच्छेदकेलीपटीयान् ॥ p. 13.

†The two verses are—महामहीभृतः पुत्री शिवानन्दितमानसा । तेनोढा पार्वतीतुल्या यज्जा नाम यशस्विनी ॥.................निश्चलमतिशक्तिदधानं धरां सेनारक्षणदक्षमुग्रमहसं व्यावृत्तविद्वेषिणं ॥ सानन्दं शिखिनः परिग्रहतया श्रीहर्षराजं द्विजं तस्यां वीरमजीजनत्स तनयं स्कन्दोपमं भूभुजम् ॥

from our present condition, were borne in mind. We have already described the social condition of this period in Chapter II Book V, and have also explained the custom of Anuloma marriage which was then prevalent (p. 192-5). But it will bear repetition if we here state that unlike Brahmins of the present day who can only marry Brahmin wives, Brahmins could then marry Kshatriya wives but unlike what happened in ancient times when the progeny of such marriage was treated as Brahmin or later on as belonging to an intermediate caste the progeny of a Brahmin from a Kshatriya wife was treated as a Kshatriya at this period. Hence even if the bards of those times and later declared that Bappā Rāwal was a Brahmin, that could not make the *Guhila* family a Brahmin family. For this purpose it must be told that each king married a Brahmin wife and the next king was the son of that Brahmin wife. Now we have seen that chronicles distinctly state that Bappā married many wives chiefly daughters of kings and therefore even if Bappā had been a Brahmin as a matter of truth, his son Guhila or Bhoja could not have been a Brahmin, unless it was also stated that he was the son of a Brahmin wife. In fact most probably Guhila was the son of a Kshatriya princess and hence a Kshatriya. The Ātpura inscription does not mention the mothers of all kings but where it does, they are daughters of a Rāshtrakūta or a Chāhamāna or a Hūṇà* family. Similarly this Chātsu inscription where it mentions queens, mentions them as belonging to Chāhamāna or Paramāra family and hence it clearly appears that these inscription writers never looked upon the Guhila family as anything but a solar race Kshatriya family. The Guhila family in fact never had the repute of being a Brahmin family. There was nothing wrong or derogatory then that a reigning family should be known as a Brahmin family. The Chacha family of Sind was known as a Brahmin family and Mahomedan historians have recorded that Brahmins appeared bare-headed before Kasim alleging that they were kinsmen of the deceased Dahar. Similarly Al-Beruni records that the Lalliya family of Kabul kings was a Brahmin family. Therefore, had Bappā's family remained a Brahmin family, it would certainly have been reputed as such. A Kshatriya family may also, in fact can alone, be described as Brahma-Kshatra family, if it leads an orthodox Kshatriya life according to the Vedas and the Smṛitis and there is nothing wrong if the Udaipur family is so described. In fact it deserves to be so described, having always abstained from wine, as described even by Arab writers. In short even if Bappā is represented as a Brahmin by the Chītod and Abu inscriptions of V. E. 1331 and 1342 and all later records, that does not make the Guhila family a Brahmin family and the Chitod and Abu inscriptions do not represent the Guhila vaṁśa as a Brahmin Vaṁśa. Pandit Gaurishankar Ojha is apparently under a wrong impression in this

* Hūṇa is not necessarily a Mlecchha family as it is also the name of a Kshatriya family (See Hall in A. B. XXXI p. 117 note 11).

respect. 'गुहिलवंशजाको ब्राह्मण लिखा है' (p. 265) is too general a statement and it must be clearly understood that these inscriptions and some others represent Bappā alone as a Brahmin and not this family and that according to the social customs of the times, the family could not have been a Brahmin family. The fact of Bappā being looked upon as a Brahmin under a wrong idea of the gotra system, and by the misunderstanding of the word Mahīdeva did not interfere with the status of the family in the opinion of the bards themselves as a Solar race Kshatriya family. It is only we, living in a differnt social atmosphere, who are misled by the mere mention of Bappā's being a Brahmin, into believing that the status of the whole family is changed or vitiated thereby. As we have shown, Bappā's being a Brahmin would not alone detract from the family's being known as a Solar race family, even if that were true . But, as Pandit Gaurishankar Ojha has shown, the oldest inscription of Naravāhana settles the point and Bappā's being represented as a Brahmin is due to a mistake caused by a wrong interpretation of the word Mahīdeva.

And the mischief has, we think, further been aggravated by the misinterpretation of the word Ānandapura in that same verse of the Ātpura inscription. Ānandapura is now known as the name of Vadnagar and a Brahmin coming from Ānandapura means now a Nagar Brahmin. But it is clear that Ānandapura in this first verse of Ātpura Inscription means the town of Nāgahrada as distinctly stated in the Chitod inscription. In fact Dr. D. R. Bhandarkar has himself admitted that Ānandapura here is the name of Nāgahrada or Nagada and that it is the name of many other towns besides Vadnagar. It is surprising that Rai Bahadur Gaurishankar Ojha also translates it by Vadnagar and treats Ānandapura Brahmin as meaning Nagar Brahmin (p. 267). The result has been that the word Mahīdeva has led to the tradition of Bappā being a Brahmin and the word Ānandapur has led to the tradition of his being a Nagar Brahmin from Vadnagar. We have already pointed out (p. 85) that the writer of Chitod and Abu inscriptions who was himself a Nagar Brahmin does not describe Bappā as a Nagar Brahmin which he would have been too glad to do, had he thought him to be so. He distinctly describes Nāgahrada as Ānandapura (जीयादानन्दपूर्वं तदिह पुरमिलाखण्डसौंदर्यशोभि) and never thought that Bappā was a Nagar Brahmin. The Nagar tradition thus, as given in Ekalinga Purāṇa and other later records, has also to be abandoned. In fine, we have to remember that this myth of Nagar extraction like the Agnivaṅśa myth arose under a misapprehension and as Pandit Gaurishankar has conclusively shown, we have to hold that Bappā Rāwal was a solar race Kshatriya, from the Naravāhana inscription and the golden coin of Bappā.

Whether Bappā belonged to an off-shoot of the Valabhī family, which might have established itself at Nagada is a question which may here be discussed before proceeding further. Bappā's great exploit, historically speaking, was his taking the fort of Chitod and supplanting the Mori dynasty which ruled there. Round this great and dazzling exploit, it is natural that traditions should gather. The case of Bappā seems to us to exactly resemble that of Śivaji in this as in many respects. When Śivaji founded an independent kingdom defeating four Mahomedan powers, he was naturally extolled to the highest and historians and Bakharkars and even ministers would find for him some great genealogy. Consequently he was connected in his own life-time with the then best blood among Rajputs and Śivaji was believed to be descended from the Śisodia family of Udaipur. Bappā was similarly connected probably in his own life-time with the best royal blood in his time and his connection was established with the royal family of Valabhī which was then known as the best Kshatriya family, as evidenced by Harsha's giving his daughter to a king of this family who again is described by Hiuen Tsang as a Kshatriya. In fact this very connection of Bappā's family with the royal family of Valabhī which was then ruling it shows that that family was considered the best Kshatriya family and it also proves to our mind that it was also known as a Solar race family as Udaipur tradition represents it. In our view the genealogy of Śivaji as a descendant of the Śisodias of Udaipur is not a concocted story and we equally believe that the Guhila family of Nagada in which Bappā was born was similarly *really* connected with the Maitraka family of Valabhī. But what we urge is that even if this connection be looked upon as concocted by bards of the eighth and later centuries, it at least establishes the fact that the Valabhī family was then reputed to be a Solar race Kshatriya family of the best blood.

2 The Dates of Bappa's Birth, Accession and Retirement.

On the next disputed topic in connection with Bappā viz., his dates, there is again fortunately no difference practically between the view of Rai Bahadur Gaurishankar Ojha and the view adopted in this volume. Certain minor differences, however, exist and must be discussed at length. And first with regard to the date of Bappā's birth. We have taken this date to be 700 A.D. on the basis of the tradition long current in Mewad and which, as Tod has recorded, in spite of many difficulties Mewad bards and even the Maharaṇa were not prepared to give up viz., that Bappā was born in St. 191. This figure was thus a riddle before Tod and he explained it by referring the figure to an era starting from the destruction of Valabhī which he wrongly put two hundred years before it actually took place We now know from inscriptions that Valabhī kings were still ruling when Bappā rose to fortune and established rule in Chitod. The explanation of the figure which we have given (p. 75) is this that the years should be counted not from the extinction of Valabhi rule but from its founding by Bhaṭārka in 509 A.D. The figure 191 added to 509 gives 700 A.D. as the date of Bappā's birth and it fits in well with the history of the period, Man Mori's inscription at Chitod dated V.E. 770 showing that the Mori rule must have been supplanted thereafter by Bappā. Pandit Gaurishankar Ojha, has however, shown that St. 191 was the traditional date in Mewad not of Bappa's *birth* but of his *accession* to the gaddi of Chitod. Unfortunately it must be conceded that Gaurishankar is right and Tod is here mistaken (see Crooke's Tod Vol. I p. 268). The oldest edition of Tod gives this date as the date of Bappa's *birth* (p. 229); it was expected that Crooke would have added a note to the effect that the date was the date of the accession of Bappā. Probably Crooke forgot to notice this as we failed to notice. The date is, however, not only given as the date of Bappā's accession by local oral tradition but is also given in an inscription printed in the Bhavnagar inscriptions quoted by Gaurishankar Ojha (p. 272). The verse therein means that Bappā having obtained boons became endowed with fortune by the favour of Ekalinga and Hārīta in 191 (Māgha Śuddha 7) at the age of fifteen "* The fact is thus certain that St. or year 191 is the date of Bappā's accession to the gaddi of Chitod and not his birth.

How to explain this figure is, therefore, again a riddle and Gaurishankar Ojha has solved it by supposing that the figure is a mis-reading for 791 as the figure seven is often mistaken for one. The year of Bappa's accession is therefore St. 791 or A.D. 734 and as Bappā cannot be taken to be then 15 as the tradition represents, Gaurishankar thinks that the year St. 769 given by Tod for Bappā's birth may be accepted as it would make him 22 years old in St. 791 *i.e.* at the time of the taking of Chitod. In short Bappā's birth may be placed according to Gaurishankar in 712 A.D.

But it may be urged that this is not a satisfactory explanation, unless you show in what particular writing the figure seven was misread for one; in fact unless the original writing is pointed out, this explanation cannot recommend itself to us. Moreover in ancient writings especially Sanskrit verse we have usually words instead of figures denoting number. And in the only inscription where this figure is given it is given in words 'ekāgranavati' etc. There it is not possible to misread the figure. We have, therefore, to suggest another explanation and it is this that the years may be counted from the date of Guhāditya in whose reign the branch family of Guhila was forunded at Idar. That date as shown in Vol. I (p. 246) is 539 A.D. and if we add 191 to this figure we get the date 730 A.D. as the date of Bappā's accession. And if Bappā was then 30 years old as we have taken him to be, the date of his birth would be 700 A.D. as already taken.

प्राप्येत्यादिवरान् बाप्पः एकस्मिन्शतके गंते । एकाग्रनवतिसृष्टे माघे पक्षे वलक्षके सप्तमी दिवसे बाप्पः सपञ्चदशवत्सरः । एकलिंगेशहारीतप्रसादाद्भाग्यवान्भुव ॥ १२ ॥ *राजप्रशस्ति.

This explanation of the figure 191 is supported to our mind by the Raisāgar inscription itself wherein it is recorded. The figure is not given therein as that of any Saṁvat. We have seen that the verse means only that after 191 years had elapsed Bappā came to fortune. Now to determine from where this figure is to be counted, we have to take into account the story of the sarga itself wherein this verse is given. In the previous sarga the story is given how Kanakasena came from Ayodhyā and his descendant Vijayasena came to the south and he was told by a voice from heaven that he should thenceforward give up the name ending Sena and adopt the ending Āditya (p. 149 Bhav. Ins.). Accordingly in this sarga we are first told that Vijaya's son was called Padmāditya and so on and after 14 Ādityas the last Guhāditya's eldest son was Bappā. It clearly, therefore, appears from the context that the years 191 are to be counted from the time when the title Āditya was adopted presumably by Valabhī or Idar kings and that 14 kings had ruled before Bappā. A period of 191 years for 14 kings is not improbable and we have not the slightest hesitation in urging that 191 should be counted from the foundation of the Āditya family of Idar, Guhāditya and others, especially as we get at a resonable date for Bappā's accession in this way also. The date of Bappā's accession thus comes to 730 A.D.; while by supposing that some one misread 191 for 791 Saṁvat somewhere, as Gaurishankar thinks, that date comes to A.D. 734, a difference of four years only; which may even be removed if we suppose that the Idar branch was founded four years before Guhāditya came to the throne of Valabhī. The date of Bappā's birth will depend upon the view that we take of Bappā's age at accession. That the tradition that he was fifteen years old is absurd no body can doubt and he may be taken either 22 or 30 years old and the date ofBappā's birth would be 712 A.D. or even 700 A.D. as we have takan it.

We next come to the question of the date of Bappā's accession which has in the above discussion been nearly answered. The oldest Mewad oral and written tradition gives 191 as the year of that event. From what point that period is to be reckoned was a riddle before Tod which he, as we have seen, wrongly solved by holding that the period should be computed from the destruction of Valabhī. We consequently computed the period from the establishment of Valabhaī rule, thinking that was the date of Bappā's birth. As it now seems clear that it is the date of Bappā's accession we have suggested another solution and that is that the period should be computed from the rule of Guhāsena of Valabhī which began in 539 A.D.; and hence the date of Bappā's accession again comes to be 730 A.D. Pandit Gaurishankar Ojha's solution of the riddle is not acceptable according to our view as firstly the figure 191 is not given as that of any Saṁvat much less of Vikrama Saṁvat and secondly the idea that St. 791 was somewhere read wrongly by some one as St. 191 is not plausible, unless the very record, stone or paper is before us. Moreover as stated above the Raisāgar inscription which gives this period in words " one hundred and ninety one " clearly leads to the idea that the period is to be recokoned from the time of that son of Vijayabhūpa from whom the name ending of the king was changed from Sena to Āditya, undoubtedly a reference to the Valabhī dynasty. Unfortunately we do not find the name Vjiaya in the Valabhī dynasty nor many of the names given in this inscription (Bhav. Ins. p. 150) such as Padmāditya, Śivādtya and so on, except Śilāditya; which name was taken in the Valabhī dynasty by seven kings and by six of them in succession. We will refer to this list again hereafter; but it seems to us that these names are names of kings either at Idar or at Nagada sprung from Guhasena of the Valabhī dynasty. There is no record about the branch at Idar and we rely for this on oral tradition; but whether the off-shoot family reigned at Īḍar or at Nagada does not make much difference. This much is certain from this Raisāgar stone inscription dated Saṁvat 1732 or A. D. 1675, that the Mewad tradition at least in the 17th century A.D. computed 191 years from the connection of the Mewad family with the family at Valabhī and therefore presumably from Guhasena or Guhila whose rule began in 539 A.D. This gives a date for Bappā's accession somewhere about 730 A.D. which fits in properly with the end of Mān Mori's rule at Chitod his inscription at Chitoḍ being dated St. 770 or 713 A.D. as also with the inroads of the Arabs in the inner country after their conquest of Sind in 712 A.D. In short, although we have not been able to fix the date of Bappā's accession with exactitude it must have been somewhere about 730 A.D.

Lastly we have to settle the date of Bappā's abdication. Tod gives this date on the basis of Mewad tradition as St. 820. But Pandit Gaurishankar Ojha has pointed out that this figure ought to have been St. 810, as the several records noted by him give the year in words 'khachandrạdiggaja.' (Ekalinga Mahātmya and other records p. 270). But Gaurishankar has himself stated that from Bikaner records that date appears to be Śaka pañchāshṭashaṭ or 685 *i.e.*, A.D. 763 or St. 820. (Descriptive Catalogue of bardic and historical manuscripts Part II. p. 63 Bikaner State by Dr. Tesitori). Though thus there is a divergence of records, we think that St. 820 is more acceptable. For it is generally accepted that Bappā ruled long and eventually abdicated in favour of his son. If according to Gaurishankar's dates, we believe that Bappā was born in 712, came to the throne in 734 at the age of 22 and abdicated in V. E. 810 or 753 A.D. he had ruled only for 19 years and was about 41 years old. We, therefore, think that the dates which we have proposed viz. 700, 730 and 763 for the three events fit in more properly with the tradition that Bappā ruled long and abdicated in his old age. With these dates his age at abdication would be 63 or 64 and his rule would extend over 33 or 34 years. The Bikaner tradition, therefore, seems to be more correct as also the oral tradition prevailing at Udaipur as reported to Tod, and we may place

Bappā's abdication in St. 820 or A.D. 763. Although thus we have differeds from Pandit Gaurishankar Ojha's views on these points, the difference is only slight and it cannot but be recognised that he has corrected some wrong notions and based his opinions on several inscriptional records which must be placed before the curious reader, .in order that he may draw his own inference and that further light may be thrown on these dates. Minor differences being disregarded, we may take it as certain that Bappā was on the throne of Chitod in 750 A.D. in any case.

3 Bappa's Place in The Genealogy of The *Guhilots*.

This topic is the most vexed topic in connection with Bappā and the opinion of Rai Bahadur Gaurishankar on this subject is at great variance with the view adopted in this volume as he identifies Bappā with Kālabhoja of the genealogisies. It may be stated that there is not much dispute about this genealogy in other respects, it being generally accepted that the genealogy as given by the Ātpura inscription recently published by Dr. D. R. Bhankarkar is correct with its details. The inscription begins with the verse discussed at length in this volume in connection with the word Mahīdeva. But there is also a dispute as to who this Guhadatta mentioned in that verse is. The verse when translated runs as follows. "Triumphant is Śri Guhadatta the origin of the Guhila family, the king who came from Ānandapura and who was the delighter of Brahmin families." The inscription thereafter gives the successors as 2 Guhila 3, Bhoja 4, Mahendra 5, Naga 6, Śīla 7, Aparājita 8, Mahendra II and 9, Kālabhoja. Now while Pandit Gaurishankar identifies Bappā with Kālabhoja, we have identified Guhadatta the founder of the family with Bappā, on the strength not only of tradition but of the two detailed inscriptions at Abu and Chitod. Pandit Gaurishankar Ojha has given a table of the several genealogies as given in five inscriptions at page 275, viz, Ātpura dated V.E. 1038 2 Chitod V. E. 1335, 3 Abu V. E. 1342, 4 Bānapura V. E. 1436 and 5 Kumalgadh V. E. 1517; and in three of these viz. Chitod, Abu and Bānapura, Bappā is given as the founder of the family, Guhila being given as his son with desascendants Bhoja, Śīla, Kālabhoja, &c, while in the fifth Kumalgadh Bappā is given in place of Śīla and not Kālabhoja who is given in the fourth degree after him. In the first Ātpura inscription Bappā's name has not been given at all. But as Bappā is mentioned in the very beginning in the Naravāhana inscription dated 1028 *i.e.*, only six years before, it can not but be doubted that the Ātpura inscription seems to identify Guhadatta with Bappā and therefore does not mention him separately. The very fact that blessing is invoked on Guhadatta and that he is said to be the originator of the famous family of Mewad or Guhila naturally leads to the identification of Guhadatta with Bappā. Let us see now what difficulties stand in the way of this identification inducing Pandit Gaurishankar to identify Kālabhoja with Bappā and let us consider whether these difficulties are insuperable.

The first and foremost difficulty is that caused by the dates of the inscriptions of Śila and Aparājita two names in this genealogy viz., V. E. 703 and 718 or A.D. 646 and 661. Since Bappā's probable date of acesssion is 730 A.D. and since he was unquestionably on the throne of Chitod in 750 A.D., he cannot be taken to be an ancestor of the Śila of 646 A.D. or the Aparājita of 661 A.D. but must be treated as their descendant two or three degrees later. But there is nothing in these inscriptions of Śila and Aparājita to show that they are the kings of the same name in the Ātpura genealogy. They may be Guhila-vaṁśis ,but the name Guhila is also one which frequently recurs. For we actually find Guhila recurring more than once in the Chātsu inscription as also Bhatripatta and other names. The real vital question would thus be, are these kings Śila and Aparājita whose inscriptions dated A.D. 646 and 661 have been found, Guhila's ancestors or descendants ?

First we think that Guhila is both a son of Bappā and an ancestor. The Chitod and Abu inscriptions distinctly state that Guhila was a son of Bappā and Bappā retired in his favour. They also state that the family was named Guhilota from him. यस्य नामकलितां किल जातिं भूभुजो दधति तत्कुलजाताः. It does not seem to us proper that these inscriptions of so-old a date as St. 1332 and 1341 should be disregarded in this matter. The expression Guhilagotra-Narendrachandra appearing in the Naravāhana inscription dated V. E. 1028 may be explained in two ways ; either that Bappā was a moon among kings of the Guhila gotra referring to kings after him, surpassing them as the moon surpasses stars, or that Bappā was a moon to kings in the Guhilagotra referring to kings before him at Nagada born in the family of Guhila born of the Valabhī king Guhasena or of Guhasena himself. There does not appear to us any doubt as to the fact of there being two Guhilas, one before Bappā and the other a son of Bappā. The previous kings were called Guhilas and the subsequent kings Guhilots (Guhilaputras.) Probably this name was adopted to distinguish the subsequent kings from the previous kings.

In this manner practically, there remains no difference between the Ātpura inscription of 1034 and the Abu and Chitod inscriptions of 1334 and 1342. If some kings are omitted in the latter they might have been omitted because of their unimportance. The most glaring difference arises in the beginning if we take Guhadatta as none else but Guhila in the Ātpura inscription and therefore Bappā as king Kālabhoja many degrees after him. In our view there is nothing in the first verse of the Ātpura inscription to prevent us from taking Guhadatta as distinct from Guhila; the expression Guhadatta " the origin of Guhila family " does not necessarily equate Guhadatta with Guhila. The family known subsequently as Guhila family was started by Guhadatta whose son Guhila gave his name to the family. Moreover the words Jayati Śrī "May he triumph" indicate that Guhadatta was a very great king . If Bappā is brought down the list and identified with Kālabhoja what is it that made Guhadatta great or even Guhila great ? The memorable exploit of Bappā in founding an independent kingdom at Chitod goes not to the founder of the family but to a descendant many degrees below ! ! !

Rai Bahadur Gaurishankar has seen this defect and tries to show that Guhila alias Guhadatta was himself an illustrious king whose coin has been found near Agra indicating that his rule extended as far as that place (p. 283). These coins were found as many as 2000 and could not have been taken there from Mewad but they must have been current there as is inferred by Carlylle himself the editor (Cunningham's Archæological Survey Report Vol. IV p. 95). We have referred to this volume and find that this Guhila in Carlylle's opinion could not be the Guhila of the Ātpura inscription. If Śīla and Aparājita are taken to be his descendants as Gaurishankar takes them, the date of Guhila falls somewhere about A.D. 598. (We must remember that in this line we cannot use the 20 years average but only about 12 years and deducting 48 years for 4 generations from 646 A.D. we come to 598 A.D.) . Pratāpavardhana was a great king in Northern India at this time and the Maukhari family of Kanauj was also very powerful and hence Guhila could not have extended his sway as far as Agra. If we take 20 years average and more and throwing back Guhila fifty years place him somewhere about 540 A.D. he cannot be distinct from Guhila or Guhasena of the Valabhī family himself. In fact Carllyle himself suggests this when he observes. "Upwards of 2000 coins were dug up at Agra in 1869, all bearing an inscription in an ancient western form of the Sanskrit character which I read plainly as 'Guhila Śri' or 'Śri Guhila.' These might possibly be coins of Śri Gohidit or Guhila, the founder of the Guhilot dynasty of Mewar of A.D. 750, if it were not that the characters which compose the inscription on these coins appear to me to be of too ancient a form for such a late date. Could these coins then possibly be attributable to the earlier Gohila or Grahāditya or Guhāditya of the same race the son of Śilāiditya of the expelled dynasty of Valabhī or Saurāshtra, the exact date of whose reign is not certain but who probably lived about the sixth century of the Christian era." Valabhī or Saurāshtra history was not well elucidated in the days of Carllyle, but it is to be remembered that he thought that the coin was as old as the sixth century and was attributable to the first Guhadatta the origiator of the Guhilot branch. We now know for certain that Guhasena ruled from 539 to 569 A.D. and that he was an indepednent king having declared his independance of the Gupta empire which was then dying. He or his son a Guhila may very probably have extended his sway as far as Agra in the moribund state of the Gupta empire, and before the Vardhanas or the Maukharis had become powerful. It seems, therefore, very probable that there were two Guhilas who were famous, one preceding Bappā and the other following him viz. his son. It is therefore possible to explain the inscription of Śīla and Aparājita as those of two kings preceding Bappā and to hold that the Śīla and Aparājita mentioned in the Ātpura inscription are descendants of Bappā.

It is necessary to advert here to the Chātsu inscription again as it makes mention of the Guhila vaṁśa and as it is looked upon as the same Guhila vaṁśa as that of Mewad. Now this inscription gives 12 kings from Bhatṛipaṭṭa as follows :—1 Īśānabhata, 2 Upendrabhata, 3 Guhila, 4 Dhanika, 5 Auka, 6 Kṛishṇarāja, 7 Sanakaragaṇa, 8 Harsharāja, 9 Guhila, 10 Bhatta, 11 Bālāditya and 12 Vigraharāja. Now with regard to Harsharāja it is stated that "he conquered kings in the north and presented with great devotion horses to Bhoja." This evidences not only that he was a feudatory of Bhoja, but also shows that his date must be somewhere about 840 A.D., Bhoja being properly identified by Dr. D. R. Bhandarkar with the Bhoja Pratihāra of the Imperial line of Kanauj. Now if we count back eight generations to Bhatṛipaṭṭa the first king, his date comes to be somewhere about (840-160) 680 A.D. Now this clearly takes him some generations before Bappā himself of 750 A.D. whereas the first Bhatṛipaṭṭa of the Guhilot dynasty given in Ātpura inscription is 6 generations after even Kālabhoja sought to be identified with Bappā. Bhatṛipaṭṭa is therefore a name which appears both before and after Bappā, in the Guhila vaṁśa. His Guhila vaṁśa is, therefore, different from the vaṁśa given in the Ātpura inscription for we find no Bhatṛipaṭṭa between Guhadatta or Guhila and Kālabhoja. It is therefore certain that the Guhilavaṁśa of which the Chātsu inscription makes mention is a vaṁśa which preceded 680 A.D. and leads us to the same Guhila vaṁśa of which Śīla and Aparājita of 646 A.D. may have been members and which was started by Guhila or Guhasena of the Valabhī dynasty. The Guhila vaṁśa mentioned therein cannot be started by the Guhila of the Ātpura inscription as seems to be taken by Gaurishankar (p. 283).

The second difficulty (which also presented itself before Dr. D. R. Bhandarkar and which led him to identify Bappā with Khommāṇa son of Kālabhoja) is presented by the shortness of the average reign per king which we get if we identify Guhadatta with Bappā. Bappā's reign ended in 763 A.D. and if we regard Śīla and Aparājita as kings subsequent and different from those whose inscriptions have been found, since Bhatṛipaṭṭa II, whose inscription has been found dated 1000 V.E. or 943 A.D. is the sixteenth decendant from Guhila, we get for 15 intervening reigns a period of 180 years or an average of about 12 years per reign. This is very short and Bhandarkar would identify Bappā with Khommāṇa I, taking an average of 20 or 22 years. But as we have said before, to overhaul a regular genealogy merely for the purpose of recurring the usual average is not proper. For we actually see that the average for the next 4 or 5 reigns is even less than what we have obtained. For Śaktikumāra's inscription is dated 1038 V.E. and Bhatripatta II's 1000 V.E. During 38 years we have four reigns or an average of 9 years according to the Ātpura inscription itself. On the other hand if we identify Kālabhoja with Bappā whose accession date is 734 A.D. and take Sīla whose inscription of 646 A.D. has been found as his ancestor in the Ātpura line, we have only three kings before him and we shall have to assign about 88 years for three reigns giving an average of about 30 years; which Pandit Gaurishankar thinks is not unbelievable from the reigns of Akbar, Jehangir and Shahjahan. But if long reigns are not uncommon, short reigns are also not uncommon; for example, the Peishwas ruled for about 100 years only and were 1 Balaji, 2 Bajirao, 3 Nanasaheb, 4 Madhavrao, 5 Narayanarao, 6 Savai Mahdhavrao and 7 Bajirao II in all 7 which gives us an average of about 14 years. It is therefore not proper to distrust genealogies for the averages which they give and reject evidences of ancient inscriptions merely to secure any particular average, without any further reason.

It may perhaps be suggested that if Guhadatta in the disputed verse of the Ātpura inscription be taken to be distinct from Guhila as we do, he with 2 Guhila, 3 Bhoja, 4 Mahendra and 5 Naga may be taken to precede Śīla, supposing him to be the Śīla of the inscription of St. 703 or A.D. 646 and supposing Śīla's reign began about 640 A.D., by about 100 years at 20 years per reign and hence Guhadatta may be identified with Guhasena of the Valabhī dynasty whose reign began about 539 A.D. The same result follows if the pediree down to Kālabhoja identified with Bappā whose reign began about 734 A.D. be taken as we have 1 Guhadatta, 2 Guhila, 3 Bhoja, 4 Mahendra, 5 Naga, 6 Śīla, 7 Aparājita and 8 Mahendra II or 8 reigns which at 25 years per reign will take us back 200 years *i. e.*, to 534 A.D. *i. e.*, to the date of Guhasena of the Valabhī dynasty. This in fact would not be unwelcome in one way as the Ātpura inscription would properly begin with a praise of that king of the Valabhī family from whom the Ātpura branch has always been believed to have been sprung. It is not quite certain whether Rai Bahadur Gaurishankar looks upon Guhila or Guhadatta of the Ātpura inscription as identical with the Guhasena of the Valabhī dynasty. He probably looks upon that Guhadatta as some Guhila yet unidentified whose coins were found near Agra. But even if he or any one identifies this Guhadatta with Guhasena of the Valabhī dynasty, we yet think that this identification, plausible and acceptable though it may be, does not satisfy the requirements of the case. For in the first place there is then no mention in the Ātpura inscription of Bappā whose great exploit in acquiring Chitod was memorable. His name even is not mentioned nor also this exploit against the name of Kālabhoja, nor any blessing invoked on him at the beginning of the inscription or in the middle. It was impossible to ignore Bappā or his great exploit altogether in the Ātpura inscription of V. E. 1038 when we know that only 6 years before in the Naravāhana inscription Bappā is mentioned by that name and he is described there as the most illustrious of the Guhila kings. Secondly the epithet "Ānandapuravinirgata" cannot apply to Guhasena of Valabhī. For Valabhī is not yet shown to have had this name also. Ānandapura is the name of many towns and notably of Vadnagar and had Guhadatta been taken to be a Brahmin come from Vadnagar, it would have applied to him properly. But as it is certain that Guhadatta was not a Brahmin and had not come from Vadnagar, the expression " come from Ānandapura or Nagada " would well apply to Bappā, who going from that capital conquered Chitod. Dr. D. R. Bhandarkar has in his usual way ignored the word ' tad ' used in the Chitorgadh inscription (p. 170 Bengal R. A. S. New series Vol. V) when he translates the line jīyād &c. as " May Ānandapura be victorious which shines " &c., whereas the translation ought to have been " May *that* Ānandapura be victorious," meaning thereby the Ānandapura described in the previous verse (8) viz. Nāgahrada. There is not the slightest doubt (see Bhav. Insc. p. 74, 75) that this verse in the Chitorgadh inscription clearly states that the vipra Bappā came from Ānandapura alias Nāgahrada. It is well known that Ānandapura is the name of more than one town and Nāgahrada is one of these. Bappā's coming from Vadanagar is neither contemplated by the Chitod Ins. of V. E. 1332 nor by the Ātpura inscription. Therefore, we maintain that the epithets 'come from Ānandapura or Nagaday' is an epithet which can well apply to Bappā alone who from thence conquered the fortress of Chitod. It would not apply to Guhasena of Valabhī at all nor to any other Guhila who may have ruled in Nagada itself. The word ' vinirgata ' shows that the man originally came from one place and went to another and hence applies to Bappā properly who went from Nagada to Chitod. Similarly the epithet ' viprakulānandana ' applies to Bappā appropriately. The word is no doubt used for the sake of alliteration (Ānandapura and Ānandana) but the epithet ' delighter of Brahmin families ' refers to the highly religious tendencies of Bappā, to his devotion to Brahmins and ascetics. Hence we think that the line is an appropriate description of Bappā and it would be absurd to think that the Ātpura inscription giving the whole Mewad dynasty spoke not a word about Bappā or his great exploit. It seems, therefore, proper to hold that in this introductory verse we have a description of Bappā and putting together the Nāravāhana, the Ātpura and the Chitod inscriptions, we may believe that Guhadatta or Bappā was the greatest monarch of the family and hence was looked upon as the founder and that Guhila was his son.

It remains to consider how the name Guhadatta in this verse may have been used for Bappā. We have stated that Bappā was his usual name and not given to him as founder of the family (p. 76). But it is possible that he may have had another name in consonance with his family tradition and that name might have been Guhadatta which is specially mentioned in this Ātpura inscription to show his family connection. Bappā according to our view belonged to a branch family from the Valabhī family reigning at

Nagada and according to the Raisagar inscription detailed above the kings of this Guhila vaṁśa called themselves by names ending in Āditya. These names from the beginning are given therein as 1 Padmāditya, 2 Śivāditya, 3 Haradatta, 4 Sujasāditya, 5 Sumukhāditya, 6 Somadatta, 7 Śīlāditya, 8 Keshavāditya, 9 Nāgāditya, 10 Bhogāditya, 11 Devāditya, 12 Āsāditya, 13 Kālabhojāditya, 14 Guhāditya. " These are the 14 Ādityas " so says the Raisagar inscription and " the eldest son of the last was Bappā " (Bhav. Ins. p. 150). Now probably these are imaginary names but the name Śīlāditya occurs therein and the inscription found dated 703 V. E. is of one Śīlāditya and not of Śīla (see Report Western circle for 1909 p. 48 referred to by Dr. D. R. Bhandarkar Indian Antiquary XXXIX). It must be borne in mind that the tradition is that the Valabhī kings separating from Valabhī were called for 14 generations by names ending in Āditya and these names are given with Āditya at the end. When from Bappā and his son Guhila a new branch began, so to say, the names never used Āditya at the end and accordingly we find in the Ātpura inscription no name ending in Āditya. The Śīla, therefore, mentioned therein may be taken to be different from the Śīlāditya whose inscription of V. E. 703 has been found. But what we chiefly draw the attention of the reader to here is that the last name among the fourteen is Guhāditya. We also find that in one or two names the word Āditya is changed into datta probably for the sake of easy pronunciation. It is, therefore, natural that Bappā may have had a name in the beginning ending in Āditya itself, softened into datta ; nay we even think that Guhādatta in this first verse of the Ātpura inscription stands for Guhāditya and is used in this form to suit the exigency of the metre. Bappā was practically the last and the greatest of the Āditya kings of Nagada and having conquered the famous Chitod fortress and established himself in the sovereignty of the Moris, he became the starter of a new line of kings which became known through Guhila, his son and successor. Such is our view of this verse and this inscription and we place it before the reader with some diffidence, differing as we do from the view of Gaurishankar Ojha. We may state in the end again that we are not justified in giving up the Ātpura inscription of V. E. 1035 as amplified by the Abu and Chitod inscriptions of V.E. 1332 and 1341 and as repeated again in the Bānapura Inscription V. E. 1496 which tersely gives the genealogy as follows 1 Śri Bappā 2 Śri Guhila 3 Bhoja 4 Mahendra 5 Śīla 6 Kālabhoja 7 Bhatṛipaṭṭa 8 Sinha &c. It must be pointed out that if later inscriptions change the order a little, they are to be corrected by previous inscriptions. The rule of Pūrvaprāmāṇya applies forcibly to inscriptions also but unless statements in inscriptions are unbelievable or contradicted by older inscriptions, they must be believed. Hence we are not prepared to identify Bappā either with Kālabhoja or with Khommāṇa but place him at the head of the genealogy given by the Ātpura inscription.

APPENDIX VI.

NOTE.—RECENT RESEARCH AND THE LIGHT IT THROWS ON THE HISTORY OF THIS PERIOD.

I

Professor Velankar of Wilson College, Bombay has recently discovered a copper-plate grant made by a Śilāhāra king of Thana in Śaka 915 or A.D. 993, which will shortly be published by him, but which we have had an opportunity of inspecting before publication; and we were surprised to find therein not only a complete genealogy of the Rāshtrakūtas of Malkhed, who were the overlords of these Śilāhāras of Thana but a correct reflection of the political condition of India in the tenth century A.D. It must be remembered that this grant was made after the fall of the Rāshtrakūta dynasty in about 974 A.D., and the grant actually contains expressions of sorrow over the destruction of Rattarājya by Tailapa. This clearly shows how the rule of the Rāshtrakūtas was popular even among the feudatory chiefs; for who would be disposed to deplore the downfall of their overlords after the destruction of their power? The genealogy given in this copper-plate grant, of the Rāshtrakūtas does not differ from the one we have given. Thus we are assured that the genealogy hitherto accepted is substantially correct. The grant highly extols king Kṛishṇa, grand-father of Kakkala in whose reign the Rāshtrakūta power came to an end and declares that his sovereignty was accepted by the whole of India from the Himalaya to Ceylon and from the western to the eastern ocean. As this eulogy comes from a grant made by an entirely different line of kings and after the loss of their power by the Rāshtrakūtas, it may be taken to be based on substantial truth. In the following śloka* the exact political condition of India at this time is portrayed. " The Chola trembled with fear and the lord of

---

*चोलो लोलो भियाभूद्गजपतिरपतज्जान्हवीगव्हरान्तः ।
वाजीशश्वासशेषः समभवदभवच्छैलरन्ध्रे तथान्ध्रः ॥
पाण्ड्येशः खाण्डितोऽभूदनुजलधि जलं द्वीपपालाः प्रलीना ।
यस्मिन्दत्तप्रयाणे सकलमपि तदा राजकं न व्यराजत् ॥

It may be noted that Gajapati and Hayapati became in later times hereditary titles of certain lines of Kings.

elephants slipped into the ravines of the Ganges. The lord of horses was sorely troubled while Āndhra took refuge in mountain holes. The king of the Pāṇdyas was foiled and the kings of maritime countries took to the sea. When Kṛishṇa took the field, all kings lost the colour of their faces." We recognise here the power of the Cholas just rising, while the lord of elephants was the king of Bengal and the lord of horses was the king of Kanauj. We have already noted that Kanauj was strong in cavalry and Bengal in elephant force. Āndhra and Pāṇdya were the next important kingdoms in India but fast declining as we shall see in the next volume. It is not strange, therefore, to conceive that the supreme power of Kṛishṇa the 11th Rāshtrakūta king was felt all over India.

The Bhadāna grant of the same Śilāhāra king has already been published in Ep. Ind. III. (p. 257) and contains similar expressions of regret over the fall of the Rāshtrakūta kingdom. But it is dated four years later viz., 997 A.D. and though it extols the power of the same Kṛishṇa and gives the whole line of the Rāshtrakūtas, it does not contain the above quoted verse about Kṛishṇa and hence the importance of the earlier grant.

In these grants as in some others, the kingdom of the Rāshtrakūtas is distinctly called Rattarājya and Ratta means clearly the Marāthas. The latter word came into use generally hereafter.. The Rattarājya mentioned in the Skanda Purāṇa is this very kingdom of the Rāshtrakūtas and Skanda Purāṇa therefore cannot have been composed before their rule *i. e.*, before 750 A. D.

II. Pratihara Line.

II. Rai Bahadur Gaurishankar Ojha has recently published a new Pratihāra inscription which adds a further king to the Pratihāra genealogy named Mahendrapāla II. (See Pratāpgadh Inscription Ep. Ind. XIV p. 182). The inscription is dated 1003 (A.D. 946) as the figure is read by Pandit Gaurishankar and it recites the whole genealogy from Maharaja Devaśakti, giving the mother of each king and his favourite deity as usual. The genealogy of the Pratihāra Imperial line given at page 113 does not give Mahendrapāla II who makes this Pratāpgadh grant and who is stated therein to be a son of Vināyakapāla. Now the Khajuraho inscription of Yaśovarman (Ep. Ind. I) speaks of Hayapati Devapāla son of Herambapāla; and this Devapāla is considered to be the same Devapāla spoken of in the Siyadoni Inscription (Ep. Ind. I) of Saṁvat 1005 or A.D. 948 as meditating on the feet of Kshitipāla. But Pandit Gaurishankar thinks that these two can not be the same persons as Hayapati is not a title of the Pratihāra kings of Kanauj. However on this point we may be certain that by 'Hayapati', only kings of Kanauj are meant. As we have already shown, they were, even according to the accounts of Arab travellers, strong in cavalry and we find in the above Śilāhāra grant the word Vājīśa used clearly with reference to the king of Kanauj. Hence though Kanauj kings had not the title 'hayapati,' nor did they call themselves so, other kings and their documents described them usually as 'lords of horses' much as the Rāshtrakūtas called the Pratihāras Gurjaras though the latter did not call themselves so. We may, therefore, feel sure that the Hayapati Devap āla son of Herambapāla spoken of in the Khajuraho inscription from whom the image of Vaikuntha was obtained by Yaśovarman is the same Devapāla spoken of in the Siyadoni inscription as son of Shitipāla and ruling from Kanauj. The genealogy which Pandit Gaurishankar Ojha gives on the supposition that the Devapālas are different need not, therefore, be considered. But the genealogy which he gives on the supposition that the two are one must be given here, and it is as follows.

VII Mahendrapāla I
(903, 909 A. D.)

- IX Bhoja II — 910
- X Mahīpāla, or Kshitipāla alias Herambapāla or Vināyakapāla — 917, 931 and 941
  - Mahendrapāla II — 946
  - XII Devapāla — 948
  - XIII Vijayapāla — 960
    - XIV Rājyapāla — 1018

We may, however, add two observations. It is possible that Mahendrapāla may be another name of Devapāla himself as the date 946 is very near 948 a certain date of Devapāla; and Mahendra is only an amplification of Deva. Secondly, a difficulty is further presented by the fact that the Khajuraho inscription above noted and dated Saṁvat 1011 or 954 A. D. ends with the expression "In the reign of Vināyakapāla" as stated at page 128 of this volume. We have there stated that the Chandellas still nominally recognised the suzerainty of Vināyakpāla *alias* Mahīpāla who was then dead. But if we believe that this was a reference to a living Vināyakapāla on the throne of Kanauj also acknowledged as emperor, like the last Mogul emperor acknowledged by the Marāthas and the English, we shall have to suppose that Devapāla had a son named Vināyakapāla who was on the throne of Kanauj in 954 A.D. and who after a short reign was succeeded by his uncle Vijayapāla whose certain date is 960 A.D. from the Rajor inscription of Mathanadeva (Ep. Ind. III). Until further light is thrown on this part of the Pratihāra genealogy by fresh epigraphic records, we may, however, accept the genealogy as proposed by Rai Bahadur Gaurishankar.

It is important to add that Mahendrapāla II signs the grant as Śrividagdha or simply Vidagdha. This epithet, might lead to his possible identification with Devapāla. No record of Devapāla has yet been found. Smith in his table of Prātihāra documents in *J. R. A. S.* 1909 p. 33 only refers to the Siyadoni and the Khajuraho inscriptions for evidence of Devapāla. It would be interesting to find what epithet Devapāla had taken for signature on documents as the custom appears to be with all Pratihāra emperors.

III. Paramara Line.

The above Pratāpgadh inscription (Ep. Ind. XVI) has caused another riddle, and that about the Paramāras of Dhār. A sun temple probably built at Pratāpgadh by a Chāhamāna Chief Indrarāja was granted a village at his request by one Mādhava son of Dāmodara who calls himself Mahasāmanta and Mahādandanāyaka in Ujjain under Śrīvidagdha (Mahendrapāla II). And the grant is made at Ujjain and signed by both Mādhava and Śrīvidagdha. It is not dated, yet its date must be somewhere about the date of the previous document viz., A.D. 946. Now this shows that Malwa with its capital Ujjain was still under Kanauj. But we have held that Kṛishṇa had founded the power of the Paramāras in Malwa and at Ujjain already in about 910 A.D. (p. 119); how could Mādhava then be a Viceroy of the Kanuaj Pratihāras about 946 A.D.? Of course this in one way confirms our view that the Paramāras had not come to Malwa before Kṛishṇa of 910 A.D. But it goes to show that even Kṛishṇa must be put later or that Mādhava was allowed to pose as Viceroy of the Pratihāras in Ujjain, while Kṛishṇa was virtually his own master. The suzerainty of decaying empires is often seen acknowledged by habit or for the satisfaction of people, before it is finally disowned. Even the English for long acknowledged the overlordship of the Mogul emperor over Bengal though they were its real masters and had merely for people's satisfaction leased its Diwani from the Emperor of Delhi.

IV. Rashtrakuta Line.

In a recent Rāshtrakūta record published in Ep. Ind. XIV. p. 125, Dr. Sukthankar following Dr. D. R. Bhandarkar says that Kṛishṇa succeeded Dantidurga by natural succession and not by uprooting him as surmised by Fleet from the Baroda grant. We have referred to this controversy at page 145 of this volume and stated at the end of the para that we may accept the story of Dantidurga being uprooted by Kṛishṇa though given in one grant only. Mr. Sukthankar in publishing this new inscription of Kṛishṇa I, dated Śaka 694 or A. D. 772 says that as Kṛishṇa himself says nothing wrong about Dantidurga, the story of his getting into evil ways and his eventual supression may be disbelieved. We think after looking into the several documents that the story may be accepted with some variation. The Baroda grant which is dated 812 A. D. *i. e.*, only 40 years later cannot be set aside altogether. There can be no reason why a false statement should have been made so shortly after Kṛishṇa. Any statement in an inscription should be given its due weight unless we can show how an erroneous idea might have arisen. Now this account may very easily have been forgotten in later times or may have been omitted from a sense of propriety. The Kardā grant which is dated 972 A.D. may have made, after 200 years, the mistaken statement that Dantidurga left no issue since his uncle Kṛisṇa succeeded him and we may believe that Dantidurga left behind him a son who was ill-behaved and who consequently was set aside by his powerful uncle Kṛishṇa. The words in the Baroda grant are wide enough to admit this possibility; यो वंश्यमुन्मूल्य विमार्गभाजं राज्यं स्वयं गोत्रहिताय चक्रे mentions only a Vaṁśya or a person to whom inheritance goes and may include a son of Dantidurga. This indeed lays down a good maxim viz: that any rightful heir, if he is unfit to govern by his licencious behaviour should be set aside by the next heir for the benefit of the family (गोत्रहित). We see that this was done at the very next step; for we are told that Kṛishṇa's elder son Govinda was immersed in sensual pleasures and was therefore set aside by his younger brother Dhruva (Deoli grant). In fact a battle was fought between them according to the Paiṭhan grant (Ep. Ind. III. p. 167) which states that Dhruva defeated his brother Govinda though assisted by Kānchi, Ganga, Vengi and Mālava. This also shows that outsiders are ready enough to interfere in internecine quarrels; but it also shows that the Rajputs who came to the front about this period were men of strong moral fibre and the people also sided with virile and well-conducted claimants. It may, in short, be accepted that though Dantidurga was not himself ill-behaved nor was himself uprooted by Kṛishṇa, his son most probably was from the Baroda grant.*

---

* The several records of the Rāshṭrakūṭas in order of date are as follows: I The recently published Bhandak plates of Kṛishṇa I (Ep. In. XIV 772 A.D. 2. Paiṭhan grant (Ep. In. III. 167) of 794 A.D. 3. Baroda grant (Ind. Ant. XII. p. 162) of 812 A.D. 4. Bagumra grant (Ind. Ant. XII. p. 187) of 867 A.D. 5. Alas plates of Govind III. (Ep. Ind. VI. p. 209) and Samangad plates (ditto) of......7. Kardā grant (Ind. Ant. XII. p. 267) of 972 A.D. etc.

V. Palas of Bengal.

Mr. Bannerji has republished the ..smagachhi grant of Vigrahapāla III. which had been half published by Kielhorn years ago. In the present edition of the grant (Ep. Ind. XV. p. 295) we get the same genealogy of the Pālas with an additional name Jayapāla who is said to be a son of Vākpāla, brother of Dharmapāla. (See genealogy given at page 143 of this volume.) His son was Vigrahapāla I, who is mentioned in this genealogy which onwards is the same. It may further be noted that the donor of this grant Vigrahapāla III, is distinctly said to be a Buddhist.

VI. Malkhed.

I recently visited Malkhed (not Mālkhed) which is identified with Mānyakheṭa the capital of the Rāshṭrakuṭas of the Deccan. I found no trace of any large city described as "vying with the city of gods." Nor can a city exist here for the Kāngini river which runs by Malkhed, though large, runs dry in the hot season and in Malkhed itself there are no wells; nor can there be any as the ground is rocky and the rock appears to be very deep. The only thing which seems favourable is that there is an extensive fort at the confluence of a large stream with the Kāngini river on a natural eminence; which, standing in a vast plane country must have commanded it in ancient days when there was no canon. The present fort is, however, said to have been built by a Mahomedan Sardar, named Mujaffar and hence called Mujaffar Kilā. The fort is an extensive one and the present Jagirdar resides therein and the vast space inside the fort can contain a population of about 5000 souls. It is full of debris but there is a remnant of a Jain sanctuary and also a Vaishṇava Muṭh of about the thirteenth century. Oral tradition states that Mujaffar obtained the place from a Jain chief by stratagem. It is likely that there might have been an old fort at the place and Mujaffar only rebuilt it. And that fort like the fort of Rayagad built by Śivaji and made his capital might have been selected by the Rāshṭrakūṭas as a strong commanding place, for their capital, even without a large city outside it.* The statement of an Arab traveller that the capital was surrounded by mountains is no doubt inapplicable to Malkhed as the place is situated in a perfectly plain country. But if we can believe that the word mountains in the translation is incorrect and in the original Arabic, the word is merely 'rocky ground' then the description is correct as the ground in and about Malkhed is entireky stony and unfit for movements of cavalry. The fort can be held or attacked by infantry alone. Taking all these facts into consideration I think, however, that the identification of Mālkhed with Mānyakheṭa is still problematical.

---

* In ancient times, a stong fort was the *sine qua non* of capaital not a city.

End of Vol. II.

INDEX.

A

Abul Fazal 133.
Abu Zaid—a peculiarity recorded by—190 f.
—statement about ornaments and Queens in darbar of—and refutation thereof 187.
—statement of practice of suicide of—191.
Abhiyara—23.
Abu mountain or Arbuda mountain, legend of—67 f.
Abhira 25.
Addaka 116.
Administration—sources of system of 229.
—Civil and Military 229 ff.
—Civil leading to happiness 255f.
Ādisura cannot be identified 142.
Agastya 56 ff.
—origin of—86.
Agnihotra gradually disappearing 200f.
Agnikulas 9 ; 16.
—are they Gujars ? 27ff.
—correct interpretation of story of—16.
—examination of caste of—30ff.
—exploded myth of—12ff. 91.
—fancy, misconception 13.
—Gotras of supposed—50.
—mere mith ; tradition 11.
—origin of—unhistorical, misconception and of recent date 12.
—story of, accepted 13.
Agnikulas story of—first told by Chand 12f.
—story of—not correct representation of tradition but misinterpreted 15f.
Āgamas—list of different—200.
—the result of different deity worship 199f.
Ahichchhatra (City) same as Ahichchhatra of Pañchāla 92.
Ahichchhatra town 36.
Ahimsā doctrine—influence of-202f.
Āhīra 25.
Aiṅgra Mainyu 264.
Ajmīdha 58f ; 290.
Akālavarsha, son and successor of Amoghavarsha—account and exploits of—148.
Alexander—40 ; 292.
Al Idrisi—extract about religion from work of—196.
—statement of noble characters of Indians of—191f.
Al Istakhri—extracts from writings of—166.
—statement of dress of Sind, Multan etc. of—187.
Allaṭa son of Khommāṇa III 80.
Al Masaudi, an Arab traveller, 36, 105, 184f.
—extract from writings of—on caste, 181.
—accounts of—and inference therefrom 107.
—Identification of writings about India of—164ff.

Al Masaudi—evidence about languages of—168f.
Amala 41.
Amarasing Maharaja—statement about learning of ancient Rajputs of—181f.
Ambarīsha 58f.
Amitagati 122.
Amoghavarsha—devotee of Jains 148.
—son of Govind III—date, exploits and account of —147f.
Anahillapaṭṭaṇa 14.
Ananda Vikrama era, a special era, —efforts to construe—20f.
Anaṅga 23, 25.
Anaṅgapāla Tomara 159.
Aniga 23, 25.
Audhala 41.
Animal sacrifices—aversion to—1f.
Anuloma marriages checked 27f.
Anus 276ff, 282, 284ff, 297.
—progress of—294.
Anthropometry—science of—7f.
Ānandapāla—date of—157.
Ānandapura or Nagad—come from
—an epithet well applied to Bappā alone 347.
—not Vadnagara of Nagar Brahmins 85.
Ānarta,—central and north Gujarata 33, 104.
Āndhra 103.
—history of Yavana kingdom of—161.
Aparājita 345f.
Āpastamba Sūtra 57.
—explanation of rule for pravara of—61.
Arab—conquest of —4.
Arab invasion before Bappā 73.
—inKhommāna Rāsā—date of—79f
—Arab writers 162ff.
Arbuda Tīrtha 67.
Arjuna 24.
Arkabhava 25.
Armies of different kings 102f.
—manner of fighting of 245f.
—officers of—244.
—reasons and result of defects in 246.
—in general—contents of—242ff.
—standing—persons engaged there in 242ff.
—of different kings—contents of—and evidences thereof—223f.
Aryans-characteristics of—7.
—analogy from American history to the colonisation of—268f.
—analogy from American settlement to settlement of—264.
—evidence of and conclusion from two invasions of India by—265f.
—contries occupied by—265f.
—mixing with Dravidian races 27.
Asceticism—reasons of Indian feeling then and now about—199.
Assam or Kāmarūpa—history of kingdoms in—160.
Aśvalāyana 58 ff.
Aśvamukha 41.
Aśvamedha 47.
Aśoka 100, 323.
Atilāṅgada 40f.
Atisindhu 41.
Atri 56ff.
Avanti Bhūpāla—meaning of—101f.
Avantivarman of Utpala dynasty 158.

B

Babar 36.
Bais 25.
Balhara of Mānkīra is Vallabharāya of Mānyakheṭa—some facts noted about him 162f.
Balana—a Mlechchha king 99.
Bambaṇavāhaka 41.

Banerji 354.
Bappayarāja—Vindhya Nṛipati 93f
Bappā Rāwal—4f, 26, 70ff, 99, 177, 322ff, 346f.
—accession story of—73f.
—belonged to Guhila Vaṁśa according to Naravāhana Inscription 88.
—commander-in-chief of Mori forces 73.
—compared with Charles Matrel 72ff.
—descent of—72.
—evidences and discussion of dates of birth, accession and retirement of—74ff 338ff.
—evidences of his being Brahmin 84f.
—evidences of and conclusion from the place in genealogy of Guhilots of—342ff.
—facts of life of—in author's opinion 88f.
—golden Valaya legend of—77.
—identical with Guhādatta and founder of the line 82, 85f.
—identification with Khumāna of—76.
—identification with Khumāna of—impossible 82.
—interpretation of date St. 191 of—75.
—legend of abdication of—74.
—not Brahmin 88, 232ff.
—Nagara Brahmin 85.
—number of his successors varying 78.
—proper name; similar examples 76.
—śaivait; divotee of Hārita worshipper of Ekaligna 88f.
—story of—71ff.
—successors of—77ff.
—though taken to be a Nāgara Brahmin still not foreigner 87f.
Bappā—why looked upon as brahmin ?86f.
Baudhāyana 56.
Baurā—identification of—165.
Bbhandikula—mentioned in Sāgaratala Inscription 112.
Badāmi 14.
Bālaka 41.
Bālhika 42.
Bāṇa 29, 103, 178.
—uses Rājputra as Kshatriya soldier 44.
—uses Rājaputra in good sense 45.
Begging bands—absence of—252f.
Benares 5.
Bhadra 41.
Bhandarkar—Dr. Sir —318, 321.
Bhandarkar—Dr. D. R.—9ff 27ff, 40, 65, 69, 72, 82ff, 98, 111, 113, 144, 148, 332ff, 345, 347f, 352.
—Theory of Gujars as foreigners of—mistaken 10 f.
—theory of Rajputs as descendants of Gujars of—refuted 10f.
—theory of Guhilots of—83.
—wrong interpretation of sapādalaksha by 92.
Bharadvāja 56ff, 273f.
Bhāradvāja 14.
Bharata Dauśyanti 296.
Bharatas—conclusion from reference to—in Bhāgavata 267.
—reference to—in Nirukta 268.
—inference from reference to in Rigveda 269ff.
—conclusion from reference to—in Vāyu Purāṇa 267f.
—conclusion from reference to—in Vedic Index Vol. II. 269f.
—theory of—267ff.
—wrong view of scholars about 267ff.
Bharmayaśva 59.
Bhars 8.
Bhartṛipaṭṭa son of Kālabhoja 79f

Bhaṭṭāraka 75.
Bhāṭī 25.
Bhavabhūti 44, 207.
Bhayānaka 42.
Bhāgavata Purāṇa 20f.
Bhīma 70.
Bhinmāl—capital of Pratiharas according to some 99 f.
Bhīmadeva—date of—157.
Bhoja, 108, 118, 346.
—real facts discussed about the mith of murder of—120f.
—successor of Guhila 79.
—successor and son of Sindhurāja—date of accession of—discussed 120f.
Bhoja II son of Mehendrapāla—date of—106.
Bhosales not foreigners—reasons of—325f.
Bhṛigu 56ff.
—origin of—86.
Bhujabhava 25.
Bilhaṇa 189.
Biruds, special names of different kings 110.
Brahma Gupta 20f.
Brahma-kshatriya-kulīna 59.
—meaning of—62f.
Brahmins formed one caste—examples 175f.
Brahmins and Kshtriyas—privileges of chosing occupations and special features of 181f.
Brahmins and Kshatriyas—relation of—260f.
—why took to agriculture 182.
—and Vaiśyas evidences of being not given to drinking 184f, 202.
Buddhism 9, 43, 45f.
—annihilated by Pūrvamīmānsā 1.
—condition of—247f.
—decay of—1.
—overthrown and Hinduism re-established—effects 167f.
Buddhism—result of one of the great defects of—252f.
—reaction against 139.
—supplanted 197.
—two great good results of—adding to happiness 252f.
—why preferred by foreigners 168.
Buddhagupta 225.
Bülher, Dr. 116, 118ff, 122.
Bull—sacredness of—2.
Bundlekhand rulers—dates of—and epigraphic evidence thereof 124f.
Bundi kingdoms 90.
Bundikoṭa 16.

C

Castes—condition of—and effects therefrom 28, 249ff.
—authorities on main number of 177ff.
—distinction not strict 27, authorities in favour of free intercourse of food in—186f.
—further ramification of—2f.
—higher—enforced widowhood in—190.
—history of development of 28f.
—intermediate—cannot be traced 177.
—Matrimonial—history of—179f.
—Matrimonial and occupational aspects of—179f.
—not hard bound in ancient times 54, 175f.
—privileges in occupation of—181f.
—and social condition of India 175ff
—and social condition—materials for survey of 175.
—Vedic history of—misunderstood 27.
—watertight compartments of—about 300 B.C. 28.

Chand Baradai, the bard—12f. 16, 18ff, 25f, 67f, 91, 117, 125, 131.
—story of fire origin of—imaginary 97.
Chandana 94.
—Chāhmāna king 159.
—successor of Gūvaka II defeated by Rudreṇa 96.
Chandels 8, 25, 55.
—Bhars or Gonds by origin; arguments in support by Smith 130.
—coins of—and history of coins in general 128.
—examination and reply to arguments of origin of—131ff.
—genealogy and dates of—129.
—of Jajhoti or Bundelhand 124ff.
Chandra 94.
Chandragupta, the Emperor 100, 225.
Chandrarāja, Gūvaka's successor 96.
Chakrāyudha 103, 140.
—last Varmā Emperor 98.
Charles Martel 4, 72ff.
Chaṭa 42.
Chāhmānas or Chauhānas 9, 13f, 15f, 23, 27, 35ff, 50, 53, 55, 69, 90ff.
—available sources of history of—91f.
—compared with Guhilots 95f.
—descendants of Gūvaka, and of Solar race 14, 97.
—examination of arguments of Gujar descent of—35ff.
—history of—very little known 91f.
—original seat of power of—92.
—valorous and chivalrous like Guhilots 90f.
—why second in rank to Guhilots 90f.
Chāhamāna or Anahila—fabulous date of—33f.
Chālukyas of Badāmi 4, 9, 13ff, 16, 23, 27, 33f, 47, 50, 5ff. 55.
Chālukyas—examination of arguments of Gujars descent 33f.
—early history of 321f.
—of Badāmi different from Chālukyas of Anahilapaṭṭaṇa 14.
—of lunar race 14.
—origination story of 86.
—and other families compared with Bhosale, 324ff.
—and others—rule of—not foreign 328.
—theory of origin of—14.
Chālukya—Avanivarman 14.
Chāpas of Vardhamāna—account of—116.
—śaivas 116.
Chāpotkaṭa 23.
Chāvadas of Anhilwāḍ Pāṭaṇ 114ff.
—history of—not much known 114.
—important facts of—116.
—short account supported by Bombay Gazetteer and others 114ff.
Chhand 25.
Chhandaka 23.
Chitod 21.
Chūḍāsama 55.
Clans or families—names of—not to be looked into 134f.
Combinations of kings possible in Mediæval times 227f.
Coining—Art and history of—241f.
Coins—names of—241.
Countries' names not through rulers 34.
Cow—sacredness of—2.
—its slaughter a heinous crime 2.
Crooke—9ff, 14, 74f, 159.
Cunnigham 35, 37, 51f, 68, 329.
—wrong view on Gotras like Mitāksharā of—51f.

D

Dadabhai Nowroji 319.
Dadhisbaṭa 25.

Daṇḍakāraṇya 67.
Dantidurga 171, 322.
—discussion and evidences about uprootment by Kṛishṇa of—352f.
—son of Indrarāja—exploits and territory of 144f.
—story of death of—145.
Dasyu and Mlechchha—meaning of—65.
Dayitavishṇu, father of Gopāla 140.
Dāhala or Bundelkhand—extent of—40f.
Dāhima 25.
Deccan ruling families were Marāṭhās not Kshatriyas—all evidences that—329ff.
Deccan settlement 321.
Delhi 36f.
Deity—favourite—changeable—examples 197.
Deorā 23.
Devabhadra 42.
Devapāla, nephew and successor of Dharmapāla—date of—141
—Devapāla, successor of Mahīpāla —account of—107.
Devaśakti or Devarāja, brother and successor of Kakutsa—date of —100.
Devaśravas 271, 274.
Devavāta 291.
Devavrāta 271f, 274.
Dhanakaṭaka 47.
Dhanapāla poet 120.
Dhaṅga, successor of Harsha—inscriptions, exploits and extent of Empire of—126ff.
Dharaṇīvarāha, subordinate to Mahīpāla 116.
Dharmapāla, son and successor of Gopāla—exploits date and account of 140.
Dhruvabhaṭa 116.
Dhruva Nirūpama, younger brother and successor of Govind II—exploits of—146.
—defeats Mihira 104f.
Dhānyapāla 25.
Dhānyapālaka 23.
Diḍḍā, queen—some facts of—158.
Didiot 23.
Dining—inter 250f.
Divisions—usual—of countries for administration; their names and examples 230f.
Divodsāa 60, 269, 273f, 276, 281, 283, 295.
Doyāmata 23, 25.
Drāḍa 41.
Drupada 14, 291.
Draupadi 24, 44.
Drinking—generally abstained from 202.
Droṇa Bhāradvāja 14, 52.
Druhyus 276ff, 281f, 284ff, 297.
—progress of—294.
Durgāvati Rāṇi—inference by Smith from story of—and author's reply to it 133.
Durlabharāja 93f.
Durlabha 93.
—brother and successor of Vigraharāja 97.

E

Economical condition, good as result of political condition 255.
Elliot 162ff, 168.
Elorā temple of śiva 153.
Ekaliṅga Māhātmya 84f.
Ekabāhu 41.
Ekapāda 40f.
Empire never meant annexation but subordination, examples 221.
Engl'sh 102.
Ethnology 8.

F

Fleet Dr. 148, 150, 352.
Flesh eating—state of things with regard to—202f.
Foreign descent theory 7ff.
—criticised 29ff.
—loses support 17.
—refuted 15.
Foreign domination—external and internal—bad effects of—255.
—invasions, stopped 256f.
—rule characteristics of—examples and inference therefrom 319f.

G

Gājanaka—extent of—fabulous 39, 41.
Gaṅga King 146.
Gāṅgeyadeva, son of Kokkaladeva —date of—136.
Garga—explanation of—in Āṅgirasa stock 58f.
—descent of—58.
Gaura 23.
Garua 24f.
—identical with Gujar 25.
Gauḍa—Bengal—extent of 39ff.
—deśa—Thanesar 69.
Gauḍapāda—commentator on Sāṅkhya Kārika 214.
Gaurishankar Ojhā 122, 332f, 336, 338ff 345f 348, 350, 352.
—views of and authorities relied upon by—on Bappā Rāwal—332ff.
Gautama 56ff.
Gautamiputra Śatakarṇi, a śūdra 47.
Geetoe 6.
Geholts 4.
Genealogies not proper to distrust for averages 345f.

Ghaghaḍa or Rāhapa, successor of Muṇḍrāja—date of—115.
Ghārwar 8, 55, 124.
Gibbon 5, 12.
Gifts and taxes for temples 236ff.
Gohila 23.
Gohilaputra 23.
Goṇḍas 8.
Gopāla Avanti 102.
—descendant of Pratihāra Pāla dynasty—and evidence thereof 139f.
—the elected Emperor, capital and exploits of—139.
—Kshatriya and a Buddhist—account, exploits and date of—139f.
Gopāla II son and successor of Rājyapāla 141.
Gopendra 93.
Gotra—Bhāradvāja 14.
Gotras borrowed from Purohits—theory of—50; this theory a misconception 50ff.
—by descent and not by discipleship, instances 52f.
—eight—according to Baudhāyana 56.
—four—according to Mbh. and Pravarādhyās 56.
—history of—of Solar and Lunar races 56f.
—mention of—necessary 51.
—mention of—by Rajputs useless 51.
—of Brahmins, Kshatriyas and Vaishhyas—why the same 54.
—of Marāṭhā Kshatriya families 331.
—of Modern Rajputs with Gotras of their Purohits 55.
—of the Rajputs 49ff.
Gotra and Pravar 56ff.
—minute examination of—56ff.
—system—benefit of 49f.

Gotras—reasons of theory of Vijñāneśvara about 53.
Gotra Rishi founder of the family examples 87.
Gotra Rishi and Pravara Rishi, latest view of—56
—relation of and difference between 57.
—rule in śrauta sūtras and author's interpretation of it 50ff.
—śloka in Mahābhārata on 56.
—Vasishṭha 14.
Govind I 144.
Govind II son and successor of Kṛishṇarāja—some facts of—145f.
Govind III 107, 119, 140.
—Jagatuṅga, Dhurva Nirūpama's son and successor—exploits and account of—146f.
Govind IV 154.
Govindrāja—successor of Indra. III—confusion about him in different plates and account and date of him 150.
Grant Als of Yuvarāja Govind II 145, 171, 230.
—Amāgācchi of Vigraharāja III 140.
—Bhagumrā 105.
—Balavarman 106.
—Baroda 145.
—Bhadān by a śilāhāra king 350.
—Bhālgur 234.
—Bhāgalpura 140ff.
—Copperplate by a Śilāhāra king of Thana—political condition described in—349f.
—Daulpurā of Bhoja—contents of the seal there on—108f.
—Dighwa Dubauli by Mahendrapāla 106, 230.—contents of the seal of—108f.
—Khardā 120, 147ff.—date of and —inference from 151.
of karkarāja dated 812,—176.
Grant—Kavi 146.
—Khārepāṭana 147, 149f.
—Khalimpurā of Dhanapāla 139f.
—Mālwā 234.
—Navasāri 148f, 152f.
—Paiṭhan of Govind III 171, 234.
—Rādhanpūra 145f.
—Samangadh 145.—date of and inference from 144.
—Sangali 176.—date of 149f.
—Sarvanātha Mahīpāla—date of and inferences from—141.
—Vani Diṇḍori 146.
—Wardhā 144ff, 175.
Grierson Dr. 12, 172f, 265, 280, 293, 294.
—extracts from writings of—on Indian languages etc. 133f.
Gṛistmada—story of—60.
Guhādatta 83.
—distinct from Guhila and identified with Guhasena of Valabhī—result thereof not satisfying the requirements 346f.
—name—how used for Bappā 347f.
Guhasena 75.
Guhila 55, 346ff.
—son of Bappā 79.
Guhilots 8, 23f, 26, 50, 55, 69ff, 83, 90.
—are they foreigners' 83ff.
—Kings—comparative genealogy of —81f.
—line—virtues of—77.
—story of—70f.
—theory of—some extracts from —83.
Gujars—8, 10f, 17, 25, 27, 29ff.
—characters and profession of—10.
—not foreigners 31.
—Prākṛit for Gaurs 25.
Gujarāti Language 33f.
Gujarātra 40f.
Guṇāḍhya 279.
Guptas 3.

Gupta Empire 9.
Gurjars 9, 83.:
—of Bhinmāl 69.
Gūvaka 94.
—compared with Bappā 95f.
—first great king of Chauhāns of Sambhar according to Harsha stone Inscription 92f.
Gūvaka II son of Chandrarāja 94, 96.

H

Hāḍas of Bundikoṭa 16.
Hāeala plates 106.
Haihaya Keyurvarsha 14.
—Sahasrārjuna—Aryan 30.
—Record 50.
Haihayas not Mlechchhas 30.
—origin and territory of—134.
Hamira 70.
Hammira Kāvya—story of origin of Chauhāns and Pushkara lake in 14, 97.
Harbilas Śarad 92.
Hariśchandra 96, 272.
Harivaṁśa 30.
Hariyāla 41.
Harsha 1, 29, 101, 124, 148, 154, 182.
—Bāla, son and successor of Mughatuṅga 136.
—son and successor of Rāhila—account of—125.
—Śiva, family deity of 95.
Harshacharita 29, 44f, 103, 135.
Harsha—Empire of 138.
Hāritaṭa 23, 25.
Hāritas 59.
Hārita 73, 96.
Hindu India, beginning of—1f.
Hindus, against amalgamation 31.
—firm belief in Metempsychosis 201
Hinduism—condition of—248f.
—prominent feature of—2.
—and tolerance 109.
Hieun Tsang 4, 28, 37, 39, 45f, 47, 107, 117, 124f 157, 171, 206, 210f, 229, 248, 329.
Hoerule Dr. 265, 295.
Homer 22, 80.
Hūla 23, 26.
—not Hūṇa 26.
Hume 71.
Huṇas 4, 6, 9f, 26, 29f, 35f, 68f, 82f
—not Kshatriyas 26.
—mentioned as foreigners 30.
—not included in 36 families. 30.

I

Ibbetson 7.
Ibn Haukal—extracts from writings of—166.
—statement about dress by—187.
Ibn Khurdabda—information of India by 164.
—examination of the extract from work of—on caste: and its identification 178f.
Idār 72, 75.
Idols—famous—of India 199.
Idol worship of Aryans and non-Aryans 198f.
Idolatry why permitted in Hinduism and its significance 198f.
Ikshvāku 274f, 289.
Illiad 22.
Ināma villages—privileges of owners of—234f.
India—Mediæval—resemblance and difference of—with holy Roman Empire 227.
—old and new—divisions of and different kingdoms in 136.
—other kingdoms in—from 800-1000 A.D. 157ff.
—why enslaved by foreign domination 222.
Indians—dress of—187.
—food of 184ff.

Indians—how asserted right of choosing a king 222f.
—not flesh eaters—some exceptions 185f.
—noble character towords foreigners of—191f.
—ornaments—of 187f.
Indra II—story of marriage of—144.
Indra III—captured Kanauj 106.
Indrachandra 159.
Indrarāja or Indrāyudha 101.
Indrarāja of Kanauj 140.
Indrarāja III,—successor of Akālavarsha—some facts of—149.
Inscriptions—Achaleśvara 77, 81, 84ff.
—Achalagadh 82.
—Bappa's legend and interpretation there of 73.
—of Aśoka 329.
—Ātapurā 78ff, 82f, 86, 154, 301, 332f, 336, 342, 345f, 348.—examination of verse in 85ff.
—Bāṇapurā—Genealogy given in—348.
—Bharut Toraṇa 51.
—Copperplate of Benares 135.
—Benares and Bhillauri 105.
—Benares and Assam 107.
—Benares of Dhanaga—examination of contents of—124f.
—Bhāgalpurā mentioning standing army 224.
—Bijolia 50, 91ff.; translation and interpretation of beginning verse of—93.
—Bilhauri-stone 14, 135f, 238.
—Buchakalā 103f.
—of ehahāḍadeva of Ranthambhor 92.
—chātsu 334, 336; —Examination of Guhila Vaṁśa in—345.
—Chitoregadh 77, 81, 84ff 384.
—Daulatpurā and others—Date of 112.
Inscriptions —Dharaṇīvarāha —Date count of 116.
—Ekaliṅga 74, 84.
—Ghātiālā—inference from account of 111 ; reason of non-mention of Kanauj Soverign 111.
—Gawaliar Bhoja 13.
—Valabha Swāmi 235.
—Bhoja Praśasti—relating to Imperial Pratihāras of Kanauj 304f.
—Haihayas of Chedi 14.
—Harsha stone 13, 91ff, 159. interpretation of expression in by Keilhorn and author —95.
—relating to chāhamānas 302f.
—Kalachūri Haihaya 52.
—Kānheri—date of and inference from 147.
—Khājurāho 126ff, 350f.
—must be verified 84.
—Navasāri—Chālukya 73.
—Naravāhana, 80, 82, 86f, 177, 333f, 346.
—Nasika cave of Gautamī Putra Śatakarṇi 47, 329.
—Nīlaguṇḍa—date of and inference, from—147, 155.
—Nityavarsha 322.
—Pāla and Rāshṭrakūṭa 102.
—Pātanārāyaṇa 50.
—Pratāpagadh 350, 352.
—Pratihāras 29.
—Pratihāra—published by Gaurishankar—discussion of genealogy therein 350f.
—Pehewā—Date of—159.
—Rai Sāgara 340. genealogy of.
— kings in—348.
—at Rajor 31, 108.
—relibility of—71.
—Śāgaratala—of Bhoja 98, 103f.
—extract about Vatsarāja and its meaning 100ff ; 4 verses in praise of Nāgabhaṭa 103.
—Śiyādoni 106, 110, 235ff, 241.

Inscriptions—some—in original 301f.
—Sundarahill Chāchigdeva 92.
Itihāsa and Purāṇa, tradition of Kshatriyas 261f.
Itsing—chinese traveller 218.

J

Jabulistāna 35, 37.
Jackson 38.
Jagannātha records 160.
Jagattuṅga, son of Akālavarsha—account of—149.
Jahahuti 41.
Jain work—translation of and inference from a verse stating conquest of Kanauj 101.
Jainism—condition of—248.
—growth of—in different parts 203.
—not yet prominent 197.
Jaipur 24.
Jamadagni 56ff.
Jammuval 55.
Janamejaya 19.
Jarāsandha 100.
Jayachand 68.
Jayachandra 158.
Jayapāla 108.
—Date of—157.
Jayarāja 93.
Jayaśakti and Vijayaśakti 125.
Jayāpīḍa of Kakoṭa dynasty 158.
Jadeja 55.
Jādhava 23ff.
Jālandhara 40f.
—or Kaṅgrakoṭa kingdom of Trigarta—history of—158f.
Jejjaka name—derivation and date of—125.
Jhalā 22, 25, 55.
Jñāneśvara 330.
Jogarāja, son of Vanarāja—date of—115.
Johnson 11.
Juzur—kingdom of—32.

K

Kabul kingdoms, history, names of kings and dates of 157.
Kachchhamaṇḍala 40.
Kachchhavāhṭas 24f, 55.
Kakkal—successor of Khoṭṭiga—account and exploits of—151.
Kakustha or Kakkuka, nephew and successor of Nāgabhaṭa—Date of 100.
Kakutsa 23, 25.
Kalachūris of Chedi 134ff.
—branch of Haihayas—extent and date of 134f.
—genealogy of—137.
—not new branch but old one, 137.
—pure Kshatriyas and Śaivas 137.
Kalasha 23.
Kalhaṇa 22, 159.
Kali age myth—effect and reasons of—43, 46f.
—interpretation of—47.
—later than 7th century, 47f.
Kaliṅga 103.
Kālabhoja 80.
—and Khommāṇa foot-note on 82.
—Śīla's successor 79.
Kālachchhuraka 23.
Kālahayañjaya 41.
Kamalākara Bhaṭṭa 312.
Kamalu—date of—157.
Kamāsha 23, 25.
Kāmboja or Kabul 34, 40, 42.
Kāmbojas 30.
Kāmarūpa or Assam—extent of 40f.
Kanauj 13, 98ff.
—Empire—contest for—102.
Kanuj Empire—decaying—compared with Mughal Empire 102.
Kandāhara—history of kingsdom of 158.
Kāntipura 41.

Kaṇva 59, 284ff.
—Śaśakarṇa 284.
—Triśoka 284.
Kānyakubja, or Kanauj—extent of 39, 41.
Karka I 144.
Karkarāja nephew of Khoṭṭiga 120.
Karnāṭa 36f, 40, 42.
Karaṭṭapāla 23, 25.
Kashmir 40f.
—history of different dynasties in 158.
Kāśyapa 56ff.
Kausalyā Rājaputri 44.
Kāthi 25.
Kātyāyana Laugāksha—sūtra from 62.
Kavinīsa 23ff.
Keyūrvarsha, brother and successor of Bāla Harsha—some facts of—136.
Kayyaṭa 312, 314.
Kāyastha caste, one not divided 177.
Khārwars 8.
Khazar 36.
Khizars—character and profession of—10.
Khemarāja successor of Vairisiṁiha—date of—115.
Khommāṇa son of Mahāyaka 79f.
Khommāṇa Rāsā 79.
—validity of—80.
Khoṭṭiga—date and account of 120
—successor of Kṛishṇa III—account of—150.
Khumāna 70.
Khusrū Parveiz 35.
Keilhorn, 128, 131, 134f, 140f, 354.
Kingdoms—numerous—reasons of 226.
—struggle for supremacy in Kings of—222.
Kingly families non drinkers 202.
Kingly—Families ruling in Deccan; were they foreigners? its Examination 319f
—power—idea of and result and effect therefrom 220f.
Kirāta 42, 104.
Kokkaladeva of Chedi 105.
—date of—discussed 135.
—relations with other then living kings of 135f.
Kokkaladeva II son of Yuvarāja 136.
Koṅkaṇa 40f.
—laghu 40f.
Kośala 40, 42.
—kingdom 161.
—Videhas—history of—293.
Koṭapāla 23, 25.
Koṭa kingdom 90.
Kṛishṇa 286f.
—settles in Dwāraka 64.
Kṛishṇarāja, first king—date account and capital of—119.
—paternal uncle and successor of Dantidurga—exploits of—145.
Kṛishnarāja II Rāshṭrakūṭa 135.
Kṛishṇasāja III successor of Amoghavarsha III—exploits and account of—given by Wardhā grant 150.
Kshatriya families—reasons of fanciful origins of—56.
Kshatriyas formed one caste—no minor distinctions 176.
—generally temperate drinkers 202.
—Gotrochchāra forgotten 176.
—Kula of—taking place of Gotra-its reasons 176f.
—learning of 181f.
—occupation of arms of—shared by others 183f.
—Pravara Rishs in Āngirasa and Bhṛigu stock 58ff.
—residing in Deccan in 1st century 47.

Kshatriyas—turning brahmins in Vedic times and vice varsa; instances 58ff.
Kumārapālacharita 22, 131.
Kumārila 260ff, 316, 329.
—achievements of—206f.
—birth place and country of 207ff.
—Date of—207.
—how learned Buddhism and his death 208f.
—important facts of date, birthplace etc. of—211.
—inference about date and political situation from political observation of—210f.
—an interesting remark of—211.
—not Dakshiṇātya 209.
—of Northern central India 209f.
Kuru 42, 290.
Kurukshetra 67.
Kushāṇas 9, 68f.
Kuvalāśva of Ayodhya 65.

L

Lachhamana younger son of Vākpati, founder of Nadal line 96.
Land—measurement of 240.
Language Bengali 173.
—Eastern Hindi 74.
—Kanarese 173.
—Kiriyā and other minor dialects 168f.
—Māgadhī 3.
—Mahārāshṭrī 3, 34.
—Marāṭhi 174.
—origin of—171.
—Sanskṛit—chief stock of others 170.
—Telagu 173.
—Western Hindi 174.
Languages—different—time and reasons of origin of 167f.
—non Aryans at the time of Kumārila and inference therefrom 208f.
—Prākṛit—once spoken languages and their period 169f.
Laṅkā 42.
Lakulīśa—śiva cult of 96.
Lakshmaṇa son of Keyurvarsha—some facts of—136.
Lalliya—date of—157.
Lāṭṭalura, capital of Rāshtrakūṭas, identification and inference 323.
Lāṭa southern Gujarat 33, 40f.
Legal writers and Kaliage myth 48
Lele 123.
Liṅgabhava 41.
Lohara dynasty of Kashmir 158.
Lohapura or Lahore—extent of—40f.
Lunar race settlements 64.
—five-races—their individual progress as evidenced in the Vedas 286ff.
Lunar Kshatriyas—Rigvedic references to—their colonisation and analogy from American history and conclusion therefrom 276ff.

M

Macdonell 293, 295, 297.
—Vedic Index of—260.
Māchipura 41.
Madras Presidency—history of kingdoms in—161.
Mādhavagupta of Magadha 139.
Mādhyamikas 69.
Maga 28.
Magadha 40, 42.
Mahābhārata 9, 27, 37, 39, 44f, 60, 64ff.
—Mīmānsa in Hindi 18, 21.
Mahadaji Scindia 327.
Mahālakshmi, mother of Allaṭa 80.

Mahāraja Vākapati, son of Chandana 96.
Mahārāshṭra 40.
—Mahomedan invasions repelled from 152f.
Mahāyaka son of Siṁha 79f.
Mahendra 41, 108, 346.
Mahendra II 346.
Mahendrapāla, son of Mihira 105f.
Mahendrapāla II may be identified with Devapāla 351f.
Mahīdeva, means a king and not Brahmin 85ff.
Mahīpāla 107, 116, 119.
—brother and successor of Bhoja II 106.
—son of Mahendrapāla—date and extent of Empire of—106.
—son and successor of Vigrahapāla II—account of—141.
Mahmud of Gazni 32, 80f, 108, 159.
—invasions of and effect thereof 141.
Mahodaya *alias* Kanauj 104.
Maitrakas of Valabhī 4, 83.
Makavaṇa 23.
Mālavas 68, 104.
Mālawa 40f.
Malaya 41.
Malhārarao Holkar 327.
Mālkhed—identified with Mānyakheṭa—some observation of 354.
Māndhātā 58.
Mandor, 25. capital town of Pratihāras according to Vaidya C.V.99.
Manikrai 96.
Manu 27.
Manubhava 25.
Marāṭhās 102.
—blending of Aryans and Nāga Vaṁśa 326.
Marāṭhās—not of lower civilisation and capacities 327.
Marāṭha Kshatriyas were ruling families in Deccan 318ff.
Marriages Anuloma—of Kshatriyas and Vaiśyas 195.
—Anuloma how treated in different Smṛitis 193ff.
—condition of—249f.
—early—misconception about 188f
—early—when came into vogue and why 189f.
Maru desert—two references in Mbh. 65.
Maṭa 23, 25.
Mathandeva 108.
Matsya 104.
Medapāṭa or Mewad 48 f.
Megasthenes 28, 178f.
Mention with foreigners does not make the first a foreigner 29f.
Mer 83.
Merutuṅga—ficticious story of—like Pṛithvirāja and Ghori 120f.
Mewad 4, 18, 26, 36.
Mexician Aztecs 298.
Mihira Bhoja 135, 148.
Mihira, *alias* Bhoja, successor of Rāmachandra—date and extent of Empire of—104.
Military officers different from civil ones 236.
Mitāksharā 53.
—Gotra dictum of—wrong 53, 56.
—pravara rule of—useless 62.
—Śrauta sūtra rule misinterpreted in—50f.
Mitra distinguishing epithet of Nagar brahmins 83.
—not Mer 84.
Mitraya 60.
Mohanlāla Pāṇḍya 23ff.
Moris of Chitod 73.
Mudgala—descent of—59.
Mugdhatuṅga, son and successor of Kokkala 136.
Mularāja chālukya 107.
Mulrāja Saloṅki, seized thekingdom of Chāvaḍās 115f.

Mulasthānapur 40, 42,
Multan 36.
—Sun temple of—fear of idol being broken by Moslems and author's view on it 197f.
Muṇḍarāja or Bhūyada, successor of Khemrāja 115.

N

Nadol 22.
Nāga 346.
Nāgabhaṭa son of Vatsarāja 140.
Nāgabhaṭa—capital of, not determined, 100.
—conquest of Kanauj Empire by—103.
Nāgabhaṭṭa, first Pratihāra king—how came to power 98f.
—probable date of accession and period of rule and conquests of—100, 104.
Nāgabhaṭṭa II 108.
Nāgaḍā 72f.
Nāgars 83.
Nāgari Prachāriṇi Granthamālā 18.
Nāgas—history and civilisation of—326.
Nāgojibhaṭṭa's Udyota, 312, 314ff,
Nahararai 99.
Nahusha 27.
Nānāsaheb Peshwā 74.
Nanda 21.
Nannuka first Chandella king—date of—125.
Nārasiṁha Chālukya 106.
Naravāhana, son of Allaṭṭa 80.
Nārāyaṇapāla, successor of Mahīpāla 141.
Nārāyaṇapāladeva, son and successor of Vigrahapāla 141.
Nationality only prevents foreign domination—examples 226.
Navasāhasṅka charita 119.
Nepāl—extent of—39, 41.
—kingdoms—history of 160.
Nesfield 7.
Nīlapura 41.
Nikumbhavara 23.
Nivṛita 41.
Nohalādevi 14.

O

Occupation of selling certain provisions 184.
Odiyāna or Orissa—extent of—40f.
Officers—translation of and inference from list of—in Bhālgur inscription 231ff.
Origin legends ficticious 97.
—stories myths 86f, 131.
Orissa kingdoms—history of—160.

P

Padhihara 25.
Paiśāchī 3.
Pakshabāhu 42.
Pālas of Bengal 138ff, 354.
—dates of—cannot be ciphered 140.
—extent of rule and exploits of—142.
—Genealogy and probable dates of—143.
—rise of —as in documents 138f.
—were Rajputs, Buddhists in name and Hindu in character 142.
Pāla suffix—meaning of—139.
Pallavas of Kāñchi 4, 47, 51.
Pampa, kanarese poet 106.
Pāmbipur 41.
Pāñchāla—North 37.
Pāñchālas—history of—as in the Vedas 290ff.
Pandit S. P. 207.
Pāṇḍu 42.
Pāṇḍuvishaya 41.
Pāṇḍya Mohnalal 18ff.
—Shyāmaldāsa 15.
Paṅgu 42.

Pāṇini—Sūtra of—different Bhāshyas on, 312f.
—meaning of sūtra of—consisting the word Rājapatra 44f.
Panipat 18.
Pargitar 58, 259ff, 278f 287.
—conclusion from the study of Purāṇas by 259f.
Parjhārs 8.
Paramāras 9, 13, 16, 23, 27, 34f, 50, 52f, 55, 68f, 117ff.
—date of—117.
—examination of arguments of Gujar and foreign descent of—34f.
—Genealogy of—123; discussed from various sources 118f.
—history of—unknown at Tod's time and represented by minor chiefs to-day; their names 117
—and Pratāpagadh Inscriptions; inference therefrom 352.
—origin of—15.
Parāśara Smṛiti 43f.
—contradicts Kaliage myth 47f.
—śloka allowing Brahmins and Kshatriyas to become agriculturists 182f.
—śloka requesting taxes for temples and Brahmins in 238.
Parvagupta of Divir Dynasty 158.
Pāradas 30.
Parihāra, 9, 13, 16, 23, 25.
Pariyātra 41.
Patañjali's Mahābhāshya 312f.
Pāṭaka 23.
Pāṭaliputra 100f.
Pāyagunde Mahādeva-chhāyā on Udyota of—312ff.
Pijavana 274.
Political condition in India 220ff, 229
Poros 292.
Prabandhas—ficticious account of—114
Prabanda Chintāmaṇi 39, 114, 119.
—list of kings in Pātan 116.
Prabandha-Kośa 35.
Praśasti of Hemādri 324.
—Nāgpur 118.
—Udepur 118.
Pratāpa 70.
Pratāpavardhana 29.
Pratihāras of Kanauja 8, 23, 25, 27, 31ff, 50, 69, 98ff.
—chief events from foundation of 108f.
—capital of; its situation 99.
—descendants of Lakshmaṇa 13.
—explanation of arguments appearing to show—as Gujars 31f.
—of Ghatiala inscription 111ff.
—Imperial line of Kanauja—Genealogy of 113.
—minor dynasty of—calling Gurjar Pratihāras for distinction; not Gujars themselves 31ff.
—names of—Arynas 31.
—never call themselves Gujars in inscriptions 31.
—neither Gujars nor foreigners 98.
—not insignificant power in 9th century 98.
—peculiarity of Grants of—109f.
—form of writing of grants similar to that of Harsha grants 108f.
—origin 32f 86 of 98f.
—power of —declining 106f.
—represented as Sūrya-vaṁśis 31.
—of Solar race 13.
—why called Gujars 105.
Pratiloma marriages checked 27f.
Pravar matter made clear by some Sūtras 61f.
—and Pravara Rishi 57.
—Rishis—reasons of—being 3 or 5; 57.
—a special provision for Kshatriyas 61.
—system uncertain affair 54.
Pṛithu 60.
Pṛithvīrāja, 12ff, 18ff, 25, 80, 90, 91, 99, 136.

Prithvirāja Rāsā, 12ff, 18ff, 25f, 85, 93, 96.
—additions in, unseparable—19.
—authenticity of questioned—18.
—authority and popularity of—like Mahābhārata 19.
—compared with Mahābhārata 18f.
—concious attempt in—to imitate Mahābhārata 19.
—dates of—not wrong 20ff.
—nucleus by chand 21; authentic and ancient 18f.
—points of similarity with Mbh. 19f.
—verses in—misinterpreted; author's interpretation 22f.
—kings 36 in—unhistorical 91.
Prithvīraja Vijaya 14, 35.
Prosperity period of India—factors which led to, 247ff.
Pulakeśin 116, 154, 329f.
Pulakeśin II. 148.
Pulastya 42.
Puṅgala 40, 42.
Punjab—some other kingdoms in, 159.
Purāṇas, not historical authorities; its reasons 262.
Purāṇic age—historical facts misinterpreted in—278ff.
—Gods 2.
—statements —regarding Rajputs valueless, interpolations 43.
Puru 270, 278.
—Śatapatha Brāhmaṇa interpretation of—Macdonnell's and author's views thereon 270.
Purus 270, 276ff, 282ff, 297.
—progress of—288f.
Purukutsa 58f, 271, 274, 276, 283f 290, 296, 297f. [277f.
Pururavas—inference from story of
Pūrva Mīmānsā, annihilator of Buddhism 1f.
Pushyabhūti 2.
Pushkarāraṇya 67.
Pushkara Tīrtha 67.

R

Race—fusion of—after settlement 27.
Rādhā—Mādhava-Vilāsa—Champū by Jayarāma Pindye 318.
Rāhila, successor of Vijaya—date, account and exploits of 125.
Rahmni kingdom and try for its identification 163f.
Rājapāla 23, 25.
Rājyapāla, successor of Nārāyaṇapāla—account and date of 141.
—successor of Vijayapāla and fall of Kanauj Empire 108.
Rājataraṅgiṇi 22.
Rājaśekhara 31, 35, 188.
—plays Bālabhārata and Pāṇḍava of—106.
—Guru of Mahendrapāla 105f.
Rājendralāla 127.
Rajput applied to illegitimate progeny 43f.
Rajput clans—identification of 23f.
—clans list of—as old as chand 25.
—clans 36 in number, their history 22f.
—families almost all worshippers of Śiva, their list 203f.
—not new word 43
—word meaning of 43ff.
—word, as old as Pāṇini and Mahābhārata 45.
—word, in Mahābhārata in good sense 44.
—why prominent in 9th century 45f.
Rajputs—chivalry, Heroism, orthodoxy of faith and struggle against foreign faith of 4.
—descendants of Vedic Āryans 7, 69; an evidence of 49f.
—fighting with Turks, Afghans and their independence 5.

Rajputs founded a Hindu Empire 69.
—Gaur 69.
—Gotras of—by descent from times immemorial 53.
—Gotras and Pravaras of—as in Vedic Sūtras 49f.
—Indo-Āryans 5.
—a mixed caste in Pārāśara Smṛiti and Śūdrakamalākara 43f.
—not pure Kshatriyas according to Purāṇas 43.
—not ugras 48.
—prominence in politics of 3f.
Rajputana—Aryan settlements in 64ff.
—Gazeteer wrongly omits Gūvaka I 94.
—historical proofs of immigrants in—before Rāṭhods 68f.
—inhabited by Ābhirs and others 64ff.
—not inhabited by Āryans for long 64.
—order of Aryan Settelemnts in 66f.
—settlemnts through foreign pressure 68.
—southern Gujarat 31f.
—very inhospitable 64.
Rājputra used in the sense of Kshatriya in Mbh 44.
—denotes high born Kshatriya 44.
Rajvade, V. K. 155, 320, 323ff 327f.
—examination of theory of Deccan Marāṭhās of—318ff.
Rāma, 24, 272, 275, 287, 295.
Rāmachandra, son of Nāgabhaṭṭa —date of—104.
Rāmāyaṇa 9, 65f.
—reference to Maru (Rajputana) and Ābhirs in 66.
Rāmpur 37f.
Raṇḍel 25.
Rāṇoji Scindia 327.
Rapson—Prof. 357.
Rāshṭrakūṭa—meaning of —144, 152.
Rāshṭrakūṭas 32, 47, 102, 144ff.
—condition of Mahārāshṭra before —152f.
—dates of first kings mentioned in grants of 144.
—early history of—322ff.
—extent of Empire of 153f.
—Genealogy of 156.
—government, army and religion of—154f.
—list with dates of kings of—151.
—and Marāṭhās compared 153f.
—names of kings of—153.
—origin of—144.
—period of suzerainty in Deccan of—151.
—rise and monumental works of—153.
—same as Rāshṭrikās 323.
—Social status of—154f.
—some general remarks about 152ff
—unlike Chālukyas went to the heart of Empire 154.
Raṭarājya or Rāshtrakūṭa, extent of 40f.
Ratnāditya, successor of Yogarāja 115.
Rāṭhods 8, 23, 50, 55, 90.
—originally Rāshṭrakūṭas of the Deccan 328.
—last immigrants historically known 68.
Ravi 23ff.
—Śasi, Jādhava not clans but races 24f.
Rāwal—meaning of 72.
Religion-one—Vedic religion being held supreme 196f.
—Vedic—side by side idolatry 201
Religious condition of India 196ff, 247ff.
Research—value of—11, 17.

Revenue administration—inference from—as evidenced from Daulatpurā grant of Bhoja 239.
—administration—inference from—as evidenced from Śilahāra grant 239f.
—land tax and other dues paid by villagers 234.
—officers—rights and appointments of—as evidenced from grants 235f
—and pay of officers generally paid in kinds 235.
Rights of descendants of kings religiously respected in India 222.
Riksha 41.
Rishi—meaning of 57.
Risley—Sir, 294.
—observation of—265f.
Rohillas 102.
Romaka 42.
Rosajuta 23ff.
Rudreṇa, Tomara king, 159.

S

Sabaktagin 108.
Sahadeva 291,
Sahya 41.
Saindhava 23, 103.
Samarasi 18, 21, 70.
Samarasiṁha 81.
Samrāṭs—history of—100f.
Samudragupta 100.
Saṅga 70.
Sañjaya 41.
Sapādalaksha 36f, 40, 92.
Sapardalakshāṇa 35, 37.
Sassanian coins 35.
Sati custom 190.
Saurāshṭra 40f.
Sauti 18.
Sāhaṇapura 41.
Sāmanta—date of—157.
Sāmantadeva 99.
—and Gūvaka I—probable dates of 94f.
Sāmbhar or Sayambhara 37, 40f, 90ff, 281.
—first seat of power of Chauhānas 92.
Sāmrājya and Samrāṭ—idea of—long since Mbh. 100f.
Sārasvata Maṇḍala—Northern Gujrat 33.
Scythians 10.
Sadāvara 23, 25.
Shahābuddin Ghori 90.
Shāhu of Sātāra 74.
Shasi of Sind 74.
Shyāmaldāsa 18.
Shyama Sundaradas 18.
Silāra 23.
Siṁha, son of Bhartṛipaṭṭa 79.
Siṁhala 42.
Siṁharāja 94.
—Vākpatirāja's elder son, 96, 159.
Sind 40.
—history of kingdoms in 157.
Sindha 41.
Sindhurāja, brother and suscessor of Vākpati 118, 121.
Sirohi 90.
Sītā 24.
Skandapurāṇa, 36f, 39f, 92, 199.
—Arbuda Khaṇḍa 68.
—date of—39f.
—list, examination and identification of 39f.
—list of countries and villages in 39ff.
—mountains and rivers in 40f.
Smṛiti law of Anuloma marriage 193ff.
—law predominent—no new legislature and result therefrom 225.
Smṛiti Atri—extract from 308; evidence on interdining of 252.
—Āpastamba—extract from 309.

Smriti Brihaspati—extract from 309.
—Daksha—extract from 310.
—Gotama—extract from 310.
—Kātyāyana—extract from 309.
—Manu—ślokas of treating Anuloma marriage and status of Śūdra Progeny 193.
—Manu and Yājñavalkya—view on Anuloma Brahmin marriage of 194.
—Parāśara and Vyāsa—statement about marriages in 189f.
—Parāśara extract from 309.
—Saṁvarta—extract from 309.
—Śaṅkha—extract from 310.
—Uśanas—extract from 308f.
—Vasishṭha—extract from 311.
—Vishṇu—extract from 308.
—Vyāsa—evidence on interdining of 251; Vyāsa extract from 310.
—Vyāsa—śloka of—on caste—its explanation 179f.
—Vyāsa and Auśanasa views on Anuloma marriages of 194.
—Vyāsa and Parāśara—view on Anuloma Śūdra marriage of—193f.
—Yājñavalkya—view on Anuloma Śūdra marriage of 193.
Smṛities—extracts from important [308ff.
Smith V.—6, 8, 10f, 18, 38, 69, 98ff, 104, 107f, 124f, 128ff.
—wrong view of—about the origin of Chandells 130ff.
Salonkhi or Chālukya 14.
Solar and Lunar Races—arguments and conclusion of—resumed 294ff
—kingdoms and peoples of 292f.
—Kshatriyas how descendants of Pravara Rishis ? 58f.
—of India in the Vedas 259ff.
—Order of authorities 262ff.
—Rigvedic references to the conflict of—and conclusion therefrom 281ff.
—Race idea—reasons of origin of 298.
—some important facts in the history of 265ff.
—traditions of—through absurd historically important 12.
Somaka 291.
Spaniards fighting with Moors 5.
Sṛiñjaya 291.
Strirājya 42.
State—rights of—234f.
Sub-castes small due to overthrow of Buddhism 3.
Sudāsa 269, 271ff, 276, 282f, 290 295.
Suḷaimān merchant—identification and contents of work of—162ff.
—extract of his work on caste 181.
—inference from evidence of—showing political condition 221f.
—inference from statement of—about kings army 222f.
—story of an ascetic of—and statement in general about asceticism of—200.
Sukṛit Saṅkīrtana 114.
Sukthankar Dr. 352f.
Suicide in sacred places 191.
Spurious work without nucleus not popular 19.
Surjmal Bhat 16, 25, 91.
Sūryamukha 41.
Sussanian 36.
Suśarman 158.
Śabaraswāmin 329.
Śakas 4, 6, 8ff, 28, 30, 68.
—and Yavanas not admitted in Indian caste 28.
Śaktikumāra, son of Naravāhana 80f.
Śaṅkara and Kumārila—little historical evidence about and sources thereof 206.
—account of life, works and travels of 213ff.

Śaṅkara—controversy of with Maṇḍana Miśra 214.
—date of 218f.
—death of 217.
—doctrines of 212f and result therefrom 217.
—foundations of 4 Mathas by 215.
—greatness of 215.
—Native place and date of 213.
—Prof. Pathak's internal and external authorities about date of 218.
—views of Vidyāraṇya and Veṅkaṭeśvara on date of—not correct 219.
—why Prachchhanna Buddha and causes of his success 212f.
Śaṅkaradvijaya—inference from statement of—about Kumārila 207
Śaṅkaragaṇa, son and successor of Lakshmaṇa 136.
Śaraḍa Harbilas 14, 37.
Śaśāṅka of Karṇasuvarṇa 139.
Śasi 23ff.
Śaśibhava 25.
Śatrughna 272, 274, 287, 295.
Śauraseni 3.
Śāhi, king of Kīra 107.
Śākambhara 36f.
Śākambarī—family of 35.
Śālivāhana 80.
Śātavāhana, Āndhra Emperor 134.
Śīla 345f.
Śīla and Aparājita-foot-note on 82.
—Bhoja's successor 79.
Śilāditya 75.
Śisodias 4.
Śiva cult, revival of 2.
Śivadesha 41.
Śiva worship prominent 116, 203f.
—worship origin and history of—204.
Śivāji 5, 72f.
—belonged to Northern Rajput family of Śisodias 324f.
Śivālik hills 35ff, 40.
Śīyaka or Śrī Harsha, son of Vairisiṁha—exploits of 119.
—date of 118ff.
Śrauta Sūtras 54, 60.
—dictum of 58.
Śrīchandra 93.
Śrīvallabha, son of Kṛishṇa 101.
Śuchibhava 25.
Śuchivarman 81.
Śūdrakamalākara 44, 48, 312.
—refutation of Varṇa dictum in 315.
Śūdras, agriculture occupation of 183.
—and others drinkers 212.
Śuktimān 41.
Śunahotra 58.
Śunahśepa 272.

T

Tafik kingdom—account and identification of—mentioned by Sulaiman 163.
Tailapāla 120, 151.
Takkāṇa 35, 37.
Tāka 23.
Takshaśilā 292f.
Tantrapāla 159.
Tāntric worship—disappearance of 2
Tapas and sannyāsa 199f.
Tapasvis origin and growth of 200.
Taura 25, 55.
Taxes—system of 230.
Temples of favourite deities—custom of building of 197f.
Thānesar 29.
Tod, Col. 7, 13, 16, 22ff, 50, 70f, 73ff, 78ff, 90, 98f, 117, 159, 338f 341.
Tod's Annual 9.
—Rājastān 14.
Tomara 40, 42.

Tod's Kingdoms at Delhi—history of 159.
Town—general administration of 236.
Traditions—reliability of—of Brahmins and Kshatriyas 260ff.
Transubstantiation—doctrine of 12
Trasadasyu 58f, 271, 274, 276, 283f, 290, 296.
Trilochanapāla—date of 157.
Ṭriksha 59.
Ṭritsus 269.
Tuṅga Rāshṭrakūṭa 141.
Turushka 104.
—in Sāgaratala—explanation of 112f
Turvaśas 276ff, 281ff, 297f.
—progress of 288.

U

Udayana 21.
Udepur 24.
—Museum Library 23.
—Praśasti 15, 50.
U. P. and Oudh under Kanauj Emperors 160.
Upanishad Chhāndogya 287. statement in 26f.
Uttaṅka legends in Mbh 65, 67.

V

Vadhryaśva 295.
Vadhvaryaśva 60.
Vāghila 55.
Vāguri 41.
Vaidya—points of difference of—from Pargitar 260ff.
Vairisiṁha, successor of Ratnāditya 115.
—Vajraṭa, successor of Kṛishṇarāja 119.
—date of—118f.
Vaiśampāyana 18f.
Vaiśyas formed one caste, no minor distinctions 177.
—non-drinkers 202.
—originally agriculturists; left it 182.
Vajradāman, a Kachchavāha Chief 108.
Vākpati chauhāna 159.
—*alias* Munja—date of 118f.
—son and successor of Śīyaka—account and exploits of 120.
Vākpatirāja 93f.
Valabhī 72, 75.
Vālmikī 272.
Vaṁśa Bhāskara 16, 25, 91.
Vanrāja, ancestors, birth, foundation of Empire at Anhilwāḍa and Date of 114f.
Vāpyaṭa, grandfather of Gopāla 140.
Varāha Mihira 34, 39.
Vararuchi 34.
Vardhamāna 40, 42.
Vardhanas 3.
Varendeka 42.
Varendu 36, 40f.
Varmas of Kanauj 4.
Varṇa dictum—date of—316f.
'Varnas Brahmins and Śūdras only'—origin and examination of the dictum namely—312ff.
Varṇas—historical comment on 313f
Vasiṣṭha 12f, 15f, 52, 56ff, 269ff.
—born of Urvaśi 86.
Vāsudeva Vāhman—legends of 35.
—sussanian king 37.
Vatsa (Allahabad) 104.
Vatsarāja, son of Devaśakti—date and conquest of Kanauj of—100ff
Vāyu Purāṇa 58f.
Vedic literature 261.
Velankar, Prof. H. D. 349.
Velākulas—interpretation of 40.
Vena 60.
Veṅgi kingdom 161.
Vernaculars, modern, beginning of

[3.

Vidarbha or Berar, 40, 42, 103.
Vigraha 93.
Vigrahapāla I, nephew and successor of Devapāla—date and account of 141.
Vigrahapāla II, successor of Gopāla II, 141.
Vigrahapāla III, made Amagachhi grant 141
Vigraharāja, son of Siṁharāja 94, 96f.
Vijaya, successor of Nannuka—date of 125.
Vijñāneśvara 51ff, 62, 316, 330.
—theory of Kshatriya gotras of—a misconception 87, 325.
Vikramārka—date of 116.
Vikrama 20f.
—śaka 20f.
Villagers—description of—in different grants, 233f.
Vinayāditya 154, 182.
Vindhya 41.
Vindhyaśakti 161.
Viprakulānandana, well applied to Bappā 347.
Virāṭa 42.
Viśāladeva 20f.
Vishṇuvardhana 59.
Vishṇu worship, prominent in Hinduism 2.
Viśvāmitra 15, 56ff, 271ff 296.
Vithikā, meaning of 237.
Vyāsa 18f, 29.
Vyāghramukha, Chāpa family king ruling at Bhinmāl 99f.

W

Walid Khalif 79.
Wars—good result of 257f.
—international—effect of 256ff.
—occasional, lead to progress 225.
West Coast kingdoms 161.
William the conquerer 328.
Words—good and bad meanings of—; latter later growth 43.

Y

Yadus 276ff, 281ff, 297f.
—settlement and progress of 286ff.
Yadu Vaṁśa separate from Chandra Vaṁśa 24.
Yādavas 16, 286f.
—early history of 324.
Yājñavalkya 28.
—smṛiti 50.
Yamakoṭi 42.
Yaśaskaradeva 158.
Yaśovarman, son of Harsha 139, 154, 207.
—exploits and date of 125f.
—Chandel 107.
Yāsana 42.
Yantika 23, 25.
Yavanas 4, 30.
Yayāti 270, 277ff, 287f, 297f.
Yudhishṭhira 20.
—śaka 20f.
Yue-chi 6, 8.
Yuvarāja II, brother and successo of Śaṅkaragaṇa and contemporary of Muñja 136.
Yuvanāśva 58f.

ERRATA

(Mistakes of comma, long or short a, i, u and single letters have been omitted.)

Incorrect	*Correct*	*Page*	*Line*
Shyamaldas Pandya	Kaviraj Syamaldas	15	27
the seasons	the six seasons	20	11
संकरत्वात्सवर्णानां	संकरात्तर्वैवर्णानां	27	31
these	there	36	39
precedes	follows	45	5
dictum)-चक्षते	dictum..चक्षते)	56	15,16
the	their	68	15
contemporaries ?	contemporaries ;	82	26
and Sāmantadeva	Sāmantadeva and	94	20
by	renown by	100	9
703	705	101	26
Rāshtrakūtas	Chālukyas	121	34
813	831	125	9
this	the	141	10
856 934	836 914	149	20
hold	held	153	32
regal	regnal	163	10
Pampas	Pampa's	173	13
through..Bhili)	though..Bhili	174	9—11
sacrifice	sacrifice"	183	7
India	Indians	191	14
the mankind	mankind	200	20
merits	merit	201	37
in Gujarat..into the	into Gujarat..in the	203	35
time"	time	208	30
Kumārila"	Kumārila	209	13
union	unison	212	6
389	3889	218	9
languages	language	226	21
शोकशिका	शोकशिका	238	11
it is	they are	250	28
that Viśvāmitra	Viśvāmitra	272	16

Incorrect	*Correct*	*Page*	*Line*
Purāṇa's	Purānas	279	29
शुभ्रे	शुभ्रे	280	16
forded	forded it	282	24
पूरम्	पूरुम्	283	36
कात्म	काण्व	284	27
Ghora	Ghaura	285	34,38
Hindus	Aryans	288	25
Brahmanas	the Brāhmaṇas	292	17
द्विजः...मत्स्योपेत्य	द्विजाः...मात्स्योपेथ	315	9,13
Kṣhatriya	Kshatriyas	316	34
निमम—	निमग्नो	322	30
to	or	327	23
relies	relies	332	27
दाबिरे-	दागिरे-	333	43
Bhāsha	Bhāskara	334	14
विद्वेपिणं	विद्वेषिणं	335	42
तमय	तनयं	,,	43
Śhivādtya	Śivāditya	341	8
Iuscription	Inscriptions	345	3
recurring	seeuring	345	44
epithets	epithet	347	21
Shitipāla	Kshitipāla	351	1
supression	suppression	353	7
Krisna	Krishna		17
Smagachi	Amagachhi	354	3
capaital	a capital	,,	43

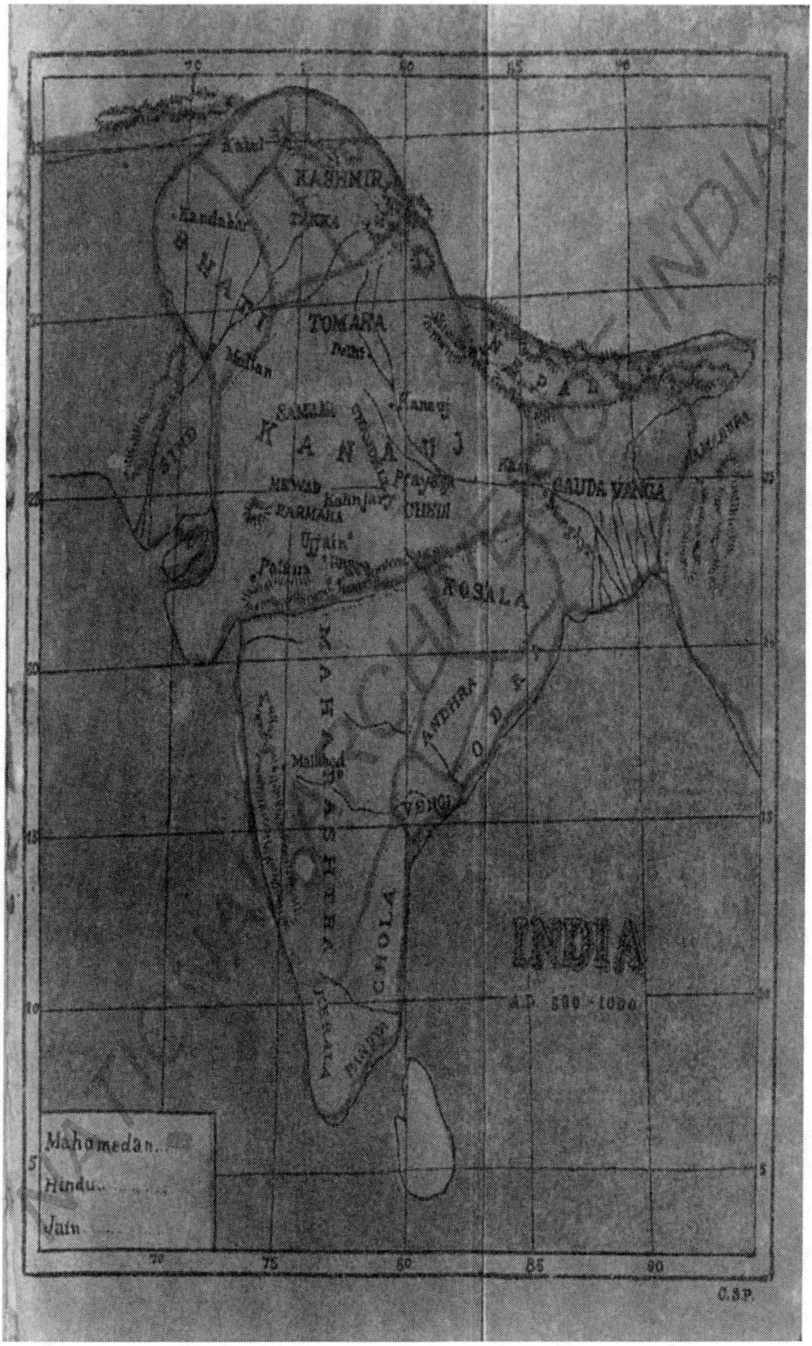

KASHMIR
Kabul
TOMARA
Multan
K A N A U J
Kanauj
Prayag
CHEDI
MEWAR
PARMARA
Ujjain
GAUDA VANGA
KOSALA
ANDHRA
O D R A
VENGI
Malkhed
CHOLA
INDIA
Mahomedan
Hindu
Jain
70
75
80
85
90
5
C.S.P.